Islam and th

How do modern Muslims adapt their traditions to engage with today's world? Charles Tripp's erudite and incisive book considers one of the most significant challenges faced by Muslims over the last sixty years: the challenge of capitalism. By reference to the works of noted Muslim scholars, the author shows how, faced by this challenge, these intellectuals have devised a range of strategies which have enabled Muslims to remain true to their faith, whilst engaging effectively with a world not of their own making. The work is framed around the development of their ideas on Islamic socialism, economics and the rationale for Islamic banking. While there are those who have resorted to confrontation or insularity to cope with the challenges of modernity, most have aspired to innovation and ingenuity in the search for compromise and interaction with global capitalism in the twenty-first century.

CHARLES TRIPP is Reader in Politics with reference to the Middle East in the Department of Political and International Studies, School of Oriental and African Studies, University of London. His many publications include *Iran and Iraq at War* (1988, with Shahram Chubin), *Iran–Saudi Arabia Relations and Regional Order* (1996, with Shahram Chubin) and *A History of Iraq* (2000, 2002).

Islam and the Moral Economy

The Challenge of Capitalism

Charles Tripp
University of London

CAMBRIDGE
UNIVERSITY PRESS

CAMBRIDGE UNIVERSITY PRESS
Cambridge, New York, Melbourne, Madrid, Cape Town, Singapore, São Paulo

Cambridge University Press
The Edinburgh Building, Cambridge CB2 2RU, UK
Published in the United States of America by Cambridge University Press, New York

www.cambridge.org
Information on this title: www.cambridge.org/9780521682442

First published 2006

Printed in the United Kingdom at the University Press, Cambridge

A catalogue record for this book is available from the British Library

ISBN-13 978-0-521-86377-3 hardback
ISBN-10 0-521-86377-5 hardback
ISBN-13 978-0-521-68244-2 paperback
ISBN-10 0-521-68244-4 paperback

for
Emily and Rhiannon

Contents

Acknowledgements

Writing a book which deals in some measure with the moral problems of debt and repayment has made me acutely conscious of the debts of gratitude that I owe to all those who have helped me in my work. They have been many, both institutional and individual, and I would like to express my thanks to them all for having advised and assisted me along the way.

In particular, I would like to thank the Nuffield Foundation and the Arts and Humanities Research Board for the grants which helped to support my research and to provide the precious time needed for writing, free of teaching and administrative duties. In this respect, I would also like to thank my colleagues in my department and in the library at the School of Oriental and African Studies whose support gave me the time needed to complete this project and whose expertise helped me greatly in my research. I also acknowledge with gratitude the assistance of the staff at the Dar al-Kutub al-Misriyah, at CEDEJ and at the American University in Cairo, at the library of the Mu'assasat Al al-Bait, at Jordan University Library and at the American Center for Oriental Research in Amman, as well as at the British Library and at the library of the London School of Economics and Political Science.

There are many who have helped me during my research, who have given advice and encouragement and whose own work has sent my thoughts along paths that I might not otherwise have followed. In particular, I stand indebted to Hind and Mohsen Muhammad, James Piscatori, Muhammad Abd al-Halim, Sami Zubaidah, Fred Halliday, Sudipta Kaviraj, Ben Fortna, Kathryn Dean, Bill Hale, Eberhard Kienle, Malise Ruthven and Ali Rahnema. Finally, no book can appear without the confidence of the publisher in the project and in the author. I would therefore like to thank Marigold Acland, Senior Commissioning Editor at Cambridge University Press, for the faith she has shown in my work.

I cannot discharge the debts I owe to all those who have made this book possible, but I hope at least that it can stand as a token of my gratitude to them.

Glossary

chador	lit. tent, thus cloth covering a woman's body
faqih (pl. *fuqaha'*)	jurist
fatwa	judgement
fiqh	jurisprudence
hadith	saying or tradition of the Prophet Muhammad
halal	permitted
haram	forbidden
hijab	woman's head covering or veil
ijma'	consensus
ijtihad	independent interpretation of a legal or theological question in Islam
infitah	lit. opening, thus the opening of the economy to private and foreign capital
ishtirakiyah	socialism
jahiliyah (adj. *jahili*)	lit. ignorance, thus the period prior to the Islamic era
jihad	effort or struggle (on behalf of Islam)
mal	wealth
maslahah	welfare
milk	property
mudarabah	contract in which a lender puts up capital and a borrower invests time, energy and expertise
muhtasib	inspector of markets and public morals
mujahid (pl. *mujahidun*; Persian *mojahed*)	struggler, fighter
mujtama'	society
murabahah	contract in which a lender buys goods on behalf of another party and charges that party a fee
musharakah	contract in which both borrower and lender make a financial investment in a venture
mu'tazilah	school of speculative theology in medieval Islam

nass	text
purdah	(female) seclusion
qiyas	analogy
riba	interest
salafi (pl. *salafiyun*)	one who follows the example of the earliest Muslims
shari'ah	Islamic law
shirk	polytheism
sunnah	legally binding precedents established by the rulings of the Qur'an and the traditions of the Prophet Muhammad
surah	chapter of the Qur'an
tafsir	exegesis (of the Qur'an)
tanzimat	nineteenth-century reform movement of the Ottoman Empire
'ulama (sing. *'alim*)	Islamic scholar
ummah	(Muslim) community
wali al-amr	principal political authority
watan	fatherland
zakat	alms, thus alms tax

Introduction

Vivid but contrasting images come to mind when considering Islamic responses to capitalism. The burning towers of the World Trade Center in New York in September 2001 have become powerful icons of the early twenty-first century, representing for some a violent rejection of the power of global capitalism at the heart of its main marketplace by Muslims who believed they were doing the work of God. Yet images of a different kind of response, less shocking but more substantial, have long been available. Since the 1970s the financial press and then the global media have reported extensively on the rapid growth of Islamic banks and on the opening of Islamic banking facilities by bastions of conventional capitalism such as Citibank and Chase International. Here too the initiative has been justified with reference to distinctively Islamic injunctions.

Both cases, radically different as they are, represent forms of engagement by Muslims with a world shaped by industrial capitalism. Furthermore, both owe much to distinctive debates during the past fifty years or so among Muslim intellectuals who have developed contrasting answers to the question of how a Muslim should act in the world. Those for whom these actions had meaning – self-immolation in an act of merciless violence or the pursuit of ethically sanctioned profit – can draw upon a repertoire of Islamic terms, narratives and prescriptions familiar to many, but assembled in particular combinations according to a logic that is not exclusive to Muslims, let alone to an abstracted 'Islam'. The fact that those responsible for these contrasting courses of action believe themselves to be acting upon specifically Islamic grounds is not irrelevant, but their actions are also shaped by the economic and political structures with which they are engaging.

Consequently, this book seeks to examine why such different responses can be justified with reference to a repertoire of identifiable Islamic beliefs, and why it can provide Muslims with valid reasons for acting in such contradictory ways. The intention is to understand how those who do not simply happen to be Muslim, but who see themselves as providing guidance and example to other Muslims, have tried to meet the challenges of industrial capitalism. Other studies have done much to illuminate, for instance, Islamic jurists' writings on aspects of commercial life, financial institutions and the relations of production and markets underpinning a capitalist economy.[1] There are also many original contributions to the study of the encounter between Islamic traditions of thought and those of a predominantly Western European modernity.[2] However, relatively little has been published which assesses the specifically Islamic responses to capitalism as a social and economic phenomenon.[3]

As Braudel has pointed out, the term capitalism is primarily political, first used by some of the harshest critics of a process which, during the industrial revolution, moved out from the relatively restricted commercial and financial fields to colonise all of social and economic life. At its heart lies a series of negations or exclusions, founded upon new understandings of property and labour, and increasingly incorporated into the legal, coercive apparatus of the political order. This process and its formidable defences were condemned by many. Proudhon, for example, characterised capitalism as a regime, founded on private property, in which 'capital, the source of income, does not generally belong to those who make it work through labour'.[4]

As a historical phenomenon, since the seventeenth century the organisation of economic life that became the capitalist system has taken numerous forms, embodied in systems of mass industrial production, in networks of financial institutions and in the organisation of firms. Different countries and different histories have lent to capitalist enterprise in any particular place and time specific aspects, such as attitudes to labour, to the role of the state or to the environment producing considerable and substantial diversity. Furthermore, the ways in which various parts of the world first experienced the beginnings of capitalist enterprise and the transformation of their economies have

---

[1] See Maxime Rodinson, *Islam and Capitalism* (London, 1974), and Peter Gran, *Islamic Roots of Capitalism* (Austin, TX, 1979).

[2] See Aziz Al-Azmeh, *Islams and Modernities* (London, 1993); Leonard Binder, *Islamic Liberalism* (Chicago, 1988); John Cooper, Ronald Nettler and Mohamed Mahmoud (eds.), *Islam and Modernity* (London, 1998); Hamid Enayat, *Modern Islamic Political Thought* (London, 1982); Albert Hourani, *Arabic Thought in the Liberal Age* (Cambridge, 1962); Fahmi Jad'an, *Usus al-taqaddum 'ind mufakkiray al-islam fi al-'alam al-'arabi al-hadith* (Beirut, 1981); Malcolm Kerr, *Islamic Reform: The Political and Legal Theories of Muhammad Abduh and Rashid Rida* (Berkeley, 1966); Abdallah Laroui, *Islam et modernité* (Paris, 1987).

[3] A notable example of this, however, is the chapter by Joel Beinin, 'Islamic responses to the capitalist penetration of the Middle East', in B. F. Stowasser (ed.), *The Islamic Impulse* (London, 1987). There have also been a number of complex and sound analyses of responses to specific aspects of modern capitalism – especially the banking sector and the underlying principles of the economy – in a distinctively Islamic idiom. See, for instance, most recently, Timur Kuran, *Islam and Mammon – The Economic Predicaments of Islamism* (Princeton, 2004), and Clement M. Henry and Rodney Wilson (eds.), *The Politics of Islamic Finance* (Edinburgh, 2004).

[4] Fernand Braudel, *Civilization and Capitalism 15th–18th Century*, vol. II: *The Wheels of Commerce* (London, 1983), pp. 231–9.

shaped the particular ways in which people have responded and adapted. This, in turn, has led to numerous debates, such as that between Brenner and Wallerstein, concerning the 'essential nature' of capitalism itself.[5]

For the purposes of this study, capitalism is understood as a system of economic life made distinctive by its combination of three spheres – the imaginative, the productive and the institutional. Imaginatively, capitalism has been associated with a view of human rationality which places a premium on individual self-interest, ends–means calculations and a largely utilitarian calculus of benefits. In many respects such a view of economic sociability produces, but has also been constituted by, the ways in which capital itself and its potential has been imagined, whether as raw materials, financial resources, machinery or final product.

These are represented as commodities, without moral ties, capable of being owned as private property, subject to calculation and valued insofar as they contribute to a productive process measured by the margin of profit. This, in turn, is generated by developing consumption, focusing on the satisfaction of individual wants and tying the imaginative construct of the rational, possessive consumer to the growth of the economy. Historically, the formidable power of capitalist enterprise has been seen to work, seeking out markets and profits, creating product innovation through rapid technological development, and proliferating the range of commodities on which the system depends.

These processes have generated institutional innovation, and have transformed pre-existing institutions, such as markets, financial organisations, legal systems and the territorial state. In doing so, capitalism as process and as imaginative construct has become enmeshed in other ways of viewing the world, different legacies and normative systems, making for social conflict and discontinuity, but also encouraging the adaptations which have been so much a feature of the history of global capitalist development.[6] The capacity of capitalism to be reinvented in the wake of the crises to which it has inevitably been prone has been one of the distinctive features of such a system, historically confounding those in the Islamic world and beyond who have seen crisis as the harbinger of self-destruction.

In fact, many of the characteristic features of capitalism have long existed. Some emerged and made sense initially only within a moral and legal universe particular to Western Europe, marked by a distinctive, if changing,

---

[5] V. D. Lippit, *Capitalism* (London, 2005), pp. 5–12. Robert Brenner, following Marx, argued that the key to understanding capitalism lay in the relationship between property owners and those who only had their labour to sell, whereas Immanuel Wallerstein focused more on the production of commodities for a world market. It was the global range of the market, he claimed, that distinguished capitalism from all previous systems.

[6] Kathryn Dean, *Capitalism and Citizenship: The Impossible Partnership* (London, 2003), pp. 26–9.

epistemology.[7] What is exceptional is the degree to which, during the past three hundred years, they have combined to form the core of a motor-in-history in an unprecedented way. Yet there is much within capitalist practice that can establish affinities with aspects of local cultures. Its colonising power has partly been due to its capacity to disembed practices from pre-existing moral and social constraints, isolating them and recombining them in ways more conducive to acceptance of global capitalist enterprise – an acceptance facilitated by the appearance of familiarity which has been part of the historical changes in attitudes towards profits, commodities and exchange.

For instance, commodities have been present since humans first produced for the purpose of exchange. However, under capitalism, processes of commodification have taken over the lifeworld in ways which are startling in their implications, beginning with labour and ending with the designation of thoughts, ideas and social relations as commodities. This has been made possible by the role of the market, another ancient institution which now holds a position of institutional, even normative dominance without parallel, shaping the imagination of the social world, encouraging further commodification and dictating very particular and in some respects restrictive forms of exchange.[8]

Exchange practices themselves capture much that is distinctive about capitalism. Ideas of exchange form part of a complex web of imagining the world and evaluating it, producing particular business enterprises, legal systems and states to enforce the rules.[9] This is directly relevant to Muslim responses, since rulings on fair exchange are central to all the major juristic schools of Islam. In fact, one can argue that many contemporary Islamic responses to capitalism stem from anxieties about unlicensed or unfair exchange, leading to various strategies devised to 'tame' the process and to make it authentically yet also productively part of an Islamic system, reinforcing, rather than undermining, the solidarities and trust of transactions.

---

[7] See, for instance, Ruthven's argument about the cultural and religious connection between the Christian idea of the *corpus mysticum*, the development of the fiction of the 'legal personality' from the traditions of Roman law and the emergence of the corporations which were the necessary precursors of the capitalist revolution: Malise Ruthven, *A Fury for God* (London, 2002), pp. 251–7. See also D. Chakrabarty, *Provincializing Europe* (Princeton, 2000), pp. 6–18; R. Dilley (ed.), *Contesting Markets* (Edinburgh, 1992), pp. 3–6; Ellen Meiksins Wood, *The Origins of Capitalism* (New York, 1999), pp. 2–7, 70–8.

[8] Immanuael Wallerstein, *Historical Capitalism* (London, 1996), pp. 14–18;, Antony Giddens, *The Consequences of Modernity* (Cambridge, 1991), pp. 55–61, 79–83, 101–9; Alan Macfarlane, *The Culture of Capitalism* (Oxford, 1987), pp. 225–6; Peter Berger, *The Capitalist Revolution* (Aldershot, 1987), pp. 19–27; T. Bottomore, *Theories of Modern Capitalism* (London, 1985), pp. 6–11; Robert Heilbroner, *The Nature and Logic of Capitalism* (New York, 1985), pp. 137–40; S. Narotzky, *New Directions in Economic Anthropology* (London, 1997), pp. 94–7; Dean, *Capitalism and Citizenship*, pp. 29–36, 88–95.

[9] John Davis, *Exchange* (Buckingham, 1992), pp. 7, 28, 39–45.

For many Muslim intellectuals the key question has been whether symbolic exchange and material exchange are in harmony, and whether appropriate mechanisms can be found to translate like into unlike and vice versa. This has often focused on debates about money, introducing characteristic fears and prohibitions. Both in the Islamic world and elsewhere, the fear is that money, detached from the objects which give it value, has a free-floating, amoral power, representing a serious threat to the social order and the ethical community. It is thus not surprising that in Islamic thought, as in a number of other great ethical traditions, restrictions have been devised to control monetary exchange, attempting to keep it tied to actually existing objects.[10]

These anxieties have also raised the question of the sites of exchange and the nature of what can properly be exchanged – a crucial part of the history and promise of capitalism, but also a major cause for concern in Islamic, as well as other pre-capitalist ethical traditions.[11] In a capitalist system, the market is not only the major site for the exchange of commodities, but becomes the supreme institution and dominant metaphor for most social transactions.[12] Money and the search for profit become the measures of all things, completing the circle of disembodied cash transactions in which ethical constraints are no longer considered part of the process, except prudentially. This model of rationality colonises the ethical world, suggesting that it is the model for a universal rationality, its triumph evident in the ethically sanctioned freeing of 'human nature' to become the agent that will reproduce capitalist enterprise.[13]

The combined force of these processes helps to explain the restless power of capitalism, as well as its capacity to shock pre-existing ideas of the moral economy. In part this is due to the perceived inhumanity of a system that depends so heavily upon the commodification of labour for its power. In part, however, it is also due to its ability to induce those who act and work within its terms of reference to dissolve and reconstitute all social relations, all goods

[10] J. Parry and M. Bloch (eds.), *Money and the Morality of Exchange* (Cambridge, 1989), pp. 2–3. See also Simmel's ambiguity about money as both an instrument of personal freedom, but equally, by the same token, a mechanism of social dislocation that has brought about 'instability, disorder and dissatisfaction': Georg Simmel, *The Philosophy of Money*, ed. David Frisby (London, 1990), pp. 108–30, 399–404.

[11] Arjun Appadurai (ed.), *The Social Life of Things: Commodities in Cultural Perspective* (Cambridge, 1986), 'Introduction', pp. 6–13; Ben Fine and Costas Lapavitsas, 'Markets and money in social theory: what role for economics?' *Economy and Society* 29/3 (August 2000), pp. 360–76; R. Friedland and A. F. Robertson (eds.), *Beyond the Marketplace: Rethinking Economy and Society* (New York, 1990), pp. 6–10; Davis, *Exchange*, pp. 75–8; G. Dalton (ed.), *Primitive, Archaic and Modern Economics – Essays by Karl Polanyi* (Boston, 1968), pp. 107–10.

[12] Dilley, 'Contesting Markets', pp. 10–12, 25–6.

[13] Dilley, 'Contesting Markets', pp. 18–23; Parry and Bloch, *Money*, pp. 4–6; Simmel, *Philosophy of Money*, pp. 429–31, 441–5.

and services, on its own terms. It is not simply that the morally offensive aspects of capitalism provoke, but also that its transformative potential attracts.[14] It is this which helps to explain the ambivalence of Muslim responses to a phenomenon which some see as an existential threat, but others see as an opportunity for Muslims to re-inscribe themselves into world history. For some, such as Tal'at Harb in Egypt in the early 1900s or the 'virtuous capitalists' of the Sarekat Islam in Java, resentment focused more on the non-Muslim identity of those who commanded the system and who had rigged it to serve their own ends. For many, however, the prime concern has been for the moral economy as a whole – often based upon an idealised picture of the past, both recent and ancient. This has prompted efforts in the Islamic world to devise a discourse of equal power that would break the circle of capital–market–exchange–profit–capital which so dominates social life and dictates the culture of exchange under capitalism.

In some respects, this is an idealist and a self-consciously moralising position, dealing less with the structural or institutional mechanics of capitalist enterprise than with the assumptions, values and consequences associated with capitalism as a historical phenomenon. However, whether Muslim or not, people engage with and react to aspects of capitalist practice without necessarily reflecting on capitalism as such, or its moral foundations. Counterstrategies corresponding more closely to people's notions of propriety and trust demonstrate the appeal of other systems, without setting themselves up as alternatives to capitalism itself. One example is the fund transfer system known as *hawalah* (promissory note) practised by many migrant workers from Pakistan, India and Bangladesh. Relying on interpersonal transnational networks of trust, which avoid the formal banking institutions associated with the dominant global capitalist economy, this practice is common among South Asian Muslims. It is, in this sense, a response by Muslims to the conditions of global capitalism. However, it is not a specifically Islamic practice, in the sense of being justified with reference to authoritative texts within any particular Islamic tradition, or of being confined to Muslims alone. In fact, it shares its main features with similar practices found among migrant workers and transnational communities of different backgrounds who nevertheless stand in much the same relation as each other to the dominant powers in the global division of labour.[15]

---

[14] James C. Scott, *The Moral Economy of the Peasant – Rebellion and Subsistence in South East Asia* (New Haven, 1976), pp. 2–7; Karl Polanyi, *The Great Transformation* (Boston, 2001), pp. 71–80.
[15] For an extensive and thoughtful discussion of *hawalah*, see Roger Ballard, 'A background report on the operation of informal value transfer systems (hawala)', available at http://www.art.man.ac.uk/CASAS/PDF papers/Hawala.pdf, and 'The impact of kinship on the economic dynamics of transnational networks: reflections on some South Asian developments', paper

In this study, however, the main focus will be on those who have tried to understand and to respond to capitalism, and above all to the moral freight of capitalism, from a self-consciously Islamic perspective. Some have confined themselves to publishing their views of how to guard or extend specifically Islamic identities and the interests of the imagined Islamic community in a world where material growth, technological achievement and economic power are not simply divorced from Islamic principles, but may be in conflict with them. Others, theorising about the kind of world that is coming into being, have tried to engage actively with it, or have urged Muslims to do so. Underlying both approaches has been the desire to challenge unthinking acceptance of the way the world is and to alert people to the imbalances of power inherent in forms of capitalist domination.

In this respect, many of the self-consciously Islamic writers have been concerned, like the early Christian socialists, utopian socialists, anarchists and Marxists, to identify not simply the injustice underpinning capitalist practice, but also the processes giving capitalism its power, but possibly contributing to its undoing. Muslim intellectuals have therefore trodden a path influenced by other critiques of capitalism, even while drawing upon resources distinctive of Islamic schools of thought. This has produced a wide variety of responses, reflecting the diversity of contemporary Islamic communities and their engagement with the world. They may all draw upon a broadly similar repertoire of idioms, but how they combine and interpret them will depend on their circumstances and partly also on the imaginative forms and even the normative concerns associated with the emergence of modern industrial capitalism itself. This dialectical logic has influenced the organisation of the responses, and the construction of alternatives, both imaginatively and in practice.

For many of the authors studied here, the problem of capitalism has been seen largely in idealist terms, with a focus on attitudes sanctioning capitalist practice and growth. Thus effective defence is organised around trying to change the assumptions which make these processes seem both normal and even laudable. Many Muslim intellectuals have tried to induce a shift in the way people value social transactions, alerting people to the price they are paying for uncritical engagement with a system that takes no account of their identity, or of the sublime nature of the moral code they must follow as Muslims. The aim has been to make individual Muslims impervious to the material attractions of a profit-oriented system of economic life, leading some to stress the moral regeneration of the individual. Others, however, with a

presented to a workshop on Transnational Migration, Princeton University, 29 June – 1 July 2001, available at http://www.transcomm.ox.ac.uk/working-papers.htm; also Mohammad El-Qorchi 'Hawala', *Finance and Development* 39/4 (December 2002), available at http://www.imf.org/external/pubs/ft/fandd/2002/12/elqorchi.htm.

more collective understanding of the task, have tried to imagine how the community as a whole could organise to disrupt the historical trajectory of what seems to be an all-conquering economic system.

However, the Islamic social critics, fearful of what capitalism was doing to their communities and their values, were faced by a double challenge. On the one hand, their views of society, social cohesion and public utility were informed by the very categories that had made possible the imagination of a world transformed by the expansion of capital, the organisation of human labour and the calculation of social utility. They tried to reclaim these for a distinctive Islamic order, but their reasoning was often vulnerable to the influence of that which they were seeking to criticise. Interpretations of Islamic obligations were coloured, often shaped, by these same imaginative constructions. As with other proposed alternatives to capitalism, their visions seem less like radical alternatives, and more like projects competing on the same terrain, judged therefore by broadly similar criteria.[16]

The consequences of this invasive logic were even more obvious in those projects which moved from the purely imagined sphere to that of practical action. An imagined alternative can at least be presented as under normative control. This form of reasoning, sometimes circular and often apologetic, can prevent the putative consequences from deviating from accepted Islamic values. However, in the search for effective social agency, the problem of an extraneous logic of action shaping the outcome is much greater. This is well exemplified by the delight with which gold markets welcomed the call for Muslims to return to the use of the gold dinar by the transnational Islamist group, al-Murabitun. Its spokesmen saw it as an alternative currency that would unite Muslims and undermine the financial system of modern capitalism, but the effect was simply to boost demand for a highly marketable commodity within the existing system.[17]

This is an extreme form of a more general dilemma facing Muslim intellectuals, leading to different forms of engagement. Some came to believe that the modern state, suitably directed towards the fulfilment of Islamic goals, would be the best mechanism for establishing an effective Islamic alternative, but they often found themselves entangled in the secular logic of the state. Whether those who ruled the state were using appeals to Islamic tradition

---

[16] Appadurai, *The Social Life of Things*, pp. 13–16; Robert Heilbroner, *Behind the Veil of Economics* (New York, 1988), pp. 189–99; Jon Mulberg, *Social Limits to Economic Theory* (London, 1995), pp. 12–35; Louis Dumont, *From Mandeville to Marx: The Genesis and Triumph of Economic Ideology* (Chicago, 1977); see also Baudrillard's critique of Marxism in Jean Baudrillard, *The Mirror of Production*, tr. Mark Poster (St Louis, Mo, 1975).

[17] Bill Maurer, *Mutual Life, Limited: Islamic Banking, Alternative Currencies, Lateral Reason* (Princeton, 2005), pp. 122–35; report of Granada conference, published 12 July 2003, available at http://news.bbc.co.uk/go/pr/fr/-/1/hi/world/europe/3061833.stm.

cynically or with fierce conviction, the outcome was similar. In the final analysis, the determination to strengthen the state as an apparatus of power both vis-à-vis its associated society and the outside world, and the pressing short-term calculations of political advantage, tended to override larger and more far-reaching ethical concerns. Thus, prudential considerations, in which prudence is measured by the relative success of engaging with the world as it is through the medium of the nation state and the national economy, began to outweigh all other considerations for those preoccupied with the material forms of power. However, politically, this has led to critical engagement with the state, as idea and as apparatus – engagement which has taken such diverse forms as the violent rejectionism of Al-Jama'at al-Islamiyah in Egypt or the acceptance of the free-market, parliamentary republic in Turkey by the Adalet ve Kalkinma Partisi (AKP).

A similar argument could be made for those who looked to the creation of distinctively Islamic financial institutions as a way of harnessing economic growth for the benefit of the Muslim community at large. These institutions took two directions. Either they became the institutions of national economies, such as the Iranian banking system, which, whilst they undoubtedly benefited those Muslims within the jurisdiction of the state, although by no means all equally, became a recognisable subsidiary of a global economy that owed nothing to distinctively Islamic principles or practices. Alternatively, they developed as private financial institutions, initiating the dynamic expansion of Islamic banking witnessed since the 1970s and providing Muslims with ethically sound vehicles for full participation in global markets of capital and commodities. In both cases, the response to the dominant capitalist order has been distinct, but largely integrative in effect. For the many who have participated in these activities or who have justified them in the terms of Islamic jurisprudence, they have provided one answer to the question of how to lead a good Muslim life in the world of capitalist modernity.

However, there have been other responses, drawing equally upon traditions of Islamic jurisprudence. Faced by the power of these examples and the transformations embraced by their fellow Muslims, a number of intellectuals developed responses that were primarily symbolic. They have been troubled not simply by capitalism, but also by a subversive rationality grounded in the assumptions and norms which made capitalism both thinkable and desirable. They have responded in ways which aim for autonomy and ethical self-sufficiency, drawing upon a repertoire familiar to Muslims and invoking a value system that does not depend for its validation upon the working out of 'Islamic' institutions upon a terrain already demarcated by capitalism itself.

This remains an aspiration for those who insist on the impossibility of synthesis between Islamic and non-Islamic values. It has led to attempts to create a 'guarded sphere' as an imaginative and social construct within which an ideal of Islamic life can be led under the oversight of those who can unfailingly distinguish right from wrong, the Islamic from the un-Islamic.[18] The ideal and the practical aspects of this response come together in the role conferred on women and in the institution of the 'Islamic family' – spheres represented as insulated from the world and claimed, therefore, as the foundation of an authentically Islamic response to that world. For others, the symbolic response can imply spectacular violence, the violent act represented as a way of jolting out of their complacency those who have been co-opted unthinkingly or have taken for granted the way the world is constituted.

However, the 'symbolic turn' cannot wholly escape from the logic of practice and the requirements of acting effectively in the world. In the case of the 'guarded sphere', it becomes difficult to sustain the assumption that Muslim women can be ascribed a purely symbolic and homogeneous identity, conferred upon them by male coreligionists. Even where Muslim women have themselves subscribed to part of this narrative, they have increasingly seen themselves as actors in their own right, able to determine their own forms of engagement with the world through state institutions, property ownership or economic enterprise. The power of worldly engagement takes over, seized by women who, although fully aware of their Islamic identities, understandably refuse to see themselves simply as ciphers in a repertoire of symbols devised by men.

Similarly, a paradox arises in connection with symbolic violence. Its effective organisation requires structure, motivation and mobilisation – all of which may depend upon a range of other contexts and processes. Furthermore, the symbolic does not come out of a vacuum. On the contrary, it forms part of a communicative system which may itself be subject to rules that make it less autonomous than may be supposed by the protagonists. The idiom will be shaped to some degree by the situation which calls for a distinctive response.

In order to understand the dynamics and the dilemmas faced by Muslim intellectuals in mapping out alternatives to the dominant capitalist order, the contours of their discourse must be determined. Capitalism has not been a problem that has engaged all the major thinkers of the contemporary Islamic world, many of whom have paid scant attention to capitalism as such, even if most have dealt with aspects of social interaction and power relations integral to the phenomenon of capitalist expansion and colonisation. However, during the twentieth century there emerged a significant number of Muslim intellectuals who were often influenced by each other's writings, even though they

---

[18] More ambitiously, the Taliban tried to make the whole of Afghanistan a 'guarded sphere' with predictably disastrous and self-defeating results – see Ahmed Rashid, *Taliban: The Story of the Afghan Warlords* (London, 2001).

themselves wrote at different periods and in different parts of the world. They wrote primarily as Muslims, but they had been open to a range of different influences, some from Islamic sources, some from the secular liberal and socialist debates of their own or previous eras. What unites them further is the belief that capitalism is a distinct kind of problem and that Muslims and others can find answers to that problem in the traditions of Islam.

This study, therefore, seeks to understand the repertoire of distinctively Islamic responses, in order to form a picture of the 'alphabet' of identifying markers from which particular vocabularies of social action have been constructed.[19] At the same time, it looks at the processes which have shaped the articulation of these vocabularies, their terms and their grammar, examining how and why they were put together as they were. Consequently, this is not an account of the political economy of the countries where Muslims mostly live. It is not argued here that self-consciously Islamic thinking about capitalism has been simply a reflection of the material vicissitudes of the political economy at the time, important as aspects of this may have been in suggesting themes or highlighting issues of particular concern. Nor is this an intellectual biography of those who have voiced these sentiments, in part because the consistency and indeed continuity of many of the responses and their forms soon become apparent, regardless of where the writers themselves are situated in terms of country or moment in history.

The intention is, rather, to understand the logic of ideas, the forms of imagination and thought which were called into being by the sensed need to respond to a phenomenon that was transforming human transactions across the globe. In this regard, the central question is how these responses have been formed from a distinctive Islamic 'alphabet', but shaped by a grammar already out there, external to the tradition, which is nevertheless intrinsic to the endeavour. This involves examining the implications of that tradition and how it is understood when it is thus constructed – the self-conscious and reflexive reconstruction of those elements which are intended to guarantee an adaptive and responsive authenticity. It is, therefore, an attempt to understand powerful but contrasting ways of engaging with the world, all distinctively Islamic, but with radically different implications for Muslim responses to capitalism and its institutions.

No attempt has been made here exhaustively to catalogue responses across the Islamic world, let alone to suggest that being Muslim necessarily triggers a specific kind of response. On the contrary, it is the variety of responses which is striking, as well as the degree to which many of them share their

---

[19] I am indebted to Sudipta Kaviraj for this imaginative way of representing the process by which distinctive articulations of contemporary ideologies may draw upon much wider, prolific and often ambiguous cultural traditions, symbols and beliefs.

structure, but understandably not their idiom, with the ways in which others, in very different settings and traditions of thought, have sought to grapple with the moral and practical complexities of capitalism. In this sense, therefore, although the great majority of authors cited are situated in the Arabic-speaking world, the elements of a self-consciously Islamic alphabet used by different writers to articulate their responses have been common to all those who identify themselves with reference to Islam, regardless of their linguistic inheritance. This has produced a variety of answers, but again, within a certain range which recurs from the Arabic-speaking to the Malay-speaking worlds.

The similarity of this range to those found in secular discourses, as well as in other religious and normative idioms, suggests that, whilst the alphabet may be distinctive to Islam, the logic governing its formation into a consciously Islamic vocabulary and grammar may owe as much to the conditions associated with the development of capitalism itself and the worlds it has created. Understanding this aspect highlights the fact that there are many ways of being Muslim in the world, subject to the processes of change which have continued to transform social and economic life. None can remain untouched by the world, but this does not necessarily imply acceptance of that world as it is.

1   The 'social problem'

The developments in this chapter are bracketed by two distinctive phases of European imperialism in the Middle East, North Africa and Asia: first as intrusive power, bringing into local worlds the material and imaginative forms that made European imperialism such a formidable global force in the eighteenth and nineteenth centuries; second as retreating power, leaving behind states based on colonial creations, tied to a global economic system reflecting the values and interests of the departing imperial states. Between these two ragged events the peoples subjected to the forces unleashed thereby tried to understand what was happening to them and to their communities, impelling them to respond in ways that would allow them to engage with a world in the process of creation.

Most prominently, the response to these developments was articulated by those in charge of the states and empires which confronted European power as a threat to their political and military security. In the Ottoman Empire in the eighteenth century, for instance, it was initially thought that adopting European military technologies would be enough to guard the realm from further encroachment. This proved to be illusory. However, the very failure of this approach, painfully visible in the military reverses of the empire during this period, gave heart to tradition-minded critics of reform. They had argued perceptively that technology, far from being neutral, would bring with it changes in attitudes and ethics that would threaten the core of the Ottoman Islamic order.[1]

This argument had considerable influence in the late eighteenth and early nineteenth century, but it also provided the very rationale for Sultan Mahmud's extensive administrative, military, legal and educational reforms in the 1830s. He was persuaded not only of the benefit of the material innovations coming from the West, but also of the need to change the ways in which his subjects behaved, so that they could successfully adapt to developments which had conferred such military and economic power on the

---

[1] Niyazi Berkes, *The Development of Secularism in Turkey* (New York, 1998), pp. 51–63.

13

states of Europe.[2] Thus, the reforms which followed were not confined to the military or administrative spheres, but also shaped economic life.

Epitomised to some degree by the 1838 commercial treaty between Great Britain and the Ottoman state, profound changes then took place. The treaty opened up the empire to foreign trade, leading to the direct incorporation of agriculture and industry into the capitalist world market, with banks, financial institutions, joint stock companies and other distinctive forms of European capitalist organisation beginning to dominate the economic landscape. For the Ottoman state this meant a growing indebtedness and concessions to European trading power in the form of the Capitulations. For many sectors of the Ottoman population the consequences were dramatic and often unsettling. Some regions became directly affected by fluctuations in the world market through their production of specialised agricultural commodities. In others, traditional industries collapsed in the face of competition from manufactured goods produced in Europe, and everywhere large numbers of peasants abandoned the countryside and migrated to the cities.[3]

Similar processes were affecting other parts of the Islamic world, whether in Southeast Asia, India, Iran or North Africa. In these territories, the responses of local rulers reflected the condition of their states and the coherence of their administrations. For instance, attempts by the Persian statesman Amir-i Kabir to respond to a similar set of circumstances – the linking of sectors of Persian agriculture to the uncertainty of the world market and the decline of traditional manufacturing – were not particularly successful.[4] However, as in the Ottoman case, they represented an effort to engage with a new capitalist economic order, armed with new forms of knowledge. This was in part technical, but it was also administrative, indicating the concern of governments to use such knowledge for the benefit of the state – well captured in the Ottoman institution of the *tanzimat* era, the Board of Useful Affairs.

However, governments' views were informed by and in turn influenced those whose concerns were not strictly utilitarian. As the early responses had shown, serious reflection had begun not simply on the nature of the challenges thrown up by external forces, but also on the vulnerabilities of local communities. With the more sustained development of a critical and reflexive attitude to their own environment, traditions and customs, those who were

[2] Berkes, *Development of Secularism*, pp. 89–132.
[3] Zafer Toprak, 'From liberalism to solidarism: the Ottoman economic mind in the age of the nation state (1820–1920)', in R. Motika, C. Herzog and M. Ursinus (eds.), *Studies in Ottoman Social and Economic Life* (Heidelberg, 1999), pp. 171–84; Berkes, *Development of Secularism*, pp. 137–54.
[4] Charles Issawi (ed.), *The Economic History of Iran 1800–1914* (Chicago, 1971) pp. 14–19, 130–42, 292–300.

determined either to reform or conserve were obliged to think about – and devise a vocabulary to describe and fix in the imagination – the object of their concern. It was this that led to the 'discovery of society'.

1.1   Discovering society

For many of the early observers of European power in the Islamic lands, whether in the Ottoman, the Qajar or the Mughal empires, the exceptional nature of that power lay not so much in military prowess, but in the order established in the aftermath of conquest. This promised wide-ranging transformations in the lands so rapidly conquered. As 'Abd al-Rahman al-Jabarti's observations of the French in Egypt make clear, European technology did not tell the whole story. There was something equally potent in the way the French organised and generally comported themselves, puzzling and even repulsive as some of these practices were to al-Jabarti.[5] What began as a description of the marvels (*'aja'ib*) of the exotic, became increasingly an attempt to understand these forms of behaviour as part of a system, sustained not simply by the machines of material power, but by the imaginative and moral framework in which their use made sense.

Furthermore, it was obvious that the exoticism of these systems rapidly diminished as they began to have an impact on the lives of those Muslims who were drawn into their web of power. They became integral to the lives of many across the Islamic world, stimulating efforts to understand the nature of these new forms of behaviour, their moral sanctions, the discipline they encouraged and the power they granted to those who engaged with them. These were subjects of fascination for thinkers and writers from the Islamic lands during the long nineteenth century.

However, in entering this new field of social knowledge, a number of problems arose. Firstly, the very object of study needed to be identified. Material forms of power were cognitively familiar, since they were seen as improvements on existing technologies. More challenging to the existing vocabulary and imagination were the human relations associated with these forms of power, whether in war or in economic production. The old epithets – *al-ifranj* (Franks), *rumi* (Roman) and *kafir* (unbeliever) – that both described and distanced these phenomena no longer served their purpose. They did little

---

[5] 'Abd al-Rahman al-Jabarti, *'Aja'ib al-athar fi al-turajim wa-l-akhbar*, vol. IV (Cairo, 1905), translated as *Napoleon in Egypt: Al-Jabarti's Chronicle of the French Occupation of Egypt 1798* (translation of the ms. *Ta'rikh muddat al-faransis bi-Misr*), ed. and tr. S. Moreh (Princeton, 1993), pp. 61–77, 109–11. Abu Lughod suggests that al-Jabarti and Niqula al-Turk tended to ignore 'French political concepts of state and society', in part because of the very conceptual unfamiliarity of these ideas: Ibrahim Abu-Lughod, *The Arab Rediscovery of Europe* (Princeton, 1963), pp. 20–5.

to capture the essence of the processes which drove the new technologies. Nor were they reassuring for those concerned about the implications for their Islamic identities. Aspects of these innovations had obvious benefits, enthusiastically endorsed by some Muslims who yet remained deeply suspicious about their origins, since they suggested a strengthening of one faith at the expense of another. It was not surprising, therefore, that a vocabulary which described human community less in terms of faith and belief and more in terms of a universal functionality should have had a growing appeal.[6]

In the Islamic lands, a secular, functional discourse on human affairs paradoxically provided those who adhered strongly to a sense of distinctively Muslim community with an apparently neutral, universal vocabulary that promised to explain the nature of the transformations with which they and their communities were confronted. Responses could therefore in theory be judged according to the ways in which these changes improved or impaired the functioning of this community, without weakening or diluting the faith that lay at its heart. It was not until later in the twentieth century that fears developed about using seemingly neutral language that in fact carried a distinct and significant normative freight.[7]

Central to the new vocabulary of ontological understanding was the concept of 'society' itself. In European thought its meanings had changed in significant ways, reflecting the changes taking place in societal relations, both structurally and imaginatively.[8] New meanings, embodied in changed usages, carried with them different ways of conceiving of social action, making certain acts significant and valued, whilst marginalising others.[9] Indeed, the very changes in the ways people lived their lives, brought about by the momentous developments of 'the Great Transformation', were intimately

---

[6] A similar process had taken place in post-Enlightenment Europe: see E. Troeltsch, *The Social Teaching of the Christian Churches*, 2 vols. tr. O. Wyon (Louisville, KY, 1992), vol. I, pp. 280–305; B. Stiltner, *Religion and the Common Good* (Lanham, MD, 1999), pp. 17–43.

[7] See Muhammad Yahia, *Fi al-radd 'ala al-'ilmaniyah* (Cairo, 1985), pp. 31–40; Yusuf al-Qardawi, *Al-Islam wa-l-'ilmaniyah* (Cairo, 1987), pp. 191–208; Gamal Sultan, *Ghazw min al-dakhil* (Cairo, 1988), pp. 35–53, 57–86. Even one of the leading figures of the Islamic reform movement, Jamal al-Din al-Afghani, was concerned. See *Al-Radd 'ala al-dahriyin (Refutation of the Materialists* – 'Abduh's rendering of al-Afghani's original title *Refutation of the Naturalists (neitshiriyye')*), ed. Shaikh Muhammad Abu Rayyah (Beirut, 1981; originally published in Cairo in 1885), although Turner rightly observes that 'in one sense the authors of Islamic reform were Rousseau, Comte, Spencer and Durkheim'. B. Turner, *Weber and Islam*, Max Weber Classic Monographs VII (London, 1998), pp. 144–8.

[8] Raymond Williams, *Keywords* (London, 1983), pp. 291–3.

[9] M. Foucault, *The Order of Things* (London, 1980), pp. xv–xxiv, 50–63, 250–63. Bourdieu has something similar to say in relation to changing rules of practice and how this is understood and given significance by actors habituated to other practices. P. Bourdieu, *In Other Words*, tr. M. Adamson (Cambridge, 1990), pp. 76–86; and *The Logic of Practice*, tr. R. Nice (Cambridge, 1990).

associated with the emergence of a new vocabulary, or the new usage of existing words.[10] In particular, there was a need to capture the sense of movement and change, and to respond to a perceived crisis, favourable as some may have been towards the direction of change.[11] The nature of this crisis was located variously in the individual, in groups, in social norms or in social bonds, depending upon the preoccupations of the writer concerned, but the general concern was to understand how this affected the fabric of society as a whole.

At this time, writers across the Islamic lands, in common with and influenced by European writers, were developing a vocabulary to enable them to classify and analyse events in their own countries. Mitchell has listed some of the terms used by mainly Egyptian writers to provide a conceptual grasp of the hitherto unacknowledged forces that were thought to be shaping their world. In particular, he brings to our attention the al-Azhar-trained writer Husain al-Marsafi's work *Risalat al-kalim al-thaman* (Essay on Eight Words) published in 1881. A professor at the newly established Dar al-'Ulum, al-Marsafi sought to explicate the key words associated with the emergence of modern nationalism which would, he argued, if properly used, help Egyptians and Muslims to deal with the political crisis unfolding at the time. In doing so, he displays a characteristic hybridity of conception and vocabulary which mixes contemporary French thought with that of Ibn Khaldun, supported by the textual authority of the Qur'an and the *hadith*.[12] In these endeavours, the effort to find a term for 'society' itself was central. This was not the apparently simple search for linguistic equivalence. Rather, it involved no less than the imaginative reconstruction of the prism through which human affairs would be observed, profoundly shaping the understanding of the forces that bound people to each other.

Some of this can be seen in the terms used to describe the newly apprehended phenomenon of 'society'. Many refer to the idea of organisation

[10] Polanyi, *The Great Transformation*, pp. 116–35.

[11] Views of the nature of that crisis – and the new beginnings to which it might be giving birth – differed, but it can be argued that thinkers as diverse as Marx, Weber, Durkheim and Spencer, in depicting society, all made aspects of social crisis and transformation central to their work. See E. Durkheim, *The Rules of Sociological Method*, tr. W. D. Halls (London, 1982), pp. 85–107; P. Wagner, 'Crises of modernity: political sociology in historical contexts', in Stephen P. Turner (ed.), *Social Theory and Sociology* (Oxford, 1996), pp. 97–110; C. Schilling and P. A. Mellor, *The Sociological Ambition* (London, 2001), pp. 43–8, 58–68.

[12] Timothy Mitchell, *Colonising Egypt* (Cambridge, 1988), pp. 119–21, 131–7. Characteristic of this, for example, was al-Marsafi's discussion of the meaning of *al-watan* (fatherland) in which he outlines both the physical phenomenon of a bounded territory and the spirit that infuses it and gives political and imaginative significance to the word. Hasan al-Marsafi, *Risalat al-kalim al-thaman*, ed. Ahmad Zakaria al-Shalaq (Cairo, 1984), pp. 85–108. Among the other words were *al-ummah* (nation/community), *al-hukumah* (government), *al-hurriyah* (freedom) and *al-tarbiyah* (education).

(*al-intizam al-'umrani* (civilisational organisation), *al-jami'iyat al-muntazi-mah* (organised association)) – variations from the root *nazama* (organise), implying an overseeing intelligence. Others make direct reference to the concept of the *ummah* or community [of faith], as in al-Tahtawi's explanation that his term for 'society', *al-hay'at al-mujtama'iyah* (the collective form) is equivalent to *majmu'at al-ummah* (the whole community). But he also used other terms for 'society', such as *al-ijtima' al-bashri* and *al-jama'iyah* – all derived from the root word *jam'*(collection, group or plurality).[13] Increasingly, it was a derivation from this root, *al-mujtama'*, with its association as descriptor of both a place (meeting place, place of assembly) and a moment of encounter (gathering, assembly), which came to mean 'society' both for secular and for self-consciously Islamic writers in the Arabic-speaking world. It is tempting to say that the language by which the phenomenon of society became known followed the kinds of social change referred to by Tönnies in the transition from *Gemeinschaft* to *Gesellschaft*, whereby the term *al-ummah* expressed the former and the more impersonal neologism of *al-mujtama'* corresponded to the latter.[14]

There was no such mechanical reflection, but an echo does exist in the fact that, whether in Europe or in the Islamic lands of the Middle East, people were searching for new vocabularies with which to describe and understand the changes occurring in economic and social life in the long nineteenth century. The challenge was to find ways of apprehending social relations founded upon the functional interactions brought into being through industrial capitalism and the commodification of labour, as well as the particular forms of urbanisation and political discipline associated with the development of a capitalist society.

It is precisely in this setting that functionalism plays such an important role in shaping the way in which society as a phenomenon comes to be apprehended. Functionalism – the idea that social formations all have distinct roles

---

[13] Al-Tahtawi's work is characterised throughout by the attempt to relate neologisms, such as fatherland or nation, to analogous formations in Islamic history, backed up by the appropriate affirmation and moral commendation of such terms – or their equivalents – by the Prophet Muhammad, the rightly guided Caliphs and other authoritative figures. See, for example, his treatment of *al-watan* (fatherland) in *Kitab manahij al-albab al-misriyah fi mubahij al-adab al-'asriyah*, in Rifa'ah Rafi' al-Tahtawi, *Al-A'mal al-kamilah*, part 1, ed. Muhammad 'Imarah (Beirut, 1973), pp. 249–62. For his formulation regarding society, see also his *Kitab al-murshid al-amin li-l-banat wa-l-banin*, in *Al-A'mal al-kamilah*, part 2, pp. 312, 473–6; Mitchell, *Colonising Egypt*, p. 120.

[14] Whether this corresponds in a strict historical sense to the meanings Tönnies attached to the terms is open to debate. However, it is clear that for many of the Islamist writers, *al-ummah* (community of faith), idealised, did indeed correspond in the imagination to the organic, 'natural' community signified by the term *Gemeinschaft*. F. Tönnies, *Community and Association*, tr. C. P. Loomis (London, 1955), pp. 16–29, 37–9, 74–7.

to play in a division of labour, the end point of which is the 'proper function-ing' of society as a whole – was a common trope of nineteenth century thought. The teleological understanding of social action taken beyond the conscious purposes of the actors themselves, the idea not simply that society was more than the sum of its parts but that it worked, with greater or lesser success, towards the achievement of some given end, was a form of social imagination that shaped thinkers as diverse as Marx, Comte and Durkheim.[15] Diverse as their writings were, they tended to share the assumption of an overarching imperative, a collective moral intelligence, which social forma-tions embodied and, in changing, helped to transform. The key differences could be said to lie in the widely differing notions of the nature of this imperative and of the constitution of the metanarrative that informed human societies and their histories. In this respect, the argument amongst the differ-ent schools of social theory was indeed a moral argument, concerning the norms and practices that constituted a well-ordered society and thus, by contrast, the contradictions, frictions and problems that contributed to its dysfunctionality.

The relevance of this for debates within the Islamic world is that here too functionalism made intellectual and moral sense, not simply because of the powerful influence of European writers whose works were being avidly read in translation and in the original by the late nineteenth century. These writings were in part so influential because although they introduced new terms and references, they were set within a framework of functional explanation that had great local resonance. In Islamic thought, the dominant social imaginary is the subservience of human society to the will of God. Service to the Creator is the goal of existence, social and individual, and, insofar as the moral purpose enshrined in such service is only possible in the company of other beings, the telos of society is evident. This was the function by which society should be judged.[16]

Equally powerful was the related 'organic analogy' which compared human society to the human body, using the notions of corporeal unity to describe and understand the relationship of the parts to the whole. Again, this could take various forms, with some authors, such as Jamal al-Din al-Afghani, seeking to associate specific social functions with particular parts of the body, such that the analogy seemed almost to serve as an explanation in and of itself.[17]

---

[15] Robert Merton, *On Theoretical Sociology* (New York, 1967), vol. II, pp. 73–114; Dorothy Emmet, *Function, Purpose and Powers* (London, 1958), pp. 45–87; R. Fletcher, *The Making of Sociology*, 2 vols. (London, 1971), vol. II, pp. 671–8.

[16] This is already visible in al-Tahtawi's writings – see al-Tahtawi, *Kitab al-murshid* in *Al-A'mal al-kamilah*, part 2, pp. 445–6, 525–9.

[17] Jamal al-Din al-Afghani, *Al-A'mal al-kamilah*, ed. Muhammad 'Imarah (Cairo: 1968), pp. 340–6, 352–7; al-Afghani, *Al-Radd 'ala al-dahriyin*, p. 89; Mitchell, *Colonising Egypt*, p. 155.

Others used it to describe, indeed to justify, the division of labour in society, as well as the associated hierarchies of power and status. Drawing upon a tradition of Islamic natural philosophy analogous and related to European medieval ecclesiastical views of the body politic and the natural, God-given order of society, writers such as al-Tahtawi, al-Afghani, al-Marsafi and 'Abduh were able to assimilate the new concepts of society and of nation into an established idiom.[18]

In doing so, they were particularly receptive to the ideas and metaphors of those European social theorists who were preoccupied by the strength, vitality and, conversely, the pathology of society. Thus, Herbert Spencer, with his ideas of the health of discrete societies and his view of societal competition, transmitted a form of social Darwinism into the Islamic lands.[19] For some, this evoked an echo of the writings of the fourteenth/ fifteenth-century historian Ibn Khaldun (d. 1406 CE). His accounts of the flourishing and decay of dynastic states, of the importance of forms of social solidarity and of the unending struggle for survival by competing social entities had been important and early articulations of a theory of history, understood as the development of power and authority through particular social formations.

The significance of Ibn Khaldun in the nineteenth century was that he appeared to provide an authentic, independent and indigenous set of tools for understanding Middle Eastern society. The fact that he was writing as a Muslim and yet appeared able to regard Islam dispassionately, as a factor in social explanation, made his writings appealing to very different kinds of people. Certain Muslim authors wanted to draw on an indigenous tradition and saw his works as invaluable. A number of European writers read Ibn Khaldun as an early sociologist who could provide a key to understanding the specific conditions of Islamic, Arab or North African society and saw in his general propositions concerning society and social solidarity the universality of a functionalist language of social explanation.[20]

In this respect, therefore, it was scarcely surprising that authors like Gustave Le Bon became highly influential in the Arab and Islamic worlds

---

[18] Al-Azmeh, *Islams and Modernities*, pp. 79–84; Muhammad 'Abduh, 'Hukumatuna wa-l-jam'iyat al-khairiyah', in *Al-A'mal al-kamilah*, part 2, ed. Muhammad 'Imarah (Beirut, 1980), pp. 7–9; al-Marsafi, *Risalah*, pp. 134–5; al-Tahtawi, *Al-A'mal al-kamilah*, part 1, p. 247; al-Afghani, *Al-A'mal al-kamilah*, pp. 347–51; 'Madi al-ummah wa-hadruha wa-'alaj 'ilaliha', *Al-Manar* 9/9 (1324/1906) pp. 664–72.

[19] Herbert Spencer, *Structure, Function and Evolution*, ed. S. Andreski (London, 1971), pp. 63–74, 107–17, 148–77.

[20] Aziz Al-Azmeh, *Ibn Khaldun in Modern Scholarship* (London, 1981) pp. 49–58, 181–8; Ahmed Zayed, *The Development of Social Science in Egypt*, in Cairo Papers in Social Science, vol. xviii, monograph 3 (Cairo, 1996), pp. 49–50.

primarily, but also elsewhere, both among determined secularists and self-conscious Islamists. Indeed, one of the appeals of the kind of language, analysis and organicist analogy used by functionalist writers like Le Bon and indeed Durkheim is that they could appeal both to convinced materialists, such as the Young Ottomans/Young Turks, and to those, like Muhammad 'Abduh in Egypt, who wanted to guard the Islamic identity of society whilst trying to recast the way in which Islamic obligations were traditionally thought of.[21]

It is here that one can see the plasticity of functionalism and of functionalist explanation as a form of social theorising. Although framed as an objective, universal language for understanding social processes, its very universality is based upon the ease with which it can be melded to suit a range of given ends. The common feature must be the teleological nature of the enterprise, not necessarily the telos itself. It is this which provides the criteria against which the functioning of society and, by implication, its various parts can be judged. It became evident that the functionalist 'science of society', defined with reference to the telos of advanced industrial capitalism, was preparing the ground for the acceptance of many of the values linked to accompanying ideas of 'social improvement' and 'social progress'. Thus, criteria of worth and even social categories hitherto associated with the European 'other' became incorporated even into the discourse of those seeking to reconstruct a distinctively Islamic social solidarity, as shown by Rafiq al-'Azm's use of the categories of 'individual' and 'community' in sketching the outlines of reinvigorated and distinctively Islamic society.[22]

Seeing society through the prism of functionalism helped to define the 'social problem'. This took a variety of forms. One noticeable theme, visible in early European sociology and taken up by some Muslim intellectuals, was the dark side of industrial and technological progress, focusing on the ways in which internal social bonds were being undermined, weakening the cohesion of society and promising an uncertain future. Here dysfunctionality was equated with the fragmentation and anomie induced by the conditions of life associated with the advance of industrial capitalism, the dissolution of social bonds and the problem of reconstituting an order that was not doomed

---

[21] Sukru Hanioglu, *The Young Turks in Opposition*, (New York, 1995), pp. 10–13, 21–3, 200–3; Mitchell, *Colonising Egypt*, pp. 123–5; Al-Azmeh, *Islams and Modernities*, pp. 81–2; see also Gustave Le Bon, *La civilisation des Arabes* (Paris, 1884), pp. vi–xi, 656–77. He called his approach to understanding society and civilisation 'l'embryologie sociale', p. viii. As early as 1898 this book was translated into Urdu as *Tamaddun-i 'Arab*, tr. Syed Ali Asgar Bilgrami (Madras, 1898).

[22] Rafiq al-'Azm, *Tanbih al-afham ila mutalib al-hayat al-ijtima'iyah wa-l-islam* (Cairo, 1899) – cited in Jad'an, *Usus al-taqaddum 'ind mufakkiray al-islam fi al-'alam al-'arabi al-hadith*, pp. 493–9.

to self-destruct through its own internal contradictions.[23] Thus, many of the Islamic writers were discovering society through the discovery of what was pulling it apart. Identification of the phenomenon, understanding its ills and setting forth the remedies that would keep it together and strengthen its distinctively Islamic identity were the simultaneous preoccupations. This was not simply the disinterested study of society as a generic phenomenon, but the attempt to understand the roots of social power.[24]

1.2   Property and social power

One major set of preoccupations understandably arose from the differentials of prosperity between European and Islamic societies. This was based not simply on the obvious financial and commercial power of the expanding European empires, but also on the observations of numerous travellers from the Islamic lands to the industrialising states of Europe. For people such as Rifa'ah al-Tahtawi from Egypt, Khair al-Din al-Tunisi from Istanbul and North Africa, Malkam Khan from Iran or Syed Ahmed Khan from India the dynamic urban economic activity of the great European cities, their relative social order and their evident technological invention and wealth inspired and challenged them to reflect upon their own societies. The challenge was how best to capture this energy and how to reproduce the visible strengths of European societies through the transformation of their own.

For many, the key to prosperity lay in the disposition of property, but this was also the nexus of distinctive Islamic obligations. The challenge for many was to ensure that reforms in one sphere, so evident at the time in the Ottoman Empire and in British India, should not compromise the obligations in the other. For al-Tahtawi in Egypt or al-Qasimi in Damascus prosperity came in part from the advanced level of technology available to industrialists and farmers, allowing better use of natural materials and a more efficient, productive cycle of industry and agriculture.[25] However, they were also aware

[23] Georg Simmel, *The Sociology of Georg Simmel*, ed. K. H. Wolff (New York, 1950), pp. 409–24; Gustave Le Bon, *Psychologie des foules* (Paris, 1896), pp. 1–47; Auguste Comte, *The Crisis of Industrial Civilization*, intro. R. Fletcher (London, 1974), pp. 111–38.

[24] Muhammad Husain Na'ini, *Tanbih al-ummah wa-tanzih al-millah* (first published in Najaf, 1909; Persian translation published 1951), in Tawfiq al-Saif, *Didda al-istibdad: al-fiqh al-siyasi al-shi'i fi 'asr al-ghaibah* (Beirut, 1999), pp. 278–300, 315–23, 328–42; 'Abd al-Rahman al-Kawakibi, *Taba'i al-istibdad wa-masari' al-isti'bad*, in *Al-A'mal al-kamilah*, ed. Muhammad Jamal Tahhan (Beirut, 1995), pp. 524–34.

[25] Rifa'ah Rafi' al-Tahtawi, *Manahij al-albab al-misriyah fi mabahij al-adab al-'asriyah*, in *Al-A'mal al-kamilah*, part 1, pp. 323–47; D. D. Commins, 'The Salafi Islamic Reform Movement in Damascus 1885–1914: Religious Intellectuals, Politics and Social Change in Late Ottoman Syria' (Ann Arbor: University of Michigan Ph.D., dissertation 1985), pp. 233–5; Muhammad Jamal al-Din al-Qasimi, *Dala'il al-tawhid* (Beirut, 1984), pp. 101–3.

that it was not simply technological change that allowed these processes to develop, but also people's relationship to the means of production. Here the question of ownership and property arose.

Attitudes such as these, especially amongst those who had been sent to Europe by their governments, helped to suggest a distinct agenda for reform on their return to their homelands. Nowhere was this change felt more dramatically or with greater concern in these largely agricultural societies than in the introduction of laws reforming and reshaping landownership.[26] Piecemeal and incomplete as these reforms were in practice, the introduction of private property in the ownership of land, and the erosion both of customary forms and of forms sanctioned under Islamic law, introduced a number of different trends into the debate. Some of the returning Ottoman elites had been so impressed that they advocated wholesale adoption of European social forms precisely to preserve and strengthen the Ottoman state. Dismissive of traditional, religious knowledge and enthusiastic for the advantages of positivist science as the key to progress, they found themselves increasingly in a position where the essentially secular objective of the preservation of state power became their prime concern.[27]

For those who were more concerned that the Ottoman state should protect a distinctively Islamic society, the attitude to traditional Islamic rulings on property ownership and on the legal framework which should regulate it was more mixed. In some respects, the ground had been prepared for legal innovation by the long-standing Ottoman institution of decree laws, made by the authority of the Sultan and providing a legal framework (*kanun*) distinct from that of the *shari'ah*. In addition, forms of landownership and usufruct, as well as rules regarding the sale and the alienability of property, had long existed which owed little if anything to specifically Islamic injunctions, even if they had been sanctioned over the years by successive Islamic authorities. Nevertheless, the significant change during the nineteenth century was the

---

[26] K. H. Karpat, 'Some historical and methodological considerations concerning social stratification in the Middle East', in C. A. O. Van Nieuwenhuijze (ed.), *Commoners, Climbers and Notables* (Leiden, 1977), p. 99; K. Karpat, *Studies in Ottoman Social and Political History* (Leiden, 2002), pp. 339–51; S. J. Shaw and E. K. Shaw, *History of the Ottoman Empire and Modern Turkey* (Cambridge, 1977), vol. II, pp. 114–15; A. K. S. Lambton, *The Persian Land Reform 1962–1966* (Oxford, 1969), pp. 20–30; Farhat Ziadeh, *Property Law in the Arab World* (London, 1979), pp. 1–13. In India under British rule there was considerable disturbance as a result of the land regulation, registration and reform processes associated with the incorporation of Indian agricultural produce into an expanding capitalist market. In North India and East Bengal, in particular, protests were articulated in a distinctively Islamic vocabulary, by movements calling for the re-establishment of Islamic values – see Qeyamuddin Ahmad, *The Wahabi Movement in India* (Calcutta, 1966), pp. 1–64; B. Metcalf, *Islamic Revival in British India: Deoband 1860–1900* (Princeton, 1982), pp. 52–63, 68–71.

[27] Hanioglu, *Young Turks*, pp. 10–13.

extension of the secular, civic codes to take over areas of life hitherto subject to the jurisdiction of the *shari'ah* courts and the consequent relegation of the latter to a diminished sphere of social intercourse.[28]

Nevertheless, in writing about property, the overwhelming preoccupation was still with its specification under the rulings of the *shari'ah*, as in previous centuries, but now with wider circulation, given new printing methods, new media and increasing literacy. These writings followed a recognisable form in which property – its qualities, attributes, restrictions and disposition – was minutely investigated in the light of the *fiqh*. This was largely a self-sufficient literature in which the purpose was to lay before other scholars, judges and members of the literate public the most authoritative interpretations of the forms that property might legitimately take and the uses to which it should properly be put. Insofar as there was a manifest engagement with the contemporary world, it was in the nature of some of the questions put to the *fuqaha'* by people concerned about the correct way of acting in situations that seemed to be without precedent. Increasingly, even for the most tradition-minded scholars, principles and terms associated with the contemporary meaning of property in a capitalist society began to intrude.[29]

This transition became increasingly apparent in the writings of those who did not see themselves primarily as jurists, but who reflected upon the larger questions of the Islamic constitution of their societies and the nature of progress. This becomes apparent in the writings of al-Tahtawi whose vision for the development of Egypt, although informed by his concern to ensure the observance of the *shari'ah*, was founded on an understanding of the 'public good'. He equated this with material progress, with developments in the productive potential of the land and the establishment of industry, but also saw it as conforming with the *shari'ah*, suggesting that forms of property ownership could be diverse, as long as they were compatible with *al-maslahat al-'umumiyah* (the public benefit or common good). It was from this that he developed something like a labour theory of value which gave due

---

[28] A. H. de Groot, 'Modernist attitudes in Ottoman official Islam (1856–1918)', in C. van Dijk and A. H. de Groot (eds.), *State and Islam* (Leiden, 1995), pp. 51–4; Hanioglu, *Young Turks*, p. 10; Halil Inalcik, 'Turkey between Europe and the Middle East', in *From Empire to Republic – Essays on Ottoman and Turkish Social History*, Analecta Isisiana XIX (Istanbul, 1995), pp. 143–8; Ilber Ortayli, 'Ottoman family law and the state in the nineteenth century', in *Studies on Ottoman Transformation*, Analecta Isisiana X (Istanbul, 1994), pp. 149–59.

[29] Baber Johansen, *The Islamic Law on Land Tax and Rent* (London, 1988), pp. 19, 98–121; Muhammad al-Hajj al-Nasir, *Al-Islam wa-intiza' al-milk li-l-maslahat al-'ammah* (Rabat, 1991), pp. 70–91; 'Abdallah bin 'Abd al-Ghani al-Hanafi, *Al-Nur al-badi fi ahkam al-aradi* (ms. in the Dar al-Kutub al-Misriyah – *fiqh hanafi* 563, 1807).

consideration to the role of peasants and their labour in the development of the land and the creation of prosperity.[30]

Similar considerations also shaped the thought of Muhammad 'Abduh, where social utility became an important criterion for judging the commendability of social institutions, including the character and disposition of particular forms of property. He represented it as a criterion that is neutral in some respects vis-à-vis the society to which it is being applied, the assumption being that anything which contributes to the material prosperity and cohesion of the society as a whole must be of benefit. Insofar as this criterion is being explicitly applied to a distinctively Islamic society, an attempt is made to give this newly developed term of 'social utility' an 'Islamic' pedigree by equating it with the term *maslahah* (benefit) as used by the *fuqaha'*, particularly of the Maliki school, but also by al-Tufi (d. 1316 CE) and Ibn Taimiyah (d. 1328 CE), both Hanbalis.[31]

The power of the idea of 'public utility' and the assertion of its apparent equivalence to a commendable concept in the Islamic tradition was also visible in the writings of Shakib Arslan who saw no contradiction between his vehement repudiation of the political influence of European imperialism and the wholesale adoption of a form of utilitarianism as the most effective way of strengthening and developing distinctively Islamic society.[32] In his view, this criterion would allow the Islamic community to acquire anything it needed, as long as it benefited the community as a whole. Thus, a link was being made between the material assets necessary for wealth creation and the legal preconditions. Some, such as the Young Ottomans and Young Turks, saw the implications of this and welcomed it. Others, such as Malkam Khan in the Qajar Empire, saw no contradiction between this and Islamic principles, since he believed the latter provided authority for any course of action that contributed to the general betterment of

---

[30] Khaldun al-Husry, *Origins of Modern Arab Political Thought* (Delmar, NY, 1980), pp. 23–8; al-Tahtawi, *Manahij al-albab* in *Al-A'mal al-kamilah* part 1, pp. 250–1, 307–19.

[31] 'Abduh, *Al-A'mal al-kamilah*, part 1, pp. 673–9; Muhammad 'Abduh, 'Adalat al-shari' wa-taqdim al-maslahah fi al-mu'amalat 'ala al-nass', *Al-Manar* 9/9 (1324/1906), pp. 745–70, citing Najm al-Din al-Tufi, as well as Jamal al-Din al-Qasimi (d. 1914). *Maslahah* in the sense of something that would be beneficial to a human being was used by Maliki jurists to supplement the use of *qiyas* (analogy) when trying to judge whether something not specified in the body of authoritative texts was commendable or not. The assumption was that God would always favour anything that was beneficial to human beings and that, therefore, where judgement could not depend upon analogy alone, it needed to be supplemented by a judgement about the beneficial effects that a human being could be expected to derive from a particular object, institution or course of action. Hourani, *Arabic Thought in the Liberal Age*, pp. 20–1, 344; Kerr, *Islamic Reform*, pp. 115–18.

[32] Shakib Arslan, *Limadha ta'akhkhara al-muslimun wa-limadha taqaddum ghairuhum* (Cairo, 1939), pp. 58–76, 82–107; William L. Cleveland, *Islam against the West: Shakib Arslan and the Campaign for Islamic Nationalism* (London, 1985) pp. 115–18.

mankind.[33] Jamal al-Din al-Afghani, although he used different arguments to reconcile the institutions of capitalist modernity with those of a distinctively Islamic order, also contributed to this trend by suggesting that the material well-being of Muslims in the modern world would be the main criterion for determining what was acceptable in the reinvigoration of Islamic society.[34]

In the writings of Ahmad Khan in India, these transitions were even more obvious. Concerned about the material conditions of his fellow Muslims in India in the nineteenth century, not only vis-à-vis the British, but also in relation to the non–Muslims – Hindu, Sikh and Parsee – he was determined to dispel the emerging myth that Muslims could not participate in the development of the country because of the reactionary nature of their religious beliefs. He saw it as his duty to take on the forces of Islamic conservatism, and to shape the vocabulary and the imagination that would release the creative powers of the Muslim community, in the economic development of society as a whole and the raising of their standard of living in particular. For example, his concerns for social cohesion, social progress and social equity influenced his rejection of the hitherto standard prohibition of *riba* (interest) among Islamic scholars. He asserted that this prohibition should only apply to the debts of the poor who borrowed money from necessity. It should not apply to those whose expanding commercial ventures contributed to the public good.[35]

For Ahmad Khan and his followers in the Aligarh movement, society was a natural phenomenon, and since God had laid down the laws of nature and revealed the principles of Islam, there must be a necessary agreement between them. Thus social problems came from the malfunctioning of society and anything that contributed towards its proper functioning must of necessity be in accordance with Islamic principles. For him, if the most impressive model of a fully functioning society at the time, which was delivering the greatest good to the greatest number, was that of capitalist and industrialised Europe, then this must be the aim towards which Muslims must aspire. Although they certainly had their differences and, to a large degree, read very different political imperatives into their interpretations of progress, there

[33] N. Keddie, *Iran: Religion, Politics and Society* (London, 1980), pp. 56–7; H. Algar, *Mirza Malkam Khan* (Berkeley, 1973), pp. 72–6, 179–80. It should be said, however, that Khan, who converted into and out of Islam, may have had an uncharacteristically broad view of the Islamic tradition – and, some would allege, an instrumental, if not opportunistic, attitude to Islamic precepts and their use to support an essentially secular, reformist agenda.

[34] N. Keddie, *An Islamic Response to Imperialism* (Berkeley, 1968), pp. 41–5; al-Afghani, *Al-A 'mal al-kamilah*, pp. 255–60.

[35] J. M. S. Baljon, *The Reforms and Religious Ideas of Sir Sayyid Ahmad Khan* (Lahore, 1970), pp. 34–49.

was much here that linked the thought of Ahmad Khan to that of al-Afghani. In part, this may have been because of the common influence which they both acknowledged of the writings of Khair al-Din al-Tunisi.[36]

The Tunisian/Ottoman statesman and writer Khair al-Din al-Tunisi (c. 1825–89) was preoccupied with the question of the relative power of Europe vis-à-vis the Ottoman Empire. Impressed by the power and social order of the European states, he suggested that the Muslim state could be strengthened by the adoption not simply of the technology of Western Europe, but also of European institutions of governance. Only this, he argued, would provide the framework of security, stability and justice needed for the flourishing of economic life and the material progress required to maintain a fully functioning society. A properly regulated state, in harmony with the society it organised, would secure property, encourage profit from innovation and foster the kind of social and economic power which he so admired in European joint stock companies, for example. Orderly capitalism within the framework of an orderly state was in his view the foundation of progress and, he was careful to point out, fully congruent with Islamic ideals and teachings.[37]

It is also possible that some of the similarities between the positions of al-Afghani and Khan, despite their differences, may have been due to their familiarity with the writings of Mill and other utilitarian, as well as functionalist, European social theorists. However, it was also partly an outcome of theorising about society at this period. In the writings of European social theorists and political economists a dominant image of the social was establishing its hegemony. Whatever the setting, the cultural background or even ideological proclivities of the individual, as soon as an author engaged with this discourse, it was difficult to imagine 'society' without some reference, implicit or explicit, to this functionalist idea which in turn informed the criterion of social utility.

In the context of the time, it is thus significant that the virtues of different forms of property ownership are initially discussed in social terms, rather than in terms of individual rights, although Rafiq al-'Azm is to some degree an exception to this.[38] Nevertheless, underlying the understanding of the

---

[36] Aziz Ahmad, *Studies in Islamic Culture in the Indian Environment* (Delhi, 1999), pp. 55–62; S. Muhammad, *Sir Syed Ahmad Khan – A Political Biography* (Meerut, 1969), pp. 179–200; W. C. Smith, *Modern Islam in India – A Social Analysis* (London, 1946), pp. 10–12.

[37] These ideas are most evident in his influential book, first published in 1867 in Arabic and subsequently translated into Turkish and French. Khair al-Din al-Tunisi, *Aqwam al-masalik fi ma'arafah ahwal al-mamalik*, ed. Al-Mansuf al-Shannufi (Tunis, 2000), vol. I, pp. 93–122; for a good English translation and useful essay on Khair al-Din, see L. Carl Brown, *The Surest Path*, Harvard Monographs XVI (Cambridge, MA, 1967).

[38] Al-'Azm, *Tanbih al-afham*, cited in Jad'an, *Usus al-taqaddum*, pp. 490–9.

productive benefits and social utility of particular kinds of property arrangements, there is an – often unspoken – assumption about the nature of the relationship between the individual and property ownership. In contrast to European Enlightenment ideas which linked property ownership to individual self-realisation, debates about property in the Islamic lands in the nineteenth century, even where these are conducted in broadly secular terms, do not give sole or even prior claim to the individual. On the contrary, the property debate is set very consciously within the framework of the state and the expectations vested in it. Social utility elides into state utility, but this shifts the focus of much of the writing to the reform of state institutions, gearing them to the rule of law and the respect for the security of tenure which are the antithesis of arbitrary rule, despotism and tyranny.[39]

This was the period of the *tanzimat* in the Ottoman Empire and particularly of the Egyptian land laws of 1847, 1855 and 1858 and of the Ottoman Land Code of 1858. These marked a determined and self-conscious effort by state administrators and public servants to regularise the tenure and title to land across much of the Islamic world. Sometimes this involved innovation, but in some places it effectively recognised existing states of affairs which had developed piecemeal over the years. In the debates surrounding the drafting of these laws and in the *fatwas* which followed their enactment and which sought to give people guidance on the consequences for their own claims to land, one can see the themes of social utility and state benefit intertwined. The codification also made people think self-consciously about the relationship of the established, existing body of *shari'ah*-sanctioned rules surrounding property ownership.[40] At the same time, whether in the Ottoman Empire, Egypt, the Qajar Empire or in British India, property constituted a link between state, especially in regard to individual citizens' rights before the law, and society, in the sense of social utility and the achievement of prosperity, both individually and collectively.

[39] G. W. F. Hegel, *Elements of the Philosophy of Right*, ed. Allen Wood (Cambridge, 1991), pp. 77–84; Alan Ryan, *Property and Political Theory* (Oxford, 1984) pp. 119–32; Huri Islamoglu, 'Property as a contested domain: a reevaluation of the Ottoman Land Code of 1858', in R. Owen (ed.), *New Perspectives on Property and Land in the Middle East* (Cambridge, MA, 2000), pp. 30–4.

[40] Kenneth M. Cuno, *The Pasha's Peasants – Land, Society and Economy in Lower Egypt, 1740–1858* (Cambridge, 1992), pp. 179–97, particularly interesting for citing the *fatwas* of Shaikh Muhammad al-'Abbasi, a Hanafi jurist who held, with others, for example, that the undivided property of a household is held as a 'proprietary partnership' – *sharikat al-milk*. In the Balkans and Anatolia even full property (*milk*) of peasant households was regarded as indivisible, despite Islamic rulings, to preserve the viability of units of production. The same practice seems to have been current in Egypt as well. See also K. Cuno, 'The origins of private ownership of land in Egypt: a reappraisal', *IJMES* 12 (1980), pp. 248–55.

In this respect a new vocabulary and a new imaginative framework were emerging in which property was no longer seen simply in the apparently fixed categories to which it had been assigned by the traditionalists of the *fiqh*. In this realm, property, its description and its regulation, was thought of as a matter of hermeneutics, whereby the true meaning and designation of the phenomenon could be derived internally from within the Islamic tradition and the numerous, but finite number of texts upon which its interpreters could draw. However, from the nineteenth century onwards, it was increasingly difficult to conceive of property without its 'social function' (*al-wazifat al-ijtima'iyah*) – a term that was to become very familiar from the writings of those who saw themselves as responsible for ensuring that property and its disposition should always be kept within distinctively Islamic guidelines.

In this way, distinctively Islamic discourses about property began to change. The highly traditional form of jurists' commentary on the understandings and specificities of different kinds of property continued to be written. However, in tandem with this, and sometimes making use of its references to the *hadith* literature and to the works of previous jurists throughout Islamic history, writings appeared across the Islamic world which brought together a variety of novel concepts, linking them through the changing discourse on property. Thus, the individual proprietor was linked to a functional view of society and to social well-being (or harm) through the use made of property and through the latter's various forms. Equally, and in parallel, the proprietor – and citizen – formed a direct relation with the state, mediated through property and the legal framework that would ensure the proper ordering of society and the guarantee of proprietorial rights, as well as the performance of the duties expected of the proprietor. Furthermore, these functions of an orderly society were to be carried out under the sanction of Islam.

With the notion of social power and the proper functioning of society to the fore, the question arose of how best to capture the energy, dynamism and wealth of the new economic forms. It was not simply their existence as institutions, but the processes of which they formed a part, and thus the material progress and social cohesion that they were thought to foster, which attracted many to the technology and property forms of a capitalist and industrial society as the most effective means of reinvigorating Muslim societies. The social virtues of industry and of the accompanying imaginative forms of internalised discipline were extolled, both as a way of countering disorder and the potential chaos of a mass, urban society, and also as a way of transforming relations between the members of the society. At the same time, it was clearly acknowledged that moderation and fairness be respected in relations between the propertied and the propertyless. The concern was that ownership should be informed by a moral sense which would safeguard virtue and ensure proper conduct. There was, in short, a realisation among a number of writers of the negative or dark side of economic progress, capitalism, increased productivity and commodification.

Some of these preoccupations are visible in the writings of Muhammad Tal'at Harb, the Egyptian financier and founder of Bank Misr. Like many of his generation and class, he was a great admirer of the productivity and energy of Europe, its industrial might and technological innovation. He had little doubt, therefore, about the need for capitalist enterprise to enhance and strengthen his own country. Indeed, he founded Bank Misr in large part to harness the power of capitalism to the advantage of the Egyptians, thereby freeing them from dependence on European capital and allowing them to compete with European enterprises on their own terms.[41]

However, Harb's admiration for capitalist enterprise was tempered by his fears about its European origins and values. Through Bank Misr he hoped to capture the entrepreneurial dynamism of the capitalist system whilst at the same time 'taming' it by embedding it in the dominant values of his own society, interpreted primarily as those of a distinctively Islamic community. He was thus critical of the dominant role of foreign capital in Egypt and claimed that it could have no concern for the welfare and solidarity of the Muslim community of Egyptians. It was on these grounds that he was critical of the interest charged on loans, rather than on grounds of its contravention – in being identified with *riba* – of one of the rules of the *shari'ah*. His main concern appeared to be the effects of an unmediated and foreign-controlled capitalism on the communal solidarities of Egyptian peasants, in this instance, but effectively on Egyptian society as a whole. He had earlier voiced similar concerns about the effects of European-controlled capitalist development on the role of women in society. In his view, the traditional and thus, for him, Islamic rulings on the role and comportment of women guaranteed cohesion of the family, and thus of society as a whole. With the introduction of industrial capitalism, inspired by and associated with European ideas of female emancipation, he believed that there was a danger not only of the loss of the society's Islamic values, but also its very cohesion.[42]

As Harb's later energetic banking activities were to show, he was by no means against capitalism as a system for engineering economic growth. On the contrary, he was an enthusiast for the new financial instruments and procedures that would allow him to introduce a new dynamic into Egypt's

---

[41] Charles Issawi, 'The entrepreneur class', ch. 7, pp. 124–7, in S. N. Fisher (ed.), *Social Forces in the Middle East* (Ithaca, NY, 1955); Mourad Wahba, *The Role of the State in the Egyptian Economy* (Reading, MA, 1994), pp. 28–31.

[42] Muhammad Tal'at Harb, *'Ilaj misr al-iqtisadi*, ed. Ra'uf 'Abbas Hamid (Cairo, 2002), pp. 31–3, 37–46; Eric Davis, *Challenging Colonialism: Bank Misr and Egyptian Industrialisation 1920–1941* (Princeton, 1983), pp. 86–102, citing also Tal'at Harb's book on the role of women, *Fasl al-kitab 'an al-mar'ah wa-l-hijab* (Cairo, 1901).

economic life. Nor was he against establishing effective and useful links with foreign capitalists and enterprises, if he thought it would increase the growth prospects of the Misr Group of companies – indeed, their profitability often demanded it. He was, however, opposed to foreign – European – control of the process and believed that capitalism, properly guided and directed, and informed by Islamic and traditional values, could contribute to the strengthening of the emerging Muslim states, with Egypt to the fore.[43]

In the light of the subsequent development of the Misr Group and its inevitable implication in global capitalist processes, as well as its engagement with, rather than banishment of, the foreign capital which Harb was claiming to deride, it is questionable whether he could be said to have succeeded in his vision of a capitalism 'tamed' by powerful local values. However, as a response to capitalism at the time, its ethnic origins and the controlling interests behind its major enterprises, Harb was voicing sentiments which had a parallel elsewhere in the Islamic world. This was the case in the early 1900s when the Indonesian Sarekat Islam was formed around a powerful indictment of 'sinful capitalism' (foreign-owned), as opposed to 'virtuous capitalism' (indigenous enterprises owned by Muslims).[44]

Others, however, less enchanted by the potential of capitalist development, feared the effects of capitalism on the moral economy. Acquisitiveness, centred on the commodification of goods and relationships, and based upon individual property rights, sanctioned by the pursuit of individual self-interest, were being reproduced by an expanding capitalist economy and threatened the pre-existing ethical framework of economic life. These concerns in the Islamic world followed lines similar to those visible in the writings of Christian socialists and others during the nineteenth century.[45] For a number of Muslim writers, the preoccupation with the moral economy took two forms. Firstly, the ethical regulation of human transactions was seen as part of God's purpose, and a necessary bulwark against the fracturing of society. Secondly, and specific to the discourse of those concerned about a distinctively Islamic society, there were fears about the particular identity of a society undergoing these changes. Both in the nineteenth and in the twentieth centuries, this fear raised the question of the price that a Muslim community

---

[43] Robert Vitalis, *When Capitalists Collide* (Berkeley, 1995), pp. 41–9; Wahba, *Role of the State*, pp. 30–2; R. L. Tignor, *State, Private Enterprise and Economic Change in Egypt 1918–1952* (Princeton, 1984), pp. 70–2.

[44] Curiously, this organisation became a haven for some of Indonesia's early communists, until they were forced to leave in 1921. C. van Dijk, '"Communist Muslims" in the Dutch East Indies', in van Dijk and de Groot, *State and Islam*, pp. 80–4.

[45] Charles Raven, *Christian Socialism 1848–1854* (London, 1920) pp. 63, 89–91; Noel Thompson, *The Market and its Critics* (London, 1988), pp. 49–55, 135–50.

might have to pay for success in a world not of its making, seeking to benefit without succumbing to its corruption.

1.3   Education to restore the moral economy

Loss of autonomy can be felt in a number of ways. For many in Asia and Africa in the nineteenth century, the most immediate and apparent cause of their loss was the intrusion of Western European economic and imperial power. Whether or not this extended to administrative control, indigenous rulers, states and empires were enmeshed in the commercial and financial networks which accompanied the globalisation of European capital and power. For some, the impact was direct and often devastating. Impoverishment, redundancy and the potentially dire consequences of unpredictable and apparently uncontrollable economic change led to a variety of reactions. In those parts of Asia and Africa where Islam was not simply the dominant religion but where it also provided the idioms through which social and ethical relations were expressed, a variety of responses became visible.

For instance, in India in the early nineteenth century, the so-called 'Wahhabi' movement among poor peasants and impoverished craftsmen sought to re-establish a moral order of greater apparent simplicity and strength by looking back to an image of Arabia at the time of the Prophet Muhammad. Claiming to be a movement to reinstate a 'pure' Islam and to free it from the corruption and accretions of scholarly obscurantism and popular superstition, it held up the ideal of the original Islamic order as the proper framework for a society that had apparently lost its moral bearings. It soon moved beyond the stage of assertion and instruction and became a movement of direct action against both the corrupt political and financial elites who were benefiting from the licence of the new order, and the new industrial machinery that represented the technology of dispossession and marginalisation. Although politically suppressed as a movement, the sentiment of outrage at the violation of the moral economy lived on.[46]

However, concern for the condition of the moral economy was not confined simply to those whose material position had been worsened by the transformations of industrial capitalism. There were those who were perturbed by the

---

[46] Smith, *Modern Islam in India*, pp. 10–11. In this respect, it also bore a close relation to the movements that had emerged in Europe, from the seventeenth century onwards, using the vocabulary and symbols of an idealised, pristine Christianity, free of church control, to provide the foundations for an economic and political order in response to the sensed collapse of a moral economy coming under the pressures of early capitalism. Troeltsch, *Social Teaching*, vol. II, pp. 710–12; G. Winstanley, 'The True Levellers' standard advanced', pp. 77–95 in G. Winstanley, *The Law of Freedom and Other Writings*, ed. C. Hill (London, 1973); see also pp. 20–31, 36–42.

degree to which capitalist forms constituted a largely faceless and decentred force of huge transformative power. Through material incentives, it could change the way people thought of themselves and the world, encouraging new forms of association and reinforcing a value system linked to material growth. These powerful forces were felt to be shaking the foundations of the moral economy. They were assigning new values to hitherto unconsidered, even reprehensible styles of behaviour, and seemed to undermine many of the values associated with an ideal Islamic order. Those who responded in an Islamic idiom were reacting sceptically to the benefits of material progress and were articulating the perturbation of societies undergoing legal, economic and political change. They were also giving voice to an idealised and consciously 'Islamised' version of the moral economy. This provided a touchstone of authenticity, as well as terms of reference for the projected reconstruction of an integral Islamic order.

For someone like Jamal al-Din al-Afghani, this moral core was best expressed in the notion of cooperation and social solidarity. He was primarily concerned about the loss of political power by the states of the Muslim world, and specifically by the Ottoman Empire in the face of European imperialism. However, al-Afghani also gave some thought to the dangers of capitalism and industrialisation, not simply to existing Muslim societies, but also to the ideal of a Muslim society constituted as it should be. In this respect, his worries revolved around both capitalism and its socialist antithesis. He was more preoccupied with the normative order conveyed by capitalism, as well as its intellectual foundations, than by the material conditions or consequences of the commodification of labour and industrial production. Thus, he used his essay 'Refutation of the Materialists' to attack the kind of materialist thought which he believed denigrated the role of religion and which appeared to promote moral egotism as the sole standard of worth. The material power of the capitalist system and its Muslim enthusiasts, such as Syed Ahmad Khan and his followers (a particular object of al-Afghani's dislike), were seen as helping to dissolve the social bonds which gave Islamic society meaning as well as order. For al-Afghani, it was therefore incumbent upon Muslims to act in concert to re-establish a moral order founded on the social solidarities of brotherhood and cooperation.[47]

He articulated this in his essay *Al-Ishtirakiyah fi al-islam* (Socialism in Islam) written in the 1890s, in which he held up an Islamic socialism founded on brotherhood and social solidarity as a bastion against the materialism both of capitalism and of its class-based socialist critique. The latter he saw as violent, divisive and likely to lead to the breakdown of order and the

---

[47] Keddie, *Islamic Response to Imperialism*, pp. 65–70, 77–9.

repudiation of all existing ethical standards. By contrast, he sought to advocate the 'true socialism' of Islam. This he believed to be founded on brotherhood and cooperation, modelled on the example of the Prophet Muhammad and kept in place by an awareness of the normative priorities of religion. For al-Afghani this was far from the egalitarianism preached by Western socialists and constituted, on the contrary, a moral order in which everyone accepted their place and was not tempted to indulge in the kind of 'excess' which he associated with Western capitalism and socialism.[48]

Some of these themes were taken up, although with different emphases, by his disciple Muhammad 'Abduh and by Rashid Rida. As far as 'Abduh was concerned, capitalist accumulation and the qualities promoted by capitalism diminished the power of such moral restraints as compassion, mercy, solidarity and cooperation. He saw this as a sad commentary in itself on the moral harm of the excesses of capitalist acquisition and commodification, but also believed it would lead, through resentment and class hatred, to the ills of disorder and upheaval which al-Afghani had identified as a major failing of socialist remedies. In many respects, 'Abduh was concerned about the effects of excess, as he would put it, whether of a capitalist or a socialist variety. This was perhaps most evident in his willingness to sanction certain forms of financial transaction – most notoriously in the charging of interest – where that seemed on balance to contribute a clear social benefit.[49]

Rashid Rida developed this idea further, judging all economic arrangements and social prescriptions in the light of the benefit they were thought to bring to the community as a whole. This was not a materialist judgement, but rather an idealist one concerning the respect for and protection of the community's Islamic ethics. Possibly wary of the direction in which 'Abduh's more utilitarian criteria had led him, Rida came back full circle to the view that a society which obeyed the *shari'ah*, properly interpreted, would be immune to the material seductions of capitalism and to the egalitarianism and disorder promised by socialism.[50]

[48] Al-Afghani, *Al-Ishtirakiyah fi al-islam*, in *Al-A'mal al-kamilah*, pp. 413–23; Ahmad Muhammad Radwan, *Ishtirakiyat al-islam* (Cairo, 1950), pp. 113–17; Sami Hanna, 'Al-Afghani: a pioneer of Islamic socialism', *The Muslim World* 57/1 (January 1967), pp. 24–32.

[49] 'Abduh *Al-A'mal al-kamilah*, Part 1, pp. 323–6 and part 3 (1980) pp. 160–9; Some of the reasoning that might have led him to this position is evident in the more orthodox setting of 'Abduh's explication of the Qur'anic phrase '*Wa la ta' akulu amwalakum bainakum bi-l-batil*' ('and do not consume your wealth in useless things'), *Al-Manar* 7/19 (1322/1904), pp. 721–8; J. Beinin, 'Islamic responses to the capitalist penetration of the Middle East', in B. F. Stowasser (ed.), *The Islamic Impulse* (London, 1987), pp. 88–90.

[50] Muhammad Rashid Rida, *Al-Khilafah* (Cairo, 1988) pp. 69–77; Muhammad Rashid Rida, *Al Riba wa-l-mu'amalat fi al-islam*, ed. Muhammad Bahjat al-Bitar (Beirut, 1986) pp. 161–9; Radwan, *Ishtirakiyat al-islam*, (1950) pp. 118–19; Kerr, *Islamic Reform*, pp. 187–204.

A similar preoccupation with the solidarity of the Islamic community and the erosion of the normative bonds which hold it together under the pressure of industrial capitalism was visible in the writings of the Syrian Rafiq al-'Azm. He asserted that Islamic civilisation must be based on 'public solidarity' (al-takaful al-'amm). For him the shari'ah, properly observed, provided the only possible framework for a moral economy that ensured solidarity, cooperation and the independence of the individual to act within boundaries that would be just and equitable. He was careful to distinguish his views from those of European socialism which he saw as a justifiable critique of the practices of industrial capitalism, but as 'contrary to the natural laws of society' and to individual happiness in its insistence on egalitarianism and profit-sharing. On the contrary, he defended the right of the property owner to retain the profit for himself, if this was the result of effort, but he also recognised the need to channel and restrain the profit motive. For him the damage that unlicensed competition inflicted on the values and relationships that underpinned the moral economy was all too evident. The only remedy was to bring both social solidarity and individual effort into harmony under the guidance of the shari'ah.[51]

In many respects, this normative response to the depredations of capitalism had much in common with contemporary Arab writers who were Christians and who were therefore not seeking to advocate Islamic or shari'ah-based solutions to the social problem, defined as the problem of the moral economy. They too were concerned about the loss of social solidarities, the damaging effect of materialism, acquisitiveness and the consequences of unbridled egotistical competition. A number of them were equally critical of European socialists' advocacy of class warfare and of egalitarianism and common ownership. Farah Antun, for example, whilst critical of the economic exploitation which he saw as integral to unrestrained capitalism, believed that a fairer distribution of wealth, a spirit of cooperation and respect for natural justice would restore the kind of social solidarities that were both cause and effect of a healthy moral order. In this regard, it was significant that he too made reference to the importance of religion in sustaining such an order. He not only cited the 'socialism' of early Christianity as an inspirational example, but equally praised what he characterised as the 'socialism' of the early Islamic community.[52]

---

[51] Jad'an, Usus al-taqaddum 'ind mufakkiray al-Islam, pp. 490–9.

[52] These sentiments come out strongly in Antun's allegorical story: Farah Antun, Al-Din wa-l-'ilm wa-l-mal, ed. Adonis al-'Akrah (Beirut, 1979), pp. 57–80. See also Dr al-'Akrah's 'Introduction', pp. 18–41; D. M. Reid, The Odyssey of Farah Antun (Minneapolis, 1975), pp. 114–16.

Some of these themes were echoed by 'Abd al-Rahman al-Kawakabi in his book *Taba'i al-istibdad wa-masari' al-isti'bad* (Cairo, 1903). He too was preoccupied with the damaging moral and social effects of acquisitiveness, greed and unrestrained competition in economic life. For him these were not the result of capitalism as such. Rather, modern industrial capitalism was the latest manifestation of a form of tyranny and oppression that had afflicted mankind in various forms throughout human history. Thus, in his account of history, oppression and wealth acquisition were intimately connected, with one reproducing the other in a symbiosis that helped to explain the will to power and, in doing so, drove ethical considerations to the margin. Occasionally in history there would come a moment when through revelation, reason and exertion, the moral framework that would underpin a just order could be reasserted to redress the balance against what he characterised as the 'god of nations' and 'the secret of existence' – i.e. the power of money and selfish acquisitiveness. He too believed that such moments had arrived with the revelation of the Christian message, but it was with the establishment of the early Islamic community that the principles had been realised. These principles he called socialism.[53]

However, where he differed with a number of his contemporaries, both Muslim and Christian, was in seeing the emergence of modern European socialism as just such a moment. Rather than accusing it of undermining the moral economy of Islam, he portrayed Islamic principles of social justice and ethical economic organisation as identical with those of modern socialism. By his account, therefore, Islamic law and principles called for economic equality for all, for the public ownership of the means of production and for the right and indeed duty to work for the good of all.[54]

A slightly different conclusion was reached by Muhammad Iqbal in India who was also responding to what he saw as a moral vacuum at the heart of capitalism. Although impressed by aspects of the material civilisation of European capitalism, he was increasingly concerned by the effects of its driving principles on the moral order. In his lectures on the *Reconstruction of Religious Thought in Islam* he cited approvingly the Turkish leader of the Religious Reform Party, Said Halim Pasha, who had stated that 'modern culture based as it is on national egoism is . . . only another form of barbarism. It is the result of an over-developed industrialism through which men satisfy their primitive instincts and inclinations'.[55] Later in these lectures Iqbal delivered a powerful indictment of the ruthless competition, egotism and materialism of capitalism and of European civilisation which he believed

---

[53] Al-Kawakibi, *Taba'i al-istibdad*, in *Al-A'mal al-kamilah*, pp. 473–5.

[54] Al-Kawakibi, *Taba'i al-istibdad*, pp. 476–83; al-Husry, *Origins*, pp. 74–6.

[55] Muhammad Iqbal, *The Reconstruction of Religious Thought in Islam* (Lahore, 1968), p. 156.

had encouraged man's 'ruthless egoism and . . . his infinite gold-hunger which is gradually killing all higher striving in him and bringing him nothing but life-weariness' in 'a society motivated by an inhuman competition and a civilisation which has lost its spiritual unity'.[56]

For Iqbal, capitalism also represented a theme that had long been present in human history – that of materialism and the preoccupation with knowledge geared to the exploitation of material resources, bereft of spiritual considerations or limitations. It was this which he hoped a re-acquaintance with the ethical principles of Islam would serve to counteract. Wary at first of socialism, since he saw it as yet another manifestation of the materialist cast of mind which had also produced capitalism, he nevertheless began to consider that the Islam of sociability, cooperation and solidarity might share a good deal with a socialism that stressed community and fairness. He did not pursue this systematically. His concern was in many ways the spiritual well-being of the individual, and for him, therefore, any framework of community which allowed this to develop and which provided the individual with moral guidance was to be encouraged. In this respect, an Islam geared to social action and transformation was the instrument that would bring this about.[57]

Iqbal did not elaborate much on the agency that would not simply articulate the programme of a reformed and socially active Islam, but would also implement it in order to create the framework for a guarded sphere of renewed sociability. However, for many of those who were writing about their concern for the condition of the moral economy, the obvious agency was the state. This had been the conclusion of writers as diverse as al-Afghani, al-Kawakibi, Haddad, al-Mansuri and al-'Azm. This was even more pronounced among the Young Ottomans and Young Turks, where the reformed Ottoman state became the chief object of their attentions. Ideally, this would be both the barrier against further inroads into Muslim domains by the European imperial powers, and the agency that would guarantee respect for Islamic principles and cultural autonomy within the bounds of the empire.[58]

---

[56] Iqbal, *Reconstruction*, pp. 187–9; as Smith says of Iqbal, 'He spoke of the West (i.e. capitalism) as power without love, knowledge without spirit' and cites a couplet from Iqbal's poem '*Paygham i Afghani bi Milla*':

> What is the Qur'an? For the capitalist, a message of death;
> It is the patron of the propertyless slave.

Smith, *Modern Islam in India*, pp. 111–12.

[57] Smith, *Modern Islam in India*, pp. 101–14, 133; Iqbal, *Reconstruction*, pp. 124–80; see also Iqbal's powerful poems 'Lenin before God' and 'God's Command to His Angels', in Aziz Ahmad and G. E. von Grunebaum (eds.), *Muslim Self-Statement in India and Pakistan 1857–1968* (Wiesbaden, 1970), pp. 133–5.

[58] Hanioglu, *Young Turks*, pp. 13–16; al-Tunisi, *Aqwam al-masalik*, part 1, pp. 101–18, 136–57.

Disillusionment with the state and its capacity was also to lead some of these late Ottoman thinkers more in the direction of Iqbal's advocacy of spiritual renewal. This was particularly the case with Said Nursi who, in declaring the emergence of the 'New Said' in the early twentieth century, explicitly rejected state involvement and called instead for the reconstruction of Islamic consciousness through individual spiritual endeavour. Only in this way, he argued, could a moral order be established that was both respectful of Islamic principles and resilient enough to guard against materialism and the logic of capitalism.[59]

Whether the emphasis was on state action or individual spiritual renewal, many of these responses to capitalist penetration, or rather to the penetration of the values which underpinned capitalist expansion, had in common a view of the moral order as one which was intimately bound up with the social order, and in which, therefore, Islam had a vital role to play. For those concerned about this aspect of their societies, education became an increasingly important focus of their writings. Education brought together various strands, seeming to speak to all those who viewed religion as a kind of social cement, and influenced by trends in social thinking and in the developing 'science of society'. At the same time, it preserved the notion of order and hierarchy, since the moral education envisaged by many of these writers was unmistakably authoritarian.[60]

Technical knowledge was to be accompanied by strict moral instruction which would impress upon students the importance of the normative framework in which such knowledge could legitimately be used. This had great appeal for the state reformers of the day who sought, among other things, not simply to enhance social solidarities, but to strengthen the state founded on those solidarities. At the same time, the notion of pedagogy and moral development held great promise for those concerned about the coming generation's lack of spiritual awareness. It seemed to provide a framework for countering the evils of an increasingly materialist and acquisitive culture. In this respect, the emphasis on education could also draw in more conservative elements for whom a truly Islamic education was part of their *raison d'être*.

Thus for Ottomans such as Ahmad Djewdet Pasha (1822–95) Islam was both valuable in itself and a force that would provide Ottoman society with a strong moral core. In his view this would strengthen that society, by tightening the bonds of sociability and cooperation, and the state which presided over it. At the same time it would also present a barrier to cultural

[59] Hakan Yavuz, *Islamic Political Identity in Turkey* (Oxford, 2003), pp. 157–62.
[60] Benjamin Fortna, 'Islamic morality in late Ottoman "secular" schools', *IJMES* 32/3 (August 2000), pp. 369–93.

and normative intrusion of the kind that might fundamentally alter social bonds and weaken the enterprise. In this regard, he identified secularism as one of the more dangerous trends in that it could undermine the cohesion of Ottoman society.[61] A later Ottoman thinker, Musa Kazim Efendi, had a rather different view of secularism, even if he did share a number of Djewdet Pasha's beliefs about the need to adopt useful forms of organisation and power whilst maintaining the solidarity of society through proper attention to people's religious beliefs. In common with many Ottoman officials, however, and building upon a long-established tradition in Ottoman jurisprudence and political history, he saw no problem about making a distinction between the spiritual – the domain of the *shari'ah* – and the material – the domain of sultanic law (*kanun*). This explicit recognition of a distinction between a secular sphere of power which governed the state and the jurisdiction of Islam which provided the moral bond that cemented the society underpinning the state brought him close to many of his Young Turk contemporaries.[62]

For some of them, Islam provided a language which should be used as much for its instrumental value as for any set of normative considerations. Thus, quite self-consciously, a number of the Young Turks considered the strategy whereby modern, secular ideas and institutions, already assumed to be of vital necessity for the well-being of the Ottoman state, could be given an Islamic aura to make them more acceptable to the mass of the population. Men like Abdullah Cevdet acknowledged the power of Islam in shaping the imagination and the world view of the great majority of the Muslim population of the Ottoman Empire. It was thus a factor that needed to be addressed as a condition of political success. However, there was also an understanding that despite its value as a source of social and moral cohesion among the 'masses', the elite, confident, self-conscious and 'scientific' would operate by very different principles.[63]

Whether secularist and materialist at heart, or believers in Islam as a key component of their identity as Ottomans or Turks, the use of an Islamic idiom and Islamic symbols as part of a political project meant that they themselves and their allies needed to retain control over the interpretative processes. It was for this reason that some of their number occupied themselves re-examining the sources of the *shari'ah*, as well as the works of the *fuqaha'*, to derive support for their positions vis-à-vis constitutionalism and legal innovation, presenting in many instances a revised set of Islamic

---

[61] de Groot, 'Modernist attitudes', pp. 56–7; S. Mardin, 'Ideology and religion in the Turkish revolution', *IJMES* 2 (1971), pp. 197–211; H. Bowen, 'Ahmad Djewdet Pasha', *in Encyclopedia of Islam* (Leiden, 1960), vol. I, pp. 284–6.
[62] de Groot, 'Modernist attitudes', pp. 58–62.
[63] Hanioglu, *Young Turks*, pp. 200–1.

precepts that resembled in many ways the teachings of Islamic reformers such as al-Afghani and 'Abduh.[64]

Of course, both of the latter have been seen in a very similar light. There is much in al-Afghani's writings to support the view that he was somewhat sceptical concerning the metaphysical teachings of Islam, but saw it as a necessary guarantee of social order since it gave to the mass of the general public a set of moral bearings, without which they would be lost and disorder would ensue. Al-Afghani's critique of materialism and socialism seems more concerned about their propensity to anarchy, selfishness and disorder than about their possible offence against a divinely revealed set of norms. 'Irreligion' in this respect appears to be more threatening as a cause of social breakdown than as an outrage against God.[65] In India, as well, similar thoughts were being voiced by figures such as Syed Ameer Ali who regarded religion primarily as a moral code that encouraged social stability, especially insofar as it formed the basis for order and ethical conduct among 'the masses'. Like the elitists of the Ottoman Empire, and some of their European contemporaries, he made a distinction between the generality of the people who needed religion to keep them from straying into immorality and from causing social disorder, and the 'exceptional minds' who had a clear, dispassionate gaze wherein order was implicit, whatever individual beliefs they held about the nature, or even the existence, of the divine.[66]

As a remedy for the moral decay which was now associated with the new forces working upon society and breaking down the bonds of sociability, the proper education or instruction of the young into the normative tradition of Islam was thought to be ideal. Such views of social control, and the reconstruction of the moral economy to ensure that materialism, individualism and secularism should not displace Islamic values, were congenial both to the world view of the *salafiyin* and to that of the more secular, modernising elites. For a *salafi* such as al-Qasimi in Damascus, it was wholly fitting that there should be an elite that would instruct the general public in the ways of reconciling the advantages of modern technologies with the moral restraint of Islamic law. In his view, this would both prevent rich and poor alike from

---

[64] Hanioglu, *Young Turks*, pp. 202–3; Kemal Karpat, *The Politicization of Islam* (Oxford, 2001), pp. 370–3. Al-Kawakibi also represented those at the time who thought that religion was a key component of social order, but that the conservative religious institutions of the day, as well as such 'superstitious' groupings as the Sufis, were one of the reasons for 'backwardness' – hence the need for a purification of religion that depended upon a re-examination of the Qur'an and the *sunnah*. Al-Husry, *Origins*, pp. 55–9.

[65] Sylvia G. Haim (ed.), *Arab Nationalism – An Anthology* (Berkeley, 1964), pp. 9–15; Keddie, *Islamic Response*, pp. 42–5, 77–81; al-Afghani, *Al-Radd 'ala al-dahriyin*, in *Al-A'mal al-kamilah*, pp. 156–63, and *Al-Ishtirakiyah*, in *Al-A'mal al-kamilah*, pp. 413–23.

[66] Martin Forward, *The Failure of Islamic Modernism? Syed Ameer Ali's Interpretation of Islam* (Bern, 1999), pp. 71–87; Ameer Ali, *The Spirit of Islam* (London, 1922), pp. 174–82.

being led astray and ensure social harmony between different orders of society.[67] For reformers, both secular and self-consciously engaged in promoting an agenda of Islamic reform, such as Muhammad 'Abduh, the education and disciplining of the individual student was to serve the primary purpose of creating an inner framework for order in society. This would counteract the disintegrative tendencies of capitalist, urban modernity and would also lead to a renewed acquaintance with an Islamic ethic, interpreted to check the licence of the 'mass society' and to remedy the obscurantism of 'traditional' scholarship.[68]

The individual was to be the prime target of instruction, since, it was argued, the principles and values underpinning the moral economy could be most effectively reinforced through the attitudes of individuals. But they would be individuals acting as members of society, which would provide the setting and framework of meaning for their actions. For many of these writers, therefore, the moral economy was a sphere defined by the values and attitudes which individuals brought to their social interactions, especially insofar as that involved exchanges both material and sociable. Education, rather than radical social engineering, economic development or political revolution were seen at this stage as holding the key to the kinds of reinvigoration of the community which they envisaged.[69] This was a theme being developed in Europe in the emerging field of functionalist sociology that had such a strong influence on the ways in which society and social development were being 'discovered' and understood. For Durkheim and others, not simply the content of education, but the very process, in terms of the habits of mental and physical discipline which it inculcated, were key components in the successful reproduction of society.[70]

For many thinkers, variously situated in different parts of the Islamic world, education held the key in many ways to the 'social problem' as then identified. If one part of the problem of the 'backwardness' of Islamic societies was their antiquated educational systems, then this could be remedied by educational reform which would combine, in miniature, that which

---

[67] Commins, 'The Salafi Islamic Reform Movement', pp. 233–5; al-Qasimi, Dala'il al-tawhid, pp. 49–62.

[68] Mitchell, Colonising Egypt, pp. 119–25. As Mitchell observes, whether the advocate of educational remedies was Fathi Zaghlul or Muhammad 'Abduh, the influence of Gustave Le Bon with his organic, functionalist views of the 'crowd' and its proper instruction and discipline was particularly prominent.

[69] See 'Abduh's translation of Herbert Spencer's Education: Intellectual, Moral and Physical (1861) which, however, was never published but clearly left its mark on 'Abduh's thinking and writing – Al-Azmeh, Islams and Modernities, pp. 81–5; 'Abduh, Al-A'mal al-kamilah, part 3, pp. 160–72

[70] E. Durkheim, Durkheim on Politics and the State, ed. A. Giddens (Cambridge, 1986), pp. 174–86; Mitchell, Colonising Egypt, pp. 121–2.

many were trying to achieve in the wider field of society. Educational reform held out the promise of establishing the model for social reform more generally. The educational framework and the technical content of the new forms of knowledge would be adopted from the successful and powerful societies of industrial, capitalist Europe. However, the moral content, the key restraining values and shapers of a distinctive Islamic identity, would be provided by Islamic instruction informed by a contemporary approach to the original sources of the Islamic revelation. In this way, it was thought, a new generation would be equipped to benefit from engagement with a world of industrial and scientific progress, but would also have the moral discipline to ensure that they remained true to Islam, capable of resisting the subversive logic of material progress.

These views are apparent in al-Marsafi's *Risalat al-Kalim al-Thaman*. This was in part a call for the establishment of a national system of education, authoritarian in nature and geared explicitly to the disciplined, orderly functioning of society. The suggestion was that without such inculcation of knowledge and moral discipline, society would fragment, disorder would ensue and foreign powers would have the pretext to intervene directly.[71] Similar sentiments were echoed by Syed Ahmad Khan in India. He also saw education in the European style to be the key to social transformation and yet perfectly compatible with the reproduction of distinctively Islamic values. For him, this meant establishing a new framework of schooling in which scientific knowledge and socially useful disciplines derived from Europe could be taught. It also meant reinterpreting the basic sources of the Islamic revelation and implicitly questioning much of the traditional knowledge of Islamic scholarship as it had developed over the centuries. Again, Khan saw this as the best means of linking Muslim societies to the benefits of material progress, without letting them succumb to the materialism and unbridled individualism which drove progress in the West, but which were antagonistic to an Islamic moral order.[72]

Planning for an educational system that would meet these needs, on a scale sufficient to shape society as a whole, implied a scale of organisation that only a state could provide. For the Ottoman reformers this was indeed an integral part of the overall reform and strengthening of the Ottoman

---

[71] al-Marsafi, *Risalat al-kalim al-thaman*, pp. 125–76; Mitchell, *Colonising Egypt*, pp. 131–7.

[72] Syed Ahmad Khan, *Writings and Speeches*, ed. Shan Mohammed (Bombay, 1972); see Khan's speech on education, Meerut, 14 March 1888, pp. 196–202, and his testimony to the Education Commission 1882, pp. 90–8; C. W. Troll, *Sayyid Ahmad Khan – A Reinterpretation of Muslim Theology* (New Delhi, 1978), pp. 302–7, 310–15; Muhammad, *Sir Syed Ahmad Khan*, pp. 50–77. This philosophy underpinned Khan's various educational endeavours, ranging from the publications *Tahzeeb-ul-Akhlaq* and the *Muhammadan Social Reformer* (1870s) to the foundation and development of the higher educational establishment at Aligarh (1872 onwards).

state, both in the metropolis and in the provinces. However, it raised for them, as for their contemporaries in the Qajar Empire, the central political question of the fiscal and administrative control of the institutions of education, as well as the fiercely debated question of the nature of the syllabus. Implicit in both cases was the indictment of the existing institutions of learning by the reformers, and the fear of the more traditionally minded *'ulama* and their followers that the removal of responsibility for education from the religious hierarchy of scholars would open the way to secularism and, ultimately, a downgrading of Islamic principles. These were to be frequently and bitterly contested issues from the nineteenth century onwards.[73]

At stake in these struggles was not simply the unwillingness of entrenched elites in the religious establishments to relinquish a key role in the organisation of the state, but, even more fundamentally, contrasting views both about the best way of preserving distinctly Islamic values in public life, and about those Islamic attributes which were regarded as key elements of the faith. For some, the involvement of state power would lead to the introduction of expediency and secular state interests as the criteria for judging the curriculum. For others, the substantive changes in the curriculum had already diluted the ability of such institutions to impart the steadfast Islamic values a new generation would need to withstand the seductions of the secular, capitalist West. Nevertheless, others still saw such a programme, if conducted under the auspices of an Islamic state or ruler, as the best guarantee of strengthening a distinctively Islamic society. It is here, in the educational field, that the politics of the moral economy – and concerns about its degradation and restoration – manifest themselves. The order of the moral economy that appears to be dissolving may be a largely imaginative one, but it is a potent one for all that, occurring as it does as a regular and charged construct throughout the writings of differently situated thinkers. By its very nature it raises the question of the status of people as moral beings existing within a social framework of ethical possibility.

The self-conscious reconstruction of a distinctively Muslim society in the changed setting of the new world required an imaginative leap that could not avoid being influenced by the forms of thought, the concepts and the categories of the changing political context itself. This became a project with many different faces. However, in all of them it was a political project, since it implied a struggle over the authoritative interpretation of the sources of

---

[73] Bill Williamson, *Education and Social Change in Egypt and Turkey* (Basingstoke, 1987), pp. 54–67; Ben Fortna, *Imperial Classroom: Islam, the State and Education in the Late Ottoman Empire* (Oxford, 2002), pp. 87–129.

ethical public conduct, as well as those governing behaviour in private. The very clear functionalist reasoning underpinning it also ensured a contest over the implications for the disposition of material resources and the relationship of the systems devised for their effective exploitation with the values which theoretically provided the rationale for social action.[74]

The fact that such contests developed within the discourse of the Islamic regeneration of society and the subjection of its economic processes to Islamic norms, flowed in part from the different situations of various writers and thinkers on these topics. However, the commonalities across regions and social position stemmed also from a common search for an appropriate Islamic idiom to identify and respond to the common epistemological as well as material challenges of the capitalist transformation of pre-capitalist societies. The different readings of the import of the changes taking place, but the general sense of crisis within much of the Islamic world, made severe demands on the imaginative repertoire of those involved and brought out a clear ambiguity regarding the potential of capitalist enterprise.

This centred on the question of whether capitalism could be harnessed to the benefit of a distinctively 'Islamic society', without radically transforming it in ways that made it look unfamiliar and ethically compromised. The epistemological challenge was whether, by imagining an 'Islamic society' in terms largely suggested by the dominant frameworks of social understanding emerging from the heartlands of capitalism's origin, the task of imagining, let alone reconstituting, a distinctive Islamic sociability could ever be an autonomous endeavour and whether this, in turn, threw the whole project into jeopardy or, conversely, opened up the possibility of a powerful new beginning, very much in keeping with an adaptive, interpretative view of Islam.

The contours of the early debate amongst Muslims concerned about the cohesion, identity and security of a distinctively Islamic community, when faced by the forms of structural and imaginative transformation associated with capitalism, remained recognisable throughout the twentieth century. Sometimes the debts to particular thinkers are acknowledged. More frequently, later writers find themselves drawing upon the vocabulary and imaginative tropes developed during this period in order to articulate their responses, in part because this constitutes a key element of a modern, reflexive repertoire. In part, also, it is because they are seeking to grapple with

---

[74] Some of this tension was well captured in the question posed by the 'ulama to the Young Ottomans in the mid-nineteenth century when the latter had asserted that religion was secondary to society, even if of prime importance to the individual. To this the 'ulama had apparently asked: 'So what are the important determinants [of society], if not religion [Islam]?' Hanioglu, *Young Turks*, p. 203.

similar problems, as the globalising and commodifying logic of capitalist development draws larger segments of the world and of human relations into its orbit. The intensification of capitalist development, but also the periodic crises attending its growth, sharpen the need to develop a response – and a response that seems to call for more decisive and extensive social action than the moral exhortation and educational preoccupations of the earlier period of Islamic responses to capitalism.

2   Islamic social critics

In the decades following the momentous changes which had taken place in the Middle East during the First World War, many of the themes which had so preoccupied an earlier generation of writers remained of concern to those who saw themselves as developing a distinctively Islamic response to the 'problems of the age' or the 'problem of society'. However, they now acquired a sharper focus, as well as a sense of urgency which can be partly explained by the fact that the scope of local political and economic activity was widening as the process of decolonisation began. It was possible not only to imagine alternative futures, but also to plan for the power that would put them into practice. Nevertheless, political independence did not necessarily imply independence from a world economic order founded on capitalist principles. For an emerging bourgeoisie across the Islamic lands, this was something to be welcomed, if only the domination of European enterprises could be removed from the national economies of the Middle East. At the same time, capitalism itself was being moderated from within through Keynesian welfare economics, and challenged from without by the model championed by the USSR and its allies. Thus, the period opened up possibilities for various forms of action, stimulating the imagination of many in the region.

This raised the fear for those who were determined to reshape public life, society and economy along distinctively Islamic lines that others, inimical to Islam, were also preparing to seize this moment of historical possibility. In particular, there was concern about the activities of the communists, represented in the press and by the authorities at the time to be a real threat to the social order. In Egypt, for instance, many of those who defined their position in terms of Islamic values, whether affiliated to the Muslim Brotherhood or not, shared the fears of much of the political establishment about the dangerous potential of the small and fractious communist movement, its links with the USSR and its determination radically to reshape not simply the material circumstances of Egyptian society, but also the bases of its beliefs.[1] Similar

---

[1] Mustafa al-Siba'i 'Jawab al-islam 'ala al-mas'alat al-shuyu'iyah', *Al-Muslimun* 3/7 (May 1954), pp. 81–8; J. Beinin and Z. Lockman, *Workers on the Nile* (London, 1988) pp. 363–94;

fears and alignments can be found in Iraq and in Iran during these years.[2] In their critique of existing society, its injustices and the part played by capitalism in fostering such a detrimental state of affairs, therefore, many of the Muslim intellectuals seem to have been as much concerned about the opportunity that social decay offered to the forces of communism as about the absolute iniquity of the capitalist system itself.[3]

These concerns were echoed in a discourse that drew upon the images and arguments put forward by the earlier generation of social critics and concerned Muslims. Attention was paid, therefore, to the parlous state of social solidarity and cohesion, and the need to restore a moral economy governed by the norms of Islam. The values fostered by the material structures of capitalism (and by communism in a different context) were seen as antithetical to the values which defined the Islamic view of the life of man, relations between human beings and the place of mankind in history and in relation to the eternal. There was a question of identity at stake here, but it was not simply a question of identity. There was also a belief that to accept such values and the logic of their assumptions would be to negate the true order of things, as described and prescribed in the Islamic texts, thereby contradicting the way in which the social universe was created and blocking its proper ethical development. The results were portrayed in cataclysmic terms and, for some, evidence of the coming cataclysm was already visible. The proof was seen not simply in the disorders of the unsettled politics of Egypt, Iraq or Iran, but also in the problems of the industrially advanced countries and their emergence from two devastating world wars into the threatening environment of the Cold War.[4]

E. Goldberg, *Tinker, Tailor and Textile Worker* (Berkeley, 1986), pp. 173–9; Muhammad al-Ghazzali, *Al-Islam al-muftara 'alaihi baina al-shuyu'iyin wa-l-ra'smaliyin* (Cairo, 1953); Muhammad Ibrahim al-Dassuqi, 'Ijabiyat al-islam fi muqawamat al-shuyu'iyah', *Al-Ikhwan al-Muslimun*, 9 June 1948.

[2] H. Batatu, *The Old Social Classes and the Revolutionary Movements of Iraq* (Princeton, 1978), pp. 465–544; see also the reactions of Mehdi Bazargan and of Ayatollah Taleqani in Iran to the danger of the 'rapid spread of Marxist and materialist principles and the founding of the Tudeh Party', cited in H. E. Chehabi, *Iranian Politics and Religious Modernism* (London, 1990), pp. 117–19.

[3] Two streams were apparent: those who opposed both capitalism and communism as two sides of the same materialist coin, and those who feared communist threats to moral order and to private property. These latter were also adhering to an Islamic world view, but it was one that was explicitly founded on the benefits of private property and of a thriving commercial life: capitalist in many respects, but restrained by the moral codes of Islam. These two streams developed later into those who rejected all materialism (the anti-globalisation Islamists) and those who sought to work within an Islamic framework of property and markets (the Islamic bankers). These divisions become sharpened in the next phase (see chapter 3 on 'Islamic socialism').

[4] However, some saw the very danger of conflict within 'the West' as an opportunity for Muslims – Richard Mitchell, *The Society of the Muslim Brothers* (London, 1969) pp. 270–1; Sayyid Qutb, *Al-Salam al-'alami wa-l-islam* (Cairo, 1979), pp. 167–99.

As in the earlier period, however, there was a degree of ambiguity in these criticisms, as well as in some of the prescriptions, which explains the different forms of Islamic response which appeared as the period proceeds. Some of this was inherited from the original formulations of the 'social problem' by earlier Islamic reformers, but it also came from the very task of identifying and grappling with the actual social problems of the age, as well as with the underlying assumptions of the capitalist order. The search was for a vocabulary and a systematic structure of reasoning that would not only analyse current ills, but also prescribe solutions which, whilst being effective, would nevertheless remain true to Islam. In this endeavour, a number of themes stand out in the writings of independent social critics, as well as of those associated with the main organised Islamic critique of the existing order – that of the Muslim Brotherhood, principally in Egypt – and those who were soon to become part of state-sponsored attempts to seek legitimation for their own versions of socialism.

The first of these themes revolves around the question of social solidarity. At one level, this comprises a general lament by moralists concerned about the effects of the modern age on the decline of 'brotherhood'.[5] This has much in common with the Christian socialists' criticism of industrial capitalism and the frailty of the social foundation of religious values. Equally, reflecting socialists such as William Morris, there is some suggestion that through the reassertion of the quality of fellowship, the all-devouring logic of the capitalist system will be stopped in its tracks – whilst its productive side can flourish.[6] At another level, it captures the idea that capitalism erodes existing social structures by undermining solidarities of all kinds, atomising individuals through its particular processes of wealth creation and by the attitudes it encourages: individualism, moral egotism and the pursuit of individual happiness. Having dissolved the older social bonds, imagined as organic or integral to the identity of society, capitalism reconstitutes relations, but in ways that now seem mechanistic, functional and shorn of the values that had imbued social intercourse with meaning.

An eloquent expression of this sentiment can be found in Sayyid Qutb's writings when he says of the United States:

this country of mass production, immense wealth and easy pleasures. I have seen them [Americans] a helpless prey in the clutches of nervous diseases in spite of all their grand appearances . . . They are like machines swirling round madly, aimlessly into the unknown . . . That they produce a lot there is no doubt. But to what aim is this mad

[5] Ahmad al-Sukkari, 'Hadith al-jum'a: ikhwa', *Al-Ikhwan al-Muslimun*, 4 April 1947.
[6] J. B. Glasier, *William Morris and the Early Days of the Socialist Movement* (Bristol, 1994), pp. 142–52; M. R. Grennan, *William Morris – Medievalist and Revolutionary* (New York, 1945), pp. 77–87.

rush? For the mere aim of gaining and production. The human element has no place if their life is neglected . . . Their life is an everlasting windmill which grinds all in its way: men, things, places and time . . . What is the medicine to all this imbroglio? A peaceful heart, a serene soul, the pleasure which follows strenuous work, the relation of affection between men, the cooperation of friends.[7]

The practical and moral question becomes that of gaining power to restore social solidarities, whilst ensuring that power does not subvert the purpose – a matter of concern to many.[8] For some, this dilemma could be avoided by reasserting Islamic beliefs and values to reinvigorate a society drained of its spiritual strength by capitalism. However, it was also recognised that this must be done in a way which catches the imagination of people and provides them with what they need in relation to the causes of their alienation, as well as its symptoms. This was an acknowledgement of the arrival of the age of mass politics, understandable when coming from sympathisers of the Muslim Brotherhood, the largest mass movement in post-war Egypt.

This is where the related question of property comes into play, portrayed by many writers as a vehicle for the restoration of an Islamic order, providing the material basis for the spiritual revival that will create the social solidarity needed to restore the lost harmonies of Islamic pre-capitalist society. Thus, the attention to property is due not simply to its prominent position in Islamic *fiqh*. Its reinvention for the modern era in a distinctively Islamic sense (surrounded by the regulations devised by Islamic jurisprudence to ensure the proper handling of property – i.e. its nature, its obligations, its limits, the question of *riba*, *zakat*, etc.) is also intended to hit capitalism at its heart, providing the basis for an effective Islamic alternative that will become the material substructure or perhaps reinforcement of an ethical revolution.[9]

These reflections raise a theme that had been important in the previous era, but became ever more insistent: the question of society's interests and how to measure them. It continued the debate about the question of welfare or benefit (*maslahah*), and, crucially, the central question of how to 'read' society's interests. Here the argument was introduced regarding the need to treat society like a text, opening up a series of questions about the implications of such an approach for the way in which the authoritative texts of the tradition should now themselves be read. One of the more daring consequences of this line of

---

[7] Sayyid Qutb, 'Humanity needs us' (in English, tr. M. Hafez), *Al-Muslimun* 3/2 (December 1953), pp. 3–4.

[8] See the concerns of the Supreme Guide of the Muslim Brotherhood who succeeded Hasan al-Banna – Hasan al-Hudaibi, *Du'ah la qudah* (Cairo, 1977). It could also be argued that the Tabligh movement is founded on this very principle: see Elke Faust, 'Islam on tour: Die indo-pakistanische Bewegung Tablighi Jama'at', *Orient* 39/2 (June 1998), pp. 219–29.

[9] This is further developed from the 1970s onwards, in part out of disappointment with the experience of Islamic socialism under state aegis.

reasoning was that some writers came close to arguing that this latest 'text' either supersedes the earlier ones in many particulars, or, less controversially, that it can shape the way in which the original written texts (Qur'an, *hadith*) are interpreted in each age.[10]

In either case, it also raised the question of who would have the proper expertise to read this new text. As the understanding of *maslahah* and the relevant 'texts' moves away from the scriptural and towards the social, different forms of expertise are needed. New claims are made as to what constitutes an authoritative interpretation of the interests and well-being of the community. It is not simply that the laity is interpreting the necessary Islamic obligations, but also that different forms of expertise are thought to be relevant to the task – forms of expertise which may have an unspoken teleology and logic of their own, often disguised as the neutrality of expertise itself.[11]

Given the political circumstances of the time and the direction of the debate, the role and responsibilities of the state emerged as a key theme.[12] For the great majority of those concerned about the depredations of capitalism and the defence of the community, the state becomes virtually the agency of first resort. Although tempered by exhortations to spiritual, inner reform of individuals according to the guidance of Islam, the state looms large as the institution that will protect the 'guarded sphere'.[13] It is here that a significant break with 'traditional' thinking about the state becomes apparent. The state is now portrayed as the newly independent guardian of Islamic values, creating the circumstances for the 'reform of the soul' (*salah al-nafas*), as well as for the realisation of true *maslahah* for society. It would do this by reorganising property in a way to negate its capacity to poison social relations, curbing the commodification of life and remedying inequality. It was

---

[10] 'Abd al-Wahhab Khallaf, *Masadir al-tashri' al-islami fi ma la nass fihi* (Cairo, 1955); Shaikh Ma'ruf al-Dawalibi, 'Al-Nusus wa-taghyir al-ahkam bi-taghyir al-azman', *Al-Muslimun* 1/6 (May 1952), pp. 553–60 – both cited in E. Salem, 'Arab reformers and the reinterpretation of Islam', *The Muslim World* 55/4 (October 1965), p. 316; 'Abd al-Karim al-Khatib, *Al-Siyasat al-maliyah fi al-islam wa-silatuha bi-l-mu'amalat al-mu'asirah* (Cairo, 1976; first published 1961) pp. 14–28, in which he argues that since Islam is the 'religion of nature', human welfare must be its objective and there can be no contradiction between the welfare of the people and the requirements of Islam; Kerr, *Islamic Reform*, pp. 213–14, see also pp. 80–97; Shaikh Mustafa Ahmad al-Zarqa, 'Taghyir al-ahkam bi-taghyir al-azman', *Al-Muslimun* 3/8 (June 1954), pp. 34–41.

[11] Timothy Mitchell, *Rule of Experts* (Berkeley, 2002), pp. 50–3, 209–11.

[12] See Sayyid Abul A'la Mawdudi, *Let Us Be Muslims*, (tr. of *Khutubat* (1940), ed. Khurram Murad (Leicester, 1992), pp. 287–8; Taqiuddin an-Nabhani, *The Islamic State* (London, 2001) pp. 221–76.

[13] See Hassan al-Banna, 'Barnamij qawmi', *Al-Ikhwan al-Muslimun*, 17 December 1946, and compare with 'Iqtisadi Kabir', 'Al-Mawqif al-iqtisadi wa-wajib al-hukumah', *Al-Ikhwan al-Muslimun*, 5 November 1947.

the state which would also encourage social solidarity and cooperation to resist European capitalist encroachments and to preserve the integrity of an Islamic society.

This imaginative construction of the ideal state created expectations of a very high order. It was to allow the co-option of many intellectuals who had been trenchant critics of capitalist society by governments such as that of President Gamal 'Abd al-Nasir of Egypt in the late 1950s, with consequences that will be explored in the next chapter. Equally, it resulted in determined opposition to those governments that were reluctant to oversee and implement the Islamisation of their societies in ways prescribed by such critics as Abul A'la Mawdudi in Pakistan or Sayyid Qutb and 'Abd al-Qadir 'Awdah in Egypt. For some, this led to rejection of the path down which the logic of social criticism and the prescriptions for social reform were heading. They relied instead on the assertion of the faith as the only way of preserving the values of Islam intact in a world where not simply the material circumstances of existence, but also the dominant ideational environment, seemed to be so heavily weighted against Islam as they saw it.[14]

2.1   Social solidarity

Many Muslim intellectuals were preoccupied with questions about the identity and future of their societies – a preoccupation at the heart of their critique of capitalism. The unrestrained power of money, and an acquisitive drive that was both individualist and materialist, summarised their fears of capitalism and its instruments. Echoing a classical Islamic view, shared by many religious systems, Hasan al-Banna of the Muslim Brotherhood in Egypt lamented the fact that wealth turns people into oppressors, reiterating his belief that Islam had come to 'free the poor from golden idols and their power and their tyranny'.[15] He called for the restoration of brotherly feelings of mutual responsibility among Muslims in order to counteract the divisive influence of disparities of wealth. His contemporary, Ayatollah Taleqani in Iran developed this theme further, dwelling not simply on the ways in which great wealth could lead to indifference to the plight of the poor, but also on the ways in which wealth creation under the capitalism was undermining the very fabric of society.[16]

---

[14] C. Tripp, 'Sayyid Qutb: the political vision', in Ali Rahnema (ed.), *Pioneers of Islamic Revival* (London, 1994) pp. 165–75.

[15] Hassan al-Banna, 'Hadith al-jum'a: asnam', *Al-Ikhwan al-Muslimun*, 6 September 1946.

[16] See, for instance, the preoccupations of Ayatollah Taleqani in Iran – Seyyed Mahmood Taleqani, *Islam and Ownership*, tr. A. Jabbari and F. Rajaee (Lexington, KY, 1983; originally published in different editions 1951–1965), pp. 7–8, 49–52, 102–7; Mangol Bayat, 'Mahmud

It was during the period following the Second World War that attention focused on capitalism's corrosive effects on society in general, not simply on Islamic social order. The distinction was not always clearly made, indicating the ways in which certain writers were thinking of society, the problems it was facing and indeed the remedies open to those who would protect or revitalise it – all of which tended to take up the discourse of the Islamic reformers of the nineteenth and twentieth centuries who had helped to define the 'social problem'.[17] These concerns permeate their social commentary, shaping their criticism of both the political economy of contemporary Egypt, Iran or India, and the decline of the sociability of their communities. True to the many influences that had worked upon them, this was expressed in an idiom that was unmistakably Islamic. However, the substance of their critique often echoed a more general lament about the ways in which capitalism was undermining the constitution of society.

This was primarily an idealist critique which had adopted a functionalist epistemology to portray a properly working Islamic society, and it was the latter that constituted a model for any sound social order. The idealist nature of the enterprise was noticeable in the imaginative reconstruction of Islamic society as an ideal type, with a historical reference point in seventh-century Arabia at the time of the Prophet Muhammad and his immediate successors. Represented as the epitome of a soundly functioning society, this was the measure used by the Islamic social critics to judge later developments. However, it was also idealist in that there was rarely any empirical investigation into the precise nature of the ills associated with capitalist development in the countries of the Middle East. One exception was the group of writers in Egypt associated with the Muslim Brotherhood who did draw attention to the hardships of people thrown onto the labour market without sufficient protection, but such writing, based on lived experience, was rare.[18]

The idealist critiques took a number of forms. They drew attention to capitalism's encouragement of hedonistic individualism and to the divisiveness of social relations under capitalism: individuals were atomised as they each pursued their private ends, and only came together in mutually antagonistic

Taleqani and the Iranian Revolution', in Martin Kramer (ed.), *Shi'ism, Resistance, and Revolution* (Boulder, CO, 1987), pp. 69–76.

[17] See Sayyid Qutb, *Ma'arakat al-islam wa-l-ra'smaliyah* (Cairo, 1993), 13th edition, pp. 36–54.

[18] See Muhammad Mahmud Sharif, 'Mashakil al-'ummal', *Al-Ikhwan al-Muslimun*, 29 April 1947; M. L. A. (*mim, lam, alif*), 'Khalaf dukhan al-masani'', *Al-Ikhwan al-Muslimun*, 30 November 1947. The same issue declares that from this date p. 6 of the publication will be devoted to the workers and 'the well-being of this great struggling class [*hadhihi al-ta'ifat al-kabirat al-mujahidah*]' – see, for instance, Anonymous, "Ummal al-Iskandiriya', *Al-Ikhwan al-Muslimun*, 23 December 1947. See also Beinin, 'Islamic responses to capitalist penetration of the Middle East', pp. 95–8.

classes. In addition, the danger for specifically Islamic society was capitalism's elevation of materialism (identified with both capitalism and communism) over spirituality (identified as the defining feature of the Islamic system).
As in other critiques of the ethos of capitalism (in particular those of the
Christian socialists, the Roman Catholic Church, and the Utopian socialists),
there existed a general fear among many of these writers of the capacity of
capitalism to foster selfishness.[19] Individualism was seen as intrinsic to
capitalism, as well as, in its guise of moral egotism, to the social order of
the *jahiliyah* which the Islamic message had originally come to reform. For
Said Nursi in Turkey, for example, with his organic notion of society,
harmonious relations between individuals could only be secured by joint
service to God.[20]

This theme was echoed by many Muslim intellectuals who saw individualism as a form of anomie, separating individuals from the organic whole of
society. This was often presented as a sociological 'fact' about the way in
which capitalist society operated and reproduced itself. The suggestion was
that capitalism needed and thus encouraged a property system founded on
the private property of isolated individuals.[21] Furthermore, it was suggested
that this individuation was also a necessary aspect of labour under capitalism.
Just as there must be individual proprietors, so must there be individuals who
owned no property other than their labour. This allowed employers to use that
labour as they wished, hiring and firing as the profit motive dictated. The
mechanics of this were little discussed, but the suggested outcome – mass
and chronic unemployment – was described in some detail. It formed one of
the standard indictments of capitalism, describing the conditions necessary
for the transmission of capitalism's flawed assumptions and practices into
society, with its loosening of social bonds in the process.[22]

---

[19] W. Charlton, T. Mallinson and R. Oakeshott, *The Christian Response to Industrial Capitalism*
   (London, 1986), pp. 65–7, 85–6, 111–13; R. H. Tawney, *Religion and the Rise of Capitalism*
   (Harmondsworth, 1938), pp. 163–78, 239–44; Thompson, *The Market and its Critics*,
   pp. 135–50.
[20] Serif Mardin, *Religion and Social Change in Modern Turkey* (Albany, NY, 1989) pp. 160–73;
   Mawdudi, *Let Us Be Muslims*, pp. 218–38.
[21] Al-Bahi al-Khuli, *Al-Islam la shuyu'iyah wa-la ra'smaliyah* (Cairo, 1951), pp. 12–34, 90–1;
   Radwan, *Ishtirakiyat al-islam*.
[22] Al-Khuli, *Al-Islam la shuyu'iyah* pp. 59–71; Abu al-A'la al-Mawdudi, 'Al-Nizam al-ra'smali
   al-jadid', *Al-Muslimun* 2/5 (March 1953), pp. 48–52, and 2/6 (April 1953), pp. 71–3. Unemployment as a phenomenon was also a preoccupation of economists and of capitalism's
   critics in the industrialised countries (see, for instance, the Keynesian project in the inter-war
   period), and this clearly affected debate in the Middle East and elsewhere. There was, in
   addition, a strand in the critique of capitalism which held up the constant threat of unemployment (and thus implicitly starvation) through the commodification of labour in the market as
   one of the main engines of capitalism – and one of its more immoral features.

Individualism was also represented as a creed or belief system which undermined the ethical foundations of Islam, by focusing on the individual as a self-directed and autonomous being, detracting from the social being, or the 'worshipper' (*'abad*) in relation to God. Individualism, therefore, removed the foundational justification of the Islamic creed, since it relegated God and the divine to a category of beliefs like any other set of beliefs. This went to the heart of the unease of many Muslim intellectuals on the dangerous implications of man-made laws. It was not simply that they might neglect the *shari'ah* or incorporate erroneous readings of the sacred texts, but also that they opened the way for the humanist foundation of morality, with its accompanying relativism and uncertainty.[23]

The Islamic social critics were also concerned about another feature of social fragmentation which they attributed to capitalism: the division of society into classes. This was different to the division between rich and poor familiar to writers in the Islamic tradition since the days of the Prophet, many of whom chose the examples of proper relations between wealth and poverty to illustrate the ethical framework of social relations.[24] Class-based society was seen as different, although commentaries on rich and poor were often used as pegs on which to hang a more extensive discussion of the class system. Identification with a particular class suggested that people were basing their relations with each other on the purely material preoccupations that went into the constitution of socio-economic classes. In the view of writers close to the Muslim Brotherhood in Egypt, for example, class solidarity is fundamentally different to general social solidarity, since it is founded on the principles of greed (the proprietors) and of envy (the propertyless).[25]

The blame for this state of affairs is laid on capitalism since it has created a society for the wealthy, based on the exclusivity of private property and the solidarity that arises out of the exploitation of others. In the view of the Islamic critics this is neither stable nor commendable. It is unstable because the search for relative advantage continues to preoccupy the class of proprietors, turning them against each other and giving the lie to any genuine solidarity amongst the acquisitive individuals of capitalism.[26] At the same

---

[23] 'Abd al-Qadir 'Awdah, *Al-Islam wa-awda'na al-qanuniyah* (Beirut, 1988), pp. 54–131.

[24] As representative texts of this genre, see Abu 'Ubaid (d. 838 CE), *Kitab al-amwal* (Cairo, 1975); Abu Yusuf (d. 798 CE), *Kitab al-kharaj* (Cairo, 1972); Ibn Taymiyah (d. 1328), *Al-Siyasat al-shar'iyah* (Cairo, 1971) and Ibn Taymiyah, *Al-Hisbah* (Cairo, 1976).

[25] Muhammad Ibrahim al-Dassuqi, 'Ijabiyat al-islam fi muqawamat al-shuyu'iyah', *Al-Ikhwan al-Muslimun*, 9 June 1948; Muhammad Mahmud Sharif, 'Mashakil al-'ummal', *Al-Ikhwan al-Muslimun*, 29 April 1947; Radwan, *Ishtirakiyat al-islam*, pp. 18–21; Hasan al-Banna, 'Al-Nizam al-iqtisadi', pp. 340–3 in *Majmu'ah rasa'il al-Imam al-Shahid Hasan al-Banna* (Beirut, 1984).

[26] Mustafa al-Siba'i, *Akhlaquna al-ijtima'iyah* (Beirut, 1972) pp. 41–9.

time, it distracts people from the ethical foundations of existence and directs their attention to the material conditions of life, opening the door to other materialist creeds, such as communism, which threaten an equally devastating assault on existing social bonds.[27]

Social disintegration, acquisitiveness and class resentments are all seen as symptoms of a rampant materialism, intertwined with the understanding of individualism promoted by capitalism. By contrast, an Islamic order is represented as embodying the crucial element of 'spirituality' which counteracts materialism by reminding people of a world beyond the present and of the duties they owe to others in this world. In this sense, 'spirituality' is the key to social solidarity – and it is this that will protect Islamic society against the many threats associated with the capitalist (and communist) onslaught.[28] The twin themes of social solidarity (al-tadamun al-ijtima'i) and mutual social responsibility (al-takaful al-ijtima'i) were restated in various forms by many of those authors most concerned about the disintegration of their societies.[29] They acknowledged that disparities of wealth existed and that absolute material equality was neither achievable nor desirable, but they did not believe that this should be the basis for class formation and social division. Poverty and unemployment were written about as diseases encouraged by capitalism and by the attitudes and schisms underlying and promoted by the capitalist ethic.[30] The pathology of society had clear antecedents in the functionalism of the corporeal analogy promoted by writers of the nineteenth and early twentieth centuries, both Islamist and secular. It was this that informed those who sought to grasp society imaginatively.

The ideas of social solidarity and of mutual social responsibility clearly owed much to an ideal of society in which, despite differences, all cooperated for the common good. In a world increasingly dominated by the forces of materialism, calls for greater social solidarity suggested that the cure for the ills besetting Muslim peoples and their civilisation lay with them – in the strength of their beliefs and thus in their will. This was an encouraging message for Muslims, but it was also bound up with the idea that the distinguishing characteristic of a truly Islamic society lay in its cultivation of a spirituality that would encourage engagement with the world, rather than

[27] al-Dassuqi, 'Ijabiyat al-islam fi muqawamat al-shuyu'iyah', Al-Ikhwan al-Muslimun, 9 June 1948.

[28] Qutb, Ma'arakat, pp. 109–12; Ibrahim al-Bayumi Ghanim, Al-Fikr al-siyasi li-l-Imam Hasan al-Banna (al-Mansurah, 1992) pp. 241–50.

[29] Muhammad Abu Zahra, Al-Takaful al-ijtima'i fi al-islam (Cairo, 1964); S. A. Hanna, 'Al-Takaful al-ijtima'i and Islamic socialism', The Muslim World 59 (1969) pp. 275–86.

[30] Abu Zahra, Al-Takaful, pp. 71–7; Radwan, Ishtirakiyat al-islam, p. 99; Sayyid Qutb, 'Tabi'ah al-mujtama' al-islami' (2), Al-Muslimun 2/5 (March 1953), pp. 446–7; Abu al-A'la al-Mawdudi, 'Al-Nizam al-ra'smali al-jadid', Al-Muslimun 2/6 (April 1953), pp. 71–3.

a withdrawal from it.[31] Refocusing people's attention on the bonds that linked them with others as fellow Muslims drew attention to the conditions under which Muslim society was formed and the social obligations incumbent upon the believer if he or she were to please God. In addition, emphasis on social solidarity stressed the primacy of a specifically Islamic identity over and above the temptations of individualism and of other forms of collective identity, such as those based on socio-economic class.[32]

In these arguments a conflation was taking place between the Islamic ethical imperatives of mutual social responsibility and social solidarity to sustain a distinctive Islamic order, and their functional aspects as instruments for the reinforcement of any society. By problematising society as a natural fact, Muslim intellectuals had equated a distinctively Islamic society with the proper functioning of any society, suggesting also that harmonious relations could only be achieved through the establishment of an Islamic system. In other words, the Islamic system of social regulation and mutual social responsibility was being presented as the only true basis of social integration and equilibrium. The principal reason for this, so it was argued, was that only in a system governed by Islamic values would the potentially dysfunctional aspects of property ownership be kept in check.

2.2   Property and its social function

Underlying the idea of mutual social responsibility was the belief that it could counteract the remorseless individualism of property ownership and acquisition. Linking ownership to a goal greater than the mere satisfaction of individual wants would bring out the 'social function' (al-wazifat al-ijtima'iyah) of property – that is, the obligations of the proprietor to other members of society. This function corresponded partly to the conditionality of all property in a universe in which God had entrusted humans with its use, encapsulated in rules such as payment of zakat, which were associated with this conditional ownership. To participate in a system of zakat was not only obligatory in the terms laid down for the faith (as one of the five pillars of Islam), but was also a means whereby any individual could fulfil their ethically complete potential. Similarly, any society in which this system of monetary contribution was seriously practised would reinforce the 'spiritual' values of Islam, domesticating the 'natural' tendencies towards the making of a profit and ensuring that this was not the only impulse to social and

---

[31] Hasan al-Banna, 'Hadith al-thulatha: kalimat fiyada ra'i'ah li-fadilat al-murshid al-'amm', Al-Ikhwan al-Muslimun, 8 April 1948; Salah al-Din Fakhr al-Din, 'Ma huwa al-islam?' Al-Ikhwan al-Muslimun, 21 June 1948.
[32] Qutb, Al-Salam al-'alami, pp. 103–21, 142–66.

economic activity. The intention was to strengthen the society in which this was encouraged, imbuing it once again with the power necessary to thrive, through social order and cooperation, and to defend Islam against the mundane encroachments that came with the seductions of materialism.[33]

It was understandable that property should have become a focus, embodying as it does contrasting ways of thinking about society, social power and identity. Its definition contains valuable information on the legal structure of a society, since it is pre-eminently an instance of the attachment of legal prohibitions and permissions to the objects of the material world. It thereby gives an indication of the assumptions on which the social order is founded and the values being promoted. Property is also a medium through which people act in fulfilment of their own ambitions, whether in pursuit of self-realisation or of social integration. It is thus a marker of identity, symbolising those qualities valued by the society – a token and indicator of the moral economy – as well as a means of their realisation.[34] It is in this capacity that property is of particular interest to those Muslim intellectuals concerned about the workings of capitalism in the twentieth century.

Discussions of property allowed them to draw on a substantial corpus of 'traditional' writing, in the works of the jurists who had devoted considerable attention to the question of property and its proper disposition under Islamic law. As the Egyptian writer 'Abd al-Qadir 'Awdah stated quite forcefully, Islam was a religion which concerned itself in some detail with the question of property.[35] Indeed, property as *milk* or *milkiyah* (that which is owned) or *mal* (wealth) had been the subject of certain defining injunctions from the outset of the Islamic revelation. At the same time, discussion of property allowed the Islamic social critics to link an identifying Islamic tradition with prescriptions for the disposition of the things of this world. Amongst intellectuals close to the Muslim Brotherhood in Egypt, but also elsewhere, the need to stress the relevance of Islamic values to the material aspects of life was apparent, since they wanted to refute both the claim that religion was relevant only to the things of the spirit and the allegation that Islam was either

---

[33] One of the clearest statements of this position which became influential in many parts of the Islamic world was by the leader of the Syrian Muslim Brotherhood, Mustafa al-Siba'i. Despite the use made of his writings later for rather different purposes by the Egyptian government of Gamal 'Abd al-Nasir, in the mid-1950s, he was already expounding his views on the means of enhancing 'mutual social responsibility' and the intimate connection between this and the Islamic message. See al-Siba'i, *Akhlaquna al-ijtima'iyah*, pp. 41–9, and *Ishtirakiyat al-islam* (Damascus, 1960), pp. 174–84.

[34] C. B. Macpherson, *Property – Mainstream and Critical Positions* (Oxford, 1978), pp. 1–13; D. Pels, *Property and Power in Social Theory*, (New York, 1998), pp. 18–46; Ryan, *Property and Political Theory*, pp. 1–13.

[35] 'Abd al-Qadir 'Awdah, *Al-Mal wa-l-hukm fi al-islam* (Cairo, 1977), pp. 9–35.

silent on the material conditions of the mass of the people or buttressed the status quo.[36]

The starting point for most of the discussions of property is the orthodox view that all property belongs to God in the final analysis. From this perspective, human beings are simply the trustees placed in charge by God to ensure that his property is used fruitfully and in a morally commendable way. The conditions of the trust are then explained and encompass the *shari'ah* rulings on the permitted forms of property acquisition and disposal, listing those which are forbidden, those which are permitted and encouraged, those which are merely commended or discouraged and those which are morally neutral. However, other than in the hands of the most legalistic of the jurists, the identifying of property and its place within an ethical and a social universe begins to take on different and innovative aspects.[37] More dramatically, in the writings of those who are responding to the condition of society and who are determined to reconstitute and reinvigorate an Islamic social order, the discussion of property, its qualities and its potential assumes a dynamic form which links it directly to the vision of a modern, yet distinctively Islamic society.[38]

In this sense, the Egyptian writer 'Abd al-Qadir 'Awdah is typical of similarly concerned Islamic social critics of the period, even if his conclusions and his reasoning may not be identical. In his writings two different understandings of property develop: one comes from the assumption of a hypothetical state of nature in which man's instinct to accumulate is awakened by the realisation that nature can be made to yield wealth for the individual by being transformed into property; the other depends upon the projection of God as a moral overseer, and for this purpose it is claimed that everything is the property of God. This usage of 'property' is less a legalistic description of the kind commonly understood by the Islamic jurists than a hypothetical construction to allow him to assert that God owns all creation and that no human being, therefore, can have an absolute right to call anything his or her own. Since humans hold everything on trust from God, they are

---

[36] Hasan al-Banna, 'Hadith al-juma': thawrah', *Al-Ikhwan al-Muslimun*, 19 September 1946; M. A. (*mim, alif*), 'Risalatuna', *Al-Ikhwan al-Muslimun*, 11 April 1948; Taleqani, *Islam and Ownership*, pp. 72–8.

[37] For traditionally framed but contemporary commentary on property, see Shaikh Ahmad Ibrahim, *Al-Mu'amalat al-shari'at al-maliyah* (Cairo, 1936); Abu al-Nasr Ahmad al-Husaini, *Milkiyah fi al-islam* (Cairo, 1952); Shaikh Muhammad Abu Zahra, *Al-Milkiyah wa-l-nazriyat al-'aqd* (Cairo, 1939); Shaikh 'Ali al-Khafif, *Al-Milkiyah fi al-shari'at al-islamiyah* parts 1 and 2 (Beirut, 1969); Shaikh Hasanain Muhammad Makhluf, *Al-Mawarith fi al-shari'at al-islamiyah* (Cairo, 1956).

[38] Sayyid Qutb, *Al-'Adalat al-ijtima'iyah fi al-islam* (Cairo, 1977), pp. 87–107; Shaikh Taqi al-Din al-Nabhani, *Al-Nizam al-iqtisadi fi al-islam* (Amman, n.d.).

obliged to abide by certain regulations if they wish to enjoy the fruits of his creation in this world and his pleasure in the next.[39]

However, the conclusions which he and others draw from these commonly held beliefs give an indication of the changing nature of the property debate during the mid-twentieth century, and link his arguments to concerns about actual property relations in the postcolonial world. In their writings there is an echo of the uncertain acceptance of the institution of wholly alienable private property, despite the fact that this had been formally instituted in Egypt and elsewhere in the former Ottoman Empire for nearly one hundred years, and, as far as real estate and transactional capital were concerned, had existed for much longer than that.[40] Possibly to avoid the full implications of recognising private property rights, a number of writers make a distinction between ownership of property (the material thing: land, machinery, factors of production) and the ownership and enjoyment of 'usufruct'. This proves to be a difficult distinction to make. On a practical level, it is scarcely possible to separate fixed capital assets used to generate profit ('usufruct') and those assets created when profit is reinvested to increase capital. On a theoretical level, God may well be designated as the sole owner, but property here takes on a very different meaning to human property relations: in the latter case, ownership and the quality of property is pre-eminently social, whereas the 'property of God' is clearly a-social and absolute.[41]

'Awdah and others are principally concerned about what property has become under the conditions of modern capitalism and how it might be reconfigured to strengthen a distinctive Islamic society in the contemporary world. This is what distinguishes the tenor and substance of their writings from those of the legally minded interpreters of the *shari'ah*. For instance,

---

[39] 'Awdah, *Al-Mal wa-l-hukm*, pp. 17–35; 'Abd al-Qadir 'Awdah, *Al-Islam wa-awda'na al-siyasiyah* (Cairo, 1967), pp. 38–54; Muhammad Salih, 'Al-Fikr al-iqtisadi al-Islami', *Al-Muslimun* 1/2 (January 1952), pp. 165–8; 'Anonymous' in a later issue was even more forthright: 'capitalists are stupid when they claim that to which they have no right' and 'the relationship of man to wealth is that he is a trustee, no more, no less': *Al-Muslimun* 1/5 (March 1952), pp. 502–7.

[40] T. Aricanli and M. Thomas, 'Sidestepping capitalism: on the Ottoman road to elsewhere', *Journal of Historical Sociology* 7/1 (March 1994), pp. 25–47; Cuno, *The Pasha's Peasants*, pp. 198–207; H. Islamoglu, 'Property as a contested domain: a reevaluation of the Ottoman Land Code of 1858', in Owen *New Perspectives on Property and Land in the Middle East*, pp. 4–7, 18–24, 29–42.

[41] 'Awdah, *Al-Islam wa-awda'na al-siyasiyah*, pp. 29–38; Mahmud Abu al-Sa'ud, 'Istighlal al-ard fi al-islam 2', *Al-Muslimun* 1/3 (February 1952), pp. 271–3, and 'Istighlal al-ard fi al-Islam 3', *Al-Muslimun* 1/4 (March 1952), pp. 382–6. This has echoes of the debate about the 'rights of God', another construction which becomes interestingly transformed in the writings of 'Awdah and others as they seek to socialise them and, in doing so, have to look for an agency other than that of God – a deputy worthy of the name, which turns out to be 'society' or the 'community'.

when criticising the institution of property in modern Egypt, 'Awdah sees it as solely at the disposal of the individual, free of any concern other than that of his own advantage. Under these conditions, the instinct to accumulate dominates and restrictions on the methods of accumulation and the uses of wealth fall away, creating an unlicensed society. Like other social critics of the time, he wants to bring property back under control, to ensure that it plays its part in the realisation of a truly Islamic society. Yet the idea that God's ownership makes all creation open to all humanity to enjoy must be tempered by his assertion that all humans individually have the right to possess the yield of wealth, even if not to be the final owner. Evidently there are grounds for considerable difference if the two precepts of 'universal right to enjoyment' and 'individual right to yield' are to be seriously pursued – and the tensions this generates form a notable feature of 'Awdah's writings, and in the writings of others.[42]

On the one hand, this leads 'Awdah and others to stress the key role of the 'society', understood as the community, to resolve these tensions, arguing that since God made wealth for the benefit of society as a whole, it should be the latter, not any individual that must act with regard to wealth and property. These, it is suggested, flow from the 'rights of God' instanced in this case by God's right to ultimate ownership, and by the role of society (standing in for 'humanity') as the agent of God on earth.[43] On the other hand, it is also argued that the right of individuals to profit from wealth and to possess its usufruct must be taken seriously and that society should have no role here, except to regulate ownership claims. These can be alienated, bought, sold and passed on in inheritance. Indeed, given the detailed regulations regarding such transactions, some of them laid down unambiguously in the verses of the Qur'an, it would be difficult for contemporary critics to suggest otherwise.[44]

---

[42] M. Umer Chapra, 'Mawlana Mawdudi's contribution to Islamic economics', *The Muslim World* 94/2 (April 2004), pp. 164–8 – a tension which Mawdudi thought to overcome by stressing the spiritual and moral dimension of Islam and the need to begin with the 'reform of the individual', thus ensuring that – at least from the idealist perspective – there could be no conflict between these claims. 'Awdah, *Al-Islam wa-awda'na al-siyasiyah*, pp. 33–7; al-Siba'i, *Akhlaquna al-ijtima'iyah*, (lecture of May 1954), pp. 41–9.

[43] In this respect, it is interesting that Qutb brings to the fore the verses of the Qur'an stressing mankind's collective role as *khalifah*, or agent/inheritor of God on earth – for instance, *Al-Qur'an* Surah 6 (*al-An'am*) verse 166, Surah 10 (*Yunus*) verse 14, Surah 27 (*al-Naml*) verse 62, Surah 35 (*Fatir*) verse 39, takes on a collective, rather than an individual interpretation. Sayyid Qutb, *Fi zilal al-Qur'an*, 5 vols. (Beirut, 1967), part 8, pp. 90–102, part 11, pp. 127–9, part 28, pp. 134–7; see also Muhammad Qutb, *Al-Insan baina al-maddiyah wa-l-islam* (Cairo, 1980) pp. 111–40.

[44] See, for instance, the Qur'anic verses dealing with the laws of inheritance: *Al-Qur'an*, Surah 2 (*al-Baqarah*) verses 180–1, 240 and Surah 4 (*al-Nisa'*) verses 6–14, 176; or those dealing with

However, there is an attempt to qualify this by suggesting that the right to this kind of property – the ownership of usufruct – is also conditional upon the benefit both the individual and the society should derive from it. This move shifts the argument squarely onto the more familiar terrain, as far as European social and political theory is concerned, of the competing claims of individual and society. It is not a terrain which can be immediately encompassed within a traditional Islamic idiom and one can witness in the writings of the Islamic social critics the emergence of a distinctively Islamic vocabulary and set of ethical criteria to describe and to adjudicate between the competing claims of these relatively new and unfamiliar phenomena of 'individual' and 'society'. In general, there is a difficulty in specifying the relative weight of the two claims; nor is there much guidance as to the criteria which would allow common measurement and comparison of competing claims. Indeed, given the difference in the nature of the understanding of 'property' underlying these claims, it is difficult to know how such a standard of comparison could be established.[45]

These different understandings of property give rise to significant and creative ambiguities which were explored in the developing debate about the respective property claims of the community or society and the individual across the Islamic world, framed both in secular and self-consciously Islamic terms. In fact, it is noticeable that the self-consciously 'Islamic' and 'secular' debates about collective versus individual claims to property follow broadly similar lines, apparent not just in 'Awdah's writings, but in those of a number of others in Egypt, Iran and beyond, all of whom influenced the debate.[46] Three different kinds of argumentation appeared. The first concerned the substance of the tradition with which these writers sought to identify themselves. The second had to do with the nature of political contestation within Egypt, Iran, Iraq and elsewhere during these years, as the relative merits and disadvantages of capitalism and communism were hotly argued and ideals of collective or liberal paths to development were promoted by the governments concerned. The third was the encounter between idealised property rights and the reality of a variety of forms of ownership, based on a mixture of accepted practices, Islamic propriety and codes of positive law which defined and implicitly protected private property.

---

usury (*riba*) and profits from trade that make a sharp distinction between them, as well as with commercial and financial transactions: Surah 2 (*al-Baqarah*) verses 274–83.

[45] Mahmud Abu al-Sa'ud, 'Istighlal al-ard fi al-islam 4', *Al-Muslimun* 1/5 (March 1952), pp. 461–4; Abu al-A'la al-Mawdudi, tr. Muhammad 'Asim al-Haddad 'Al-Nizam al-ra'smali al-jadid', *Al-Muslimun* 2/2 (December 1952), pp. 180–5.

[46] Abu Zahra, *Al-Takaful*, pp. 14–27; Taleqani, *Islam and Ownership*, pp. 131–44.

As far as the first was concerned, the 'tradition' with which these writers sought to identify themselves had its uses, but also its problems. In part this may have been due to their own ambiguous attitudes towards that tradition and the sometimes eclectic nature of their selections from thirteen centuries of Islamic jurisprudence. More than that, however, there was an ambiguity in the nature of the enterprise which has been characteristic of the modern Islamic, as well as of various nationalist approaches to 'tradition'. Muslim intellectuals were looking back at 'tradition', therefore, with a sensibility that was largely a product of a modern search for identity, called into being in part by the nature of the threats they confronted in the twentieth century, and the strategies with which they hoped to meet those threats. Their sensibilities were unsurprisingly a product of their time, not simply because they addressed contemporary challenges, but because they incorporated a critical self-reflexivity which is itself a marker of modernity, and this made them ambivalent about the nature of tradition and about the role it would play in defining the new 'Muslim self'. It was a modern sense of crisis that led to the search for an identifying 'tradition' in the writings of the Islamic jurists. It was not surprising that they discovered one. However, it was also not surprising that it should have contained so many ambiguities.[47]

Nowhere is this more visible than in the question of property and its status. A distinctively modern epistemology produced a particular reading of what it was that the Islamic 'tradition' had to say about the nature of property. Seeking to reconcile the apparently contradictory or potentially conflicting strands found therein led those who were seeking a specifically Islamic solution to try to bring about a harmony founded on categories that would have been incomprehensible to the authors of the supposedly authoritative interpretations, the classical jurists themselves. In other words, the contemporary writers were clearly informed by the debate about socialist collectivism versus liberal individualism which was so evidently a child of capitalism. They were also influenced by the ambient debate about economic injustice and the unequal distribution of wealth in Egypt and elsewhere at the time, and sought in the writings of the jurists' adjudication between collective and individual rights to property, even though this was far from the jurists' concerns. The latter had expressed themselves forcefully from time to time about the problems of wealth and the dangers which this represented for the soul of man. However, they were preoccupied with wealth as the source of

[47] D. W. Brown, *Rethinking Tradition in Modern Islamic Thought* (Cambridge, 1996), pp. 1–4, 27–42; Al-Azmeh, *Islams and Modernities*, pp. 77–88; P. Chatterjee, *Nationalist Thought and the Colonial World – A Derivative Discourse* (London, 1993) pp. 4–17, 167–71; Laroui, *Islam et modernité*, pp. 68–80; R. Meijer, *The Quest for Modernity: Secular Liberal and Left-Wing Political Thought in Egypt 1945–1958* (Richmond, 2002) pp. 11–14.

power for good and evil, rather than the relationship of forms of property ownership to such questions as social cohesion.[48] There was sufficient material, however, both in the writings of the jurists and in the *hadith* of the Prophet, to allow 'Awdah, Qutb and others to draw a number of conclusions about the ideal forms of property in the Islamic system.[49]

In such circumstances, it is not surprising that their conclusions were ambiguous, as in 'Awdah's assertion that 'society must not touch the property of the usufruct/profit, except to settle ownership rights. Indeed Islam forbids this, unless it is required' or that 'Islam allows freedom of possession to an unlimited extent – but demands that society limit this . . . if the public welfare demands this'.[50] The repeated use of the term 'society' in contrast to the individual focuses attention on the question of public interest, giving rise to a debate about how this interest can be determined. In some cases, it becomes clear that those seeking to promote a distinctively Islamic approach were trying simultaneously to avoid the accusation of being apologists for the status quo, or of being communist fellow-travellers because of their social criticism.[51] This led some to embrace a form of Fabian socialism and to call themselves 'moderate socialists': advocates of the mixed economy which was proving so potent a model of development at the time. In Iran, for instance, the emergence of a group in the 1940s calling themselves the 'God-worshipping socialists' was characteristic of this trend, and in Egypt the writings of Khalid Muhammad Khalid captured the same spirit, outlining a distinct position that would be developed in the 1950s and 1960s into the forms of argument and apologia labelled 'Islamic socialism'.[52]

Insofar as these concerns went to the heart of a distinctively Islamic critique of capitalism, two particular themes come out in a variety of ways. The first is the belief that in capitalist systems there exist untrammelled property rights. The second has to do with capital as a disembodied force which yet has vast power to shape people's lives. In both cases the fear was that an absence of social rules to keep the acquisitive instinct in check would inevitably encourage an individualist pursuit of self-interest and advantage. In contrast to this, the various conditions attached to wealth creation and its disposal in the works of Islamic jurisprudence, as well as certain redistributive

[48] Muhammad al-Ghazzali, *Al-Islam wa-l-manahij al-ishtirakiyah* (Cairo, 1954), pp. 56–9.
[49] See Nasir, *Al-Islam wa-intiza' al-milk li-l-maslahat al-'ammah*; a useful index of *hadith* relating to wealth and property can be found in 'Abd al-Salam Dawud al-'Abbadi, *Al-Milkiyah fi al-shari'at al-islamiyah* (Amman, 1977), part 3, pp. 245–74.
[50] 'Awdah, *Al-Islam wa-awda'na al-siyasiyah*, p. 37.
[51] Ahmad al-Sharabasi *Al-Ishtirakiyah wa-l-din (Imanuna* no. 2) (Cairo, 1962), pp. 8–10; Ahmad al-Sharabasi, *Al-Islam wa-l-iqtisad* (Cairo, 1965), pp. 206–8.
[52] Ali Rahnema, *An Islamic Utopian – A Political Biography of Ali Shari'ati* (London, 1998), pp. 30–4; Khalid Muhammad Khalid, *Min huna nabda'* (Cairo, 1950), pp. 73–162.

taxes, are held up as mechanisms that will bring these dangerous forces under control, directing them towards the creation of wealth for praiseworthy ends and avoiding the dangers of rampant acquisitiveness.[53]

2.3   The problem of money

It is in this connection that the problems of money come to the fore. Money in pre-capitalist systems has been described as a pre-eminently 'protocapitalist' feature of the economy, in the sense that it embodies all the aspects of capital which have made the latter so productive – and disturbing – a force. Whether the system in which it is employed will become predominantly capitalist will, of course, depend upon many other factors, the identity and relative weight of which remain a matter of debate.[54] However, the features of money that make it so amenable are its characteristic of 'wealth in circulation', its transferability or alienability and the possibility of converting it into all the forms of factors of production – land, labour, machinery, even ideas in the sense they can be purchased as commodities and added to the productive enterprise. Marx appreciated the 'wealth-in-circulation' aspect of money, but also, as a critic of what this means for human relations, was aware of its alienating capacities.[55] In this, he was following a long tradition of uneasy moralists who inveighed against the dangers inherent in the nature of money. Thus money is not simply 'protocapitalist' in a material sense, but also in an ethical or normative sense. It introduces some of the moral dilemmas brought out on a larger scale by capitalism and the historical wariness of money can be seen as foreshadowing the critique of the capitalist system as it began to colonise local economies. Much of this concern focused on the need to keep the disturbing features of money in check through systems of ethics and power which would, in theory, diminish its potency as a social disruptor.[56]

Aristotle had condemned the practice of lending money at interest, because, as he said, 'it makes a gain out of money itself, and not from the natural object

---

[53] See, for example, the very characteristic setting out in *Al-Manar* in the 1930s of the rules governing the ownership of legal wealth as laid out in the *Surat al-Tawbah* in the Qur'an: *Al-Manar* 32 (1932) pp. 246–9.

[54] Simmel, *The Philosophy of Money*, pp. 228–57; Parry and Bloch, *Money and the Morality of Exchange*, pp. 2–3; M. Mauss, *The Gift: The Form and Reason for Exchange in Archaic Societies* (London, 2004), pp. 71–2.

[55] Karl Marx, *Capital* (Harmondsworth, 1977–9), vol. I, pp. 188–244; S. de Brunhoff, *La monnaie chez Marx* (Paris, 1967) pp. 32–64; B. Fine and C. Lapavitsas, 'Markets and money in social theory: what role for economics?' *Economy and Society* 29/3 (August 2000), pp. 367–71; Parry and Bloch, *Money*, pp. 5–7.

[56] C. E. Staley, *A History of Economic Thought: From Aristotle to Arrow* (Oxford, 1992), pp. 3–8; Thomas Aquinas, *Selected Political Writings*, ed. A. P. d'Entrèves (Oxford, 1965), pp. 171–5.

of it'.[57] This was taken up both by the Church Fathers and by Muslim scholars who could also cite the prohibitions on usury in the Qur'an, but this concern is echoed in civilisations which had no connection with the classical or the Islamic worlds. For those who placed themselves in the Islamic tradition, numerous *hadith* of the Prophet, Qur'anic injunctions and other established authorities contained warnings about the power of money, expressed as *mal* (strictly, 'wealth'). These were used by twentieth-century Muslim intellectuals and developed both as a critique of capitalism and as the basis of an economic system grounded in Islamic values.

One of the principal themes coming out of the writings of various classical Islamic jurists and taken up by modern intellectuals was the idea derived from a saying attributed to the Prophet Muhammad that 'wealth is the test of my community', implying its capacity to test their moral fortitude.[58] The test facing Muslims is whether they will succumb to the acquisitive instinct, ignoring various claims on their wealth and the restrictions on the ways in which it can be earned. In the view of many of the Islamic social critics of the twentieth century, this is precisely what capitalism encourages people to do. Echoing other critics of capitalism, they condemn it for removing all restrictions on the acquisition and spending of money, promoting accumulation and the commodification of everything, thus making money the measure of all things. What they fear is that under capitalism the universal equivalences of a monetary economy will no longer be a convenience (as money was depicted to be in their reading of Islamic history), but will become the driving force, colonising all spheres of life, free of moral restraint.[59]

Of particular concern is the effect of unlicensed exchange on the moral economy. Greed, selfishness and the impulse to exploit others had long been a target of moralists. Now it seemed that capitalism had elevated these vices to the status of virtues, on the basis that they promote economic growth and the general welfare of the community. In the view of the Islamic social critics, the rules of exchange under a system where everything can be commodified and can have a purely monetary value – and thereby a potentially open-ended equivalence – is a world without moral bearings. Historically, exchange cultures (norms governing what it is permissible to exchange for what) are some of the most ingrained and elaborated, touching on profound sensibilities about the licit and the illicit. They provide, therefore, some of the distinctive

---

[57] Aristotle, *The Politics*, ed. S. Everson (Cambridge, 1990), p. 15.

[58] The *hadith* is 'Every community has a test and the test of my community is money/wealth' (*Inna li-kul ummah fitnah wa-fitnah ummati al-mal*). Abu 'Isa Muhammad bin 'Isa bin Surah al-Tirmidhi, *Kitab al-zuhd*, no. 26 (*hadith* no. 2336), in *Al-Jami' al-sahih*, ed. Ibrahim 'Awad (Beirut, 1963) part 4, p. 569.

[59] Qutb, *Ma'arakat*, pp. 38–45; al-Khatib, *Al-Siyasat al-maliyah*, pp. 42–55.

repertoire invoked to guard against the potentially open-ended, all-devouring commodity exchange system of developed capitalism which unceasingly threatens to break the rules on commodification and exchange associated with an established moral economy. In the Islamic lands, no less than else-where, this represented one of the more alarming aspects of capitalism – alarming in part because the very profitability of such a system made it highly attractive to some.[60] Furthermore, the centrality of interest mechanisms to capitalist development highlights an instrument of growth viewed by most Muslim intellectuals as explicitly prohibited in the Qur'an (insofar as they equate interest with *riba*), touching also on a long-established and deep-seated revulsion at the idea that 'money should breed money', seen in Rashid Rida's citation of a range of classical jurists such as al-Razi, al-Taftazani, al-Baghawi, al-Jurjani and Ibn Rushd.[61]

These concerns relate to the 'socially disembedding' capacities of money.[62] Precisely because money, as a common unit of exchange, can represent anything, it is freed from association with any particular material object, individual or set of social relations or ethical priorities. In a capitalist environment, this enabling feature of money becomes even more powerful, since it is reinforced by norms which sanction the commodification and monetary valuation of increasing numbers of human artefacts and relations. Working in tandem, the logic of monetarisation and the imaginative and social power of commodification combine to colonise ever larger spheres of human activity. Even in the pre-capitalist Islamic world, with the introduction of promissory notes as part of the mechanisms of long-distance trade, money was capable of losing its explicit association with the materiality of specific coinage or metals, with particular rulers and indeed with the world and values of Islam, insofar as the system extended beyond the domains of Islamic law.[63] This initiated a controversy over bills of exchange (*suftajah*), partly because of the fiscal implications, but also because of the assessment of the differential risks run by the two parties to the investment, a key consideration in both classical and contemporary accounts of a salutary economic order.

Such concerns sharpen fears for the existing moral order, regardless of the apparent material benefits promised by the fully monetarised capitalist

[60] Polanyi, *The Great Transformation*, pp. 71–80, 171–5; Scott, *The Moral Economy of the Peasant*, pp. 2–7; Macfarlane, *The Culture of Capitalism*, pp. 225–6.
[61] Rida, *Al-Riba wa-l-mu'amalat fi al-islam*, pp. 19–41; al-Khatib, *Al-Siyasat al-maliyah*, pp. 150–6.
[62] Polanyi, *Great Transformation*, pp. 71–80; Parry and Bloch *Money*, pp. 4–5.
[63] Braudel, *The Wheels of Commerce*, pp. 555–9; A. L. Udovitch, 'Credit as a means of invest-ment in medieval Islamic trade', *Journal of the American Oriental Society* 87 (1967), pp. 260–5; A. L. Udovitch, *Partnership and Profit in Medieval Islam* (Princeton, 1970), pp. 170–6, 212–15.

economy.[64] Nevertheless, these benefits were readily acknowledged. In this context, material wealth, including monetary wealth, is seen as something desirable, even necessary, if the Islamic obligation of paying *zakat* is to be fulfilled and the recommendation to perform acts of charity is to be carried out. Thus, considerable space is devoted to extolling wholesome forms of monetary exchange, such as interest-free loans, donations to charity, contributions to the central treasury of the Islamic state, or commercial transactions which increase the sum of wealth. Indeed, wealth creation is cited as a recommended, even a required activity, as when 'Awdah, al-Siba'i, al-Ghazzali or Taleqani claim that an individual must forgo his claim to property if he fails to exploit it and use it productively.[65]

In order to sustain this side of the argument, the Islamic social critics of the 1940s and 1950s and their successors make a distinction between profit from trade and profit from lending money at interest. However, the wealth which Muslims are enjoined to increase owes its origins to the capacity of a monetary economy to sustain and promote growth, through investment of capital in ventures which will succeed in making a profit because, in crude terms, the monetary value of the return is greater than the monetary value of the original outlay. In this sense, money could be said to have bred money, since all forms of capital and wealth are in principle exchangeable or transformable into monetary units. This is indeed why Marx spoke of money as pre-eminently the token or representation of capital-in-circulation. However, its mediation through goods and services avoids its prohibition and, furthermore, Taleqani argues, there can be nothing reprehensible about such wealth creation if it is being carried out under the auspices of an Islamic authority and within the framework of an Islamic system.[66]

In a form of argumentation common to the new idealist Muslim intellectuals, the existence of an Islamic society sanctions all transactions, since otherwise they would be prohibited and would not occur in the first place. The idealism and the circularity are obvious. Nevertheless, such deductions from the ideal opened up the imaginative space for the later development of ideas of an 'Islamic economy' as an answer to capitalism. Here, the capacity of a monetary economy to increase the general level of prosperity and to be a force for good, if properly directed, is seen as the other face of money-as-capital. Such ideas laid the groundwork for the development of the phenomenon of 'Islamic banking' which was to prove so successful in the late

---

[64] P. Bourdieu, *Practical Reason – On the Theory of Action* (Cambridge, 1998), pp. 104–7.
[65] 'Awdah, *Al-Mal wa-l-hukm*, pp. 9–14; al-Ghazzali, *Al-Islam wa-l-awda'al-iqtisadiyah*; Taleqani, *Islam and Ownership*, pp. 88–96; Rodinson, *Islam and Capitalism*, pp. 14–18.
[66] Taleqani, *Islam and Ownership*, pp. 112–22.

twentieth century, enjoying a distinctive but by no means antagonistic relationship with the capitalist system – a form of accommodation that caused
unease among those who saw themselves as the inheritors of the tradition of
Islamic social criticism.

Money as a form of property, but also a token of that property, bears the
imprint of the dominant system in which it circulates. By the same reasoning,
and certainly in the eyes of contemporary Muslim intellectuals, money, for all
its disembedding qualities, can be made responsive to Islamic values. In doing
so, it becomes the vehicle whereby property, as a social relationship and the
embodiment of a certain ethical order, can be brought fully under the aegis of
an Islamic order. For many of these writers, the problem is not therefore
property or money as such, but the system of which they form a part which
may be detrimental to social solidarity and to Islamic community. The imaginative attempt to reconstruct the moral economy leads to a self-consciousness
about the enterprise in which Islamic values as social values are being re-
framed, with the consequence that in the twentieth century there is a tendency
to see the moral economy as something that emerges from the needs of
society and is of benefit to all society. This leads to consideration of how to
judge society's interests and how best to ensure that they are protected within
the framework of a particular – distinctively Islamic – property regime.

2.4   Maslahah – society's interests

It was not surprising that discussion of the dangers of capitalist property
relations to a distinctly Islamic sociability should have led to discussion of
'society's needs'. The debate was characteristically informed by functionalist,
organicist arguments about what society 'needed' in order to cohere and what,
in particular, Islamic society needed in order to be in a position to remain true
to itself and to resist the encroachment of other social forms and other ideals.
The two elements were conflated in the increasingly prominent thesis that
whatever was conducive to social solidarity was obligatory in the sense of an
injunction or recommendation sanctioned by Islam, leading some writers,
such as 'Abd al-Wahhab Khallaf and Mustafa Zaid in Egypt, to claim that
this had the same binding power as the explicit injunctions derived from the
texts of the Qur'an and the *sunnah*.[67]

This argument had important consequences, since it coloured the ways in
which the authoritative texts were themselves interpreted, especially insofar

---

[67] Khallaf, *Masadir al-tashri' al-islami* (1955); Salem, 'Arab reformers and the reinterpretation
of Islam', pp. 316–18; see also the uses made of the writings of Najm al-Din Tufi (d. 1316 CE)
on *maslahah* in Mustafa Zaid, *Al-Maslahah fi al-tashri' al-islam wa-Najm al-Din al-Tufi*
(Cairo, 1954).

as the complex question about public versus private rights was concerned. It also shifted attention away from the texts and towards the condition of society. This became a kind of text in itself, subjected to scrutiny under the apparently traditional methodologies of *al-masalih al-mursalah, sadd al-dhara'i', istislah/istihsan,* and *'urf.*[68] Equally, it was clear that this shift demanded a corresponding shift in the expertise required to interpret the new 'text', its rules and its requirements, changing thereby the authority of the interpreters. The foundations of *ijtihad* were no longer strictly defined with relation to the episteme of Qur'anic exegesis. On the contrary, the new disciplines of economics and sociology as forms of knowledge seemed to provide both the framework of understanding and the data through which arguments about society could be framed. This led both to the development of state-based rationales for public ownership, as in Egypt under Nasser or Iraq under 'Abd al-Salam 'Arif, and to the burgeoning field of Islamic economics, emerging under the impulse to respond both to capitalism and to state socialism.

Increasingly, the perspective shifted away from the pious believer who had hitherto been the focus of concern, towards the effects of that individual's actions on the well-being of society as a whole. Here a noticeable shift takes place from *al-'abad* (the servant (of God)) to *al-fard* (the individual), equated with private, and from *al-ummah* (the community (of believers)) to *al-mujtama'* (the society, or collection of individuals), equated with public. Despite the changes in terminology and the opening up to another form of reasoning, the ethical associations of the earlier formulations were retained, such that 'society' or 'the public' were identified with the Islamic *ummah* and the moral imperative to take all necessary measures to defend it. In the light of this reasoning, the social consequences of certain actions with regard to property were emphasised and their moral worth was judged with reference to these consequences. A process had begun whereby social outcomes and their perceived desirability shaped the criteria for assessing the discrete actions of individuals. This was at the heart of the very notion of 'social justice' – a concept that had little or no precedent in the traditions of Islamic thought, but which was increasingly equated in contemporary Islamic thought with the requirements of divine justice, as became evident in the writings of Qutb in Egypt, Mawdudi and Hifz al-Rahman Sihwarwi in South Asia and Mehdi Bazargan in Iran.[69]

---

[68] For an explanation of these terms see pp. 71–3 below.

[69] Qutb, *Al-'Adalat al-ijtima'iyah,* especially pp. 20–107; also Mawdudi, *Let Us Be Muslims,* pp. 218–38, and Abul A'la Mawdudi, *Witnesses unto Mankind* (translation of *Shahadat Haqq*) (Leicester, 1986), pp. 31–3; Hifz al-Rahman Sihwarwi, *Islam ka iqtisadi nizam* (Delhi, 1942), cited by Aziz Ahmad, *Islamic Modernism in India and Pakistan 1857–1964* (London,

Defining the individual or the private in this context was not to advance a dispassionate view, but rather one that was fully informed by the outrage caused by the damage which capitalism was alleged to be causing to society and to the Islamic values and identity of that society.[70] It was scarcely surprising that, in such an environment, the 'public good' and 'social bene-fit/welfare' (al-maslahat al-ijtima'iyah) should become the yardsticks by which social transactions would be judged, and property, as the concrete expression of individual versus collective rights, became the medium for the rulings which followed. However, determining the public or society's interest was a methodological, as well as an empirical challenge.

Contemporary Muslim intellectuals found little guidance in the corpus of the Islamic traditions with which they were familiar. The traditional jurists, saw the problem from the perspective of the ideal pious believer and had devoted little time or space (or imagination) to the other side of the equation: the condition of society that would result from certain kinds of conduct. The acquisition or disposal of property was thought to be meritorious, insofar as it tallied with their interpretation of the revealed truth and moral impera-tives laid down by God. The justifying rationale would be the effect that property transactions might have on divine judgement of an individual. Although in a relatively minor key, there was an idea that harm to others would make certain courses of action impermissible, as well as the need for an environment that encouraged pious conduct in general.[71]

The focus on the social consequences of individual actions had reversed the perspective. Nevertheless, as with the elaboration of the debate on property itself, it was not too difficult to find analogies and precedents that could be used both to justify the new concern with social consequences, and to provide methods that could sanction such conclusions. This led to a particular em-phasis on early Islamic history, sometimes looking at the Prophet's response to new and challenging situations, or, more frequently, invoking the experi-ence of the rashidun Caliphs who needed to administer an expanding political realm in conformity with Islamic precepts. The novelty of much that the early Caliphs encountered and the fact that they could not always find explicit guidance in the legacy of the Prophet meant that they had to fall back on general principles and to extrapolate, insofar as it was possible, from these guidelines sufficient detail to be useful in specific situations.

1967), pp. 201–4, 221–2; see also Mehdi Bazargan cited in Chehabi, Iranian Politics, pp. 62–4.

[70] Hasan al-Banna, 'Hadith al-thulatha: kalimat fiyadah ra'i'ah li-fadilat al-murshid al-'amm', Al-Ikhwan al-Muslimun, 8 April 1948; Radwan, Ishtirakiyat al-islam, pp. 23–9, 99.

[71] In this respect, a key hadith was 'la darar wa-la dirar' ('do not harm [others] and do not harm [others] in retaliation'). See the discussion of this hadith in Al-Manar 9 (1906), pp. 752–70; Zaid, Maslahah, appendix, pp. 14–48; Kerr, Islamic Reform, p. 97.

The readings of early Islamic history were largely conventional and derived from the standard sources, and subject therefore to some of the same problems of authenticity and narrative invention.[72] The principles of selection were appropriate to the case, in that they focused on episodes that concerned the disposition of property. In particular, the Islamic social critics stressed those incidents where the Caliphs, or governors acting under their authority, laid down rulings giving the community's claims greater weight than those of any particular individual, or stipulating the conditions under which an individual could retain title to property, generally by sharing some portion of it with others.

One striking and recurrent example of this was the invocation of the figure of Abu al-Dharr al-Ghaffari, whose reported attitude to the selfish abuse of private property led him into several confrontations with the governor of Syria, Mu'awiya, later to become Caliph. This theme was developed at great length in the 1960s, when officially sanctioned 'Islamic socialism' was being elaborated. However, for the earlier Islamic social critics, Abu al-Dharr's great quality was that, as a companion of the Prophet, he could be said to have been a direct transmitter of the Prophet Muhammad's thoughts on property. He could also be portrayed as someone enraged by the abuse of private property, aware of its dangers for the public good and awake to the fact that constant vigilance was needed if the seductions of property and the ills of selfishness were not to overtake the Islamic community. In this respect, he was used to bridge the gap between a traditional juridical and moralistic discourse on the evils of wealth and greed and a more contemporary discourse on the nature of property, the problems of materialism and the rights of the individual versus the rights of society.[73]

However, the writers concerned were not merely content with providing examples from the past in order to furnish precedents for the present. Rather, what they sought were rules of derivation and interpretation that could be used to help them in their contemporary predicament. They seemed to be looking for a methodology sanctified by ancient usage, but not so tied to its time of origin as to be of little use some thirteen centuries later. They appeared to find these qualities in various traditionally sanctioned methods of ethical reasoning that allowed judgement on the relative merits of courses

[72] R. S. Humphreys, *Islamic History – A Framework for Inquiry* (London, 1991), pp. 69–103.

[73] U. Haarmann, 'Abu Dharr – Muhammad's revolutionary companion', *The Muslim World* 68/4 (October 1978), pp. 285–9; Rodinson, *Islam and Capitalism*, p. 25; Al-Bahi al-Khuli, *Al-Ishtirakiyah fi al-mujtama' al-islami* (Cairo, 1963), pp. 47–94; A. J. Cameron, *Abu Dharr al-Ghifari – An Examination of his Image in the Historiography of Islam* (London, 1973); Taleqani, *Islam and Ownership*, pp. 108–11.

of action for which there was no obvious textual guidance and which were not amenable to *qiyas* (analogy) or *ijma'* (consensus).

Foremost among these was *al-masalih al-mursalah* (lit. delegated or transmitted interests or benefits), traditionally used by jurists to give a ruling on something based on the benefits it produced. If similar benefits were produced by actions for which sanctioned precedents could indeed be found, then the course of action in question was to be permitted. *Al-masalih al-mursalah* required, therefore, a judgement about social and individual consequences, and also demanded a capacity for social knowledge and judgement, allowing a relatively open-ended attitude to new forms of activity, organisation and behaviour. *Sadd al-dhara'i'* (lit. blocking of the means) was included by some jurists within the larger field of *al-masalih al-mursalah*, since it referred to a similar judgement, but in this case about negative consequences. Thus, if a course of action initially allowed because of its supposed positive outcome is judged instead to have negative consequences, then it should be forbidden.[74]

These approaches permitted interpretation and judgement beyond the confines of the sacred texts, but further guidance was needed concerning outcomes that would suggest prohibition or permission of particular courses of action. These were found in the notions of *istihsan* (lit. to regard something as right, to approve of something) and *istislah* (lit. to consider something useful or suitable). Both terms had enjoyed considerable usage by jurists over the centuries. Abu Hanifah (d. 767 CE) was credited particularly with the innovative use of *istihsan* which set up 'the requirements of everyday life' as the standard by which to judge actions.[75] Some jurists had been wary of the potentially open-ended possibilities of *istislah* and *istihsan* and had tried both to ensure that judgements about human welfare, contingent as they must be, should not contradict the *shari'ah*, and to confine the substantive content of *maslahah* (human benefit) to a limited and agreed number of aspects of human existence. Others, however, had been more relaxed about this.[76]

A common feature of these methods is that they oblige the observer to examine the nature of the community or society and thus to judge the effects of actions upon it. Similarly, they all – even *'urf* (custom) – require some attempt to grapple with the question of *maslahah* (benefit or welfare) since this provides the common justifying principle. They appeared, therefore, to suit the temper of the age, suggesting that the discovery of society's needs is possible and commendable. Indeed, the understanding of human interests as

---

[74] Husain Hamid Hasan, *Nazriyat al-maslahah fi al-fiqh al-islami* (Cairo, 1971), pp. 4–12.

[75] Enayat, *Modern Islamic Political Thought*, p. 148.

[76] See, for instance, the contrast between al-Ghazzali (d. 1111 CE) and al-Tufi (d. 1316 CE) as described in Kerr, *Islamic Reform*, pp. 80–101.

composed of necessities (*daruriyat*), needs (*hajiyat*) and preferences (*tahsinat*) led Muhammad 'Abdallah al-'Arabi, for instance, to acknowledge the contingency of the undertaking by asserting that 'you cannot rule only according to the welfare or interests [*maslahah*] already established in the *shari'ah* because the interests of people are made anew and it may be that what are considered the needs and necessities of people in one era are interests which have no parallel in the period of the ruling in question'.[77]

In this regard, a theme linking both traditional and contemporary commentaries is the underlying assumption that the *shari'ah* cannot require anything that contradicts human welfare. However, different ideas about the implications of this for what is forbidden or permitted are marked by a variety of attitudes, allowing a fairly wide range of interpretation. Ibn Taimiyah (d. 1328 CE) represents one view which could be seen as conservative and traditional – but which could also open the door to more innovative interpretation. He held that if something appears beneficial but is without obvious justification in the *shari'ah*, then either the *shari'ah* is being misinterpreted or it is not really beneficial at all and may have concealed disadvantages.[78] For others, it was axiomatic that the *shari'ah* must endorse contemporary understandings of social welfare, both individual and collective. Thus, if a traditional reading seemed to suggest something that was seen now as unacceptable or contrary to human well-being, the traditional reading must be revised.

In some respects, this comes close to equating human needs and the measures necessary to secure them with the commands of God. Furthermore, there is an implicit belief that, in using such methods, apparently authorised by previous generations, the Islamic nature and identity of the society, as well as the interests of its members, would be preserved, providing Muslim intellectuals with the authentic tools of analysis for engaging with the world. Thus, an authority as eminent as al-Ghazzali (d. 1111 CE) was often cited because his systematic approach seemed to supply unequivocally clear and authentic criteria for determining what constituted the welfare (*maslahah*) of every Muslim and indeed of all mankind: the protection of a person's religion, person, mind or reason, offspring and wealth.[79]

---

[77] Muhammad 'Abdallah al-'Arabi, *Al-Tanzim al-hadith li-l-dawlat al-islamiyah* (Cairo, 1969).

[78] Kerr, *Islamic Reform*, p. 87; Taqi al-Din Ahmad Ibn Taimiyah, *Ma'arij al-wusul ila ma'rifat anna usul al-din wa-furu'ahu qad bayyanaha al-rasul*, translated into French by Henri Laoust as *Contribution à une étude de la méthodologie canonique de Taki-d-din Ahmad b. Taimiya* (Cairo, 1939) pp. 102–12; see also Henri Laoust, *Essai sur les doctrines sociales et politiques de Taki-d-Din Ahmad b. Taimiya* (Cairo, 1939) pp. 541–75.

[79] Abu Hamid al-Ghazzali, *Al-Mustasfa min 'ilm al-usul*, ed. Muhammad Mustafa Abu al-'Ala (Cairo, 1970), pp. 250–9; Hasan, *Nazriyat al-maslahah*, pp. 5–7, refers to the views of al-Ghazzali, al-Tufi and al-Khawarizmi. Cook also cites similar usage and a similar appeal to

However, the methods could also undermine the authority of some of the texts of commentary. With new preoccupations, novel or hitherto little-considered forms of reasoning come to the fore. This is a case of the ends suggesting the means. The ethical objective and the new terms in which it is expressed bring with them new forms of reasoning. In part this is due to the fact that the terms themselves are not neutral. On the contrary, they come with a history and a host of associations in terms of the moral universe for which they are providing a descriptive basis. For instance, they introduce new rules of evidence, giving weight to different social phenomena and altering in some measure the authority of specific kinds of reasoning. These phenomena seemed largely meaningless or irrelevant to tradition-minded *'ulama* who were largely marginalised, insofar as the dominant debates were concerned. By the same token it brought to the fore the journalists, social commentators, political activists and those *'ulama* engaged in politics who felt they not only had something to say, but also the means and the authority to do so. In Egypt, this was very characteristic of the members and sympathisers of the Muslim Brotherhood, and in Pakistan of those associated with the Jamaat-e-Islami, as well as of the Movement of God-Worshipping Socialists and its successor organisations in Iran.[80]

However, as this trend became increasingly influential, it provoked the suspicion that the new preoccupations were distorting properly Islamic priorities, making Muslims susceptible to the reasoning, values and ideologies of the Western societies where these concerns had originated. In many respects, this suspicion was justified. Those who believed that a new direction should be taken to preserve Islamic identity in the modern world did face the problem of deciding which aspects of which traditions they would accept. This was the challenge of the creative interpretative possibilities of *ijtihad*. The new Muslim intellectuals had to fashion their own criteria of relevance in order to have some yardstick of significance and utility when sifting through the Islamic tradition. One strategy employed was to refer to those features which they claimed had been of prime relevance to the early Muslims – whom they still imbued with greatest authority – according to their reading of the traditions and the texts. These readings were of course coloured by their contemporary preoccupations, dependent to some degree on rules and forms of reasoning that were very much of their time, bringing with them a sense of

established authorities in M. Cook, *Commanding Right and Forbidding Wrong in Islamic Thought* (Cambridge, 2002) pp. 507–11.

[80] 'Iqtisadi' (an economist), 'Ma huwa al-iqtisad?' *Al-Ikhwan al-Muslimun*, 5 October 1946; 'Risalatuna', *Al-Ikhwan al-Muslimun*, 11 April 1948; K. Zebiri, *Mahmud Shaltut and Islamic Modernism* (Oxford, 1993), pp. 74–7, 132–8; Ahmad, *Islamic Modernism*, pp. 208–22; Beinin, 'Islamic responses to capitalist penetration of the Middle East', pp. 91–101; Rahnema, *An Islamic Utopian*, pp. 24–9.

creative possibility and social engagement that was liberating for some, but clearly of concern to others.[81]

These tensions and the direction of the thought of the social critics, whether or not they were originally trained in the institutions of traditional Islamic learning, such as Al-Azhar, led them to advance their claims to expertise in the fields on which they commented. As far as most of them were concerned, they established their Islamic credentials largely by being Muslims and by demonstrating an active Muslim sensibility – a distinctly modern condition of subjective expressionism as an important qualification for becoming a social critic. The most obvious example of this is Sayyid Qutb's multi-volume commentary on the Qur'an, *Fi zilal al-Qur'an* (In the Shade of the Qur'an).[82] In addition, they familiarised themselves with enough of the Islamic tradition, formally understood, to be able to draw on its texts and methodologies for their purposes. In many ways, however, authority was shifting elsewhere. In particular, the discursive field of 'social science', encompassing the study of society and of the economy, was demanding its own categories of expertise and establishing its own criteria of relevance. For those who wished to make authoritative statements about society or the economy, the mastery of, or at the very least familiarisation with, these new disciplines seemed to be crucially important.[83]

For the Islamic social critics, uneasy or dissatisfied with the role of the *'ulama* and the condition of the strictly 'Islamic sciences', these disciplines brought with them new promise. Influenced by the positivist temper of some of the founding texts in these disciplines, many came to believe that the proper ends of society could be rationally discovered. Linked to an unshakeable belief in the truth of the Islamic message and its universal applicability,

---

[81] Mahmud Abu al-Sa'ud, 'Al-siyasat al-iqtisadiyah fi al-islam', pp. 51–6, and 'Isa 'Abduh Ibrahim, 'Hawl al-siyasat al-iqtisadiyah', *Al-Muslimun* 2/9 (July 1953), pp. 66–72; Al-Bahi al-Khuli, 'Min fiqh 'Umar fi al-iqtisad wa-l-mal', *Al-Muslimun* 3/4 (February 1954), pp. 55–9.

[82] Qutb, *Fi zilal al-Qur'an*. Ostensibly traditional in the sense of a *surah*-by-*surah* commentary, *Fi zilal* in fact contains very few references to the works of others, and those that do occur appear to be divided equally between 'classical' and modern commentaries, with a significant number of non-Muslim sources used as references for particular points of explanation. See also Olivier Carré, *Mystique et politique* (Paris, 1984), pp. 31–40; Abul A'la Mawdudi, *Towards Understanding the Qur'an*, 7 vols., translation of *Tafhim al-Qur'an* by Z. Ishaq (Leicester, 1988–). In some respects quite similar in form, it too is a *surah*-by-*surah* commentary, with very few references overall. There is a noticeably higher proportion of references to 'classical' authorities and commentaries than in Qutb's case, but there are also conspicuous references to non-Islamic sources, such as *The Encyclopedia Britannica*.

[83] See the two articles by Zaki Mahmud Shabanah, 'Mu'alim ra'isiyah fi siyasat iqtisadiyat islamiyah', *Al-Muslimun* 3/2 (December 1953), pp. 65–9, and 3/6 (April 1954), pp. 52–8; also the series of five articles by Mahmud Abu al-Sa'ud, 'Barnamijuna al-iqtisadiyah', *Al-Muslimun* 3/6 (April 1954), pp. 37–43, 3/7 (May 1954), pp. 48–55, 3/8 (June 1954), pp. 74–9, 3/9 (July 1954), pp. 68–72, 3/10 (August 1954), pp. 65–74.

this created a marked and apparently powerful alliance between Islamic beliefs and a positivist attitude – despite specific denials of its influence.[84] It also created problems of a practical nature. Most obviously, there arose the question of the agency that was to be entrusted with both the discovery of human needs and the policies needed to meet them. This led to the privileging of state power, a radical break with the decidedly cautious treatment of the state by generations of Islamic jurists. For the new Muslim intellectuals, however, the state alone had the potential to shape policy and to implement the prescriptions which would make society whole again, restoring both its sociability and its Islamic identity. The problem, as they were to discover in the coming decades, was that the state's logic was rather different – Islamic themes might be used to justify policy, but the creation of an ideal Islamic society was neither the sole intention nor the outcome.[85]

[84] Sayyid Qutb, 'Nizam rabbani', *Al-Muslimun* 3/1 (November 1953), pp. 15–23.
[85] C. Tripp, 'Islam and the secular logic of the state in the Middle East', in Abdel Salam Sidahmed and Anoushiravan Ehteshami (eds.), *Islamic Fundamentalism* (Boulder, CO, 1996), pp. 54–60.

3   Islamic socialism

In much of the writing associated with the Islamic social critique of the 1940s and early 1950s, a decisive role had been assigned to the state. It was the state which would both defend society against the depredations of capitalism and lay the foundation for its Islamic reassertion. This not only followed the line of reasoning mapped out in the early part of the century, but also reflected the changing political economy of much of the Islamic world. The peoples of the Islamic world and the Middle East had experienced capitalism through the intrusion of the modern state as the vehicle of a capitalist order, despite the dominant liberal myth of capitalism freeing people from state regulation. It was the state which embodied a certain kind of power and which provided the legal framework for the flourishing of capitalism.

With the movements of decolonisation, national independence and state development that marked the 1950s and 1960s, it was not surprising that the newly sovereign states in the Islamic world should have been seen as having the potential to fulfil the role given to the idealised state in the arguments on social reform. By the same token, governments from Algeria to Iraq found in the writings of the Islamic social critics a rich source for a vocabulary of authentication and justification in an idiom which had wide popular appeal. By taking this up, they added to and developed the emerging repertoire of Islamic social criticism, but made it serve the purposes of states that were driven by another, unmistakably secular logic. Nowhere was this more in evidence than in Egypt, one of the principal sites for the development of a distinctive Islamic social critique of capitalism in the 1930s and 1940s. In the 1950s and 1960s, under the republican regime of Gamal 'Abd al-Nasir (Nasser), it became the terrain for competing visions of development – centralised socialist state planning versus free enterprise liberal capitalism – expressed in both a secular and a distinctively Islamic idiom.

The promise of full independence and the gradual withdrawal of imperial forces in theory created the conditions in which Muslims could realise their full potential, principally by establishing a society that would respond to their interests and conform to their values. In this context, the state was seen as something that would allow Muslims to achieve what they had long been denied, conjuring up images of prosperity, social solidarity, even destiny. Much of this, of course, was a matter of fierce dispute. In one of the many echoes of contemporary debates among secular Arab nationalists, it raised questions about the jurisdictions of specific governments, their connection to the territorial limits of their states and the bounded sovereignty this implied, which was often hard to reconcile with expectations about an idealised Islamic state that should properly regulate a society designated simply as 'Islamic'. Thus, the identity and direction of the state remained central to the debates and discussions in which Muslim intellectuals of the day took part.

Adding sharpness to this debate was the projection of the overwhelming power of the state, in part an outcome of the distinctive reasoning of the Islamic social critics, in part a testimony to the optimism of the age. For many of the Muslim intellectuals, the state's power should be commensurate with the importance of its moral purpose and social function, implying that limits could no more be placed on this than on the reach and enforceability of the *shari'ah*. It should ensure conformity and protect its society from the harm emanating from the global economy. In a distinctive way, the historical suspicion of Islamic authorities for state power, its potential for abuse and its rapacity, was overcome. It gave way to idealised historical reconstructions of the state of the early Caliphs, or to an equally idealised state of the future, the power of which was to be paramount, but which was described more in terms of ideal outcomes, rather than in terms of its specific institutional mechanisms or relations with already existing society.

At the same time, for all critics of the status quo, whether Islamic or secular, the power of a reinvigorated state was seen as necessary to break the social hierarchies which had emerged through the peripheral capitalist systems and the semi-tutelary forms of state which had dominated Egypt, Syria, Iraq and Iran. Equally, the state would provide protection to the local economy and society, allowing them to thrive in a global economic order in which the newly independent states were at a marked disadvantage.[1] Given the fragmentation and weakening of local society, it was suggested, only the state, properly directed, could deploy sufficient force to ensure the reconstruction of a successful, just and independent social order.

Although clearly influenced by secular, socialist critics of capitalism and imperialism, it was important for many Muslim intellectuals to differentiate themselves from a movement based on assumptions they could not share. During the 1960s, this led to some unease about the degree to which the Egyptian state, for instance, had appropriated the language and idiom of

---

[1] Meijer, *The Quest for Modernity*, pp. 173–90, 208–30; Wahba, *The Role of the State in the Egyptian Economy*, pp. 75–81; Steven Heydemann, *Authoritarianism in Syria* (Ithaca, NY, 1999), pp. 55–72; Samira Haj, *The Making of Iraq 1900–1963* (Albany, NY, 1997), pp. 83–99.

Islamic social criticism. For all its claimed appeals to a historical Islamic tradition, as well as to the Islamic reformers of the preceding century, the Nasserist state's elaboration of the edifice of 'Islamic socialism' was more closely tied to its immediate interests and to secular ideas of socialist development than to the views expressed in earlier engagements with the term, developed by such writers as Jamal al-Din al-Afghani, Rashid Rida, 'Abd al-Rahman al-Kawakibi or even originally by Mustafa al-Siba'i.[2]

Nevertheless, there was sufficient optimism in its earlier phases, as well as sufficient co-optive power deployed by the new republics, to appear to champion two issues close to the heart of Islamic critiques of capitalism. Under the direction of the radical officers who came to power in the 1950s and 1960s, states across the Middle East took up the cause of the redistribution of wealth, particularly in land, deploying arguments based on social justice and on the social benefits of collective as against private ownership of the means of production. This was also linked to a renewed emphasis on social harmony and solidarity – a secular corporatist vision which had a marked affinity with the views of Muslim intellectuals regarding the body of society.

One of the claimed social benefits of the state's trusteeship of property, elaborated upon both by independent writers and by those in Egypt involved in the Nasserist project, was its capacity to restore the lost harmony of society. This had the virtue of countering class-based analysis of social injustice and the prediction – even prescription – of class warfare. The notion of social concord within a corporate state, idealised by many Muslim intellectuals, also appealed to governments of the day because it avoided the social disruption implied by class conflict, asserted the overarching authority of the state and helped to neutralise Marxist critiques of the government's role and of the interests shaping the government's views. These were to form the major themes of 'Islamic socialism' during this period. Inevitably, fears about what they might mean for a distinctive Islamic identity if driven by the interests of a secular state apparatus helped to create a backlash against those who had been too easily taken in by the promises of Nasser's Egypt in its heyday.

---

[2] Jamal al-Din al-Afghani, 'Ra'ihu 'ala al-ishtirakiyah (al-Susialist)', in Muhammad Basha al-Makhzumi (ed.), *Khatirat Jamal al-Din al-Afghani al-Husaini* (Beirut, 1931), cited in Hanna 'Al-Afghani: a pioneer of Islamic socialism', pp. 24–32; Rashid Rida, 'Al-Ishtirakiyah wa-l-din' (in vol. I of *Al-Manar*), cited in Radwan, *Ishtirakiyat al-islam*, pp. 118–19; S. A. Hanna, ch. 9, in S. A. Hanna and G. H. Gardner (eds.), *Arab Socialism – A Documentary Survey* (Leiden, 1969), pp. 217–24; al-Husry, *Origins of Modern Arab Political Thought*, pp. 74–6; Mustafa al-Siba'i, 'Ishtirakiyat al-islam', in *Al-Mahadarat al-'ammah 1958–9*, no. 7 (Damascus, 1959). But see also Tahhan's critique of Muhammad 'Imarah's attempt to read into 'Abd al-Rahman al-Kawakibi's works principles congruent with Arab Islamic socialism: al-Kawakibi, *Al-A'mal al-kamilah li-l-Kawakibi*, pp. 59–60.

3.1   Islamic socialism and state development

Emerging out of the social criticism that had so marked the writings of Muslim intellectuals in Egypt, Syria, Iran and elsewhere, the idea of 'Islamic socialism' focused on curing the ills of society as perceived at the time. In particular, it was presented as a solution to the divisive effects of unequal property ownership. Redistributive measures would both alleviate poverty and provide a basis for a society in which those without property had some claim on property owners. At the same time, figures like the Shaikh al-Azhar in the early 1960s, Shaikh Mahmud Shaltut, and others in Egypt suggested controversially that a permanent form of property transfer could be made under Islamic rulings, ensuring that everyone would thenceforth have a sufficiency and that the welfare of the whole would not be damaged by the claims of individuals.[3]

For governments concerned about economic development and about the limits which the global economic system placed on their control over their own national economies, these were useful arguments. In Egypt under Nasser, in Syria in the 1960s, in Iraq under 'Abd al-Salam 'Arif, and in Algeria under the FLN the official sponsorship of a distinctive 'Islamic socialism' went hand in hand with the development of its cognate 'Arab socialism', for very similar reasons. It promised an independent path to economic development, based on popular appeals to social justice, yet it excluded the Marxist parties on the grounds of cultural and religious specificity.[4] By the same token, of course, government adoption of this rationale made it vulnerable to trans-formation by distinctive state interests – the 'secular logic' of the state. At the same time, a capitalist logic worked through the state since this remained the dominant form, imaginatively and structurally. Even in the guise of pursuing a 'socialist path to development', such a state could not avoid promoting some of the very features of capitalism that were so objectionable to those

---

[3] Mahmud Shaltut, *Al-Islam wa-l-takaful al-ijtima'i* (Cairo, 1960), pp. 18–22, and 'Al-Ishtira-kiyah wa-l-islam', *Al-Jumhuriyah*, 22 December 1961, translated in *Orient* 20 (1961) pp. 163–74. Karpat suggests this was a riposte to the growing unease of the Syrian Muslim Brother, al-Siba'i, about the role assigned to the state in the Nasserist version of Islamic socialism – Kemal Karpat (ed.), *Political and Social Thought in the Contemporary Middle East* (New York, 1982), p. 126. See also al-Khuli, *Al-Ishtirakiyah fi al-mujtama'al-islami*, pp. 98–111; Muhammad 'Abdallah Al-'Arabi, *Al-Dimuqratiyah al-qawmiyat al-'arabiyah baina al-dimuqratiyah al-shuyu'iyah wa-l-dimuqratiyah al-ra'smaliyah* (Cairo, 1961), pp. 120–2; al-Sharabasi, *Al-Ishtirakiyah wa-l-din*; Ahmad 'Abd al-Jawwad al-Dumi, *Al-Minhaj al-ishtiraki 'ala daw' al-Islam* (Cairo, 1964).

[4] J. C. Vatin, 'Popular puritanism versus state reformism: Islam in Algeria', in J. Piscatori (ed.), *Islam in the Political Process* (New York, 1983), pp. 110–19; R. Vallin, 'Muslim socialism in Algeria', in I. William Zartman (ed.), *Man, State, and Society in the Contemporary Maghrib* (New York, 1973), pp. 50–64.

concerned about the cohesion and identity of a distinctively Islamic society. This was indeed the core of the criticism of the state voiced at the time by Sayyid Qutb in Egypt and by the group Al-Qiyam al-Islamiyah in Algeria.[5]

Such a state was the dominant form, recognised as the regulator and protector of society's interests. Where these were interpreted in terms of the socialism understood by the Fabians and the Islamic socialists, the functions of the state itself were not fundamentally rethought, even if its moral purpose and direction were to be distinguished from the liberal, capitalist order that had characterised its predecessor. The institution of private property might be downgraded, but the state would preside over a productive society, acting as the distributive agent of a proportion of the surplus gained through capitalist economic activity sufficient to maintain a welfare system for the general public while keeping the momentum of capitalist growth going. There was a secular, liberal and capitalist logic at work which was eventually to antagonise many of the Islamic and Marxist critics of the status quo, implying as it did bad faith by those in charge of the state, in whom such hopes for a fundamental revision of social relationships, property relations and ethical foundations had been invested.

In some respects, however, it meant that they were having to come to terms with the consequences of their own imagined response to the dominant socio-economic order. This can be seen as distinct from – although often contingently connected with – the peculiar form of authoritarian government that emerged to dominate, for example, the Egyptian state under Nasser. In a bid to break the power of the established systems of domination and of the groups and classes which profited most, the Islamic socialists and social critics had invested the ideally imagined state with an overarching and unanswerable capacity, as well as authority. Thus, Egyptian writers such as 'Ali 'Abd al-Wahid Wafi and al-Bahi al-Khuli could not easily separate the state from the ruler, partly because of the repeated use of the term *wali al-amr* (person in charge) to denote state power and decision making, and partly because of a tendency to refer back to the examples of the four *rashidun* Caliphs (the Prophet Muhammad's four immediate successors) to justify various forms of state activity.[6]

From this perspective the state becomes a command system and is worthy of obedience insofar as those commands are rightly guided, by the *shari'ah* and by its dominant interpretation. Only in such a context, it was suggested, could a state arise capable of bringing about the changes needed, without

---

[5] John P. Entelis, 'Political Islam in the Maghreb', in John P. Entelis (ed.), *Islam, Democracy, and the State in North Africa* (Bloomington, 1997), pp. 57–9; F. Burgat and W. Dowell, *The Islamic Movement in North Africa* (Austin, TX, 1993), pp. 247–57.

[6] D. N. Crecelius, 'The Ulama and the State in Modern Egypt' (Princeton: Princeton University Ph.D. dissertation, 1967), pp. 374–8; al-Khuli, *Al-Ishtirakiyah fi al-mujtama'al-islami.*

succumbing to the logic of capitalist or secular action. By the 1960s and 1970s this was being expressed by Muslim intellectuals as diverse as Ayatollah Khomeini in Iran and then Iraq, by Muhammad al-'Awwa in Syria and later by Hasan al-Turabi in Sudan.[7] However, as the experience of practical statecraft showed, the realisation of such an ideal was problematic. It is open to question whether any state, as an organisation of social power, whatever its rationale or symbolic representation, can escape the secular logic inherent in struggles for domination, as the history of the Islamic caliphate itself had borne out. Regardless of the personal piety of those involved, there was little escaping the fact that many of the measures of social and political innovation were based on a calculation of what would work most successfully in the world. Whilst the distinctive Islamic character of the social order was a high priority, so too was the need to ensure its security and prosperity in a world that could not be equated with the Islamic order itself. Steps would be taken which owed little to a distinct Islamic tradition, but a great deal to practical statecraft.[8]

Contemporary experience bore this out in Egypt after the 1952 *coup d'état* which overthrew the monarchy, and in Pakistan's early political direction, despite expectations that this state established for Muslims would also be a distinctively Islamic state.[9] In the Egyptian case, the growing role of the state in the economy, from the earliest land reform measures of 1952 through the nationalisations of foreign companies in the mid-1950s, showed that the government was trying both to mobilise private capital and to plan, manage and direct the properties which were now owned by the state itself. In the government's search for capital to develop the Egyptian economy, the pragmatic and essentially secular logic of state enhancement predominated. State management, and with it the management of a planned economy, generated their own concerns which, when stripped of mythical disguises (themselves also aimed at the increase in productivity and the appropriation of surplus by the state), could be equated in many important respects with the business enterprise of a capitalist economy.[10]

---

[7] Ayatollah Ruhollah Khomeini, *Islamic Government*, tr. Joint Publications Research Service (New York, 1979); Muhammad Salim al-'Awwa, *Fi al-nizam, al-siyasi li-l-dawlat al-islamiyah* (Cairo, 1983; first published 1975), pp. 129, 146–7, 190–260; Hasan al-Turabi, *Hiwarat fi al-islam, al-dimuqratiyah, al-dawlah, al-gharb* (Beirut, 1995), pp. 68–71; Hasan al-Turabi, *Al-Siyasah wa-l-hukm: al-nuzum al-sultaniyah baina al-usul wa-sunan al-waqi'* (Beirut, 2003), pp. 23–89, 509–27.

[8] Tripp, 'Islam and the secular logic of the state', pp. 51–69.

[9] K. K. Aziz, *Party Politics in Pakistan* (Islamabad, 1976), pp. 139–59; Seyyed Vali Reza Nasr, *The Vanguard of the Islamic Revolution: The Jama'at-i Islami of Pakistan* (London, 1994), pp. 28–43, 116–55.

[10] Ali E. Hillal Dessouki, 'Politics of income distribution in Egypt', in Robert Tignor and Abdel-Khalek Gouda (eds.), *The Political Economy of Income Distribution in Egypt* (New York,

Part of this strategy of appropriation was a search for suitable and effective language that would persuade people that what was happening was both necessary and desirable. It is in this context that Nasser's government encouraged elaboration of the themes of the Islamic critique of capitalism. In doing so, it both adopted much of the Muslim Brotherhood's critique, and tried to use whatever justifications were most effective for its own developing project.[11] In this strategy, the Islamic element was important, but it was not the principal one. However, it did interweave even more thoroughly Islamic and secular rationales in ways which both reinforced the mixed nature of the Islamic response to capitalism and made it difficult to extricate from the demands of a state not of its own making.

Some of the consequences became apparent later, but they were seen by Qutb and others as a symptom of the dangers inherent in seeking to introduce, for instance, standards of 'welfare' or 'social need' that derived from sources and considerations extraneous to the *shari'ah*. From this perspective, obeying the commands of God was synonymous with human welfare and the public good, since that was presumed to be God's intention. Equally importantly, this view strove to make the argument theoretically self-sufficient, asserting that no contingent set of priorities, such as those deriving from government preoccupations, nor any external criteria, could tell Muslims what was in their best interest. Subsequent arguments by the Egyptian *'alim* Yusuf al-Qardawi showed that this would be a difficult, even logically impossible position to hold, whilst simultaneously asserting normative autonomy. It was precisely such a form of synthetic reasoning which Sayyid Qutb, for instance, was determined to avoid in his later writing, having acknowledged that he was as susceptible to the logic of these arguments as anyone else in his earlier years.[12]

One of the most obvious fields to engage both governments and Muslim intellectuals was that encompassing competing claims to property. In Egypt, the land reforms of 1952, the expropriation of British and French properties in 1956, the nationalisations of 1960, and finally the nationalisations and further land reforms embodied in the July Laws of 1961, saw the state justifying its

---

1982), p. 73; Abdel Khalek Gouda, 'The open door policy in Egypt: a search for meaning, intepretation and implications', in H. M. Thompson (ed.), *Studies in Egyptian Political Economy*, Cairo Papers in Social Science 2/3 (Cairo, 1979), pp. 82–4.

[11] Mahmud 'Abd al-Halim, *Al-Ikhwan al-Muslimun – ahdath sana'at al-ta'rikh* (Alexandria, 1986), part 3, pp. 371–81; O. Carré and G. Michaud, *Les Frères Musulmans 1928–1982* (Paris, 1983), pp. 49–75; John Waterbury, *The Egypt of Nasser and Sadat* (Princeton, 1983), pp. 317–20.

[12] Sayyid Qutb, *Ma'alim fi al-tariq* (Cairo, 1988), pp. 117–23, 184–7; see also Muhammad Qasim Zaman, 'The 'ulama of contemporary Islam and their conceptions of the common good', in A. Salvatore and D. F. Eickelman (eds.), *Public Islam and the Common Good* (Leiden, 2004), pp. 129–53.

actions with reference to various criteria. Many of these were explicitly secular, such as the notion of national development, greater efficiency and greater social justice. However, self-consciously Islamic justifications for these measures were also published, helping to define 'Islamic socialism' during these years. As such, it included many of the points raised by Islamic critics of the pre-1952 status quo, to establish the respective claims of the individual and the community. Thus, attention was paid to Qur'anic injunctions on inheritance, as well as to those verses explicitly encouraging various forms of property use by individuals. But, at the same time, reference was made to the 'social function' (*wazifah ijtima'iyah*) of property, to ensure that the impulse to create wealth did not harm the maintenance of the 'social balance'. Al-'Arabi, al-Siba'i and others wanted to stress that ownership is conditional upon the use of property to benefit society as a whole, enhancing the general level of prosperity, as well as ensuring that the claims of others, through *zakat*, charity, inheritance and the observance of the prohibitions on oppression or injustice (*zulm*) should be met.[13]

Avoiding extremes of wealth and poverty, to sustain a harmonious relationship between the members of a society, become important parts of the vision of a restored moral framework for a distinctively Islamic society, seeking to give meaning, effectiveness and ethical purpose to property in the restoration of a moral economy which has been disrupted by capitalism and by the attitudes it encourages towards property and wealth creation.[14] In Egypt, the state-sponsored journal *Minbar al-Islam* became the forum for the indictment of capitalism, providing a space for attacks on exploitation, class divisions and on the power of capitalism to transform anything and everything into private property, subjecting it to the rules of the market and encouraging competition for personal profit. It is this that stands accused by al-Ghazzali, al-Bahi al-Khuli and others of corroding the solidarities of a society that adhered to the Islamic ethic. Commodification thus becomes the enemy not simply of sociability, but of virtue.[15]

---

[13] Al-Siba'i, *Ishtirakiyat al-islam*, pp. 16–17. *Zulm* is a general designation for prohibited forms of economic activity, such as the charging of interest (*riba*), gambling, monopoly, forcible seizure, theft and trade in goods which harm individuals and society as a whole; Muhammad 'Abdallah Al-'Arabi, *Al-Milkiyat al-khassah wa-hududuha fi al-Islam* (Cairo, 1964).

[14] Al-Sharabasi, *Al-Islam wa-l-iqtisad*, pp. 206–12; Mansur Nasim, 'Al-Mal baina al-na'mah wa-l-naqmah', *Minbar al-Islam* 26/11 (January 1969), pp. 197–8; Muhammad Ibrahim Hazmah, *Ishtirakiyat al-islam wa-l-ishtirakiyat al-gharbiyah* (Cairo, 1961), pp. 48–54.

[15] Muhammad al-Ghazzali in Ahmad Farraj, Ahmad al-Sharabasi et al. (eds.), *Al-Islam din al-ishtirakiyah* (Cairo, 1961), pp. 87–90; Ali Abdel Wahid Wafi, 'Private ownership in Islamic law', *Minbar al-Islam* (English edition) 2/1 (January 1962) pp. 53–4; Al-Bahay al-Kholy, 'Free and restricted ownership', *Minbar al-Islam* (English edition) 2/4 (October 1962), pp. 31–5.

Islamic socialism thus brought together two powerful indictments of capitalism within contemporary Islamic discourse: its social dysfunctionality and its power to disorder the moral universe. These are not identical criticisms. They owe their origins to two different ways of imagining the social world, finding their inspiration, respectively, in modern notions of society and social function, and in pre-modern ideas of the harmony that should exist in human interactions, reflecting the balance of the God-given universe. Thus the detailing of the 'social function' of property is informed to a large degree by modern understandings of the 'public' in social discourse and helps also to define the concept, to give it weight and symbolic meaning. It carries with it understandings that there are claims of a largely contractarian nature that can regulate relations between public and private and that the mediating element in this – the currency of agreement – is property itself. Whatever authorities are cited, therefore, to support the tilt one way or the other – towards private or public interest in matters of property disposal – the imaginative framework of appropriate calculations will owe much to ideas of social utility and contractarian considerations familiar from the development of secular European thought.[16]

On the other hand 'social balance' corresponds to a pre-modern notion of the moral economy, reflecting in human relations the balance and proportion of God's ordering of the universe. Far from being contractarian in conception, this derives from an imagination governed by cosmological notions of proportion, balance and the divine harmony of creation, animate and inanimate. In this imaginative field, property and society take on very different features since they are the terrain of a distinctive set of relationships between human beings and their Creator. In some respects, they are part of an ideally seamless whole. The danger of rupture is ever present, however, not simply in the new forms of human organisation and power introduced in this case through capitalism, but also in the new forms of imagination, as the writings of both Muhammad Iqbal in India and of Ali Shari'ati in Iran pointed out, if in slightly different and distinctive ways.[17]

This opened up the possibility that the two ways of thinking about the restoration of a distinctively Islamic sociability, far from reinforcing each other, might actually diverge, making for the creative tension out of which

[16] See, for instance, J. S. Mill, *Principles of Political Economy* (London, 1909), pp. 199–237; A. Ryan, 'Public and private property', pp. 223–45 and S. I. Benn and G. F. Gaus, 'The liberal conception of the public and the private', pp. 31–65 in S. I. Benn and G. F. Gaus, *Public and Private in Social Life* (London, 1983); D. Gobetti, *Private and Public: Individuals, Households and Body Politic in Locke and Hutcheson* (London, 1992), pp. 2–10, 93–105.

[17] Sheila McDonough, *The Authority of the Past – A Study of Three Muslim Modernists* (Chambersburg, PA, 1970), pp. 31–4; Hamid Dabashi, *Theology of Discontent* (New York, 1993), pp. 142–4.

came the ideas that were to be developed in the decades following the demise of the state socialist experiment in many countries in the Islamic world. However, whilst the major emphasis was on the development of a critique of the effects of capitalism, the two reinforced each other, providing a powerful and appealing indictment of the ills of a system based on capitalist principles with multiple resonances.[18]

These arguments and the accompanying debates in the secular press coincided with the preoccupation of many in Egypt and elsewhere in the developing world at the time about the role of private capital in sustaining economic development. Commentators such as Shaikh Shaltut reproduced in their own idiom arguments that social utility required both the productive use of capital and the conditions that would ensure that it was used for generally beneficial ends.[19] This implied concern about the wilful nature of private capital. The fear was that it worked according to its own logic and with its own priorities, carving out for itself an area of productive social life that respected neither national boundaries nor the cultural values and ethical beliefs of specific peoples. Capital investment followed profit, and in a world dominated by a capitalist economic order where the opportunities for profit appeared limitless, a state could only 'capture' capital by using its coercive capacity to transfer ownership to the state itself. The effect this would subsequently have on the productivity of capital was to be a subject of heated debate in Egypt and elsewhere thereafter. However, for those writers concerned about the erosion of Islamic values by the working of a capitalist logic, it underlined the need to assign a dominant role to the state.

For the Islamic socialists, the state, armed with the programme of Islamic socialism, was to be the vehicle that would capture capital, putting it to productive use for the benefit of society as a whole. This involved the regulation of all forms of property ownership to ensure that they contributed to a thriving, but also an Islamic society to develop. The role assigned to the state by many of those writing from a self-consciously Islamist position at the time in Egypt, for instance, was partly due to the fact that the state was the main sponsor and consumer of their writings. Part of the attraction of 'Islamic socialism' for Nasser's government was that it allowed the government to define the terms of its socialist experiment, allegedly without owing a debt to external socialist or Marxist authorities, and would also allow the government to calibrate the degree of its radicalism with respect to property relations. This is captured well in the words of Kamal al-Din Husain, an ex-Free Officer,

---

[18] Hazma, *Ishtirakiyat al-islam*, pp. 9–16.
[19] Compare Shaltut, *Al-Islam wa-l-takaful al-ijtima'i*, pp. 16–22, and Al-'Arabi, *Dimuqratiyat al-qawmiyah*, pp. 120–2, with writings in *Al-Ahram al-iqtisadi* of the time: *Al-Ahram al-iqtisadi* 163, 10 June 1962, pp. 50–1.

close to the Muslim Brotherhood, in 1960: 'Our socialism is not imported, it does not aim at allowing the state full ownership of the means of production; but protects private property and stipulates the freedom of private initiative and its equality of opportunity with the private sector.'[20]

However, the heavy emphasis on the role of the state was also partly a logical consequence of the ways in which the Islamic socialists had imagined power, especially insofar as they laid great stress on the ideal construct of the *wali al-amr* in their thinking about the link between moral precepts and social practice. Some form of commanding presence had always been posited as necessary – a force or authority that would delegate for God in the sense of ensuring that his commands would be carried out in this world. In the Egyptian case, it was the determination and ruthlessness of the government under Nasser that ensured that it alone was in a position to set itself up as the *wali al-amr* in question, identifying the real presence of the Egyptian state and government with the idealist construct of the Islamic writers' argumentation. This was ubiquitous, if not always as obvious as the photograph of Nasser entitled '*Za'im al-'urubah wa-l-islam*' (The leader of Arabism and of Islam).[21]

At the same time an elision takes place between the identity and interests of the state not simply with the *wali al-amr* but with the society as a whole. It is claimed that the state or government (often used interchangeably) speaks through and for the collectivity of the people, and possesses the rights and duties of the people in its entirety – particularly with regard to property. From this it is argued that since all wealth belongs to God and since the people are the servants of God, all wealth must belong to all the servants of God, regardless of the identity of the officially registered owner. As Shaikh Shaltut remarked, 'it [property] is guarded by all for the benefit of all'.[22] This makes private property clearly subordinate to the interests of the community, as defined by the government – a theme stressed by Muhammad Ghallab at the time: 'Private ownership of the means of production remains legal within the limits set by the economic needs of the life of the society. This means that it is not a fixed right . . . but must defer to all the rights of others in organising the welfare of

---

[20] *Al-Ahram al-Iqtisadi* 117, 1 July 1960, and, as the Minister of the Economy Ibrahim Qaissouni said at the time, 'Egyptian socialism' would be 'propertied socialism' (*ishtirakiyah tamlik*): *Al-Ahram al-Iqtisadi* 140, 15 June 1961. Cited in Wahba, *Role of the State*, p. 79. When the government brought in more radical nationalisation measures, Kamal al-Din Husain was forced out of his official post since he objected to the Charter's references to 'scientific socialism', the widespread nationalisation of private property and the neglect of Islam as the prime source of social values. Dessouki, 'Politics of income distribution in Egypt', pp. 71–2; Beinin, 'Islamic responses to the capitalist penetration of the Middle East', pp. 101–4; Enayat, *Modern Islamic Political Thought*, pp. 139–50.
[21] See the frontispiece of Jami'at al-Azhar *Al-Muhadarat al-'ammah li-l-mawsim al-thaqafi al-awwal* (Cairo, 1959).
[22] Shaltut, *Al-Islam wa-l-takaful al-ijtima'i*, pp. 20–1.

society.'[23] Furthermore, as al-Bahi al-Khuli made clear, these rights were solely in the hands of the ruler (here designated as *al-imam*): 'The ruler is entitled at any moment to take from the wealthy in order to satisfy the material, spiritual, hygienic, educational and military demands of the society.'[24]

In one variation of this argument, clearly influenced by the equally power-ful contemporary discourse of nationalism, property is seen as the means whereby individuals can discharge their duties both to God and to the father-land (*al-watan*). There is not a precise equation of the rights of God with the rights of the fatherland (*haqq Allah wa-haqq al-watan*), but rather a suggest-ive form of equivalence. They are treated as much the same category of obligation. Both are seen as being necessary conditions attaching to anyone's legitimate claim of property ownership. Both constitute a necessary part of an integrated and truly Islamic society. The rights of God in this respect are seen as consisting of both necessary conditions, such as the payment of *zakat*, as well as recommended courses of action which the individual can choose to follow or not, such as giving to charity. The rights of the fatherland, on the other hand, are construed as the collection of taxes to 'enhance the necessary public welfare of the community'. Only once the owner of wealth has discharged these duties can he/she be permitted to use his/her money, and even then only within the limits laid down by God and enforced by the state (*wali al-amr*).[25]

In addition to the question of overarching rights, the state also becomes the repository of the expertise required to understand the needs and thus the well-being of society, encapsulated in the use made of the concept of *maslahah* (benefit/interest/welfare). By this reasoning, because it can uncover and pronounce on social needs, the state is given authority in understanding and interpreting Islamic obligations, based upon the assumption that the aims of the latter were taken to be the benefit (*maslahah*) of society as a whole. As certain *'ulama* had feared, the technical knowledge of social expertise, often amassed through the resources and apparatus of the state, begins to colonise the world of religious learning and interpretation of the tradition, and consti-tutes, therefore, one of the more radical new departures in the emerging discourse of 'Islamic socialism'.[26]

Here the state, or rather the government, was given a broad mandate to judge the general or public interest, but Muslim intellectuals differed in their views on the relevant criteria – and the full significance of these differences

[23] Muhammad Ghallab, 'Al-Milkiyah baina al-i'tidal wa-l-jasha'', *Minbar al-Islam* 19/12 (May 1962), pp. 47–50.
[24] El Kholy, 'Free and restricted ownership', p. 40.
[25] Al-Sharabasi, *Al-Islam wa-l-iqtisad*, pp. 209–11; see also Wafi, 'Private ownership in Islamic law', pp. 53–5.
[26] Brown, *Rethinking Tradition in Modern Islamic Thought*, pp. 116–22, 133–9.

was to emerge in later debates. Nevertheless, the great majority of those who wrote on this topic took the notion of public welfare seriously, and at the same time demonstrated the relative inadequacy of the 'tradition' of understanding the meaning of *maslahah* (welfare or benefit) when dealing with it as a social, rather than as an individual phenomenon. Although al-Ghazzali's five criteria of welfare were invoked at intervals, it was difficult to transfer these largely individual concerns to the larger collective stage of society without doing considerable violence to the intention and spirit of the initial ruling. Even so confident a scholar as Yusuf al-Qardawi displays considerable unease when the consequences of translating some of the new understandings of *maslahah* into policy-based prescriptions become apparent.[27]

Some writers did cite classical or traditional definitions, developed in a very different setting and with different resonances, as if there were nothing problematic in such a transfer. It scarcely helped in any practical sense, but it did act as a form of reassurance that the writer had remained 'true' to the Islamic heritage, although such a manoeuvre seriously compromised the notion of heritage itself. In the context of the development of 'Islamic socialism' in the 1960s, the search for some defining criteria of public interest led eventually – and in some cases after a relatively brief attempt to derive them from exclusively and 'authentically' Islamic sources – to the assertion that it was up to the government to decide on the public interest. As numerous contributors to *Minbar al-Islam* asserted, this was something that it was not only incumbent on the government to discover, but that it would have little difficulty in discovering.[28] Of course, the very latitude granted to the state by such a position, and the radical implications of its adoption, clearly did alarm some of the more tradition-minded writers, such as Muhammad Abu Zahra, sympathetic as they may have been to the overall thrust of the 'progressive' interpretation of Islamic obligation.[29]

Possibly to reinforce the benefits of these innovations, a theme which began to gain prominence was that which stressed how much an increase in productivity and in the gross national product would enhance the general

---

[27] See Muhammad Qasim Zaman, 'The 'ulama of contemporary Islam and the conceptions of the common good', in Salvatore and Eickelman, *Public Islam and the Common Good*, pp. 133–9.

[28] El Kholy, 'Free and Restricted Ownership', pp. 36–7; al-Bahi al-Khuli, 'Fi Ta'mim al-murafiq', *Minbar al-Islam* 19/5 (October 1961), pp. 47–53; 'Abd al-Mun'im al-Nimr, 'Al-Ta'mim fi al-islam', *Minbar al-Islam* 19/8 (January 1962), pp. 98–101; Shaikh Hasan al-Ma'mun, 'The Mufti answers your questions', *Minbar al-Islam* (English edition) 3/2 (April 1963), pp. 64–7. See, for instance, Ahmad al-Sharabasi, who is reflecting on the prohibitions of *riba* and of drunkenness and suggests that Islam forbids them for social reasons, only citing the Qur'an as a kind of post facto validation of his argument: Ahmad al-Sharabasi, *Al-Din wa-l-mithaq* (Cairo, 1965), pp. 106–11.

[29] See Muhammad Abu Zahra's caution about the rules for deriving the content of *maslahah* in 'Ahkam al-islam li-maslahat al-insan', *Minbar al-Islam* 19/5 (October 1961), pp. 37–9.

interest or public welfare. This echoed the secular rationale for the 1961 natio-nalisations which took so large a section of Egyptian commercial and industrial life into state ownership. The argument was that private capital operated according to other incentives and that therefore encouraging the entry of private capital into the development projects envisaged by the Egyptian gov-ernment would never succeed. Thus, by taking these same sources of capital into state ownership, more efficient use could be made of capital since it would now be devoted exclusively to the goals of national development which the government had decided were the appropriate ones for Egypt to follow.[30]

In other words, an argument from efficiency, based on the discovery, through superior means of knowledge, of the best techniques of wealth crea-tion and capital investment was being used to justify the expropriation of private property.[31] This raised the issue once again of the nature and location of the expertise needed to interpret public welfare and interest more generally, placing traditionally trained Islamic scholars at a disadvantage, but privileging the new Muslim intellectuals who were familiar with the disciplines compris-ing the 'science of society'. If the *nass* had changed, from literary text to social text, so too had the skills necessary for its interpretation.[32] Moral exhortation was no longer enough. Now was the time that called for social expertise.[33]

In this respect, prominence was increasingly accorded to the question of technique and its part in increasing the well-being of the public. Technique in this sense meant both technology and administrative skills. For the Muslim intellectuals, nature had been created by God for the benefit of mankind and there could be few restraints on the technologies that should be employed to increase the productivity and wealth of Islamic societies. They shared with secular counterparts in the non-Islamic, as well as Islamic worlds, an optimism, but also a naiveté about the benefits of technology and industrial

---

[30] Ahmad al-Murshidi, 'Ma huwa . . . kaif . . . wa-limadha? al-Takhtit', *Al-Tali'ah*, 6 June 1965, pp. 16–25; Mahmud 'Abd al-Mun'im 'Azmi, 'Tatawwur fikrat al-takhtit fi iqtisadina al-qawmi', *Al-Tali'ah*, 6 June 1965, pp. 26–9; Khalil Hasan Khalil 'Al-Qata' al-'amm . . . fi al-nizam al-ra'smali, wa-l-qata' al-'amm . . . fi al-nizam al-ishtiraki', *Al-Tali'ah*, 8 August 1965, pp. 15–23.

[31] See Nasser's comments on the 'science of administration' and its claimed neutrality and social utility, quoted in Wahba, *Role of the State*, p. 99.

[32] Zebiri, *Mahmud Shaltut and Islamic Modernism*, pp. 72–7, 162–6; Al-'Arabi, *Dimuqratiyat al-qawmiyat al-'arabiyah*, pp. 58–61; 'Abd al-Nabi Hasan Yusuf, 'Al-Islam wa-l-takhtit al-iqtisadi', *Minbar al-Islam* 26/9 (November 1968), pp. 55–7.

[33] Of course, as people reflected upon this and upon the shortcomings of particular governments, as well as the disadvantages of leaving the initiative and the development of new policies to act upon this new knowledge solely in the hands of the state, the argument was developed that this could as well, and possibly better, be entrusted to private individuals and concerns, rightly guided and less prone to the manifold pressures of statecraft – an acknowledgement, in short, that the secular logic of the state could be best avoided through recourse to private initiative. See the emergence of 'Islamic economics' and 'Islamic banking' partly in response to disillusionment with the 'Islamic socialism' of the state in chapter 4.

expansion. This was characteristic of the period prior to full awareness of its ecological drawbacks. It was for a later generation of Muslim intellectuals to elaborate on this and on the social cost, but even then there was little exploration of either the inner logic of technical and scientific advance, or the social and intellectual consequences of technology.[34]

A similarly optimistic view was visible in their attitude to the beneficial effects of new administrative techniques. The idea was common that a properly directed state could adopt various administrative techniques without affecting the basic purpose or character of the society. This was at odds with actual experience. Indeed, it could be said that the innovatory administrative techniques of the modern state in the Islamic world had introduced rationales that had in turn shaped the way people thought of state organisation as such. This was evident in the writings of Muslim intellectuals, from the Palestinian Taqi al-Din al-Nabhani to the Syrian Sa'id Hawwa.[35] This reflected a similar lack of acknowledgement of the normative power of criteria of administrative efficiency among those writers who wanted to suggest that techniques for the discovery and realisation of the public interest were neutral and carried no ideological baggage.[36]

Inevitably, such a view further reinforced the role of the state as the arbiter of the public interest. The comments of Shaikh Muhammad al-Ghazzali and others at the time concerning the congruity of 'social balance' determined by the government and the Islamic message showed how the state's administrative techniques, which owed nothing to a distinctively Islamic tradition, could colonise the field of public welfare and thus determine which reading of Islamic obligations should apply in the changing circumstances of the time.[37] This also encouraged the tendency to read backwards from the assertion that everything that was in the public interest was also in God's interest, to suggest that what was in the public interest must *therefore* be in God's interest.[38]

---

[34] Some, however, saw technology as a carrier of cultural values that might be harmful to an Islamic order more for what they conveyed than for the inner logic in the sense used by Marcuse and elaborated upon by Habermas. See J. Habermas, 'Technology and science as "ideology"', ch. 6 in *Toward a Rational Society*, tr. J. J. Shapiro (Cambridge, 1989), pp. 81–122; Hasan al-Turabi, *Al-Iman wa-atharuhu fi hayat al-insan* (Jiddah, 1984), pp. 269–301.

[35] An-Nabhani, *The Islamic State*; Sa'id Hawwa, *Jund Allah* (Beirut, 1988), pp. 40–3; Asghar Ali Engineer, *The Islamic State* (New Delhi, 1980); Khalid Muhammad Khalid, *Al-Dawlah fi al-islam* (Cairo, 1981). It was this very feature that was at the heart of the critique of contemporary Islamism by Muhammad Sa'id al-'Ashmawi, *Al-Islam al-siyasi* (Cairo, 1987), who attacked its claims to an authentic exclusivity on this basis.

[36] See, for instance, al-Bahi al-Khuli, 'Al-mujtama' al-ishtiraki huwa al-mujtama' al-insani fi mafhum al-islam', *Al-Tali'ah*, 6 June 1965, pp. 60–8.

[37] Al-Ghazzali in Farraj, al-Sharabasi et al., *Al-Islam din al-ishtirakiyah*, pp. 87–90; Muhammad al-Madani, 'Fi itar al-ishtirakiyat al-islamiyah', *Majallat al-Azhar* 33/8 (January 1962), pp. 940–5.

[38] It was this phenomenon which Malcolm Kerr describes in *Islamic Reform*, pp. 80–97.

Such a move introduced the potentially open-ended and contingent measure of the public interest into understanding and interpreting the 'rights of God', opening the field not simply to diverse interpretations, but also to the dominant power at the time, encapsulated in the state. Inevitably, this was seized upon by the Egyptian government at the time (and others subsequently) to justify and legitimise state activities with reference to Islamic values, raising for some the spectre of everything they had learned to fear about the *mu'tazilah*.[39] For others, such as Sayyid Qutb, this line of reasoning sparked a repudiation of some of his earlier assumptions and led him into headlong confrontation with the state, precisely because it seemed to bear out his charge that a state invested with such wide and absolute authority was indeed the focus of a modern form of 'idolatry'.[40]

3.2   Social harmony and the moral economy

Although the state was almost universally portrayed as the principal agent of effective social action, one of the main preoccupations of those Muslim intellectuals who saw 'socialism' as the antidote to capitalist exploitation and fragmentation was the question of social solidarity. The restoration of a distinctive Islamic sociability became the aim. Imagining the ways in which people could be persuaded to rediscover their common bonds, to work cooperatively together and to place social activity, especially that geared towards the acquisition and disposal of property, in a proper ethical setting, was the task which the early Islamic socialists set for themselves in advancing their critique of capitalism. Taking up and developing the term 'mutual social responsibility' (*al-takaful al-ijtima'i*) as the framework for a restored moral economy became the concern of Egyptian writers such as Muhammad al-Bahi, Shaikh Shaltut and Ahmad al-Sharabasi.[41]

---

[39] The *mu'tazilah*, a rationalist movement in the Abbasid Empire, influential during the ninth century CE (813–47 CE/198–233 H), had been associated with views concerning the nature of the Qur'an – that it was created and thus contingent, rather than uncreated and thus eternal – and with the ambitions of three Abbasid Caliphs which came to be equated by some with a willingness to encourage the powerful to interpret and possibly change aspects of the *shari'ah*. See Albert Nader, *Le système philosophique des Mu'tazila* (Beirut, 1956), pp. 99–113; see also Abu al-Husain al-Basri's views on the contingency of *ijma'* (consensus) in different generations in M. Bernand, *L'accord unanime de la communauté comme fondement des statuts légaux de l'Islam* (Paris, 1970), pp. 73–6. Rightly or wrongly, the *mu'tazilah* had come to be regarded with suspicion as Muslims who were willing to allow the contingencies of power and of reason not simply to interpret, but also to shape the divine law.

[40] Charles Tripp, 'Sayyid Qutb: the political vision', in Rahnema, *Pioneers of Islamic Revival*, pp. 165–83.

[41] See, for instance, Muhammad al-Bahi, 'Al-Islam din al-mustawa al-fadil fi al-insaniyah', *Al-Muhadarat al-'ammah*, pp. 73–9; Shaltut, *Al-Islam wa-l-takaful*, pp. 4–15; Ahmad

Mutual social responsibility would eliminate extremes of wealth and poverty and would ensure that the worker would be respected and his or her rights guaranteed – and furthermore that 'the individual would not be looked at as a factor of production, but as a being with a spirit and preferences and feelings'.[42] This was in many respects a Fabian view of society and of socialism. It owed some of its distinctiveness to the Fabian influences transmitted through the early writers and thinkers about socialism, both secular and Islamic. However, it also owed something to the common roots it shared with Fabian socialism as a particular kind of response to industrial capitalism, looking back to an imagined pre-capitalist social order of organic linkages, sanctioned by an ethic of mutual respect and steeped in the values of traditionally accepted revealed religion.[43]

For the Fabians, these antecedents could be found in the Christian socialists of the early nineteenth century. The Islamic socialists drew upon different images and a different tradition, but shared much of the underlying imaginary conception of society and its nature. In particular, they shared the belief in the natural 'organic' character of society in which individuals had distinct roles to play that were equally valued, since they contributed to the well-being and solidity of the whole – the worth of which was taken to be a self-evident truth. In this respect, al-Sharabasi, for instance, deployed images both of 'society as body', in which the different organs worked in harmony towards the same end, and 'society as building', in which the different parts of the edifice combined to hold it up.[44] Such an understanding of socialism meshed well with the preoccupations of those who were beginning to discover society, to protest against its injustices and yet remain true to their own traditions. In these various idioms, therefore, there is a correspondence of imagery, a coincidence of the positive associations of what was thought to be fitting, establishing a certain plausibility for socialism at the level of metaphor and thus acting as a powerful vehicle for socialist ideals.[45]

---

al-Sharabasi, 'Al-Mal wa-l-ishtirakiyah fi al-islam', in Farraj, al-Sharabasi et al., *Al-Islam din al-ishtirakiyah*, pp. 115–16; Al-Sharabasi, *Al-Islam wa-l-iqtisad*, pp. 147–51.

[42] 'Abd al-Rahman Bakr, *'Alaqat al-'amal fi al-Islam* (Cairo, 1970), p. *ha*, see also pp. 72–94, and Hazma, *Ishtirakiyat al-islam*, pp. 61–3.

[43] W. Wolfe, *From Radicalism to Socialism: Men and Ideas in the Formation of Fabian Socialist Doctrines 1881–1899* (New Haven, 1975), pp. 151–75, 215–32; E. R. Norman, *The Victorian Christian Socialists* (Cambridge, 1987) pp. 1–34.

[44] Al-Sharabasi, *Al-Islam wa-l-iqtisad*, p. 139; Ahmad al-Sharabasi, *Baina al-din wa-l-dunya* (Cairo, 1970), p. 43 – he also used 'society as a family' where its members are assigned different but integral roles in an organic whole.

[45] See al-Dumi, *Al-Minhaj al-ishtiraki 'ala du' al-islam*, pp. 94–105. The word for socialism itself – *ishtirakiyah* – was derived from the root *sh-r-k* which has both positive and negative connotations in Islamic thought. On the positive side, it denotes partnership, cooperation and sharing; on the negative side, it can be associated with idolatory and polytheism (from the notion of allowing other beings to share in the attributes of God). This ambiguity thus permits

One of the Muslim intellectuals most closely associated with the development of this view of socialism was Mustafa al-Siba'i, leader of the Muslim Brotherhood in Syria from the mid-1940s. His direction of the Muslim Brotherhood in the lively and contested arena of Syrian politics during the late 1940s and early 1950s was associated with campaigns against both the influence of foreign capital in the economy and the growing power of landowners, whose embrace of capitalist principles was threatening traditional solidarities in the countryside.[46] This political activity was accompanied, and eventually superseded by, his role as one who sought to explain the contribution of Islam to curing the ills of contemporary society.

In particular, he did not flinch from using the term 'the socialism of Islam' (*ishtirakiyat al-islam*), defining it essentially as the sociability of an Islamic society in which the bonds of cooperation and mutual assistance would be kept in place and strengthened by a legal framework based on the rules of the *shari'ah*. Thus, he argued, the rights to life, freedom, knowledge, respect and ownership would be defined in a way which promoted an Islamic conception of people's relationship to one another and to God – and would also be protected against external aggression and internal corruption.[47] For al-Siba'i – and for others – 'socialism' in this sense meant above all the restraints that 'would prevent the individual from using capital to oppress and exploit the masses', as well as 'the realization of social solidarity among citizens in order to eradicate poverty, deprivation, hunger and sickness', and the protection and advancement of the five components of a person's interest (*maslahah*) outlined in the classical tradition by al-Ghazzali.[48] From his perspective, attention to the ethic of cooperation and social solidarity not only made Islamic society a better place, it had also made it, historically, a strong society – 'the foremost society in the world'.[49]

This vision of a unified and cooperative society, in which the members worked selflessly for the good of the whole, lent itself admirably to the corporatist and authoritarian purposes of Nasser and his government in Egypt. Whilst the government itself retained tight control of the measures they thought necessary to promote public welfare, the ground had been prepared

the use of the term with very different resonances. Interview with Kamal Abu al-Magd, Cairo, 13 May 1997.

[46] Umar F. Abd-Allah, *The Islamic Struggle in Syria* (Berkeley, 1983), pp. 91–9; 'Abd al-'Aziz al-Hajj Mustafa, *Mustafa al-Siba'i – rajul fikr wa-qa'id da'wah* (Amman, 1984), pp. 49–54, 60–71; Doreen Warriner, *Land Reform and Development in the Middle East* (London, 1957), pp. 71–112; Birgit Schaebler, '"Practicing Musha": common lands and the common good in southern Syria under the Ottomans and the French', in Owen, *New Perspectives on Property and Land in the Middle East*, pp. 241–307.

[47] Al-Siba'i, *Ishtirakiyat al-islam*, pp. 59–128.

[48] Al-Siba'i, *Ishtirakiyat al-islam*, pp. 9 and 173–85.

[49] Al-Siba'i, *Akhlaquna al-ijtima'iyah*, pp. 48–9.

with the idea that social harmony and solidarity were desired by all who favoured a reconstitution of society after the onslaughts of capitalism and imperialism. This mixture of imperatives is captured well, for instance, in the writings of Muhammad al-Bahi, formerly of the Muslim Brotherhood, and in the early 1960s Minister of Awqaf in the Egyptian government. He attacked capitalism not simply for causing class divisions in society, but also for destroying the self-sufficient ideal of the independent craftsman working for himself. At the same time, he indicted it for the power that capital granted some over the lives of others, for the drive to accumulate for the sake of accumulation, and for the charging of interest (*riba*) which undermined its ethical character because it contravened the rules laid down by God and harmed the weak.[50]

For Shaikh al-Madani and Shaikh al-Ghazzali, close to the government in Egypt, the refounding of a moral economy would be made possible by instruments such as *zakat*, or the explicit prohibition of *riba*. These measures were not simply praiseworthy because they were laid down by divine decree. They were also believed to be instrumental in restoring harmony to a society disrupted by class antagonisms and driven by the acquisitiveness, competition and commodification unleashed by capitalism.[51] In this and other writings, Muslim intellectuals were calling for a reinvigorated moral economy which would ensure that individuals' material transactions would nevertheless be set in a context of social justice and ethical respect by keeping the 'spiritual' side of such transactions in the forefront of people's thoughts. Thus, sociability, whilst it had an obvious material face in the social organisation of individuals, also had a non-material dimension which both acted as a cement through imaginative empathy and imbued it with value.[52]

Thus, in Egypt in the 1960s the 'Socialist Decrees' were justified by Nasser and his Islamic socialist apologists with reference not simply to general Qur'anic injunctions, but also to the effects which differentials in property had on the fabric of society. The redistribution of land, the nationalisation of businesses and the expropriations of property were therefore linked directly to the project of social solidarity and corporate interdependence. Furthermore, it

---

[50] Muhammad al-Bahi, *Al-Islam wa-nuzum al-hukm al-mu'asirah* (Cairo, 1965), pp. 18–24.

[51] Shaikh Muhammad Muhammad al-Madani, 'Da'a'im al-ishtirakiyah fi al-islam wa-l-takaful al-islami', pp. 75–81, and Shaikh Muhammad al-Ghazzali, 'Hawl wasa'il al-tamaluk wa-taqyid al-milkiyah', pp. 82–6 – both in Farraj, al-Sharabasi et al., *Al-Islam din al-ishtirakiyah*.

[52] 'Abd al-Rahman al-Sharabini, 'Al-Ishtirakiyat al-islamiyah', *Minbar al-Islam* 19/11 (April 1962), pp. 63–7; 'Abd al-Ghani 'Awad al-Rajahi, 'Ishtirakiyatuna al-islamiyah', *Minbar al-Islam* 21/3 (August 1963), pp. 70–2, and 'Abd al-Ghani 'Awad al-Rajahi, 'Ishtirakiyatuna al-islamiyah', *Minbar al-Islam* 21/5 (October 1963), pp. 93–5; 'Isa 'Abduh Ibrahim, 'Al-Islam wa-l-ishtirakiyah', in Farraj, al-Sharabasi et al., *Al-Islam din al-ishtirakiyah*, pp. 147–8; Muhammad Farraj Salim, *Al-Takaful al-ijtima'i* (Cairo, 1965); Zebiri, *Mahmud Shaltut and Islamic Modernism*, pp. 40–1, 51–6.

was suggested that if mutual social responsibility could not emerge through the workings of the conscience and reason of individuals, then the state had a duty to intervene. As those Muslim intellectuals who hastened to extol the 'National Charter' explained, the state would be acting in full accordance with the Islamic *shari'ah*.[53] This may not have been the precise implications of the notion of 'mutual social responsibility' suggested by Mustafa al-Siba'i during the 1950s. Indeed, it could be argued that it went directly against his view of the need for individual commitment, rather than compulsion. Nevertheless, the element of compulsion, in the shape of the state as agency of last resort, was never far from his writings. This would explain why the Egyptian government of the day should have taken up and officially sponsored many editions of his major book, *Ishtirakiyat al-islam*.[54]

Al-Siba'i's reaction to his adoption by the Nasserist government was mixed. He appeared to welcome the fact that the government of the UAR was committed to a socialist programme compatible in some respects with the 'socialism of Islam' which he had outlined. Yet he was evidently also increasingly nervous about the latitude the programme granted to the state. He tried to counteract this by pointing out the many restrictions under which the state must operate were it to begin expropriating private property. Equally important was his emphasis on the voluntary nature of much of the 'socialism of Islam' if it were to have any lasting impact or moral worth. The writings towards the end of his life suggest strongly that state compulsion could be no substitute for moral regeneration and that state action might in fact hinder or subvert the process.[55]

Thus, what had begun as an attempt to outline the programme for the restoration of a moral economy, based on principles that would counter

---

[53] Shaikh Muhammad Muhammad al-Madani, 'Al-Mithaq', *Minbar al-Islam* 20/2 (July 1962), pp. 21–7; al-Bahi al-Khuli, 'Ma' al-mithaq', *Minbar al-Islam* 20/2 (July 1962), pp. 28–33; al-Sharabasi, *Al-Din wa-l-mujtama'*, Bakr, *'Alaqat al-'amal fi al-islam*, pp. 131–6. The National Charter (*al-Mithaq al-Watani*) of 1962 in Egypt was a declaration of the Nasserist government's direction of economic and political development in which the dominant role of the state was emphasised and that of private enterprise and foreign capital downplayed. It served a number of purposes, one of which was to suggest that the Charter had emerged from a national consensus and thus that all debate should now take place with reference to the terms of the Charter.

[54] See, for instance, al-Siba'i's assertion that 'although the *shari'ah* does protect the right of private property, the consensus of the *fuqaha'* believe that this right is not absolute . . . [cites the examples of the Prophet Muhammad and of the Caliph 'Umar who had distributed land and money without the consent of the owners] . . . The state may resort to nationalisation on account of social necessity [*dururat ijtima'iyah*]' Al-Siba'i, *Ishtirakiyat al-islam*, p. 164. The book was taken up by the government of the UAR and went into numerous editions, published by the government press – Enayat, *Modern Islamic Political Thought*, pp. 144–8.

[55] Karpat, *Political and Social Thought in the Contemporary Middle East*, pp. 124–6; G. C. Anawati and M. Borrmans, *Tendances et courants de l'Islam arabe contemporain*, vol. I: *Egypte et Afrique du Nord* (Munich, 1982), pp. 109–11.

the effects of capitalism and capitalist exploitation, appeared to some to be assimilated ever more closely into the project of the state. Whilst some could suspend disbelief and persuade themselves that, since the Nasserist state was carrying out measures intended to protect the country from the power of foreign capital, and to restore the 'social function' of capital within Egypt itself, the sociability which they were seeking would be restored. Nevertheless, quite apart from the shortcomings of the Nasserist state itself, a growing suspicion emerged that the state would follow its own imperative and its own logic – and this owed little to the distinctively Islamic norms which should underlie the endeavour. In short, by invoking the power of the state, there was a danger that those who espoused 'the socialism of Islam' might also succumb to the logic of state socialism. As a consequence, increasing numbers of Muslim intellectuals looked to the redefinition of an Islamic sociability that would be founded on distinctively Islamic values, separated both from capitalism and from the state socialism so prevalent in much of the Arab Islamic world at the time.

3.3   Identifying Islamic sociability

Muslim intellectuals who were concerned about the effects of capitalism on Islamic society were concerned not simply about the loss of social cohesion, but also about the loss of autonomy and the dilution of identity. They saw their societies being eroded by individualism, moral egotism, profit-oriented behaviour and commodification. This was partly a concern about the ethnicity of capitalism and the normative framework in which capitalist institutions and practices were embedded.[56] It was also in part a fear of the transformative power of a thriving commercial society, and the antagonism it might generate. In this respect, communism, as the antithesis of capitalism, loomed large in writings of the time, presented in all its worrying detail as a construct to allow the explicit formulation of a distinctively Islamic alternative.[57] In some respects, this was one of the implications of Muhammad al-Ghazzali's comment that 'Communism is the enemy at the gates and capitalism is the enemy within', suggesting not simply that capitalism was more insidious, but also that a society weakened by capitalism made itself prey to communism.[58] The

---

[56] Ruthven, *Fury for God*, pp. 251–7.

[57] This would help to explain why Muhammad Baqir al-Sadr devoted some two hundred pages to his discussion of Marxism, compared to only forty or so devoted explicitly to capitalism, in his main work *Iqtisaduna* (Beirut, 1982), pp. 15–213 (first published in 1961) – a book which was aimed precisely at discouraging Muslims from turning to a materialist communist alternative simply because they were outraged and revolted by the ills of a capitalist society.

[58] Muhammad al-Ghazzali, *Al-Islam al-muftara 'alaihu baina al-shuyu'iyin wa-l-ra'smaliyin* (Cairo, 1960), p. 14.

Islamic socialist response was, in part, due to a determination that Muslims should not be faced by two unpalatable alternatives – capitalism and communism.

One of the indictments of communism was that it 'went against nature'. This was meant to place Marxism beyond the moral pale, but it was also possibly expressing a hope that mankind would reject so 'unnatural' a set of beliefs.[59] It was clearly for those concerned with the preservation and extension of Islamic values to ensure that people did not then go towards the other extreme: that those angered by capitalism should not be drawn into the orbit of the communists; and that those disillusioned with communism should not forget all restraint and throw themselves into the selfish pursuit of profit encouraged by capitalism.[60] For this reason, it was a common trope to present Islam as a 'third way' which strikes a perfect balance between the claims of the individual and the community – moderating the extremes of capitalism and communism, respectively.[61]

This was also important when presenting Islam as a way of healing the social fragmentation promised by the individualism of capitalism and the class warfare threatened by Marxists. Both were founded upon a materialism that, in the view of many Muslim intellectuals, reduced man to a mere machine, with communism dehumanising the individual as effectively as capitalism, and both undermining the organic solidarity of society.[62] The philosophy of materialism, as well as the actual obsession with material advantage, were both part of the capitalist revolution and the danger of capitalist values. It was this that comprised the 'cultural invasion' (al-ghazw al-thaqafi) to which the Islamic countries had been subjected.[63] It was for Islam to remind people of the spiritual aspect of existence, filling the void left by these two materialist philosophies. Such a position was also important as a means of asserting that Islam was of relevance to the situation of contemporary society and was therefore capable of engaging with – and

---

[59] 'Abd al-Ghani 'Awad al-Rajahi, 'Ishtirakiyatuna al-islamiyah', *Minbar al-Islam* 21/3 (August 1963), pp. 70–2.

[60] See, for example, Hazma, *Ishtirakiyat al-islam*, pp. 7–8; Muhammad al-Ghazzali, *Al-Islam fi wajh al-zahf al-ahmar* (Beirut, n.d.), pp. 9–20, 63–76 (first published 1966).

[61] See, for instance, Ibrahim Muhammad Ismail's assertion that in the Islamic system 'the individual is not acquisitive at the expense of the community and the community does not impose upon the individual. It secures under the shelter of human justice, the good of both the individual and the community', from his book *Islam and Contemporary Economic Theories* (Cairo, 1962), cited in Crecelius, *Ulama and the State*, p. 381.

[62] Muhammad al-Bahi, *Tahafut al-fikr al-maddi al-ta'rikhi baina al-nazr wa-l-tatbiq* (Cairo, 1975), pp. 3–8 (first published 1969); al-Sharabasi, *Al-Islam wa-l-iqtisad*, pp. 203–7; Sami A. Hanna, '"Al-Takaful al-Ijtima'i" and Islamic socialism', *The Muslim World* 59/3–4 (July–October 1969), p. 283; al-Ghazzali, *Al-Islam wa-l-manahij al-ishtirakiyah*, pp. 92–7; al-Sharabasi, *Al-Ishtirakiyah wa-l-din*, pp. 5–7.

[63] Mustafa Darwish in Jami'at al-Azhar, *Al-Muhadarat al-'ammah*, pp. 251–2.

of refuting – the dominant ideologies that so marked the world of the late twentieth century.[64]

Despite the explicit rejection of materialism and of communism, there was some unease about whether a critique of capitalism characterising itself as socialist, even if qualified by the epithet 'Islamic', would also be vulnerable to an alien form of reasoning. Whether this would show itself in criteria used to judge social benefit, or in the methods used to interpret Islamic obligations, or in the close association of distinctively Islamic associations and other secular organisations, there was a concern for the unwelcome transformation of Islam itself and a possible weakening of the faith.[65] As a result, there were numerous efforts to relate the principles of 'Islamic socialism' to the sacred history of Islam. This involved citing the behaviour and sayings of the Prophet Muhammad and the four *rashidun* (rightly guided) Caliphs, particularly on questions of property distribution.[66] Similar exemplars were used to show that instruments such as social insurance had long been part of a well-ordered Islamic society, antedating the measures taken to alleviate the worst effects of capitalism in modern societies. Equally, the key 'spiritual' or moral dimension of mutual social responsibility or social solidarity was asserted to have been one of the most important features of early Islamic society and could thus plausibly be cited as having formed an integral part of a distinctive Islamic order from the outset.[67]

However, the appropriation of 'Islamic socialism' by governments in different parts of the Islamic world – Algeria, Egypt and Pakistan – as a rhetorical device, if not a programme of action, necessarily changed its content and significance. As some had feared, it altered the balance of forces and thus the possible outcomes, transforming the virtues of mutual social responsibility into something like forced cooperation with the agencies of the state. Given the predominantly secular logic under which these agencies

---

[64] Al-Dumi, *Al-Minhaj al-ishtiraki*, pp. 4–6; Muhammad al-Ghazzali, *Min huna na'lam* (Cairo, 1950), pp. 119–32; al-Sadr, *Iqtisaduna*, pp. 7–10.

[65] Y. Y. Haddad, *Contemporary Islam and the Challenge of History* (Albany, NY, 1982), pp. 30–2.

[66] See Abdurrahman Badawi, 'A pioneer of socialism in Islam: Abu Dharr Al-Ghifari', *Minbar al-Islam* (English edition) 2/1 (January 1962), pp. 49–50 and 122; al-Khuli, *Al-Ishtirakiyah fi al-mujtama' al-islami baina al-nazriyah wa-l-tatbiq*, pp. 47–94; al-Dumi, *Al-Minhaj al-ishtiraki*, pp. 64–93; al-Ghazzali, *Al-Islam al-muftara 'alaihi*, pp. 136–9.

[67] An author who was particularly energetic in this regard was Mahmud Shalabi who wrote a series of books, beginning with *Ishtirakiyah Muhammad* (Cairo, 1962), and ending with *Ishtirakiyah 'Uthman* (Cairo, 1968), which sought to demonstrate that the Prophet and the early Caliphs had the principles of 'Islamic socialism' at heart – as he states explicitly, 'we have an independent socialism, springing from our history, our beliefs and our nature'. Shalabi, *Ishtirakiyah Muhammad*, p. 72. See also al-Sharabasi, *Al-Islam wa-l-iqtisad*, pp. 139–40; al-Sharabasi, *Baina al-din wa-l-dunya*, pp. 47–52; 'Abd al-'Aziz Kamil, 'Adwa' 'ala tariq ishtirakiyat al-Islam', pp. 48–9 in Farraj, al-Sharabasi et al., *Al-Ishtirakiyah wa-l-din*.

operated, and the compromises and opportunistic pursuit of strategic and government interests, it led to reactions in all these countries against the governments which had claimed to champion an 'Islamic socialism' and against the clerics and Muslim intellectuals who had been drawn into this endeavour. In Syria, the Muslim Brotherhood under the new leadership of 'Isam al-'Attar in the 1960s made a clear break with socialism, advocating instead the virtues of private property and entrepreneurial activity guided by the *shari'ah* as the best way of restoring Islamic society.[68] In Algeria, a similar reaction set in regarding the state socialism of the FLN, hitherto endorsed by a number of Muslim intellectuals, where it was suggested that prayers said on nationalised property would be invalid.[69]

Even an independent critic, such as the Egyptian Hasan Hanafi, who was determined to keep the spirit of 'the Islamic left' alive, admitted his own ambiguity when it came to making a judgement upon the role of the state.[70] This ambiguity is most apparent in his multi-volume work on Islam and the Egyptian revolution. He reiterates the familiar claims that Islam is the religion of socialism and that the early Islamic state was a socialist state, in the sense that the Prophet Muhammad (whom he calls at one point '*imam al-ishtira-kiyin*' – leader of the socialists) encouraged cooperation, mutual social responsibility, the equitable sharing of resources and the use of wealth for the common good. He also defends Nasserist socialism against the attacks by 'Arab reaction', such as the government of Saudi Arabia, which had claimed that such socialist measures contradicted the precepts of Islam. Yet he was also aware of the uses of Islam by an autocratic government in Egypt and was evidently uneasy about the distorting effect this had on Islamic socialism.[71]

In his manifesto for *Al-Yasar al-Islami* (the Islamic Left), the title both of the short-lived journal he published in 1981 and of the movement he wanted to initiate throughout the Islamic world, Hanafi regrets the link between the phrase 'Islamic socialism' and the Egyptian state under Nasser. Nevertheless, he tries to rehabilitate the principles which initially gave rise to it, recalling Jamal al-Din al-Afghani and his efforts to resist the military and territorial imperialism of the West. Hanafi then claims that he and his movement would be attempting to counter the economic and cultural imperialism which remained even when the European empires withdrew. In order to do this, he

---

[68] Abd-Allah, *The Islamic Struggle in Syria*, pp. 128–30, 154–62; Carré and Michaud, *Les Frères Musulmans*, pp. 193–202; Sa'id Hawwa, *Fusul fi al-imrah wa-l-amir* (Beirut, 1988) pp. 218–22, 234–5.

[69] Burgat and Dowell, *Islamic Movement in North Africa*, pp. 248–51, 255–7.

[70] See Burgat's interview with Hanafi in 1988: Burgat and Dowell, *Islamic Movement in North Africa*, pp. 210–12.

[71] Hasan Hanafi, *Al-Din wa-l-tanmiyat al-qawmiyah*, vol. IV of *Al-Din wa-l-thawrah fi misr 1952–1981* (Cairo, 1989), pp. 110–37, 215–31.

identifies himself with the cause of 'reform' in Islam. Like his intellectual forebears, Hanafi shows an admiration for the *mu'tazilah*, a disdain for sufism and an enthusiasm for the *maliki* school of Islamic law, precisely because of the scope it allows for establishing what is in the best interests of the Islamic community under the heading of *al-masalih al-mursalah*.[72]

In this respect, he remains true to the spirit of Islamic socialism. His concern is that global capitalism has established a hierarchy of states and wealth in which Muslim countries generally occupy the lowest rungs. But he is also worried about the effects on the identity and sociability of Muslim societies. Like Mustafa al-Siba'i in his writings, Hanafi argues that the programme of the Islamic left will be the antidote to these corrosive and materialistic aspects of capitalist development. Thus, in place of individualism, mutual social responsibility and cooperation will be encouraged; in place of private property over which the individual has absolute rights of disposal, the claims of the Islamic community as a whole will be asserted; in place of interest-based transactions that encourage inequality and injustice, cooperative forms of exchange will combine productivity with social harmony.[73] There is little here that departs from the views put forward about the ills of capitalism and the endangered sociability of the Islamic community since al-Banna, 'Awdah and others were writing in the 1950s. Whilst Hanafi's project may sometimes unwittingly succumb to the utilitarianism to which the writings of his predecessors were prone, it is noticeable that he tries hard to insulate his project from the state and thus from its potentially authoritarian logic.[74]

These developments had a marked impact on any distinctively Islamic critique of capitalism. During these years, the self-consciously Islamic critique of capitalism had become a set of propositions or identifying markers taken up by the Egyptian government and used to legitimate or mobilise support for its programme of state socialism. Inevitably, different priorities came into play, bringing with them a logic which transformed these responses into something more directly useful for the state and thus ever more ambiguous. Hitherto, the ambiguity had largely been intellectual, concerning the principles of interpretation or the development of criteria of moral worth. Now it showed itself in other ways – most obviously in the search for effectiveness. The efficiency and capacity of the state were to become the main criteria for deciding on the practical implications of the Islamic socialist

---

[72] Hasan Hanafi, *Al-Yasar al-islami wa-l-wahdat al-wataniyah*, vol. VIII of *Al-Din wa-l-thawrah fi misr 1952–1981*, pp. 3–4, 10–22, 29.

[73] Hanafi, *Al-Yasar al-islami*, pp. 50–6; Hasan Hanafi, *Al-Yamin wa-l-yasar fi al-fikr al-dini*, vol. VII of *Al-Din wa-l-thawrah fi misr 1952–1981*, pp. 49–68.

[74] Hanafi, *Al-Yasar al-islami*, pp. 289–92.

programme. For this reason, it became instrumentalised in the service of governments, particularly in Egypt, which did not have the restoration of a distinctively Islamic moral economy as its highest priority, even if it deployed the symbolic vocabulary associated with the Islamic tradition.

One consequence of this was the acceleration that took place in the sceptical view of the state and its legitimacy which became so marked a feature of modern Islamic thought from the 1970s onwards, accelerated by the failure of the very programmes that were intended to increase productivity and thus boost the public interest. Using a cloak of Islamic legitimacy, and then tossing it aside when it did not seem to suit the purposes of the regime, caused understandable resentment. In Egypt, this coloured the ways in which the reasoning used to justify the reorganisation of society or the encouragement of social solidarity were to be interpreted. Thus the state, which had had such great expectations vested in it, was now seen by some as being as great a disruptor of society and as great a threat to an Islamic social order as ever capitalism had been or continued to be. Indeed, for some, the state and capitalism were but two manifestations of the same forces: materialism, secularism and the 'instincts' of the *jahiliyah* – egotism and tribalism.

4   Islamic economics and Islamic banks

The record of state direction of the national economy in much of the Arab Islamic world had not been a happy one. By the early 1970s, it was clear that only in oil-producing countries such as Iraq, Algeria or Libya could the immense revenue flow sustain the kind of welfare state promised by state ownership of the means of production. Elsewhere, and in certain sectors in these countries as well, state control of the economy had led to a fall in productivity, underemployment and an inability to boost either the volume or the terms of trade with the rest of the world. The vision of a just and effective alternative to capitalism, whether presented as secular or Islamic socialism, appeared to be wearing thin, both in the Islamic world and beyond, throwing into doubt many of the assumptions upon which an alternative global economic order had been based. At the same time, it had become clear to many Muslim intellectuals that, gratifying as it may have been to have seen their ideas taken up by a state as powerful as that of Nasser's Egypt, they and the values they espoused had paid a price which entailed the subordination of their cause to the dictates of a state guided not by Islamic principles, but by those of secular nationalism and authoritarian populism.

Nevertheless, the debates of those years concerning the nature of property, the claims of the individual and the community, the reconstitution of an organic social solidarity and the bases of the success of the national economy had opened up the way for the development of a body of ideas that were to be known as the field of 'Islamic economics'. For many Muslim intellectuals, this became an imaginative device to develop an alternative order, founded on Islamic principles, which would depend neither on the state nor on exhortations to social solidarity of the kind that had been pressed into the service of the socialism of the secular left. On the contrary, Islamic economics engaged directly with the key issue of the moral economy – treating it not simply as an ethical enterprise, but also as an economic one. The ambitious task was the construction of the model of an economic order based on distinctively Islamic principles, which would also be successful materially, competing with the apparently all-devouring ethos and apparatus of capitalist enterprise in the twentieth century.

A disciplinary field was therefore elaborated, intended to establish the foundations, both ethical and practical, of a functioning economy. Simultaneously, the period witnessed a variety of efforts to put some of these principles into practice, in some cases within the framework of a nation state, but increasingly in the proliferating networks of Islamic financial institutions, the majority driven by private capital, existing parallel to secular, capitalist financial institutions, within the international as well as the national banking systems. In both cases, the changing conditions of political possibility from the 1970s onwards had encouraged the realisation of these ideas. The vast oil price rises of the 1970s had seemingly altered the balance of economic power between many oil producers in the Islamic world and the industrialised states of the north. The increased revenues had also placed unparalleled resources in the hands of the governments of these states and, through them, of many private beneficiaries of the region's economies, giving a boost to efforts to create distinctive Islamic financial institutions that could depend upon substantial private capital.

It soon became apparent that this approach also contained transformative possibilities, not always imagined by those who had embarked on the task, and occasionally disconcerting to those who had thought they were founding a genuinely autonomous and in some respects insulated alternative to capitalism. The 'discovery' of an 'Islamic economics', as in the earlier case of the discovery of an 'Islamic society' – to which it was epistemologically related through positivist sociology – brought with it many of the assumptions and imaginative reconstructions of individual and society, and of their relation to the material world, which underpin the ethos of the capitalist imaginary.

This chapter centres, therefore, on two aspects of the ways in which Muslim intellectuals have sought to meet the challenge of capitalism, beyond the earlier efforts to construct an 'Islamic socialism'. The first involves the attempt to devise an 'Islamic economics' as a strategy which would transform and strengthen the power of Islamic societies whilst preserving a distinctively Islamic identity. Acknowledging the power of material factors and thus the success of capitalism in attracting human beings, many of these writers tried to ensure that all economic transactions would be tied to an Islamic ethical system whilst retaining their capacity for productive and material efficiency. A constant theme, therefore, is the effort to prevent economic transactions from unleashing a force in human nature which the Islamic revelation was designed to keep in check, partly through 'excavating' the *fiqh* for rules on trade, finance, taxation, property, *riba* (interest) and all related economic transactions.

In doing so, however, many of them were clearly influenced by the very act of imagining a separate domain of the economy. Thinking about the economy as a distinct sphere of knowledge, of understanding and of explanation of human behaviour seemed to bring its own rules, reasoning and criteria. By entering into arguments about the economy as a particular realm of human activity, many of the Muslim intellectuals seemed to accept – with various degrees of unease, some acknowledged, others not – that they were engaging with a discourse not of their own making. The struggle to make it theirs has been a constant and sometimes problematic one.

The second response to the challenge of capitalism, evident simultaneously in the last decades of the twentieth century, has taken the more practical form of trying to apply some of the principles governing distinctive Islamic economic transactions through the growing practice of Islamic banking. In both areas – the theoretical and the practical – there is an impulse to distinguish an Islamic sphere of transactions from a capitalist sphere. If measured by some abstracted and restrictive notion of 'Islamic authenticity', the endeavour would appear to have had very limited success. However, both areas have provided examples of the ways in which Muslim intellectuals have delineated for Muslims various forms of effective engagement with a world shaped by a particular capitalist modernity, whilst adhering to the spirit and even the letter of the Islamic *shari'ah*. Whether or not Muslims, variously situated, in terms of location, wealth and other conditions of possibility, will take up these responses, must depend upon a host of other factors, perhaps only a few of them having to do with their identity as Muslims.

4.1   Economics and Islamic economics

The determination by Muslim intellectuals to grapple with ideas and issues defined as distinctively 'economic' obliged them to engage with the discipline of economics itself. In doing so, they sought to respond to a series of concepts which had helped to define the discipline – concepts that were closely connected to the changes in European society brought about by the intellectual and industrial revolutions which they were used to explain. Whether critical or not of the value of these processes, economists had developed a language appropriate to the emerging imaginative sphere of the economy. Thus, accumulation, commodification and exchange, their associated institutional frameworks and their interplay, came to the fore, defining a distinct sphere of human activity, claimed by some to be divorced from the world of politics and social conflict.

Precisely to ground this claim, it had been asserted that the acquisitive drive which underpinned the emerging forms of capitalism, as well as the discipline used to analyse and predict the conditions of capital growth, were integral to human nature. Greed in the service of reason was to be the driving force of the economy, leading Adam Smith, Mandeville and others to state that its inhibition was not only unnatural, but would result in the social evils of poverty and universal misery.[1] This was a revolutionary claim and caused outrage at the time in Europe among clerics and lay people who had long held that the drive to acquire material goods corrupted both the human soul and the human community. Yet now, far from being a disruptive passion, greed and the drive to accumulate were portrayed as steadying interests.[2] Even more disturbing was the claim that private vices could produce public virtues in a system where the 'vice' in question was held up as the very model of rationality and, in a predominantly utilitarian calculus, could even be seen as a form of virtue.[3]

Materialist in conception and transformative in nature, the new understanding of rationality was associated with the kind of calculation which allowed 'more' to equal 'better' and in which the costs and benefits were by definition seen as commensurable, animating capital and commodifying human labour.[4] Where things become objects of exchange, then the boundaries of the economy, as a discursive field, will be determined by the criteria of commodification, generally products of cultural recognition that permits an exchange value to be assigned and thus an economic calculus to be worked out. In cross-cultural encounters, it is here that misunderstandings can be at their sharpest and most incongruous. What one culture – or 'regime of value' – considers a commodity, may be beyond the comprehension of another, causing deep offence or incredulity.[5] However, where the agreed lines of the commodity exist, there lie the boundaries of the economy, dictating the 'proper' object of study and the substance of calculation concerning exchange values.

In a capitalist economy, the prime site for such calculations is the market, an institution regarded as necessary, but ethically suspect in most pre-capitalist systems, including in the Islamic world. A general belief that the desire to make a profit by buying low and selling high could easily shade into various forms of sharp practice gave birth in classical antiquity and in the Byzantine Empire to the institution of the market inspector – *agoranomos* or *logistes* – most of whose functions were taken on in the early years of the Islamic Empire by the office of the *muhtasib*.[6] This was closely associated with a common view that the act of exchange itself, expressed through trade, was

---

[1] E. K. Hunt, *Property and Prophets – The Evolution of Economic Institutions and Ideologies* (New York, 1990), pp. 40–7; Adam Smith, *The Wealth of Nations*, books I–III (London, 1986), pp. 371–81; see also Locke, Petty, Mandeville, Cantillon, Steuart – in W. Letwin, *The Origins of Scientific Economics* (London, 1963); B. de Mandeville, *The Fable of the Bees: Or, Private Vices, Publick Benefits* (London, 1970).
[2] A. O. Hirschman, *The Passions and the Interests* (Princeton, 1977), pp. 9–20, 32–69.
[3] M. L. Myers, *The Soul of Modern Economic Man* (Chicago, 1983), pp. 57–60.
[4] Polanyi, *The Great Transformation*, pp. 75–9; I. Kopytoff, 'The cultural biography of things: commoditization as process', in Appadurai, *The Social Life of Things*, pp. 72–3.
[5] Appadurai, 'Introduction', in Appadurai, *Social Life of Things*, pp. 13–16.
[6] P. Crone, *Roman, Provincial and Islamic Law* (Cambridge, 1987), pp. 107–8.

morally dubious, since one party always seemed to come off better than the other in any purely instrumental exchange.[7]

This idea was slow to disperse, living on in mercantilist views of international trade, as well as in aristocratic disdain for trade as an activity. Yet with the growth of a capitalist economy, it was replaced by the increasingly powerful notion that exchange was wholly beneficial to all parties. Adam Smith and others proclaimed that exchange and barter were not simply the driving forces of the economy, but were also a vital part of what it meant to be a human being. In this perspective, money, the principal medium of exchange in a market economy, came to be seen as a positive element in the integration of society, representing the modern virtues of rationality and calculability, even if misgivings were to develop around its effects on the ethics of social interaction.[8]

The market was abstracted and universalised in the emerging discourse of economics, represented as a universal norm founded on reason and common sense, however time- and culture-bound it was in fact. Its trajectory as a concept and as a world-straddling institution under capitalism was an illustration of power at work, constituting a discourse and sanctioning it through the rewards offered to those who conformed, accepted its precepts and acted according to its rules – and conversely marginalising those who refused participation on these terms.[9] This process in turn projected the economy not simply as separable from other forms of human activity, but also as representing the epitome of human rationality – a sphere that could be measured and assessed neutrally by the criteria of economic efficiency.[10]

Given the derivation of the discipline of economics, it is scarcely surprising that these values and many of the beliefs underlying them are contingently connected with the value systems associated with the emergence of modern industrial capitalism. Regardless of ostensible moral approval or condemnation of the outcomes, both the advocates and the critics of the free market, for instance, largely agree on the contours of the disciplinary field itself, as

---

[7] Karl Polanyi, 'Aristotle discovers the economy', in Dalton, *Primitive, Archaic and Modern Economics – Essays by Karl Polanyi*, pp. 107–10.

[8] Dumont, *From Mandeville to Marx*, pp. 33–6; Smith, *Wealth of Nations*, pp. 117–21; Polanyi, *Great Transformation*, pp. 59–70; Parry and Bloch, 'Introduction', pp. 2–4, in *Money and the Morality of Exchange*; Simmel, *The Philosophy of Money*, pp. 285–91, 297–303.

[9] R. Friedland and A. F. Robertson, 'Beyond the marketplace', in Friedland and Robertson, *Beyond the Marketplace*, pp. 6–10; Davis, *Exchange*, pp. 65–73; R. Dilley, 'Contesting markets', in Dilley, *Contesting Markets*, pp. 11–23; Fine and Lapavitsas, 'Markets and money in social theory' pp. 357–82.

[10] Kenneth Tribe, *Land, Labour and Economic Discourse* (London, 1978), p. 145. That the notion of efficiency itself was derived from the discursive terms which helped to define the discipline gave the whole a pleasing self-sufficiency which some saw as deductive circularity, epitomised by the 'perfect conditions' of the economic model.

well as on many of its constituent terms. In an echo of some of the problems faced by those Islamic scholars seeking to construct an identifiably separate field of 'Islamic economics' as an alternative to capitalism, Marx's formidable critique has itself been criticised for being so implicated in the cognitive and value-laden terms of the discipline that it cannot distance itself enough to present the real alternative which Marx claimed to be advocating.[11]

Discursively, economics had created its own universe in which the participants as economic agents were to behave as prescribed since they could do no other. The assumption was that, all other things being equal, human beings would everywhere behave in much the same way towards the acquisition and accumulation of material goods. Failure to do so was ascribed to the 'interference' of affective and non-rational concerns that had distorted the underlying truth of the model. This was both circular and potentially self-serving.[12] However, there was no denying its power when linked to the processes of change associated with industrial capitalism. Thus did one narrative become hegemonic, creating its own criteria of relevance and surrounding itself with a mystique which discouraged examination of its contingent and historical constitution.[13] This was not simply an ideal construct. It also aimed to predict and prescribe how real people, living in given historical and cultural settings, would and should conduct their economic relationships. Yet it was doing so on the basis of an understanding of human nature that was ideologically charged and expressive of a particular system of values, as well as of hierarchies that clearly benefited some at the expense of others.[14]

The utilitarian calculus which established the 'economic motives' of hunger and gain and thus helped to establish an economic realm based on the alleged real motives of human beings (as opposed to 'ideal' and non-rational motives), was a powerful imaginary framework, the influence of which was felt far beyond the sphere of economics.[15] The plausibility of this

---

[11] Baudrillard, *The Mirror of Production*, pp. 21–51 – see also Jean Baudrillard, *Selected Writings*, ed. M. Poster (Stanford, 1988), pp. 3–4. For another critique of Marxism for being too implicated in the assumptions (and metaphors) of classical economics to form a radical alternative, see P. Mirowski, *More Heat than Light: Economics as Social Physics* (Cambridge, 1989), pp. 1–9, 396–401.

[12] Heilbroner, *The Nature and Logic of Capitalism*, pp. 53–69; Mulberg, *Social Limits to Economic Theory*, pp. 19–32; C. Castoriadis, *Philosophy, Politics, Autonomy*, ed. D. Curtis (New York, 1991), pp. 187–92; Gunar Myrdal, *Against the Stream: Critical Essays on Economics* (London, 1973), pp. 133–57.

[13] Mitchell, *Rule of Experts*, pp. 1–9, 82–4; Heilbroner, *Behind the Veil of Economics*, pp. 7–8.

[14] Macfarlane, *The Culture of Capitalism*, pp. 223–4; Barry Schwartz, *The Battle for Human Nature* (New York and London, 1986), pp. 153–62, 170–80, 273–88.

[15] K. Polanyi, 'Our obsolete market mentality' (1947), in Dalton, *Primitive, Archaic and Modern Economies*, pp. 59–70. Indeed, so powerful is the image of rationality projected by economics that some have seen it as 'colonising' other fields in the social sciences – projecting an imaginative fiction as the basis of a social ontology, flawed as this process may be. B. Fine,

calculus was reinforced by a market which privileged new forms of integra-tive association, introducing a great variety of social and cultural values and assumptions which included specific forms of property, particular rules of contract and even conceptions of the person. Despite the time- and place-bound nature of these values, it has been the power of capitalism to persuade people that the market was the 'natural' setting for human activity, the greatest guarantor of individual freedom.[16] The rewards of the dominant systems of the global economy ensured that many thrived in the new circum-stances, giving weight and plausibility to the values by which their success was now to be judged.[17]

Those made uneasy, or indeed who were outraged by these developments, have faced a challenge that is both intellectual, in the sense of apprehending and countering the imaginative and analytical power of these terms of refer-ence, and practical, in the sense of devising an equally effective method of engaging with the material world. For Muslim intellectuals there was a need to imagine an alternative economic order based on distinctively Islamic prin-ciples to perform a socially integrative function, incorporating Islamic values into the practices of everyday life. They were trying to create the conditions whereby economic actors, as Muslims, would take for granted the norms and practices associated with the ideals and structures of an ideal Islamic eco-nomic life.[18] In seeking to disembed an economic field from the context in which it had been developed (the market-oriented economy of industrial capitalism), they were setting themselves, often unawares, a Herculean task. The fact that they did not succeed in the way originally imagined is less important than the diversity and adaptability produced by this modern Islamic discourse, indicating salient features of the imaginative reconstruction of an Islamic moral economy in the twentieth century.

Prominent among those who first tried to grapple with these issues was the Iraqi Shi'i cleric, Ayatollah Muhammad Baqir al-Sadr. Faced by the twin dangers, as he saw it, of capitalism and Marxism, its intimate and equally materialist antithesis, he made it his mission to develop – or, as he put it, to

---

'A question of economics: is it colonizing the social sciences?' *Economy and Society* 28/3 (August 1999), pp. 403–5, 413–17; see also M. Godelier, *Rationality and Irrationality in Economics*, tr. B. Pearce (New York, 1972).

[16] G. Dalton, 'Introduction', in Dalton, *Primitive, Archaic and Modern Economies*, pp. xii–xvi, xxiv–xxvii; B. Barber, 'All economies are "embedded": the career of a concept, and beyond', *Social Research* 62/2 (Summer 1995), pp. 387–407.

[17] Heilbroner, *Behind the Veil of Economics*, pp. 16–34.

[18] This is a prescription of an accelerated reversal of the process described by Bourdieu as marking the gradual transition from a pre-capitalist to a capitalist economy – the deliberate construction of an Islamic *habitus*: Bourdieu, *Practical Reason*, pp. 104–7. See also John B. Thompson, 'Introduction', in P. Bourdieu, *Language and Symbolic Power*, tr. G. Raymond and M. Admanson (Cambridge, 1991), pp. 12–15.

'discover' – a distinctively Islamic economics. Only in this way would the Islamic world be able to defend itself effectively against the material and intellectual pressures of East and West, drawing on its own traditions to articulate that which the *fuqaha'* had neglected over the centuries. Changed circumstances required a change in the focus of clerical and lay Muslims alike, as well as innovative thinking that drew on possibly neglected aspects of the broader Islamic tradition.[19]

Baqir al-Sadr was keen to make a distinction between the science of economics and economic ideologies. The former he viewed as a value-neutral method for explaining the workings of capitalism in particular, given its origins as a science. Despite stressing the contingency of its origins and the inevitable influence of capitalist practice and values on its development, al-Sadr subscribed to the notion that economics is a neutral instrument of analysis and prediction that has universal validity, capable of explaining economic behaviour, regardless of cultural or regional variations.[20] This ambivalence marked the emerging field of 'Islamic economics', causing problems for the ability of its advocates to disengage from many of the assumptions of conventional economics.[21]

For the most part, those who contributed to the discourse of 'Islamic economics' made a good deal of this distinction, arguing that the hegemonic discourse of economics, coupled with the material power of capitalism, had led to unthinking acceptance of standard economic principles – and the assumptions about human nature and rational behaviour which underpinned them. They saw it as their task to reinfuse the understanding of economic life with Islamic values, such that Muslims would no longer have to accept as the only plausible economic doctrine one that was a carrier of norms alien to their own tradition. This was particularly noticeable among Egyptian writers of the 1970s onwards.

As the writings of 'Abd al-Hamid Mahmud al-Ba'li and of Muhammad Shawqi al-Fanjari show, there was evident unease about allowing 'positivist economics' to dictate the assumptions and methodologies of the field, since this is explicitly related to the nature of the capitalist project.[22] However,

---

[19] Al-Sadr, *Iqtisaduna*, pp. 346–9, 356–8. This was a common trope, taken up, for example, by writers in Egypt and in South Asia – see al-Ghazzali *Al-Islam al-muftara 'alaihi baina al-shuyu'iyin wa-l-ra'smaliyin*; al-Khuli, *Al-Islam la shuyu'iyah wa-la ra'smaliyah*.

[20] Al-Sadr, *Iqtisaduna*, pp. 6–7.

[21] Baqir al-Sadr reverts to this theme later in his own study, when discussing some of the methodological pitfalls of the whole endeavour, but from which he himself cannot easily escape: Charles Tripp 'An "Islamic economics"? Problems in the imagined reappropriation of economic life', in Kathryn Dean (ed.), *Politics and the Ends of Identity* (Aldershot, 1997), pp. 162–5.

[22] 'Abd al-Hamid Mahmud al-Ba'li, *Maqasid al-shari'ah wa-mushkilat al-hajjat fi al-iqtisad* (Cyprus, 1987), pp. 31–3; Mahmud Muhammad Nur, *Al-Iqtisad al-islami* (Cairo, 1978),

there is also some fear about relativism in the social sciences which could compromise the eternal certainties and values which they want 'Islamic economics' to inculcate. Rif'at al-Sayyid al-'Awadi states that there are 'two programmes of research in Islamic economics: one is the discovery of the fixed values of the system; the other is the positivist method working on manifestations that change'.[23] However, when he outlines the latter feature of Islamic economics as 'primarily defining the nature and form of relations between individuals and groups in society', it is clear that it is not going to be easy to separate the two spheres. In practice, it would be difficult to distinguish this from his characterisation of 'positivist economics' as the 'discovery of general laws . . . on the idea that the source of knowledge is mankind'.[24]

Out of these and other writings some general features emerge to distinguish Islamic economics as a doctrine, determining not simply the substance of this field of knowledge, but also the method. Influenced by the historical circumstances of its emergence, much was made of the importance of distinguishing this field from that of capitalist economics on the one hand and of communist or socialist economics on the other, even if, as Thomas Philipp has pointed out, these were often caricatures which disguised basic similarities.[25] As a rule, the definition of 'Islamic economics' begins with the assertion of the sources from which the principles and the particulars of the doctrine are to be derived: the Qur'an, the *sunnah* and interpretative reason (*al-ijtihad bi-l-ra'i*), found in both the legacy of the jurists and in the efforts of those engaged in thinking this through in the present. These are to be used, in conjunction with the example of the companions of the Prophet, the rightly guided Caliphs and the authoritative interpretations of the jurists, to establish the means by which these principles are to be realised. As in other fields of Islamic knowledge and prescription, various writers differ about the degree of latitude allowed to reasoned interpretation through *ijtihad*, as well as about the selection of jurists to be cited as authoritative sources for understanding the rules of an Islamic economy.[26]

pp. 18–20; Yusuf Kamal, *Adwa' 'ala al-fikr al-iqtisadi al-islami al-mu'asir* (Cairo, 1980) pp. 17–18; Muhammad Shawqi al-Fanjari, *Dhatiyat al-siyasiyat al-iqtisadiyat al-islamiyah* (Cairo, 1981), pp. 18–20; Muhammad Shawqi al-Fanjari, *Al-Madhhab al-iqtisadi fi al-islam* (Cairo, 1986), pp. 91–3; Muhammad Musa 'Uthman, *Nazriyat al-infitah al-iqtisadi fi al-islam* (Cairo, 1990), pp. 33–4.
[23] Rif'at al-Sayyid al-'Awadi, *Fi al-iqtisad al-islami* (Cairo, 1990), pp. 22–3, 35–7.
[24] Al-'Awadi, *Fi al-iqtisad al-islami*, pp. 44–5.
[25] Thomas Philipp, 'The idea of Islamic economics', *Die Welt des Islams* 30 (1990), pp. 122–4.
[26] Nur, *Al-Iqtisad al-islami*, pp. 53–5.

This has led to contrasting approaches among Muslim intellectuals helping to define the field. Some have concentrated both on the explication of Qur'anic verses and on the writings of the jurists over the centuries, presenting expository accounts of what these sources have to say about *riba* (lending money at interest), *zakat, 'ushr* and *kharaj* (forms of taxation or levies on wealth), the status of property, accounting and the market.[27] Others have addressed current economic concerns of a generic nature, seeking to infuse prescriptions for economic activity with an explicit set of Islamic values. These writers have tried to ensure that their exhortations remain true to the principles contained in the founding texts, but also wish to engage successfully with the economic sphere as presently constituted. For writers like al-Fanjari, al-'Awadi, Sa'd Ibrahim Salih and Rashid al-Barrawi, the task is not simply to cite the authorities of the past – although they do – but to devise a comprehensible vocabulary for the reinvigoration of people's commitment to an economy with moral purpose.[28]

However, the attempt to keep separate the domains of 'doctrinal' and 'scientific' economics runs into difficulties, affecting the delineation of the field of 'Islamic economics'. The assertion is soon made that all economics, whatever its scientific claims, is ideological, since it is based on a set of fundamental assumptions about human nature, and about how the world should operate as much as about how it does operate. This conforms with earlier claims that the discourse of economics emerged simultaneously with and was implicated in the emergence of capitalism. In many respects it is a valid and judicious reading of the subject. However, it also dilutes the distinction made between the 'science' of economics and economic 'doctrine'. As a consequence, it becomes harder for al-Sadr and others to maintain the boundaries between economics, as they understand it to have developed in relation to capitalism, and 'Islamic economics' as separate discursive fields,

---

[27] Philipp, 'Idea of Islamic economics', pp. 124–8; Farhad Nomani and Ali Rahnema, *Islamic Economic Systems* (London, 1994), pp. 45–8. See also 'traditional' approaches to the identification of an Islamic economics, such as Muhammad Hasan Abu Yahia, *Iqtisaduna fi daw' al-qur'an wa-l-sunnah* (Amman, 1988); al-'Abbadi, *Al-Milkiyah fi al-shari'ah al-islamiyah*; Rafiq Yusuf al-Masri, *Usul al-iqtisad al-islami* (Damascus, 1989); Muhammad Kamal al-Din Imam, *Usul al-hisbah fi al-islam* (Cairo, 1986); Husain 'Abd al-Muhid Hasanain Abu-'Ila, *Fiqh al-riba* (Cairo, 1989); Yusuf al-Qardawi, *Dawr al-qiyam wa-l-akhlaq fi al-iqtisad al-islam* (Cairo, 1995).

[28] Nur, *Al-Iqtisad al-islami*, pp. 85–9; al-Fanjari, *Dhatiyat al-siyasiyat al-iqtisadiyat al-islamiyah*, pp. 24–8; Rif'at al-'Awadi, 'Minhaj al-adhkar wa-l-istithmar fi al-iqtisad al-islami', *Al-Nur*, 5 May 1982; Sa'ad Ibrahim Salih, *Mubadi' al-nizam al-iqtisadi al-islami wa-ba'd tatbiqatuhu* (Cairo, 1986), p. 27; Salah al-Imam, 'Al-Iqtisad al-islami bayna al-wujud wa-l-'adam', *Al-Ahrar* 18 July 1991; T. Kuran, 'Fundamentalisms and the economy', in M. E. Marty and R. S. Appleby, *Fundamentalisms and the State: Remaking Polities, Economies and Militance* (Chicago, 1993), pp. 293–9; Rashid al-Barrawi, *Al-Qur'an wa-l-nuzum al-ijtima'iyat al-mu'asirah* (Cairo, 1975), pp. 32–8.

alerting some, such as writers close to the Egyptian Muslim Brotherhood, to the possibility that mainstream economics may colonise the Islamic sphere as well.[29]

By demarcating a field of knowledge as that of economics, even if qualified by the epithet 'Islamic', Muslim intellectuals were obliged to conform to criteria which determine what counts as an activity within that field. By accepting criteria of significance, of what counts and what does not, there is a strong possibility of an acceptance of many of the underlying assumptions, however strongly they insist on the ethical distinctiveness of 'Islamic economics'. Indeed, the very insistence by some that economics is a value-neutral science of 'how things work' could compound the ambivalence in this sphere. Such an assertion could not be made without accepting some of the epistemological certainties of neo-classical economics, bringing in their wake a host of assumptions about human nature, the primacy of a certain kind of reason and the determined disenchantment of the world.

4.2 Development and efficiency

Throughout the 1970s and 1980s, and influenced by earlier preoccupations which had been taken up by state authorities in various places, there was a practical purpose behind this theorising. Whilst the ethical differentiation of Islamic from non-Islamic economic systems was clearly at the heart of the endeavour, there was also a developmentalist purpose. Islamic economics was intended to develop an effective and workable system of economic life that would not simply be morally preferable, but would also generate real power to improve the material lives of Muslims.

The exploration of the question of effective economic institutions for the Islamic world leads to the argument that development plans devised in other cultural settings and for other societies would not work if applied to a society whose fundamental values differ from those from which the economic programme and ideas of development derive. This goes further than asserting the moral repugnance of Muslims when faced by some of the forms of transaction promoted by a capitalist economy. It argues that programmes of economic development, formulated by liberal free marketeers or indeed by socialists, will not succeed in economic terms unless they are in harmony with the values and culture of the *ummah* – the Islamic community. As a sociological observation, this conforms with much of the experience of the developmental

---

[29] Al-Sadr, *Iqtisaduna*, pp. 290–4, 335–41; Yusuf Kamal Muhammad, 'Adwa' 'ala al-iqtisad al-islami 'aja'ib . . . wa-ghara'ib'', *Al-Da'wah*, no. 60 (April 1981), pp. 19–20; also Kamal *Adwa' 'ala al-fikr al-iqtisadi al-islami*, pp. 5–9.

economics of the 1950s and 1960s and could be said to foreshadow debates about culturally appropriate growth strategies which began to characterise development thinking in the latter part of the century.[30]

However, the significance of this in the world of imagined possibility opening up in the last quarter of the twentieth century, is that it shifts the argument away from a focus on the ethical imperative, originally claimed to be the main reason for formulating a distinctively Islamic economics. On the contrary, it is more of an argument from pragmatism. As the Egyptian intellectual, Khalid Muhammad Khalid makes clear, the call is for a development strategy that will be effective in Islamic societies, where the measure of its effectiveness is defined as the elimination of the 'backwardness' of Islamic societies. The comparison is with the 'advanced' societies of the industrialised world and the criteria would appear to be wholly material. Not only does this show an understanding of a distinctively economic arena that is heavily influenced by the discourse of mainstream economics, but it also projects a programme of economic development suggested by the historical trajectory of the countries of the capitalist, industrialised West.[31]

Some writers, such as Baqir al-Sadr, are determined to qualify the purely material criteria of success and assert that it is precisely the ethical impulse of an Islamic development programme that makes it more effective: 'there is no framework, other than the framework of the economic system of Islam, in which solutions to the problems of economic backwardness can be found'.[32] However, quite apart from the validity of the claim, two different kinds of objective are being invoked. The claim about what works raises questions about the nature of the goal of 'development'.[33] More importantly, it leads to larger claims about the benefits of a distinctively 'Islamic economics' which take on a universal character. Instead of advocating strategies that will work best in a distinctively Muslim environment, an explicit comparison is made

---

[30] Al-Sadr, *Iqtisaduna*, pp. *dal* and *ha*, (in the 1982 edition, the pages of the Preface to the second edition are designated not by numbers, but by the letters of the Arabic alphabet). Lecture given by 'Abd al-Rahman Yusri in March 1991, reported in Sha'ban Abu Dharr, 'Al-haras 'ala al-kasab al-halal yazid al-intaj fi al-mujtama'', *Al-Wafd*, 20 March 1991.

[31] Rashid al-Barrawi, *Al-Iqtisad al-islami* (Cairo, 1986) pp. 5–9; interview with Khalid, Muhammad Khalid, July 1986, by Lutfi 'Abd al-Latif, 'Hadith al-shahr ma'al-mufakkir al-islami al-kabir Khalid Muhammad Khalid', *Al-Ahrar*, 7 July 1986; 'Uthman, *Nazriyat al-infitah*, pp. 89–97. This echoes debates in the nineteenth century in the Islamic world which reflected on the reasons for the 'backwardness' of the Islamic world or the 'East'. It also brings with it some of the same epistemological baggage. See chapter 1, section 1.1.

[32] Al-Sadr, *Iqtisaduna*, pp. *alif* and *ba*; see also Muhammad 'Abdallah al-'Arabi, *Al-Iqtisad al-islami wa-siyasat al-hukm fi al-islam* (Cairo, 1967), pp. 125–144, 385–94; see also report of the conference in Alexandria, 4–5 January 1989, on 'The Economic System: Understanding it and its Importance in the Present'. 'Amir 'Id,'Istratijiyah islamiyah li-hall mashakil al-mujtama'', *Al-Sha'b*, 17 January 1989.

[33] Al-'Awadi, *Fi al-iqtisad*, pp. 25–6, 97–105.

between 'Islamic economics' and 'economics', but on terrain defined by the latter.

In the first place, the argument is put forward by al-Sadr, and also by the Egyptian 'Abd al-Hamid Sarhan, that the Islamic economy provides a better and empirically more valid set of precepts for the organisation of economic life because it is based on a more accurate understanding of human nature.[34] Ironically, however, this argument runs the risk of compromising the distinctiveness of the Islamic economy, since the claim about its superiority is based not on some quality that is peculiarly Islamic, but rather on the universal category of 'human nature' and the ability of specific economic arrangements to satisfy the needs generated by this imaginative construct. As Ahmad al-Dumi acknowledges, this is very close to John Maynard Keynes's views and indeed the influence of Keynesian thinking about the mixed economy is visible throughout the emerging field of 'Islamic economics'.[35] Empirically, this claim is hypothetically verifiable and Muslim intellectuals opened the field up to the possibility of refutation. Furthermore, the grounding of their argument in an understanding of 'human nature', in a move reminiscent of that of the classical economists, suggests that entering into the field of economics obliges Muslim intellectuals to use the categories – even the criteria – associated with its discursive logic because they have been integral to its development.[36]

Al-Sadr and others who followed him were tempted to go further. They make a set of claims about the capacity of an Islamic economy to provide a model that is more stable and less prone to wild fluctuations than any capitalist economy. Consequently, they argue, it would be demonstrably more efficient, according to the criteria established by capitalist economics itself.[37] By the 1990s, this had developed into the justification of an Islamic economy in terms that were unmistakeably neo-liberal in their underlying rationale, as can be seen in the argument that free competition and the prohibition of monopoly are central to any truly Islamic economy.[38]

The direction of this debate raised the question about the best conditions for economic growth and the effective use of capital. It is commonly asserted by tradition-minded jurists and by modern Muslim intellectuals that Islam encourages economic activity and that capital should not lie idle, but should

---

[34] 'Abd al-Hamid Ibrahim Sarhan, *Al-Iqtisad fi al-islam* (Cairo, 1987), pp. 86–7; al-Sadr *Iqtisaduna*, pp. 264–8.

[35] Al-Dumi, *Al-Minhaj al-ishtiraki 'ala du' al-islam*, pp. 94–105.

[36] Nomani and Rahnema, *Islamic Economic Systems*, p. 95.

[37] Al-Sadr, *Iqtisaduna*, p. 293.

[38] Interviews with Dr Ahmad 'Abd al-Rahim al-Saih and Dr Sultan Abu 'Ali in January 1992 – 'Ziyada al-intaj mas'uliyah kul muslim', *Al-Siyasi*, 12 January 1992.

be put into motion through direct use by its owner, or by its owner's leasing of capital (*ijarat ra's al-mal*) to someone who can put it to productive use. Al-'Awadi represents this as ideally combining capital and labour in which the fruits of the productive enterprise are shared between the owners of these two factors of production. There is no suggestion that the owner of capital should not receive a return, but it is for the market or the state (considerable ambivalence exists on this score) to limit the return on capital, ensuring that it is not excessive by rather vaguely designated 'standards of Islamic ethics'.[39]

Once again, an empirically verifiable claim has been made which equates the 'Islamic economy' with the capitalist economy in a number of ways. Although the Islamic variant is stated to be superior, it suggests that they are competing on the same terrain. The problem here for the original intention behind the argument is that this terrain was not marked out by any of the individual writers or by a distinctively Islamic tradition. On the contrary, it is defined by the dominant discourse of the discipline of economics as it emerged in Europe. It is against this that the singularity and superiority of the Islamic economy is being asserted. Regardless of possible quantifiable comparisons which may not favour the Islamic alternative, this argumentative strategy runs the danger once again of dissolving the specificity of 'Islamic economics'.

The Egyptian writer Tariq al-Bishri, for example, warns against the consequences of trying to compare Islamic ideas about economic life with prescriptions – whether capitalist or socialist – for economic development. However, in doing so, he himself argues for a separation between the precepts of Islam as a religious and philosophical position and the secular principles of the economy with its varying and context-bound ideas for the effective organisation of economic life. Thus, in trying to escape the colonising power of economic discourse, he appears to have placed Islam in a separate field, concerned more with the ethics of individual conduct. His assertion that 'a large variety of socio-political systems can exist under Islam' may be historically true, but does little to advance the argument that 'Islamic economics' can provide a viable alternative to the systems currently dominating the world economy.[40]

The coming together of those systems, contingently and intellectually, has been well illustrated in Malaysia since the early 1980s. During Mahathir Mohamed's twenty-two years as Prime Minister, the liberalisation of the

---

[39] Rif'at al-Sayyid al-'Awadi, *Al-Iqtisad al-islami wa-l-fikr al-mu'asir* (Cairo, 1974), pp. 61–2, 180–9, 208–27.
[40] Tariq al-Bishri lecture at Cairo University, May 1996, *Al-'Arabi*, 10 June 1996.

Malaysian economy went hand in hand with the setting up of Islamic educational and research institutions which have contributed substantially to the publication of books, articles and research papers on aspects of 'Islamic economics'. Determined to encourage entrepreneurship and a vigorous business culture among the Malays, Mahathir provided opportunities and government patronage which helped to make the fortunes of many, creating a class of 'new rich' Muslim Malays.[41]

Partly to fend off criticism by the Islamist opposition, represented by the Islamic Party of Malaysia (PAS), that the United Malays National Organisation government was becoming too close to the West and too materialistic, Mahathir's government also founded a number of distinctively Islamic institutions, including the International Islamic University Malaysia (IIUM), the Islamic Economic Foundation, the Institute of Islamic Understanding (IKIM) and the Islamic Banking and Finance Institute Malaysia (IBFIM). IIUM in particular, through its Kulliyah (Faculty) of Economics and Management Sciences, became a major site for the production of an elaborate literature on 'Islamic economics' which often reads like standard treatments of economic questions that would be expected of any practitioner of the discipline. For the Malaysian government in the 1980s and 1990s, this was part of a strategy, therefore, to persuade Muslim Malays, whether close to the *dakwah* movement (Muslim missionary movement) or not, that full-scale participation in a thriving capitalist economy was permitted under Islamic rulings, and was individually profitable and nationally beneficial.[42]

If the Islamic economy is to compete on the same ground as any secular economic system, such as capitalism, and if it is to be judged by the same criteria of success, then it raises the question of how any possible divergence between its role as an effective economic system and its role as the protector and reinforcer of a society's distinctively Islamic ethos may be reconciled. As the critique framed by Sayyid Vali Reza Nasr implies, this has a serious effect on the claims made for an 'Islamic economy'.[43] The contemporary literature defining the field of 'Islamic economics' provides numerous examples of the competing influences at work. For

---

[41] E. T. Gomez and K. S. Jomo, *Malaysia's Political Economy* (Cambridge, 1999) pp. 117–30; P. Searle, *The Riddle of Malaysian Capitalism* (Honolulu, 1999), pp. 45–57.

[42] P. Sloane, *Islam, Modernity and Entrepreneurship among the Malays* (Basingstoke, 1999), pp. 68–77.

[43] Philipp, 'Idea of Islamic economics', pp. 130–1; T. Kuran, 'The economic impact of Islamic fundamentalism', in Marty and Appleby, *Fundamentalisms and the State*, p. 306; Sayyid Vali Reza Nasr, 'Islamic economics: novel perspectives on change in the Middle East', *Middle East Studies* 25/4 (October 1989), pp. 516–30 and 'Towards a philosophy of Islamic economics', *The Muslim World* 77/3–4 (July–October 1987), pp. 175–96.

instance, 'Abd al-Rahman Yusri (Director of the Higher Institute of Islamic Economics in Egypt) argues that an Islamic economy can be introduced by inculcating Islamic values into a successful programme of economic development. He cites the fundamental respect within the Islamic tradition for capital and its productive use in a market designated as free, but nevertheless under the moral guidance and supervision of the institution of the *muhtasib*: 'all wealth is the wealth of God and must be spent on whatever can bring a profit for Islamic society'.[44] This contrasts markedly with the ideas of Husain Shahata (Professor of Trade at Al-Azhar University) whose view of the Islamic economy closely resembles the ideal of autarkic development sketched out, but scarcely implemented, by the planners of state socialism in the 1960s: self-sufficiency in economic production, planned coordination of production and consumption of 'worthwhile things', the elimination of exploitation and the redistribution of wealth through *zakat* and other taxes.[45]

Thinking about economics appears to have led to an acceptance of the ostensibly quantitative concerns of economic discourse, suggesting that in imagining economics as a distinct sphere, whether as 'science' or 'ideology', those who wish to devise a distinct 'Islamic economics' must think in the existing categories of the discipline. Some claim that this is no threat to the project of 'Islamising' the social sciences, since the terms, principles and forces of economics had already been identified long before by various figures in the Islamic tradition.[46] However, in addition to the question of quantification, when an effort was made to determine the criteria by which the worth of an economic system could be judged, two further categories associated with economic discourse reappeared: the imagination of 'society' and the imagination of the individual. In both of these areas al-Sadr's and others' attempts to imagine distinctively Islamic equivalents – the *ummah* and *'Homo islamicus'*, respectively – bear the imprint of their origins in secular economic discourse.

---

[44] 'Abd al-Rahman Yusri, *Al-Qimah allati ajaraha* (Cairo, 1996); Ibrahim Radwan, 'Al-qayyim al-islamiyah wa-l-tanmiyah al-iqtisadiyah', *Uktubar*, 31 March 1996. *Al-hisbah* is the function of supervising market transactions to ensure fair trading practices. It also took on the wider meanings of the general supervision of law and order in society and was extended by some to the public duty to 'command the right and forbid the wrong' – see especially Ibn Taymiyah (d. 1328 CE) *Al-Hisbah* (Kuwait, 1983), English translation: *Public Duties in Islam – The Institution of the Hisba*, tr. M. Holland, ed. Khurshid Ahmad (Leicester, 1982).

[45] Husain Shahata, 'Hulul islamiyah li-l-mashakil al-iqtisadiyah al-mu'asirah', *Al-Ahrar*, 14 June 1996.

[46] 'Uthman, *Nazriyat al-infitah*, pp. 3–7. As in a number of other cases, Ibn Khaldun is frequently cited in this regard as the specifically Islamic progenitor of all the social sciences. This validating claim tends to overlook the very particular readings to which he was subject in both Europe and the Arab world during the late nineteenth and early twentieth centuries.

4.3   Social welfare and individual interest

As in the discussions surrounding 'Islamic socialism', so in the emerging discourse of Islamic economics increasing use is made of the notion of 'social/public benefit/welfare' (*al-maslahat al-ijtima'iyah* or *al-maslahat al-'ammah*). Given the terms of economic discourse and the ways in which the 'discovery' of the economy is linked to the 'discovery' of society, it is not surprising that the debate about the Islamic economy comes full circle to the question of the social costs and benefits of any economic system. The 'Islamic economy' was being put forward as a way of restoring a lost sociability without implementing secular state socialism, abolishing individualism by linking people through economic activity.

Under Islamic auspices, economic interactions were to form a key part of an Islamic order: they would increase the sum of public happiness, whilst reinforcing social solidarities and strengthening their values.[47] As Mustafa Kamal Wasfi put it, 'the Islamic system of property is based on the lofty social goal intended by the justice of the system and on the link between this goal and the popular base which is aimed at realising and protecting it'. The economic system, with property as its focus, should therefore be ordered in such a way that the owner 'is aware of his social responsibility and this ensures that he always thinks of the public good'.[48] Thus trade and other forms of economic interaction are encouraged because they not only benefit society materially, but also reinforce beliefs and values, justified in terms both of social utility and of Qur'anic sanction.[49]

However, it is noticeable that the emphasis tends to be on the welfare of society in general, rather than a distinctively Islamic society. In this respect, an element of historical contingency is introduced, leading to the argument that some kinds of behaviour may be regarded as 'harmful to society' in certain epochs, but regarded with equanimity in others.[50] Two features are

---

[47] Zaidan Abu al-Makaram Hasan, *Al-Iqtisad al-islami* (Cairo, 1977), pp. 10–13, 41; Ahmad al-Sharabasi, *Al-Din wa-l-mujtama'* (Cairo, 1970), pp. 113–17; Shaikh Zaki Hasan al-Sayyid, 'Al-Ikhwah al-islamiyah tada'u ila al-takaful wa-l-tamasir', *Minbar al-Islam* 29/3 (May 1971), pp. 74–5; 'Isa 'Abduh, *Al-Iqtisad al-islami: madkhal wa-minhaj* (Cairo, 1974). pp. 23–5.

[48] Mustafa Kamal Wasfi, 'Al-milkiyah fi al-islam', *Al-Da'wah*, no. 11 (April 1977), pp. 22–3.

[49] See, for instance, Rashid al-Barrawi, *Al-Qisas al-qur'ani: tafsir ijtima'i* (Cairo, 1978), pp. 74–107 – a good example of the genre, whereby Qur'anic accounts (in this case, those of Shu'aib and of Joseph) are interpreted in the light of contemporary understandings of 'social needs'. Mahmud Fahmi, *Madhahib islamiyah: madhhab iqtisadi fi itar min mantaqat al-'asr al-hadith* (Cairo, 1983), pp. 9–16 uses similar argumentation, although deploys different versus of the Qur'an as its authority.

[50] See, for example, 'Abd al-Halim 'Abd al-Fattah 'Umar, *Al-Masalih al-mursalah wa-bina' al-ahkam 'alaiha: dirasah usuliyah* (Cairo, 1990), pp. 173–7; Shawqi Ismail Shahata, 'Mafahim wa-mabadi' fi al-iqtisad al-islami,' *Minbar al-Islam* 33/9 (September 1975), pp. 42–6; see also al-'Arabi, *Al-Milkiyat al-khasah wa-hududuha fi al-islam*.

striking about this discussion. In the first place, there seems to be an argument that economic arrangements should be judged to be desirable if they contribute to the sum of 'social welfare' and the spiritual welfare of the individual, defined in humanist, rather than specifically Islamic terms.[51] Two very differently situated individuals, such as Baqir al-Sadr in Iraq and Muhammad Shawqi al-Fanjari in Egypt, also seem to admit a degree of historical relativism in the determination of values. On the face of it, this is a surprising suggestion to emerge in a discussion apparently driven by the fear of the erosion of belief in the timeless nature of Islamic values.[52]

The importance of this line of argument is that it could appear to elevate 'society' and 'social needs' above all else, making them arbiters of that which is desirable and the ultimate justification for the adoption of any particular set of economic arrangements. In a secular context this would be unremarkable, even if arguments might rage about how to determine the nature of 'social needs'. In a context in which the case is being made for a distinctively Islamic programme, this argument is problematic, since it suggests that the economy should be based on 'social needs'. When these are equated with 'public benefit' – understood as a mixture of social justice and a certain level of material well-being – they may overshadow the specifically Islamic character of the arrangements. Taken further, this argument makes it theoretically conceivable that the Islamic features of the economy might have to give way before more pressing demands for greater social utility.

As the debate about the importance of social utility developed in Egypt, particularly in the 1990s, some Muslim intellectuals, such as Yusuf Kamal Muhammad and 'Ali al-Salus, expressed their unease about the consequences of engaging with positivist economics, whether capitalist or socialist, precisely because of the introduction of criteria of materialist utility.[53] The question centred on how best to reassert the Islamic character of the enterprise in order to limit the secular logic of the economy. One way of doing this was to define 'public interest' to include obedience to the *shari'ah*. Thus, Tariq al-Bishri, for example, when asked about the possibility that understandings of public interest might conflict with the texts of the scriptures themselves,

[51] Interview with Dr Muhammad Shawqi al-Fanjari, March 1996, in *Al-Liwa al-Islami*, 21 March 1996.
[52] Al-Sadr, *Iqtisaduna*, pp. 260–4; Muhammad Shawqi al-Fanjari, 'Wajhah nazr islamiyah fi hall mashakil al-qata' al-'amm', *Al-Akhbar*, 30 November 1990.
[53] Yusuf Kamal Muhammad 'Adwa'ala al-iqtisad al-islami 'aja'ib . . . wa-ghara'ib', *Al-Da'wah*, no. 60 (April 1981), pp. 19–20; Dr 'Ali Ahmad al-Salus, 'Yaradd duktur al-Salus ila fadilatihi al-mufti', *Al-Nur*, 6 February 1991; Kamal, *'Adwa' 'ala al-fikr al-iqtisadi*, pp. 5–9; Muhammad Ra'fat 'Uthman, 'Al-khilaf ma' fadilat al-mufti', *Al-Nur*, 21 August 1991 – the latter two were taking issue with the ruling of the Grand Mufti of Egypt, Shaikh Tantawi, concerning the acceptability of certain kinds of interest-bearing bonds on grounds of social benefit or utility.

referred to twentieth-century jurists, such as Shaikh Ahmad Ibrahim or Shaikh 'Abd al-Wahhab Khallaf, who had cited the assertion of Ibn Qayyim al-Jawziyah (d. 1350 CE) that 'the whole of the *shari'* is of benefit' (*al-shari' kuluhu masalih*). He also referred to Imam al-Shatibi (d. 1388 CE) who held to the – conventional – view that interest or benefit consists in the protection of religion, of the self, of one's offspring, of the mind or reason and of wealth. Since this was the intention behind all Islamic legislation, according to al-Bishri, there could be no contradiction between human interests and the *shari'ah*, making obedience to its rulings intrinsic to our very understanding of social welfare.[54]

Of course, such a definition could also open the way for an understanding of benefit or utility that was centred on the individual. This was indeed one of the strategies whereby the potential conflict between social and individual claims and requirements could be reconciled. As al-Fanjari and al-Ba'li's writings show, by imagining an individual at the centre of 'society' and 'economy' who is somehow inalienably Muslim, any potential conflicts between social and individual benefit (as well as between human interests and the scriptural authorities) are theoretically reconciled.[55] Nevertheless, this individual is equally a construct of the same imaginary that has produced the economy and its associated society, and cannot escape entirely from some of the implications of its origins.

Economics is full of assumptions about abstracted individuals and their motivations which are as culturally determined and contingent upon a particular understanding of human nature as is any conception of 'society' itself. The act of imagining society in terms largely given by a pre-established social imaginary, deriving from the epistemological and ontological systems associated with capitalist industrialisation, helped to form views of 'society' in the Islamic world as elsewhere. Similarly, this singular being whose needs and wants, in combination with others, form the collectivities of society and economy, would be implicated in the understanding of an Islamic economy – as well as being the prime site for the moral struggle so beloved of writers on the Islamic economy. Thus the individual, as acting subject, but also as acted-upon object of an idealised Islamic ethical order, becomes a focus of the economy.

Al-Sadr and others developed the idea of the distinctively 'Islamic individual' – or the 'Islamic personality' (*al-shakhsiyat al-islamiyah*) as an antidote to secularising tendencies and as a control mechanism for the society and

---

[54] Tariq al-Bishri interviewed in March 1997 – 'Amir 'Abd al-Mun'im, 'Al-mustashar Tariq al-Bishri fi hiwar ma' "Al-Sha'b"', *Al-Sha'b*, 21 March 1997.
[55] al-Ba'li, *Minhaj al-fiqh*, pp. 1–9; al-Fanjari, *Dhatiyat al-siyasiyat al-iqtisadiyah*, pp. 30–2.

the economy.[56] This is the 'Homo islamicus' on which the theory and the practice of the Islamic economy is to be based. Through their understanding of and adherence to the rules of the shari'ah such individuals are assigned a key role in rescuing and maintaining the distinctively Islamic character of the society and the economy. If society is made up of such individuals, then 'social needs' and the demands of 'social welfare' cannot, by definition, contradict or overrule the requirements of Islamic obligation. Equally, an economy founded on the transactions of such individuals and the expression of their wants can become neither an instrument for unlimited acquisition and competition, nor the vehicle for social injustice. The 'Islamic personality' thereby becomes an ideal construct which will ensure the distinctively Islamic character of the economy and of the social order which that economy will develop. It is a projection onto the abstracted individual of the qualities of that order, its values and its characteristics.

Although an imaginary device, it is suggested that the 'Islamic personality' sums up the essence of what it is to be a Muslim in reality. Al-Sadr, for instance, uses it to claim that these are the characteristics which make Muslims different from all other people.[57] He goes on to assert that Muslims will always be protected by their faith from succumbing to the forces of capitalism, communism or Western influence in general – a claim belied by the very purpose of his writings and those of his many coreligionists concerned about the plight of Muslims in the modern world. If Muslims had no doubts about the correct way of behaving, whatever the circumstances, then they would be immune to the material temptations of capitalism and the intellectual seductions of Marxism. Moreover, their transactions would be unfailingly Islamic, making the need for an 'Islamic economics' largely redundant. In fact, the notion of the 'Islamic personality' is an ideal construct, an argumentative device to allow the reconciling of apparently contrary currents. It was bound to reflect the preoccupations of those concerned about capitalism and socialism; it cannot also serve as a sociological category with any real purchase upon the empirically verifiable world. In such a guise, it is too easy to refute.[58]

At the same time, al-Sadr and others develop another strand of thought which suggests that the 'Islamic personality' is less a reality than a model of

---

[56] Al-Sadr, Iqtisaduna, p. 260; Husain Ghanim, Al-Sil'at al-iqtisadiyah: dirasah islamiyah fi al-nazriyat al-iqtisadiyah (Cairo, 1986), pp. 3–16.
[57] Al-Sadr, Iqtisaduna, pp. nun and sad.
[58] Mauss, The Gift, pp. 91–103, suggests a similar process in Western economic thought and this is developed in detail in G. Kirchgässner, Homo oeconomicus: das ökonomische Modell individuellen Verhaltens und seine Anwendung in der Witschafts- und Sozialwissenschaften (Tübingen, 2000), pp. 96–156, 201–33.

ethical probity towards which all individuals must aspire.[59] It is said to epitomise the balance between social justice and the fulfilment of individual wants or needs, becoming the fulcrum upon which the project must turn.[60] Only once a sufficient number of similarly inclined individuals have been created, al-Sadr suggests, can an Islamic economic doctrine be implemented, shifting the focus to the circumstances that would encourage the development of such a personality.[61]

It is in this context that the question of the status of the self-interested individual arises. In al-Sadr's writings, for instance, there is originally a suggestion that economics as a discipline is most effective within the capitalist West because this was the culture from which it sprang and it represents an accurate description of the self-interested individuals of capitalism.[62] However, in presenting the 'Islamic personality' as the ideal towards which people should aspire, the precise nature of the individual who plays a key role in the scheme of the economy becomes central. The point is echoed in the argument of Yusuf Kamal, for instance, that the Islamic economy should be based on 'the freedom of the individual to pursue his activities so that his spirit prospers' – a freedom only restrained by the need not to harm the freedoms of others. In this view, Islamic values ensure a freedom that begins with the welfare of the individual (*maslahat al-fard*) and ends with the well-being of the public (*al-salih al-'amm*).[63] Imagining the 'economy' and the 'society' has thus produced something which looks very like the self-interested, calculating and rational individual of capitalist economics, even if endowed with an 'Islamic personality'.

This notion has been developed at considerable length by the South and Southeast Asian writers on the Islamic economy in particular – 'the calculus of utility which incorporates the hereafter' is introduced to suggest that individuals think beyond immediate gratification and that the time-frame of the utilitarian calculus must be extended to eternity. The 'Islamic calculus' retains the utilitarian idea of the calculation of pain and pleasure as the basis for moral action, but extends it beyond this world to the next: an individual must take into account the consequences of his or her actions not simply in this world, but also in the hereafter, where God's punishment or reward must be factored into the equation. It is through this longer-term calculation

---

[59] Husain Ghanim, *Al-Madkhal li-dirasat al-ta'rikh al-iqtisadi wa-l-hadari: ru'iyah islamiyah* (Al-Mansurah, 1990), pp. 123–39.

[60] Al-Fanjari, *Dhatiyat al-siyasiyat al-iqtisadiyah*, pp. 30–2; Ahmad al-'Assal and Fathi Ahmad 'Abd al-Karim, *Al-Nizam al-iqtisadi fi al-islam* (Cairo, 1980), p. 31; interview with Dr Shawqi al-Fanjari in March 1996 in *Al-Liwa al-Islami*, 21 March 1996.

[61] Al-Sadr, *Iqtisaduna*, pp. 652–8.

[62] Al-Sadr, *Iqtisaduna*, pp. 227–31.

[63] Kamal, *'Adwa' 'ala al-fikr al-iqtisadi*, pp. 13–15.

that al-Sadr, and those who have taken inspiration from him, as well as those who have found themselves caught up in the logic of his approach, claim the 'social problem' can be solved.[64]

Despite criticisms of '*Homo economicus*' as thin and culturally determined, there is some suggestion that it might constitute a kind of universal archetype. Bakri 'Atiyah claims, for instance, that the precepts of the Islamic moral economy are intended to moderate the behaviour of individuals who would otherwise behave in the self-centred and calculating way depicted in the possessive individual of capitalist economics.[65] It is suggested that a success-ful economic system such as capitalism does speak to something ineradicable in human nature. It develops these traits, rewards them and thus helps to make the economic agents which reproduce the economic system itself. The results may be morally reprehensible, as in the case of capitalism, but they can also be materially impressive. In accepting the picture of the being assumed to lie at its heart as a representation of reality, the function of Islam becomes clear: to introduce restraints on the hedonistic individual. Only then can an orderly society and an 'Islamic economy' be instituted.[66]

4.4   *Zakat* and *riba*: instruments of the moral economy

In the light of these concerns, there was a search for the best way of shaping the individual who would become the foundation for an Islamic economy, having internalised the ethical commands of Islam. It is in this context that Muslim intellectuals writing about the Islamic economy focus on two par-ticular rulings from the Islamic tradition: the injunction to pay *zakat* and the prohibition of *riba*. *Zakat* – a general levy on the wealth of individuals commanded by God in the Qur'an and enjoined by the Prophet Muhammad – is redistributive in intent since it takes from those who have and distributes to those who have not. More importantly, *zakat* represents a key component of the moral economy since it epitomises a number of ideas which help to define that economy: the notion that the individual holds property as a trustee

---

[64] Al-Sadr, *Iqtisaduna*, pp. 281–9; Muhammad Anas Zarqa, 'Islamic economics: an approach to human welfare', in Khurshid Ahmad (ed.), *Studies in Islamic Economics* (Jeddah, 1980), pp. 3–18.

[65] Dr Bakri 'Atiyah (Dean of the Department of Trade at Al-Azhar) at a seminar on 'The Islamic Economy in a Changing World', March 1992: 'Al-iqtisad al-islami fi 'alam mutaghayyir qadiyah tanaqushuha nadwat *Al-Ahram*', *Al-Ahram*, 17 March 1992.

[66] This also helps to explain the shift in terrain for a number of writers from the public field to the question of the education, upbringing and formation of the individual. Of course, this in turn leads to questions about the best institutional arrangements to encourage this – and the proper framework of public laws which will encourage, even enforce, the kind of formation that the Islamist writers had in mind. See chapter 5.

for God; the idea, therefore, that property must be used for a higher end, such as the sustenance and support of those in a less fortunate position than yourself; the idea of mutual social responsibility which ensures the 'integration of the individual into a truly Islamic society'.[67]

Some of the writers on the Islamic economy also argue that *zakat* not only represents a pillar of the moral economy of Islam, but that it is a more effective means of redistribution and economic development than existing secular fiscal instruments. It was thus held up in the 1990s as an efficient means of putting capital into circulation, of ensuring that money is channelled from the rich to the poor, of helping to cure the problems of poverty and unemployment and also of allowing the state to set up a comprehensive social security system.[68] It is noticeable that such arguments have been prominent primarily in countries such as Egypt where *zakat* has not been instituted by the state as a basis for its fiscal policies, and could thus be made to stand for much that was desired, both in moral terms and in terms of the material requirements of a developing economy.

However, the actual experience of *zakat* in those few countries where the government has organised its collection and distribution has been mixed. Not only are its effects on the overall economy negligible, but in some countries, such as Malaysia, even those sympathetic to the project have been obliged to acknowledge that it has had adverse outcomes as far as the peasantry is concerned, channelling resources away from the under-funded countryside towards the heavily subsidised cities.[69] In Pakistan, *zakat* revenue was estimated to be no more than 0.2 per cent of GDP by 1994 and in Iran, where *zakat* has been collected by government agencies, it has had no measurable impact on the inequalities of power at the heart of the political economy.[70]

---

[67] Mahmud Abu al-Sa'ud, 'Al-iqtisad fi al-dawlat al-islamiyah', *Al-Da'wah*, no 3 (September 1976), pp. 28–9; Muhammad 'Imarah at the *Al-Ahram* colloquium on *zakat*, March 1993: Fathi Abu al-'Ala, 'Nadwat *Al-Ahram* tanaqish al-zakat', *Al-Ahram*, 6 March 1993; Shaikh Yusuf al-Qardawi and Dr Muhammad Shawqi al-Fanjari interviewed in June 1995, 'Al-takaful baina al-muslimun faridah wa-laisa tarfan', *Al-Liwa al-Islami*, 22 June 1995.

[68] For instance, Dr Hamdi 'Abd al-'Azim at the *Al-Ahram* colloquium in March 1993: Fathi Abu al-'Ala, 'Al-zakat li-'ilaj mushakilina', *Al-Ahram*, 7 March 1993. See also Shaikh Mahmud Muhammad 'Abduh and Dr 'Abd al-Sami' al-Misri interviewed in May 1996: Sayyid Husain, 'Al-qada' 'ala al-batalah tahaququh amwal al-zakat', *Al-Jumhuriyah*, 31 May 1996.

[69] Abdul Aziz Bin Muhammad, *Zakat and Rural Development in Malaysia* (Kuala Lumpur, 1993), pp. 152–73. Scott makes the point that the peasantry of Malaysia were content with voluntary *zakat*, but tried to avoid paying it when it was collected compulsorily by the state – James Scott, *Resistance without Protest: Peasant Opposition to the Zakat in Malaysia and to the Tithe in France*, 4th James C. Jackson Memorial Lecture, 1986 (Townsville, 1987), pp. 424–37.

[70] Ishrat Hussein, *Pakistan – The Economy of an Elitist State* (Karachi, 1999), pp. 197–9; Izzud-Din Pal, *Pakistan, Islam and Economics* (Karachi, 1999), pp. 67–89. See also Seyyed Vali Reza Nasr, *Islamic Leviathan* (Oxford, 2001), pp. 122–4 and 144–6.

If the experience of *zakat* has not justified the hopes invested in it, then the prohibition of *riba* has become a more widespread token of a distinctive Islamic approach to financial matters – and a feature of immense symbolic resonance. *Riba* enjoys a central place in the imagination of the Islamic economy and it can plausibly be argued that its negation lies at the very heart of Islamic views of a moral economy – just as it looms large in the ideas of many Muslim intellectuals concerning the fundamental injustice of capitalism.[71] *Riba* is explicitly forbidden in the Qur'an, held up therein as something that would be a bar to individual salvation.[72] Although the root meaning of *riba* is 'increase', it is clear from the Qur'an that a distinction is being made between it and the kind of increase that might come from an investment, or the profits that would accrue from an economic transaction.[73] These are explicitly permitted, whilst *riba* is singled out for prohibition. Over the centuries the consensus of the jurists has been that *riba* should be understood as any interest charged on a loan, regardless of the willingness of the borrower to enter into an agreement by which he or she will have to repay interest as well as principal.

This consensus was based on the authority of the received texts, but also on moral repugnance at a number of features associated with the charging of interest on capital. For some, there was an assumption that people only seek loans because driven by need and that others would therefore be earning money on the basis of their misfortune. There was, in addition, rejection of the unequal burden of risk sustained by the borrower who would have to enter into a binding commitment to repay money with interest, despite the uncertainty of economic outcomes. These concerns about the injustice of interest were compounded by an Aristotelian aversion to the 'unnatural' process whereby, in the payment of interest on a capital sum, money is made from money.[74]

However, the new forms of knowledge introduced in the nineteenth century brought with them new ways of thinking about society, about the contingency of ethics and about systems of textual interpretation. At the same time,

---

[71] Al-'Assal and 'Abd al-Karim, *Al-Nizam al-iqtisadi fi al-islam*, pp. 80–5; Taqiuddin al-Nabahani, *The Economic System in Islam* (New Delhi: Milli Publications, 2002), pp. 172–6; Syed Nawab Haider Naqvi, *Ethics and Economics* (Leicester, 1981), pp. 109–23.

[72] *Al-Qur'an*, Surah 2 (*al-Baqarah*) verses 275, 276, 278, Surah 3 (*Al -'Umran*) verse 130, Surah 4 (*al-Nisa'*) verse 161, Surah 30 (*al-Rum*) verse 39.

[73] *Al-Qur'an*, Surah 2 (*al-Baqarah*) verse 275: 'they [those who "devour usury" (*ya'kulun al-riba*)] say: "Trade is like usury", but Allah hath permitted trade and forbidden usury.' *The Meaning of the Glorious Qur'an*, tr. Abdullah Yusuf Ali (London, 1983).

[74] Nevertheless, it was acknowledged by some of the most distinguished *fuqaha'* that the identification of *riba* was not always straightforward – see Ibn Kathir, "the subject of *riba* is one of the most difficult subjects for many of the scholars [*ahl al-'ilm*]", cited in Muhammad Asad, *The Message of the Qur'an* (Gibraltar, 1980), p. 622; J. Schacht, 'Riba', *in Encyclopedia of Islam* (Leiden, 1995), vol. VIII, pp. 491–3.

financial innovations opened up hitherto unconsidered forms of profit, challenging the jurists to decide which aspects of this new world of transactions was *haram* (forbidden) and which *halal* (permitted). These developments led to a re-examination of *riba*, made more urgent by the centrality of various forms of interest-charging at the heart of the capitalist project – a project which was drawing in Muslims in vast numbers across the world as investors, borrowers and consumers.

One of the most famous early instances of authoritative reinterpretation of the permissibility of interest was the 1904 judgement of Shaikh Muhammad 'Abduh, the Grand Mufti of Egypt at the time. When asked his opinion about whether it was permissible to accept returns, at a fixed and predetermined rate, on deposits with the Egyptian post office's savings fund (*sanduq al-tawfir*), he ruled that this was indeed permissible.[75] This was highly controversial at the time, but it helped to open the way for a more public acceptance of the idea of earning money on cash deposits. Unease remained, however, and is visible in the writings of Rashid Rida, 'Abduh's closest disciple. He tried to gloss 'Abduh's judgement in a number of ways. For instance, he suggested that 'Abduh had sanctioned returns on money deposited in this way on the understanding that the funds would be used for small investments by the post office in which the rules of *mudarabah* partnership would be observed. Rida also claimed that 'Abduh held that different rules applied to money lent to the state (which of course included the post office) since the state would act in a manner beneficial both to the depositor and to the community. Rida also found it necessary a couple of years later, in an article about *riba* published in *Al-Manar*, to remind people of 'Abduh's fierce condemnation of the interest charged by banks in Egypt.[76]

Regardless of 'Abduh's precise intention, his ambivalence about equating all forms of interest with *riba* echoed some of the re-evaluation that was taking place in the Islamic world concerning the limits of legality in a changing environment. In the case of *riba*, the argumentation followed patterns similar to those used with regard to other Islamic prescriptions. First of all, there appears an argument about the historically contingent meaning of the term, advanced by those *'ulama* and lay intellectuals who re-examined *riba* in the Qur'an and the *sunnah* and concluded that it referred to a specific practice in pre-Islamic Arabia. This was the doubling and redoubling of the

---

[75] 'Abduh, *Al-A'mal al-kamilah,* vol. I: *Al-Kitabat al-siyasiyah* (Beirut, 1979), pp. 678–9. 'Abduh's editor, 'Imarah, makes the point, however, that this was not among 'Abduh's published writings and we have to rely on Rida's account for the ruling.

[76] Muhammad Rashid Rida, 'Sanduq al-tawfir fi idarat al-barid', *Al-Manar* 7 (1904), pp. 28–9; Chibli Mallat, 'Tantawi on banking operations in Egypt', in Muhammad Khalid Masud, Brinkley Messick and David S. Powers (eds.), *Islamic Legal Interpretation: Muftis and their Fatwas* (Cambridge, MA, 1996), pp. 286–7.

principal if the date for repayment fell due and the debtor was unable to pay. In the circumstances of the time, the most likely outcome of such a crippling debt was the enslavement of the debtor to the creditor. It was argued, therefore, that it was the injustice and disproportional nature of this particular practice which was condemned in the Qur'an and the *sunnah*, not the forms of commercial interest charged by institutions operating in a market-based capitalist system.[77]

Following on from this, it was argued that the intention behind the prohibition of *riba* was the desire to prohibit extortionate interest as an instrument of injustice. The implication was that there was an imbalance in power and wealth between the lender and the borrower. This allowed the lender to exploit the needs of the borrower and to dictate the rate of return, maximising profits by further impoverishing the borrower. The historical conditions of seventh-century Arabia were again cited as relevant, since it was claimed that people were generally forced to borrow because of natural disaster or family tragedy. It was the injustice – and morally reprehensible nature – of charging interest in such circumstances which was seen as the reason behind the prohibition of *riba*, again limiting the nature of the transactions which fell under this prohibition.[78]

In the context of such a historically contingent argument, there was no necessary injustice in the charging of interest. If the rationale behind the prohibition of *riba* was to prevent injustice, then changed circumstances might dissolve the straightforward equation of the term with interest, as understood in a modern economy. As Shaikh 'Abd al-Mun'im Nimr in Egypt pointed out, changed conditions might alter judgements about what is or is not in people's interest at different times.[79] Using reasoning similar to that deployed some eighty years before by Muhammad 'Abduh, the Egyptian Deputy Prime Minister for Economic Affairs 'Abd al-Fattah Ibrahim justified national savings certificates and post office savings accounts in 1982 by stating that 'the government invests [these funds] in basic infrastructure projects . . . schools, religious institutes, etc. . . . all of these touch on the needs of the people . . . They do not bring in profits, but social returns.'[80] In

---

[77] Muhammad Sa'id al-'Ashmawi, *Al-Riba wa-l-fa'idah fi al-islam* (Cairo, 1996); Fazlur Rahman, 'Riba and interest', *Islamic Studies* 3/1 (March 1964), pp. 3–8, 24–41; Fazlur Rahman, *Islam*, 2nd edition (Chicago, 1979), pp. 248–254, 265.

[78] Asad, *Message of the Qur'an*, pp. 622–3; Fazlur Rahman, *Islam and Modernity* (Chicago, 1982), p. 18.

[79] Shaikh 'Abd al-Mun'im Nimr, 'Hukm al-riba . . . hal buniya 'ala al-hikmah aw 'ala al-'illah?', *Al-Siyasi*, 19 February 1984; 'Al-'Illah aw al-hikmah fi tahrim al-riba', *Al-Siyasi*, 8 April 1984; 'Hikmah tahrim al-riba' *Al-Siyasi* 15 April 1984; 'Hukm al-iqtirad li-mashru' iqtisadi yadarr munafa'ah 'ammah', *Al-Siyasi*, 22 April 1984.

[80] 'Abd al-Rahman 'Aqal, 'Amwal shahadat al-istithmar wa-sanadiq al-tawfir . . . baina shabahat al-halal wa-l-haram', *Al-Ahram* 7 July 1982.

much of the literature, it has also been claimed that the public interest (*maslahah*) would be harmed were there a blanket prohibition on all forms of interest, since refusal to pay interest would prevent Muslim states from raising loans for development. As far as individuals are concerned, then, it has been argued that failure to pay the lender interest would result in injustice, since inflation would effectively be a charge on the lender.[81]

Most notoriously – and again in Egypt – the 1989 *fatwa* of Shaikh Muhammad Sayyid Tantawi, Grand Mufti of Egypt, declared legal the interest-bearing bonds issued by the Egyptian government and underwritten by Egyptian banks. Again, Tantawi justified his decision partly with reference to public utility, since the bonds encouraged savings and contributed to the state's development plans.[82] He cited a number of twentieth-century Islamic authorities, such as Rashid Rida and Mahmud Shaltut, to support his views that there were differing interpretations about the exact form of *riba* and that post office savings and government bonds were legitimate because they contributed to the public good. Like Shaltut, he also wanted to make a distinction between a loan between two individuals and the deposit that an individual might make to a state saving scheme. These were not analogous and therefore different rules applied.[83] More controversially, but very much in keeping with Tantawi's acknowledgement that a changed economic and social environment demanded new forms of expertise, in his *fatwa* he cited a lay economic expert to support his views about the benefits of the savings schemes and their differentiation from mere cash loans between one party and another.[84]

He acknowledged that the majority of *'ulama* did not make an exception of savings certificates issued by governments, but also stated that some did so because 'the transactions of individuals with governments are like the transactions of fathers and sons' and because 'the intention [of these bonds] is

[81] Ibrahim Warde, *Islamic Finance in the Global Economy* (Edinburgh, 2000), pp. 55–6, citing also Ziaul Haque, *Riba: The Moral Economy of Usury, Interest and Profit* (Selangor, 1995); Muhammad Nayal, 'Shahadat al-istithmar – la istighlal fiha wa-la darar', *Mayu*, 20 April 1981.
[82] Rida 'Ukasha, 'Limadha zada al-iqbal 'ala shahadat al-istithmar ba'd fatwa Dar al-Ifta bi-nisba 25%', *Al-Liwa al-Islami*, 21 September 1989; see also Muhammad Sayyid Tantawi, *Mu'amalat al-bunuk wa-ahkamuha al-shar'iyah* (Cairo, 1997), pp. 165–211.
[83] 'Bayan al-duktur Tantawi mufti al-jumhuriyah hawl al-mu'amalat al-maliyah li-l-bunuk' in *Al-Ahram al-Iqtisadi*, *Al-Fatawa al-islamiyah fi al-qadaya al-iqtisadiyah*, Kitab Al-Ahram al-Iqtisadi XXVI, (Cairo, 1990), pp. 105–112. See Mahmud Shaltut, *Al-Fatawa: dirasah li-mushkilat al-muslim al-mu'asir fi hayatihi al-yawmiyah wa-l-'ammah* (Cairo, 1964), pp. 351–5; Muhammad Rashid Rida, 'Sunduq al-tawfir fi idarat al-barid', *Al-Manar* 7 (1904), pp. 28–9 and 'Ribh sunduq al-tawfir', *Al-Manar* 19 (1917), pp. 527–9.
[84] Mallat, 'Tantawi on banking operations in Egypt', pp. 291–2. The text of Tantawi's *fatwa* is reprinted in Muhsin Ahmad Khudairi, *Al-Bunuk al-islamiyah* (Cairo, 1990); see also interview with Muhammad Tantawi in December 1989 with Mahmud Mahdi: 'Mufti al-jumhuriyah yajib 'an kul ma athir fatwahu bi-sha'n shahadat al-istithmar', *Al-Ahram*, 8 December 1989.

service and the increase of production for the welfare of society'.[85] Throughout the 1990s Tantawi maintained this position and even extended it to cover
certain kinds of bank deposits, sanctioning fixed returns on an investment or
deposit. He claimed that this was not *riba*, but a fee paid to the owner of
capital by the user of capital and that any profit the latter might make over and
above the specified return paid to the depositor is like a wage for the user of
capital. On grounds of clarity, security and reliability, therefore, as well as
general welfare, he saw no problem in this kind of economic transaction – just
as, under the heading of *al-masalih al-mursalah* (benefit not specified in the
text), he believed it was in fact incumbent upon the government to oblige
banks to guarantee depositors a secure return on their investment, precisely
because 'this is considered to guard the welfare of the people'.[86] This led
Tantawi finally to state that he saw no particular difference in this regard
between banks which called themselves 'Islamic' and those which did not, but
which offered fixed returns to their depositors, providing they were all honest
and trustworthy in their dealings and invested their depositors' money in
permissible (*halal*) activities.[87] Although controversial and fiercely attacked
by those who had defined their niche in the financial markets with reference
to the claimed Islamic nature of their transactions, this opinion was also
shared by Tantawi's successor as Mufti of Egypt, Shaikh Nasr Farid Wasil,
who stated in 1997 simply that the controversy over bank interest should end
since 'there is no such thing as an Islamic and a non-Islamic bank'.[88]

Tantawi himself had no doubts about the impermissibility and moral
degradation of *riba*, and his views were a mixture of the traditionalist and
the modern, claiming that God's reason for forbidding *riba* was because 'it
damages the spirit of cooperation among people, and gives birth to enmity
and hatred . . . it also leads to class formation, creating a class of people whose
money increases without them making any effort'.[89] Where he differed from

[85] Rabi' Shahin, 'Ara' khatirah wa-jaray'a li-fadilat al-mufti lam tanshuraha suhuf al-hukumah',
Al-Sha'b, 20 September 1988. This pronouncement was in the curious context of the Mufti
being called as witness for the defence by the lawyer acting for the accused in the trial of the
Islamist group 'Al-Najun min al-Nar'. The defence was trying to implicate the Egyptian state
in un-Islamic activities and thus to justify the actions of the accused who had acted and
preached against agents of the state on grounds of Islamic probity.
[86] Muhammad Sayyid Tantawi, 'Al-haram wa-l-halal fi mu'amalat al-bunuk wa-l-mal',
Al-Ahram, 29 May 1991; 'Hal taghyir lafz fa'idat al-hafiz yaja'ul shahadat al-istithmar
halalan?' *Al-Ahram*, 24 April 1992.
[87] Ra'fat Amin, 'Tahdid al-irbah muqadaman bi-l-bunuk halal wa-aqrab ila ruh al-islam',
Al-Ahram, 2 March 1993; '"Uktubar" tasa'ul wa-l-mufti yajib', *Uktubar*, no. 959 (12 March
1995), pp. 14–15; Karim 'Abd al-Raziq, 'Fadilat al-Mufti fi liqa'ihu ma'talibat jami'at
al-qahirah', *Al-Akhbar*, 19 December 1995.
[88] Warde, *Islamic Finance in the Global Economy*, pp. 57–8.
[89] Muhammad Sayyid Tantawi, 'Al-haram wa-l-halal fi mu'amalat al-bunuk wa-l-mal',
Al-Ahram, 26 May 1991. and 27 May 1991.

many of his contemporaries in Egypt and elsewhere was in his views about which economic transactions could legitimately be equated with *riba*. Here he followed, as he acknowledged, a minority view which suggested that *riba* either referred only to a specific set of practices in pre-Islamic Arabia, or represented any form of exploitation of the weak by the strong. The radical implications of this extension of '*riba*-by-analogy' were considerable, but were not developed by the mufti – understandably in the light of his position as an official of an authoritarian state.[90]

Against Tantawi, the consensus of jurists is that *riba* refers to all interest-bearing transactions. In 1983 the Council of Islamic Ideology Report stated that 'there is complete unanimity among all schools of thought in Islam that the term *riba* stands for interest in all its types and forms'. The claim to unanimity is questionable, but there was little doubt about the broad agreement on this point amongst Islamic scholars, as endorsed by the Fiqh Academy of the Organisation of Islamic Conference in 1986.[91] This applies across a wide range of Islamic writers and scholars who might differ on other questions, but who have come together to see *riba* as equivalent to interest (*al-fa'idah*) on all kinds of loans, however large or small, whether these involve banks, government agencies or individuals.[92] For these scholars any contract which fixed a predetermined return on a loan or investment is *riba* and thus prohibited.[93]

Tantawi's views on the historically and socially contingent meanings of *riba* so alarmed some Muslim intellectuals that they attacked his authority as

[90] Muhammad Sayyid Tantawi, 'Asi'lah 'an al-riba', *Al-Ahram*, 21 November 1993; 'Abd al-'Aziz 'Abd al-Halim, 'Kul al-mu'amalat al-bankiyah wa-ghairuha halal ma damat qad tammat bi-l-taradi al-mashru'', *Al-Liwa al-Islami*, 12 December 1996.

[91] Mervyn K. Lewis and Latifa Algaoud, *Islamic Banking* (Cheltenham, 2001) p. 37, citing *Council of Islamic Ideology Report* (1983) p. 7 (the Council had been set up by the Pakistani government in 1962, under the Ministry of Religious Affairs); Ziauddin Ahmed, Munawar Iqbal and M. Fahim Khan (eds.), *Fiscal Policy and Resource Allocation in Islam* (Islamabad, 1983), pp. 8–14; Fuad Al-Omar and Mohammed Abdel-Haq, *Islamic Banking: Theory, Practice and Challenges* (Karachi, 1996), p. 8.

[92] Yusuf Kamal, 'Fa'idat al-bunuk haram', *Al-Da'wah*, no. 59 (March 1981), p 19; see the memorandum from the Shaikh al-Azhar in Egypt at the time: Shaikh Jadd al-Haqq 'Ali Jadd al-Haqq, 'Fi madhkirah akhirah li-majmu' al-buhuth al-islamiyah', *Al-Ahram*, 13 March 1992.

[93] For a similarity of views from a range of scholars see Hamdi al-Basir, Muhammad Fath Allah and Muhammad Salman, 'Mashru' wazir al-iqtisad – khuda'hu i'lamiyah!' *Al-Nur*, 31 January 1990, in which the following are interviewed: Dr 'Abd al-Hamid al-Ghazzali (Professor of Islamic Economics at the College of Economics and Political Science, Cairo University), 'Abd al-Sami' al-Misri (adviser to the International Union of Islamic Banks), Dr 'Abd al-'Azim Zahir (Professor at the College of Trade, Suez Canal University), Dr 'Ali Muhammad al-Shafi'i (Lecturer at the College of Trade, Suez Canal University), Dr al-Sayyid Rizq al-Tawil (Dean of College of Islamic Studies, Al-Azhar University), Dr 'Abd al-Rahman al-'Adwi (Professor of Fiqh at the College of Islamic Da'wah, Al-Azhar University), Shaikh Ahmad Hasan Muslim (Member of the Fatwa Committee at Al-Azhar University), Dr Salim Khalil (Professor of Fiqh at the College of Shari'ah Law at Al-Azhar University).

Mufti of Egypt, claiming that it was impermissible that he should depart so markedly from the consensus.[94] For the most part, however, those who equated *riba* with interest focused on the impermissibility of making money from money – which characterised their general understanding of interest on capital. In the words of the Shaikh al-Azhar, Jadd al-Haqq 'Ali Jadd al-Haqq, 'the *fuqaha*' agree that *riba* is the increase of money without compensation by returning money from money' (*ziyadah mal bila muqabil fi mu'awadah mal bi-mal*).[95] The claim was that earning money in this way was morally reprehensible because it involved no effort and it was unjust because it did not share the risk (of profit or lack of profit) equally between the creditor and the debtor. A fixed return on money over a fixed term seemed to violate a divinely sanctioned ethical order.[96]

At the same time, a number of Muslim intellectuals used social welfare arguments against the charging of interest, portraying it as one of the causes for the malfunctioning of the global economy. As 'Abd al-Hamid al-Ghazzali claimed, interest (*riba*) 'makes the economy susceptible to various diseases. It leads to exploitation, to loss of production, to the wasteful use of resources and ends by increasing economic problems.'[97] Writing in the Muslim Brotherhood's *Al-Da'wah*, al-Hamza Da'bas and others mixed a rejection of interest on grounds of its social disutility with more traditional reasons, such as the consensus of the *'ulama* or the implicit 'oppression' (*zulm*) in any interest-bearing relationship.[98] Other contributors to *Al-Da'wah* concentrated on the economic arguments against interest-charging and in favour of profit-sharing (the preferred form of financial relations), highlighting the impact these have on stability, economic growth and inflation. In many respects, this was the preferred argumentation of many of the new 'Islamic economists' of South and Southeast Asia.[99]

---

[94] 'Ali al-Salus, *Radd li-kitab mufti misr 'ala mu'amalat al-bunuk wa-shar'aiyatuha al-islamiyah* (Cairo, 1991); Yusuf al-Qardawi, *Fawa'id al-bunuk hiya al-riba al-haram* (Cairo, 1990). Sometimes the heat of the argument led to personal attacks of such vehemence that the Mufti sued those concerned, as in the case of Dr 'Ali al-Salus, 'Qisati ma' al-bunuk wa-l-mufti', *Al-Sha'b*, 12 October 1994; 'Ali al-Salus, 'Ya fadilah mufti misr madha baqa min al-haram?' *Al-Iqtisad al-Islami*, no. 108 (June 1990), pp. 19–23.

[95] 'Shaikh al-Azhar yashruh', *Al-Siyasah*, 12 May 1991.

[96] Hasan 'Ali Daba, 'Dr Yusuf al-Qardawi: al-hujum al-hali 'ala al-bunuk al-islamiyah fitnah kubra', *Al-Sha'b*, 21 March 1997.

[97] 'Abd al-Hamid al-Ghazzali, *Al-Arbah wa-l-fawa'id al-masrafiyah bayna al-tahlil al-iqtisadi wa-l-hukm al-shar'i* (Cairo, 1990) p. 14.

[98] Al-Hamza Da'bas, 'Dhalik bi-anhum qalu inama al-bay' mithl al-riba', *Al-Da'wah*, No. 4 (October 1976); Al-'Assal and 'Abd al-Karim *Al-Nizam al-iqtisadi fi al-islam*, pp. 82–3; Ahmad 'Abd al-Rahman, 'Al-halal wa-l-haram fi mu'amalat al-bunuk wa-l-mal', *Al-Sha'b*, 9 July 1991.

[99] Yusuf Kamal, 'Risalah ila muhafiz al-bank al-markazi', *Al-Da'wah*, no. 58 (February 1981), pp. 19–20; Al-Omar and Abdel-Haq, *Islamic Banking*, p. 12; see also M. A. Mannan, *Islamic*

Such a rationale was at least theoretically verifiable by empirical investigation, making it vulnerable to possible refutation. Thus, recourse to economics as a social science, pronouncing on measurable indices of prosperity, threatened to subject the judgement about the worth of practices condemned in the Qur'an to criteria derived from positive economics and from the contingency of history. Possibly to avoid this, an argument from moral economy was highlighted, suggesting that *riba* embodied impurity of such potency that, whatever the visible material benefits of charging or receiving interest payments, the moral effect was deeply corrupting.

For the more tradition-minded, such as Shaikh Bakri al-Sufi, Mufti of Egypt in the early twentieth century and successor to Muhammad 'Abduh, arguments about social benefit were answered emphatically by citing sources stating that anyone who mixed their money with money derived from *riba*, theft or other forbidden activities would contaminate his own money to such a degree that it would be forbidden to have any kind of intercourse with him.[100] In this regard, the prohibition of *riba* came to summarise the moral gulf which was held to separate a world ordered by Islamic ethics from a world presently governed by capitalism and by the practices which may have reinforced a certain kind of power, but which equally voided that world of moral content. In the vivid language of 'Abd al-'Azim al-Mat'ani of Al-Azhar: 'Capitalism is the child of imperialism and interest is the disruptive daughter of the mother capitalism.'[101]

4.5   Islamic banks: the argument for Islamic agency

As with the issue of *zakat*, the challenge of equating *riba* with interest lay not simply in escaping the theoretical contradictions which might arise from arguments pro and con, but in constructing a framework which would negate the principle, allowing social action under the auspices of a moral order uncontaminated by *riba*. In many respects, the idea of the Islamic bank and of an Islamic banking system appeared to offer just such a framework. Imaginatively at first, but increasingly with practical intent, the idea of establishing financial institutions in which distinctively Islamic principles

---

Economics (Delhi, 1980); Ziauddin Ahmad, *Islam, Poverty and Income Distribution* (Leicester, 1991); W. M. Khan, *Towards an Interest-Free Islamic Economic System* (Leicester, 1985); Naqvi, *Ethics and Economics*, pp. 85–141; Monzer Kahf, *The Islamic Economy* (Plainfield, IN, 1978).

[100] Al-Ahram al-Iqtisadi, *Al-fatawa al-islamiyah* p. 89.

[101] Interview with Dr 'Abd al-'Azim al-Mat'ani in September 1989, Rida 'Ukasha, 'Limadha zada al-iqbal 'ala shahadat al-istithmar ba'd fatwa Dar al-Ifta bi-nisbah 25%?, *Al-Liwa al-Islami*, 21 September 1989; see also al-Bahi, *Tahafut al-fikr al-maddi al-ta'rikhi baina al-nazar wa-l-tatbiq*, pp. 59–62.

could be put into practice began to emerge. They gained definition and plausibility as the conditions of Muslims in many countries changed. During the 1970s the massive revenue flows into oil-producing states, many of which were populated principally by Muslims, created the conditions in which some Muslims could begin to think of setting up financial institutions which were not simply reflections of the dominant capitalist order, but might even provide an alternative to it.[102] The aftershocks of the oil price rises for the economies of the industrialised states also led many to see this crisis of capitalism as a harbinger of the system's terminal decline. At the same time, disillusionment with the capacities of the state to act morally and effectively tended to favour the idea that the path to such an alternative might lie through the private financial sector. This was a conjunction of historical possibility and imaginative intent, giving the project of rethinking Muslims' relations with the dominant world order an unparalleled boost.

The impulse and the desire to join two parts of the separated life – the life of private devotion and the life of public transactions – was a powerful one, expressed for some in radical forms of political action, but for others in a determination to prosper individually and to enrich, both spiritually and materially, the surrounding society. Increasingly, such questions were being asked by people in the oil-producing states who had the financial means to do something about the answers. They were also being asked by another constituency of Muslims, less financially powerful, but of growing importance in Western Europe in particular. The expanding communities of Muslim immigrants from the Middle East and South Asia were obliged to work with and through the existing institutions of capitalist society. As they established themselves and accumulated capital, some began to feel that the acquiescence initially demanded by necessity could now give way to a more measured choice, informed by the identifying ethics of their religion. These circumstances combined to make the issue of the moral sphere defined by a distinctively Islamic ethic a crucial one as they sought to organise their economic transactions. This was visible at the beginning of the twenty-first century, for instance, in the United Kingdom with the proliferation of facilities for 'Islamic mortgages' and the opening of the Islamic Bank of Britain in 2004.[103]

In the early 1970s Muhammad Baqir al-Sadr had proposed a solution to the question of how to preserve a distinctive Islamic identity through the

---

[102] The sense of changing meanings and possibilities is well captured in the account of the emergence of Islamic banking in Maurer, *Mutual Life, Limited*, pp. 24–39.
[103] BBC News: 'First Islamic Bank to open in UK' available at http://news.bbc.co.uk/go/pr/fr/-/hi/business/3547374.stm; HSBC Amanah Finance was launched in 1998 specifically to provide *shari'ah*-compliant mortgages, and Lloyds TSB launched its Islamic Account some years later – see www.lloydstsb.com/islamicfinancialservices.

observance of Islamic norms whilst at the same time taking part meaningfully and effectively in economic life. His book *Al-Bank al-la-ribawi fi al-islam* (The Interest-Free Bank in Islam) proposed a space for economic transactions governed by the rules of the Islamic *shari'ah*, allowing the individual to ensure that his or her financial transactions could be effective, but which would not compromise his or her Islamic principles.[104] Such a scheme would not depend upon the successful completion of the more ambitious, but uncertain enterprise of the creation of an Islamic state or an Islamic economy. It emphasised individual salvation, but, as al-Sadr had made clear in *Iqtisaduna*, the foundation of the Islamic economy must be the individual Muslim, as both a moral and an economic agent. The interest-free bank was therefore intended to help in the formation of the 'Islamic personality'. In this way through the sum of their individual transactions, Muslims would create the basis for an Islamic economy. It was to be a case of private virtue leading to public virtue.

Nevertheless, al-Sadr was aware of the fact that such a bank, in order to survive as a financial institution, would have to offer more than simply an opportunity to act virtuously. It should also appeal to material interests, since it was intended to be a profitable institution, as well as a voluntary one – at least until the formation of an Islamic state. Al-Sadr was equally aware of the possibility that the demands of efficiency, in pursuit of political power or of profit, could gradually displace the Islamic ethical imperative, tempting people to adapt the authoritative Islamic text (*nass*) of the Qur'an or the *hadith* to the dominant worldly reality. This, he believed, would weaken their resolve to change the world in accordance with the commands specified in the text – a phenomenon he already detected in the tendency of Muslims to select or to ignore specific textual injunctions in accordance with the spirit of the times or according to purposes that were not distinctively Islamic.[105]

The trajectory and the arguments – and some of the problems – outlined in the writings of al-Sadr foreshadowed to some degree the actual experience of the growing sector of Islamic banking, as well as the rationales used to justify this as an appropriate structure for the re-foundation of economic life on distinctively Islamic grounds. Unease about the dominance of the capitalist economy, and specifically its financial institutions, based as they were on interest, speculation, risk and the commodification of money itself, had long formed part of an indictment of the capitalist world order by Muslims fearful

---

[104] Muhammad Baqir al-Sadr, *Al-bank al-la-ribawi fi al-islam* (Kuwait, 1970). The book was a response to a number of inquiries from citizens of Kuwait – already by the early 1970s, before the 'oil boom', a state with an impressive, oil-based GDP and per capita income.
[105] Al-Sadr, *Iqtisaduna*, pp. 358–60.

of the effects on their own moral compass – especially since they themselves had no real alternative to dealing with this world.

Some attempts had been made in the 1950s and 1960s to establish specifically interest-free Islamic financial institutions. For instance, in 1963 in Egypt, Ahmad al-Najjar set up a savings bank – the Bank of Local Deposits (*Bank al-idkhar al-mahalliyah*) – at Mit Ghamr in Daqhaliyah province. Modelled in part on a German agricultural savings bank scheme, it presented itself as an Islamic institution to the peasants, whilst al-Najjar persuaded the government that it was an effective means of mobilising local savings and investing in local development projects. Suspicious of independent initiatives, especially if they sought to project themselves as more virtuous and worthy of support than the institutions of the state-run economy, the Egyptian government of the day nevertheless supported the project, subsidising its activities and bringing it under the supervision of the public authorities.

For five years the bank became the site of a range of activities, all of which were in conformity with most agreed Islamic injunctions regarding financial transactions: deposit accounts did not pay interest, profit-and-loss share accounts provided a variable return, interest-free loans and *zakat* or social services accounts gave people the chance to contribute a proportion of their income to local charities. Its activities were largely confined to rural areas in the Nile Delta, but it did succeed in attracting some quarter of a million depositors and provided loans that helped to start up a variety of local businesses. However, in 1968 the Egyptian government closed it down, incorporating it into the conventional structure of the National Bank of Egypt. The crisis in Egypt following the defeat of 1967, and Nasser's enduring suspicion of initiatives which did not seem to conform wholly to the close centralised control of the economy, finally told against the experiment.[106]

In Pakistan in the late 1950s, a similar institution was set up to provide interest-free loans to poor farmers, whilst taking deposits from wealthier landowners on which it did not pay interest. However, it failed to grow and closed after a few years. In Malaysia, a more successful experiment was the Tabung Haji, a fund established in 1963 to help people save for the pilgrimage to Mecca. It attracted a large number of small deposits and on this basis thrived, becoming in 1969 the Pilgrims' Management and Fund Board, which reassured its depositors by investing their savings only in activities sanctioned

---

[106] Mahmoud Mohieldin, 'On formal and informal Islamic finance in Egypt', unpublished paper presented at MESA meeting Washington DC, 6–10 December 1995, pp. 12–14; Ahmad al-Najjar, 'Al-masarif al-islamiyah', *Al-Da'wah*, no. 1 (July 1976), pp. 44–5; Ahmad al-Najjar, *Nahwa istratijiyah jadidah li-l-tanmiyat al-iqtisadiyah fi al-duwwal al-namiyah* (Beirut, 1969), pp. 6–7; Ahmad al-Najjar, *Harakat al-bunuk al-islamiyah* (Cairo, 1993); Kuran, 'Economic impact of Islamic fundamentalism', p. 313.

by Islamic rulings on financial transactions. It remains a relatively small enterprise, but it has been argued that its success was the catalyst for the foundation of Malaysia's first Islamic commercial bank, the Bank Islam Malaysia Berhad.[107] Although modest in outcome, these institutions demonstrated that there existed a ready imaginative framework for distinctive forms of Islamic economic activity, resting on the mutually reinforcing grounds of Islamic values and the general welfare of the Islamic community.

With the increased financial power of the oil-producing states of the Arabian peninsula during the 1970s, it was not surprising, therefore, that concerted efforts should have been made to establish institutions that would fulfil the expectations of many Muslims – and would at the same time provide an alternative source of capital and investment possibilities to those offered by the dominant economic order. This initiative had modest beginnings and a multiplicity of sources, but with the authority of the ruling house of Saudi Arabia behind it, led by King Faisal, and backed by the financial weight of a number of Saudi and other Gulf businessmen, the idea of an Islamic bank began to take shape. So successful was it initially, in the sense of firing the enthusiasm of sufficient numbers of wealthy depositors, that something like an Islamic banking system began to emerge, given substance by transnational bodies established to define the field and to authorise the participants.

In the 1970s the Saudi-inspired Organisation of Islamic Conference (OIC) encouraged moves both to clarify Islamic financial principles and to set up an organisation that would put them into practice, leading to the creation of the Islamic Development Bank (IDB) in 1975. Forty countries participated, with nearly 70 per cent of the capital provided by four major oil-producing states: Saudi Arabia, Libya, the United Arab Emirates and Kuwait. The IDB was specifically charged with directing development funds towards poor areas, providing interest-free loans which complied with the main profit-and-loss-sharing principles of Islamic finance. It was also intended to help deepen training and expertise in Islamic finance and, above all, to show the world that there was an alternative way of organising the financing of economic development to the conventional capitalist system.[108]

The financial power of the capital behind the venture, and its public endorsement of Islamic finance, encouraged others to establish Islamic banks, the first being the Dubai Islamic Bank in 1975. Backed by private capital,

---

[107] Lewis and Algaoud, *Islamic Banking*, pp. 5–6; Wohlers-Scharf, *Arab and Islamic Banks*, p. 53; see also M. Ariff (ed.), *Islamic Banking in Southeast Asia* (Singapore, 1988).
[108] S. A. Meenai, *The Islamic Development Bank* (London, 1989), pp. 1–22, 190–8, 210–11; Majid Ibrahim 'Ali, *Al-Bank al-islami li-l-tanmiyah* (Cairo, 1982), pp. 189–210. Warde, *Islamic Finance in the Global Economy*, p. 75; Abdullah Saeed, *Islamic Banking and Interest* (Leiden, 1996), p. 13.

drawn initially from major financial families of the Gulf region, they increasingly attracted smaller clients, encouraged by the positive returns and by the possibility of interest-free loans in a setting legitimated by the proclaimed Islamic rectitude of the enterprise's transactions.[109] The optimism surrounding these early ventures, the vast sums of capital which initially financed them and the expectation of their ability to tap a great hidden potential for savings, and thus to generate economic growth, helped to emphasise their ideal and idealised functions.

Consequently, much was made of the intended role of the banks as engines of an economy that would embrace far wider and more socially valuable aims than the morally questionable and individualist characteristics of a capitalist economy. Furthermore, it was claimed that they were specifically intended as mechanisms what would help to remind people of their relationship with a divine order and with the divinely ordained 'social functions' of the property which they held in trust from God.[110] The idealised role sketched out for Islamic banks thus extended from being a motor of economic development to being a guarantor of 'faith, morals, peace of mind, the family and the society . . . to protect social and economic equilibrium'.[111]

As the mission statement of the International Association of Islamic Banks (one of the transnational organisations set up to regulate the field) asserted: 'the Islamic banking system involves a social implication which is necessarily connected with the Islamic order itself . . . Profitability is therefore not the sole criterion or the prime element in evaluating the performance of Islamic banks, since they have to match both between the material and the social objectives that would serve the interests of the community as a whole.'[112] As these and other contemporary statements make clear, their function was to safeguard and extend both the material and the spiritual aspects of the community – to ensure that in a world of changing economic conditions and possibilities the norms of the Islamic faith and its fundamental principles should be observed, protecting the community from marginalisation and impoverishment on one hand, and from secularisation and spiritual corruption on the other.

---

[109] In the following twenty years or so, over 170 Islamic banks had been established in different parts of the world, with over forty in the Gulf and the Middle East more generally, accounting for 70 per cent of the total assets of this sector – Lewis and Algaoud, *Islamic Banking*, pp. 8–13.

[110] Ahmad al-Najjar, 'Al-masarif al-islamiyah', *Al-Da'wah*, no. 2 (July 1976), pp. 44–5; Ahmad al-Najjar, 'Jalsah hiwar ma'al-duktur Mustafa Mahmud', *Al-Nur*, 8 April 1992; Mahmud al-Ansari, 'Dur al-bunuk al-islamiyah fi al-tanmiyah al-ijtima'iyah', *Al-Muslim al-Mu'asir* 37 (Nov./Dec. 1983–Jan. 1984), pp. 113–18.

[111] Ahmad 'Izzat Madani, *Al-Idarah wa-iqtisadiyat al-'amal: al-minhaj al-islami wa-l-tatbiq* (Cairo, 1986), pp. 86–8.

[112] Statement of purpose by the International Association of Islamic Banks (1990) cited in Al-Omar and Abdel-Haq, *Islamic Banking*, p. 27.

These were wide-ranging and highly ambitious ideals, deemed realisable through the various instruments the banks would use to keep their bearings within the moral compass of the economy. Specifically, they were charged with showing that the collection of *zakat* and the avoidance of *riba* could create the basis of a just, prosperous and equitable social order. They therefore had a dual mission: to increase the stock of faith and belief, and to achieve material capital growth.[113] The intent was well captured by the founder of the Faisal Islamic Bank, Prince Muhammad al-Faisal Al Sa'ud in 1979, when he claimed that the bank would pay and distribute *zakat* on its capital 'to purify it and to realise social development'.[114]

The chief instruments which would allow the banks to serve this dual purpose were derived from the practices sanctioned in the *fiqh*. These involved not simply avoiding *riba* – interpreted as interest-bearing activities – but also organising financial activity through contracts based on *musharakah* and *mudarabah*, in particular. These types of contract have a long pedigree in the economic history of the Islamic lands, but have also been widely practised in other cultures under different names. They are based on the principle that the lender and the borrower of capital share the profit or the loss associated with its use: in *musharakah* the borrower invests some of his or her own capital in a venture, whereas in *mudarabah* he or she invests primarily his or her labour, expertise and time. The point, however, is that the return on capital is neither guaranteed, since the venture may fail, nor predetermined. Only the respective shares of loss and profit are decided beforehand between the parties to the contract and, in the case of *mudarabah*, the lender must bear the entire financial cost of failure.[115] These instruments had been sanctioned by numerous jurists precisely because they ensure that any return will be the outcome of productive enterprise and a loss will not penalise the borrower disproportionately. Thus the evils of *riba*, as injustice or disproportionate risk, are avoided and the exhortation to fruitful economic activity is obeyed.

The support of political establishments in the oil-rich countries of the Islamic world, and of those leaders who looked to the oil-rich states for assistance, created an important constituency for the plausibility of the idea, and provided the necessary capital to take its part in the global financial system. However, these same ruling and business elites shied away from

---

[113] Tariq al-Bishri, *Al-Hiwar al-islami al-'ilmani* (Cairo, 1996) pp. 75–6; Al-Omar and Abdel-Haq, *Islamic Banking*, pp. 27–8; al-Ba'li, *Maqasid al-shari'ah wa-mushkilat al-hajjat fi al-iqtisad*, pp. 37–42.

[114] 'Muwaqa' jadid 'ala kharitat al-bunuk al-islamiyah', *Al-Bunuk al-Islamiyah*, no. 7 (October 1979), pp. 2–3.

[115] J. A. Wakin, 'Mudaraba', pp. 284–5, J. and D. Latham, 'Musharaka', pp. 671–2 in *Encyclopedia of Islam* (Leiden, 1993), vol. VII.

establishing Islamic banking as the cornerstone of their own national economies. Indeed, in Saudi Arabia Islamic banks found it virtually impossible to obtain licences to operate, perhaps because of the government's sensitivity to the suggestion that all other finance houses were in some way un-Islamic. The outstandingly successful Islamic bank, the Al-Rajhi Banking and Investment Corporation, was originally licensed as a conventional bank and only later declared itself an institution working to Islamic principles.[116] The interests of these rulers and of the political class were too deeply implicated in the processes of global capitalism to risk taking the radical step of moving towards a national economy founded on strict Islamic principles.

However, such experiments were tried in those countries where the capture of state power seemed to open the way for a distinctive Islamist agenda and a contemporary and radical Islamist vocabulary had emerged as the dominant discourse. Thus, between 1979 and 1983, first the Pakistani government, then the government of the Islamic Republic of Iran, and finally the government of Sudan brought in measures intended to 'Islamise' their national economies. In Pakistan, the government of Zia ul-Haq set up a commission in 1979 to study the introduction of distinctively Islamic measures in the economy, starting with the introduction of *zakat* (at 2.5 per cent) to be distributed through a nationwide network of *zakat* committees. At the same time, profit-and-loss-sharing accounts were set up, followed by the outlawing of interest in the mid-1980s. Nevertheless, it was soon clear that the attempt to fully 'Islamise' the economy and to sustain a national economy that was not deeply intertwined with the global economy was much harder to put into practice than it had been to imagine.[117]

At much the same time, the Sudanese government's 'Islamisation' of the national economy owed something to the imagination of an Islamic alternative for a poor, indebted country. But it also came out of the turbulent last years of President Nimairi's rule when he ostentatiously tried to portray himself as a just Islamic ruler. The outlawing of interest and the Islamisation of all banks, foreign and Sudanese, was a consequence of the 'September laws' of 1983. The following year the Zakat Tax Act gave the government the power to collect and distribute *zakat* and became the basis for the country's tax system. Suspended in 1985 with the overthrow of Nimairi, the Islamic laws were reimposed in 1989 by the new military National Islamic Front regime. However, Sudan also discovered that it could not isolate itself from the global economy without suffering even worse consequences. Thus, in the 1990s, despite the determined use of an Islamic vocabulary to describe and

---

[116] C. M. Henry, 'Financial peformances of Islamic versus conventional banks', in C. M. Henry and R. Wilson (eds.), *The Politics of Islamic Finance* (Edinburgh, 2004), pp. 107–11.
[117] Nasr, *Islamic Leviathan*, pp. 130–46, 165–8; Hussein, *Pakistan*, pp. 195–9.

justify the state, its policies and its institutions, the application of IMF-dictated reforms indicated that the driver of the economy was neither the Islamic banks nor the realisation of an Islamic financial ideal, but the international financial institutions of a global capitalist order.[118]

In Iran, the Islamist revolutionaries who had helped to overthrow the Shah and who had seized control of the state by 1979 saw the economy as an obvious terrain for the making of a new Islamic order. Consequently, following the nationalisation of banks in 1979, the banking sector was gradually 'Islamised'. In 1984 a law prohibiting *riba* was introduced, giving banks a year in which to convert their operations into interest-free transactions. This was happening in the setting of a war economy and of a government which was determined to maintain tight control of all economic activity. The effect, however, was to create a thriving black economy in which interest was charged and other practices forbidden in the formal economy proliferated. Furthermore, the management of the state's economy within a global framework required ever more pragmatic compromises with the dominant systems of world trade and finance – systems which were often embraced enthusiastically by those well-connected members of the bazaar and the new revolutionary establishment who had secured positions of great economic power.[119]

As far as the practice of Islamic banking was concerned, it did not take long before the logic of social action in a capitalist global order made itself felt. An ideal that had been heralded as radical and transformative was itself transformed. The logic of finance capital shaped practice and qualified the original ideal. As the Islamic financial sector grew, mobilising substantial sums of capital, many of the original intentions faded from view, or declined in relation to the profit-seeking operations of the banks. The goal of reinforcing the bonds of community, and the therapeutic ambition of restoring unity between people's material transactions and the spiritual dimension of their

[118] J. Millard Burr and R. O. Collins, *Revolutionary Sudan: Hasan al-Turabi and the Islamist State 1989–2000* (Leiden, 2003), pp. 21–4, 234–5, 254, 274–80; Elfatih Shaaeldin and R. Brown, *Towards an Understanding of Islamic Banking in Sudan*, DSRC Monograph XXI (Khartoum, 1985); International Monetary Fund, *Sudan: Recent Economic Developments* (Washington, DC, 1999), pp. 36–44, 52–4; Isaac Bior Deng Bior, *Some Reflections on Economic Liberalization in the Sudan*, Sudan Economy Research Group, Discussion Paper 32 (Bremen, 2000).

[119] Sohrab Behdad, 'A disputed utopia: Islamic economics in revolutionary Iran', *Comparative Studies in Society and History* 36 (1994) pp. 812–13; Ali Rahnema and Farhad Nomani, *The Secular Miracle: Religion, Politics and Economic Policy in Iran* (London, 1990), pp. 239–98; Ali Ansari, *Iran, Islam and Democracy: The Politics of Managing Change* (London, 2000), pp. 52–64, 168–75; S. Maloney, 'Islamism in Iran's postrevolutionary economy: the case of the *Bonyads*', in M. A. Tétreault and R. A. Denemark (eds.), *Gods, Guns and Globalization: Religious Radicalism and Political Economy* (Boulder, CO, 2004), pp. 191–217.

lives, gave way before the need for financial institutions to survive and to thrive. They needed to stay viable in a global market dominated by long-established and highly competitive institutions which had historically shaped the rules of the market itself, influencing the ethos within which it operated and the epistemological foundations of its terms of reference. The market of global capital had established a 'common sense', clothing its practices and principles with a degree of historical plausibility unmatched by any alternative – reinforcing this with sanctions that sustained its power, validating the very criteria by which that power was to be evaluated.[120]

Thus the logic of capital accumulation, the pursuit of profit and of individual interest, the operation of and competition within established markets and the accompanying forms of commodification appeared as transactions in the Islamic banking sector. Whatever the intentions of those who had projected onto the abstracted concept of the 'Islamic bank' their hopes for an engine of Islamic economic transformation, the reality of the 1980s and 1990s was that, far from challenging the dominant system of global capitalism, the institutions were seeking a distinctive niche within international financial markets. For those who directed the Islamic banks, it was important to gain recognition, both from international financial bodies and from the political elites of the countries in which they established themselves, whether these were predominantly Muslim or not. The intention was to make these institutions work – and to show that they could work well – within the established order, both political and financial. There was no attraction in marginalisation or exclusion, as experienced by the early experiments in setting up Islamic financial institutions. Thus, even though some Muslim intellectuals, such as al-Fanjari in Egypt, were uneasy about the capitalist turn of the Islamic banks and yearned for something more akin to cooperative societies, it was as recognised parts of the banking sector that they were to thrive.[121]

The 'logic' of global finance was soon at work throughout the Islamic banking sector. Most obviously, the instruments used and the contracts entered into diverged substantially from the original profit-and-loss-sharing principles of *mudarabah* and *musharakah*.[122] Bad decisions by a number of banks in the early, optimistic years of Islamic banking had led to considerable losses and diminished the attraction of this form of financing as a general rule, although it still made sense in situations where venture capital was

---

[120] Bourdieu, *The Logic of Practice*, pp. 52–65.

[121] Dr Al-Fanjari interviewed in April 1991: Ahmad Ibrahim al-Ba'thi, 'Al-masarif al-islamiyah baina al-waqi' wa-l-mustaqbal', *Al-Ahram*, 3 April 1991.

[122] One estimate places *musharakah* and *mudarabah* contracts at only 5 per cent of the total activity of Islamic banks globally by 1999/2000: Warde, *Islamic Finance in the Global Economy*, p. 136.

needed to realise major projects. Equally, for depositors looking for security and predictability, the idea of a fluctuating return which could become a loss was unsettling. At the same time, it was discouraging for some successful entrepreneurs that repayment of the loan should not simply be a fixed cost, but rather a fixed share of their profits, agreed at a time when they may have been in a weak bargaining position vis-à-vis the bank.[123]

As a result, the Islamic banks – and their clients – began to use instruments which were more predictable and could yield a profit for the banks as well as secure benefits for the borrowers. The most widespread of these is the contract of *murabahah*, whereby the bank buys commodities – either capital goods or consumer goods – on behalf of the client and adds a certain sum to the price charged to the client. The goods then become the property of the client who agrees to repay the bank the price of the goods, together with a predetermined charge, at some date in the future. This looks very like the payment of interest on a loan, and is indeed the way in which many loans are organised in the conventional banking sector. However, it is argued that it avoids *riba* since the mark-up on the price of the goods is merely payment for the bank's services. It is also argued that the bank itself runs a risk by taking possession of the goods for a time before passing them on to the borrower. Such an argument has failed to convince some scholars who are still wary of this development, partly because they can see that the mark-up tends to reflect prevailing interest rates and that the risk to the bank is negligible, given the speed of the transfer of ownership in an electronic market. Nevertheless, it is claimed that *murabahah* and other mark-up trans-actions comprise some 80–95 per cent of all investments by Islamic banks and finance houses.[124]

The drive behind these transactions is the drive to profit and to compete within an established financial market for clients. In some respects, this inverts the role originally foreseen for the Islamic banks. Instead of seeking to depart from existing practices by introducing those which are distinctive of an Islamic tradition, the trend has been to scour the Islamic tradition – the basic sources of the *shari'ah*, as well as the writings of the *fuqaha'* – in order to find ways of legitimating financial transactions developed in the larger context of global finance capital. The innovations claimed by the Islamic banking sector are effectively the methods developed by some of the

[123] Kuran, 'Economic impact of Islamic fundamentalism', pp. 308–12, 316–17; Mohieldin, 'Formal and informal Islamic finance in Egypt', pp. 26–7; Warde, *Islamic Finance in the Global Economy*, pp. 135–8.
[124] Warde, *Islamic Finance in the Global Economy*, pp. 132–4; Al-Omar and Abdel-Haq, *Islamic Banking*, pp. 14–18; Kuran, 'Economic Impact of Islamic fundamentalism', pp. 309–14; Tarik Yousef, 'The *Murabaha* syndrome in Islamic finance', in Henry and Wilson, *Politics of Islamic Finance*, pp. 63–80.

institutions to compete in and take advantage of the products and techniques which have proliferated so spectacularly in the 1980s and 1990s with the deregulation of global capital markets. This has been exemplified, for instance, by the discussion in the Islamic banking world about how to respond to the exchange and sale of 'derivatives' within a framework set by Islamic norms, as well as financial opportunities.[125]

The new departures and innovations demanded by this process of adaptation have contributed to the increasing fragmentation of the Islamic banking system. From the outset, Islamic banks had appointed '*shari'ah* boards' made up of clerics and laymen versed in Islamic *fiqh* to adjudicate on the financial instruments devised by the banks and thus to reassure those with whom the banks dealt that the practices were truly Islamic. There has been some criticism of the status and membership of these boards, particularly as regards their independence, since they are remunerated by the banks in question. However, many of the individuals concerned are established Islamic scholars with substantial followings and therefore rightly jealous of their reputations as reliable and authoritative interpreters of the *fiqh*.[126] This has not prevented some notorious lapses, as in the case of the self-proclaimed Islamic financial institutions in Egypt in the late 1980s, some of which had clearly been guilty of practices that were neither Islamic nor financially sound. In the wake of the scandal, the charge was that either the '*shari'ah* boards' had been kept in ignorance by the directors of companies like Al-Rayyan, or they had been complicit in their activities.[127]

The very number of *shari'ah* boards working for competing institutions has added to the multiplicity of possible interpretations, even if some prominent Islamic scholars, such as the Qatar-based Egyptian Shaikh Yusuf al-Qardawi or the Pakistani Shaikh Muhammad Taqi Usmani, are members a number of *shari'ah* boards. The overall effect, nevertheless, has been to weaken the drive for consensus which was one of the early goals of the Islamic banking sector. The International Association of Islamic Banks (IAIB), set up in 1977

---

[125] Warde, *Islamic Finance in the Global Economy*, pp. 139–41; Tarik Yousef, 'Islamic banking, financial development and growth', *Forum* (Cairo: Newsletter of the Economic Research Forum for the Arab Countries, Iran and Turkey) 3/3(September 1996), pp. 5–7; Zamir Iqbal 'Devising new product options for Islamic finance', pp. 14–16, and Zaki Badawi, 'A question of derivatives', pp. 19–20, *Islamic Banker*, no. 9 (September 1996).

[126] Michel Galloux, *Finance islamique et pouvoir politique* (Paris, 1997); Tarek El Diwany, 'Travelling the wrong road patiently', *Banker Middle East* 39 (September 2003) available at www.bankerme.com/bme/2003/sep/islamic_banking.asp.

[127] The scandal of the Islamic investment companies in Egypt was not of course solely due to the silence of the *shari'ah* boards – it also owed a great deal to the failure of the Egyptian government, for a variety of motives, to regulate and inspect these fast-growing companies. Sami Zubaida, 'The politics of the Islamic investment companies in Egypt', *BRISMES Bulletin* 17/2 (1990), pp. 152–61; Mohieldin, 'Formal and informal Islamic Finance; pp. 30–5.

as a regulatory body for the Islamic banking sector, expected Islamic banks to affiliate with it. In order to do so, they had to comply with measures which were meant to reassure the public that they would be dealing with a certified Islamic institution. In the 1980s there was a high degree of compliance, but increasingly Islamic financial institutions saw no particular advantage in adhering to the IAIB. The numerous international symposia and the output of the burgeoning number of research institutes and centres have enlivened the debates, but have also added to the diversity of opinions.[128]

Regardless of the original intentions, the drive to mobilise savings and to draw into the orbit of Islamic banks people who might have felt uneasy dealing with the regular commercial banks has been relatively successful. In the early years this did much to account for the profitability of many Islamic banks. It had an accelerator effect: deposits and profits rose as more and more people, encouraged by advantageous rates of return, began to create a substantial clientele. One study has shown that in Egypt, for instance, much of this growth has been at the expense of the state-run banks.[129] However, entering into competition with other financial institutions has had two significant outcomes. It has led to the realisation by some Islamic scholars that there is little difference between the commercial banks and the Islamic banks, as far as their structures and procedures are concerned. For some, such as Shaikh Tantawi in Egypt, this was no bad thing, since he believed they were all promoting a goal that was in accordance with Islamic principles, namely, the provision of benefits to the mass of their depositors, with no harm caused to anyone else.[130]

For others, such a development constituted a glaring indictment of the Islamic banks. They were reproached for having succumbed to the logic of *riba* and for having been contaminated by the very capitalist financial system that they were intended to transform. This attack came from two directions. It came from people such as Ahmad al-Najjar who had been the founder of the interest-free bank at Mit Ghamr in the 1960s. Although very much part of the Islamic banking establishment by the 1990s, he was clearly disappointed by the failure of the Islamic banks to live up to their original moral purpose.[131]

[128] Warde, *Islamic Finance in the Global Economy*, pp. 143–4, 226–30.
[129] E. G. Kazarian, *Islamic versus Traditional Banking* (Boulder, CO, 1993), pp. 187–217.
[130] Rajab al-Banna, 'Ain al-halal, wa-ain al-haram?', *Al-Ahram*, 22 July 1990; Muhammad Sayyid Tantawi, 'Shahadat al-istithmar wa-kul ma yashbuhha min al-mu'amalat halal . . . halal . . . halal', *Al-Wafd*, 26 September 1993.
[131] Ibrahim 'Abd al-'Aziz, 'Al-bunuk al-islamiyah: wa-l-si'r al-jadid li-l-fa'idah', *Al-Siyasi*, 24 February 1991; al-Najjar, *Harakat al-bunuk al-islamiyah – haqa'iq al-ahl wa-awham al-surah*. See also the concern that 'materialism' was becoming the dominant framework for thinking about the Islamic economy and Islamic banking, contrary to the hopes of those who thought they had seen in it a genuine alternative to capitalist materialism: Bill Maurer, 'Engineering an Islamic future', *Anthropology Today* 17/1 (February 2001), pp. 10–11.

Criticism also came from those who suspected that the use of the epithet 'Islamic' by institutions was a marketing ploy and a way of discrediting their business rivals.[132]

In reality, the Islamic banks had challenged neither the idea nor the institution of the capital market which is at the heart of global capitalism. On the contrary, they have created a niche in that market for themselves. They have attracted those who felt morally uneasy about conventional, interest-based banking and whose sense of propriety in economic transactions has been better catered for by institutions which avoid interest and invest in activities that are *halal* under Islamic law.[133] However, in addition to ideas about specifically Islamic propriety and identity, part of the attraction of many of these institutions has been their promise of above average returns, free of government-imposed rates and of government control. For some this promises greater profit and for others it corresponds with a belief that Islamic identity is better protected through private institutions than by a state preoccupied by power.

Nevertheless, the state has not been slow to appeal to this constituency. As early as 1981 one of the Egyptian state-owned banks, Bank Misr, advertised the opening of a chain of branches throughout Egypt which would operate 'in the service of the Islamic economy and all of the transactions of which will be in conformity with the rulings of the Islamic *shari'ah*', under the inspection of the *'ulama* of Al-Azhar.[134] By 1990, in Egypt alone, there were sixty-two Islamic branches of twenty-three conventional banks, some of them private, some in the state sector and some joint ventures. The lack of separate identities and the belief that these funds would be amalgamated with the conventional funds of the parent bank helped to reinforce the impression that this was simply a marketing ploy to attract the clientele that had moved to the Islamic banks. Soon there appeared dedicated Islamic sections of a variety of conventional banks, many of them long-established pillars of American and European finance, such as Citibank, Union des Banques Suisses, HSBC and Deutsche Bank. They made great play of their *shari'ah* boards and of the separation of the assets of these sections from those of the parent bank in a successful attempt to attract the deposits of those who wished their funds to be held under rules that conformed with their own values and identity. Thus had a capital market been created in which Islamic financial products could be developed by any resourceful

---

[132] A. Buccianti, 'Guerre d'usure entre banquiers "laiques" et "islamiques" en Egypte", *Le Monde*, 12 March 1997; see also the series of articles in the Egyptian periodical *Akhbar al-Yawm* attacking the Islamic banking sector for hypocrisy, 15 February 1997, 22 February 1997, 1 March 1997.

[133] Maurer, *Mutual Life*, pp. 39–42.

[134] Full page advertisement by Bank Misr in *Al-Da'wah*, no. 63 (July 1981), p. 2.

entrepreneur, or, as the report on BNP Parisbas's creation of an Islamic banking team in Bahrain in 2003 had it, it would 'tailor a new portfolio of exotic shariah-compliant investment products'.[135]

Islamic banking, far from challenging global capitalism, has become an integral part of the global financial system. It has developed its own regulatory bodies, many of which conform with those of the conventional banking sector more generally and others which ensure compliance with Islamic norms, not simply in transactions, but also in charitable contributions and development assistance. This is a small fraction of their activities, but it seeks to reassure investors and others of the integrity of these institutions, while the accounting measures are intended to guarantee their financial integrity.[136] Those who deal with these banks act from a variety of motives, but it seems clear that, like the customers of other banks, they are looking for institutions that offer secure returns on their deposits. At the same time, like those who invest in the Co-operative Bank in the United Kingdom, or in the proliferating ethical investment funds, they are reassured that their funds will not be used in ways which contravene their principles. It would be difficult to argue, however, that these considerations are always more important. Ethical concerns clearly count for something, as indicated by the marked increase in post office savings in 1989, following the Mufti of Egypt's pronouncement on the legality under the *shari'ah* of interest-bearing bonds.[137] However, it is also noticeable that in Egypt, once the rates of return of the Islamic and the conventional banks came into line, and the government removed many of the regulations complicating dealings with state-owned banks, the inflow of deposits to the independent Islamic sector slowed down. Eventually, the situation stabilised, with Islamic banks accounting for a significant, but relatively small proportion of total deposits.[138]

---

[135] www.bankerme.com/bme/2003/sep/private_banking_1.asp; Mohieldin, 'Formal and informal Islamic finance in Egypt', pp. 24–5; interview with Fahmy Huwaidi, Cairo, 15 May 1997.

[136] Al-Omar and Abdel-Haq, *Islamic Banking*, pp. 109–14; Nomani and Rahnema, *Islamic Economic Systems*, pp. 162–86; see also C. H. Moore, 'Les banques islamiques: intermédiation politique et financière dans les pays arabes', pp. 135–51, and V. Nienhaus, 'Le côntrole bancaire et la politique des banques centrales: étude comparative', pp. 172–9, in G. Beaugé (ed.), *Les capitaux de l'Islam* (Paris, 1990).

[137] Rida 'Ukasha, 'Limadha zada al-iqbal 'ala shahadat al-istithmar ba'd fatwa Dar al-Ifta bi-nisbah 25%?', *Al-Liwa al-Islami*, 21 September 1989.

[138] By one estimate, in 1990 the total deposits of the Islamic banking sector only amounted to 10 per cent of the banking sector as a whole. Mohieldin, 'Formal and informal Islamic finance in Egypt', p. 28. Kazarian, *Islamic versus Traditional Banking*, pp. 189–217, suggests it might be slightly higher for certain deposits, but concurs that the overall impact on the Egyptian economy is slight.

The determination by a number of contemporary Muslim intellectuals to develop an imaginative sphere and an institutional arena that would restore the moral economy which capitalism had so dramatically eroded produced the field of Islamic economics and the system of Islamic banking. It has been an ambitious and problematic undertaking. It was ambitious because it seemed to challenge the discursive and material power of a well-entrenched and globally dominant capitalist order. It also sought to realise an ideal that may never have existed. The imagined sociability, solidarity and ethical completeness of the Muslim *ummah* had never been a historical reality, even if the model, based on an understanding of the early Muslim community at the time of the Prophet, has retained its inspirational power throughout the centuries.

The social bonds, systems of value and normative frame of economic transactions, which capitalism had disrupted and altered across the world, had particular local origins. In many places, these had been sanctified by appeals to an Islamic set of prescriptions, but they had themselves also sometimes influenced local views about what was truly Islamic. The attempt to re-found the moral economy, on the basis of a re-conceptualised Islam, could disrupt the identifying practices of a local community. It also suggested that the framework for rethinking the economy itself came from the then dominant model of economics. This owed nothing to a specifically Islamic set of concerns or values, yet it clearly shaped the way in which an Islamic economy was imagined.

The hybridity of the undertaking raised problems for some, but for others it was a source of considerable potential. Many who developed an Islamic economics wanted to devise a way of thinking about economic life independent of the dominant paradigms of neo-liberal economics. This proved to be as problematic an undertaking as that which had faced an earlier generation of Muslim thinkers when they tried to imagine a distinctive and unique Islamic society and, in doing so, had found that the discipline of sociology had so shaped their views of society that it coloured their views of a properly functioning Islamic society. The same could be said of the power of the discipline of economics to shape views of the economy, Islamic or otherwise. For some this was not a problem, since they wanted mainly to ensure that the core values of Islam and the ethical order it promoted would not be dissolved with the dissolution of so much else undergoing capitalist transformation. However, for those whose fear of capitalism caused them to see in Islamic economics, for instance, a serious and powerful alternative to the dominant capitalist global economic order, there could only be disappointment and frustration.

A similar process has been at work in the sphere of Islamic banking. Early writers had seen in Islamic banking a distinct and genuine alternative to the capitalist financial system. It would not only reconstitute the financial power of Muslim communities, but would also restore the moral economy of Muslims, serving as the engine of equitable development for resource-poor regions of the Islamic world. These hopes have not been borne out in practice. Instead, the Islamic banks and finance houses have become a recognisable part of the landscape of advanced capitalism, catering to – indeed creating – a particular section of the market. So well integrated have they become into the web of global financial institutions that they are both trusted and effective within that world. This aspect of Muslim engagement with global capitalism was reinforced in 1999 when both the New York and the London stock exchanges launched indexes of companies judged to be ethically sound as far as Islamic principles are concerned, reassuring Muslim investors that their funds could grow without harming their moral values.[139]

Insofar as these institutions provide some Muslims with financial security and with a sense that their investments accord with their Islamic obligations, they perform an important service. They have become a way of reinforcing a certain kind of identity in the modern world. The role they now play may be very different to that envisaged by Muhammad Baqir al-Sadr and others at the outset, but they have nevertheless contributed to the transformation of Muslim identities and to new ways of thinking about being Muslim. For those who focus on the benefits of the Islamic banking system, whether as individuals or as members of specific communities which have found new possibilities through these institutions, they are providing a way of engaging with the world, which is congruent with various facets of an Islamic identity.

They are not alternatives to capitalism. On the contrary, they have shown that the practices of global capitalism, whatever its origins or initially disruptive effects, can be incorporated into a world of meaning that is validated by reference to distinctive Islamic idioms. From the alphabet of Islamic symbols and beliefs can be fashioned a vocabulary of accommodation with a capitalist order. This is not arbitrary, but has been shaped by the forces working upon Muslims during the past few centuries and by the logic of capital accumulation itself. For other Muslims, of course, less inclined to accept the end result and alert therefore to the costs of such a form of engagement, both for the individuals concerned and for what it means to be Muslim in their view, the Islamic character of such developments is a sham. For these, the unreconciled, the fundamental logic that drives this sector remains that of secular, materialist capitalism and it is to counter this that more radical strategies have been devised.

---

[139] F. Bohkari, 'Indexes clear the way for investors', *Financial Times*, 26 October 2000, in which the performance of the Dow Jones Market Index and the FTSE's Global Islamic Index are examined.

5   Repertoires of resistance: Islamic anti-capitalism

Those who have tried to respond to capitalism have discovered that its power is not simply material power, but also imaginative, helping to structure the way in which people engage with the world by shaping the way they see it. For those Muslims concerned about the identity and integrity, let alone the autonomy of their societies and their value systems, the danger of this had been only too visible in the latter part of the twentieth century. State-sponsored attempts to introduce 'Islamic socialism' had succumbed to the logic of a state that was secular in intent and constitution, seemingly owing little to anything distinctively Islamic. Equally, the attempt to engage with capitalism, through the projection of the Islamic economy and Islamic banks, had mainly served to reproduce forms of capitalist accumulation. Although in technical conformity with the *shari'ah*, these forms had done little to promote a distinctively Islamic ethos in contradistinction to the imperatives of capitalism. On the contrary, they had become part of the institutional and imaginative structure of global capital as new commodities were devised for new markets, driven by a general and urgent desire for profit.

Consequently, parallel with the efforts by Muslims to engage with and adapt a world of capitalist enterprise to match their values, there were those Muslim intellectuals for whom such engagement seemed to be tantamount to capitulation. Their concerns were sometimes sharpened by earlier hopes they had once entertained in the 1940s and 1950s about the potential for autonomous action in the period of decolonisation and independence, but the world of public institutions, whether political or financial, had let them down. Their attention focused, therefore, on the reinforcement of a system of distinctively Islamic values, such that the social order would increasingly reflect them and, in doing so, would also embody and reproduce them. In many respects, from different parts of the Islamic world, both geographically and with reference to different traditions, Sayyid Qutb in Egypt and Ali Shari'ati in Iran, embody these preoccupations. In their writings, subjectivist method and social prescription come together in distinct but related ways, to form a discourse that seeks symbolic autonomy as well as social transformative power. In this way, they both hoped that capitalism and the ideas associated with it would be stopped in their tracks, brought up against the unshakeable faith of those who adhered to Islam, as they understood it.

Their predominantly idealist approach, in which there could be no doubt that the material world was shaped by the world of belief, inevitably led to an emphasis on the symbolic as a distinct sphere of effective social action. This would encompass a set of values to which those familiar with the vocabulary would respond, making symbolic representations strategic tools. However, symbolism of this kind was not simply instrumental in design. It was also part of the way in which the world was constituted for those who held firm to the belief that social order could be changed by the faith of Muslims. Precisely because it drew directly on a repertoire of words, beliefs, images and metaphors linked to the broad sweep of Islamic history and scholarship, it was thought to be immune to the many influences that accompanied a capitalist world order. The realm of the symbolic, as well as generating a power in itself, was held to insulate the Muslim community from the insidious values of capitalist and materialist discourses.

Concentrating on the symbolic also held out a possible answer to the problem of social action. The structuring of action was seen as one of the main problems confronting those who sought to recreate a distinctive Islamic order in a world shaped and directed by the power of capital, of nation states and of class-based politics. To engage with this world, even if to challenge it, risked entry into a framework of action determined by the very world one was challenging – whether this was in the field of state politics or of the national economy. However, if the contest was largely symbolic, then this promised to liberate the challengers from the logic of the world being challenged.

In the latter part of the twentieth century, therefore, one of the powerful forms of Muslim response to capitalism has involved the turn to symbolic action and resistance in a number of spheres. By imagining a world within a world, insulated from surrounding forms and re-imbuing the transactions of everyday life with symbolic or religious significance, a number of Muslim intellectuals have sought to devise a protective shield, intended to deflect the invasive logic of the states and financial systems that have carried capitalism and its values around the globe. This constitutes a significant part of the Islamist discourse on gender and the family. It is also integral to certain views on the value and efficacy of violence as a way of dealing with the world. In both these cases, the forms of action advocated by various Muslim intellectuals can plausibly be seen as a way of acting effectively in a world not of their own making whilst avoiding the compromise which capitalism has encouraged in state, economy and the frameworks of analytical thought.

5.1   Sayyid Qutb and Ali Shari'ati: the power of subjectivity

Sayyid Qutb (1906–66) and Ali Shari'ati (1933–77) were Muslim intellectuals located in some respects on the margins. Wary of engagement with the institutions of established Islamic scholarship, let alone with the institutions of state or financial power which they felt had done so much to subvert the message of well-intentioned Islamic reformists, their very distance gave them the critical space sometimes necessary for a radically different perspective, as well as for expressing a convincing moral argument. It lent their writings an authority which appealed to those who felt themselves equally alienated from the establishments of their own societies, and their trenchant criticisms provided a repertoire of expression for the inarticulate fears and resentments of many who saw worldly power as an immovable and malign force. For that reason, their writings have a resonance that goes far beyond their original readership. They have often been taken up by others very differently placed who nevertheless share a sense of outrage at a world order apparently founded on the very values which they believe the Islamic message was intended to dispel.

They expressed revulsion at the world that European capitalism had brought into being, but they also grappled with the problem of imagination and social action if Muslims were to guard their communities from the disordering and reconstitutive power of capital. They were alert to the need for an epistemological break with the assumed foundations of knowledge – social and prescriptive – that had accompanied the global expansion of empires founded on capital accumulation and the commodification of labour. In different ways, Qutb and Shari'ati believed that a range of idealist responses would make Muslims look again at the world they had taken for granted, imbuing them with the defences needed against both the seductive 'common sense' of a capitalist, consumerist order, and the materialist critique of that order represented by socialism. For both of them, this would be the beginning of an imaginative recasting of the world, an opportunity to establish a community of Islamic belief that would serve as model and inspiration for a new generation educated in the values of a system that would negate the apparently overwhelming power of materialism.

This idealist position not only reflected their understanding of the strength of the original prophetic mission in the Hijaz of the seventh century, but also encapsulated their views of power. This was ultimately generated by divine will and transmitted to humanity through the words and commands that expressed, indeed embodied, that will. To obey the guidance contained therein was thus to become a vehicle for the kind of power which only God could exercise. It would be this inner impulse of absolute certitude – and rectitude – that would allow engagement with the world from a position of strength and the establishment of an autonomous area of distinctively Islamic sociability.

For both writers it was epistemologically necessary that 'imagining Islam' should owe nothing to other systems of thought, making an absolute break between one system of thought and another, between one set of ethical assumptions and another. For Qutb the construct of *jahiliyah*-as-antithesis of Islam, and for Shari'ati the Cain–Abel distinction, separated the world as it had been constituted by capitalism and imperialism and the imaginative realm of the truly Islamic society. These were dialectical devices that deliberately eschewed synthetic outcomes, preferring instead uncompromising negation of the thesis. Their individual projects were therefore directed towards the imaginative reconstruction of Islamic society which would avoid the neo-utilitarianism of the Islamic reformers, the barely disguised positivist econo-mism of the Islamic financial writers, or the stark secular logic to which those who had pinned their faith on the nation state had been subjected.

By privileging the ideational, they were situating the struggle between Islam-in-the-world and a range of antithetical forces on the level of the symbolic. This had an instrumental purpose, since both Qutb and Shari'ati wanted to reorganise distinctively Islamic defences, by opening the eyes of Muslims to their situation, by educating them for the coming struggle, thereby mobilising them for an effective response to the forces of materialism repre-sented by capitalism and its auto-critique, socialism. The individual and the society were to be invigorated and defined with reference to the symbolic universe of which their obedience to God's commands was a crucial part. It formed a key element in the ways in which Qutb and Shari'ati understood their faith. Their own imaginative engagement with Islam was visible in their lack of patience with much of traditional *fiqh*, the immediacy and poetry of their own interpretations, and their determination that this should be a world that was self-referential. Symbols such as these could only have meaning in a distinctively Islamic context, thereby foreclosing the possibility of ambiguous engagement with the legacies and reasoning of systems outside an Islamic repertoire.

It was during Sayyid Qutb's ten-year imprisonment in Egypt (1954–64) that he began to clarify his position regarding a Muslim's engagement with the world. In his slowly developing and increasingly popular Qur'anic com-mentary, *Fi zilal al-Qur'an*, he developed his ideas about the distinctiveness of the Islamic message – and the need to insulate Muslims from the surround-ing world of ignorance and alien values.[1] He moved away from his previous utilitarian understanding of the effects of capitalism on the welfare of

---

[1] Qutb, *Fi zilal al-Qur'an* (Beirut, 1967).

Muslims to a position in which the sole criterion was to be the word of God, written down in the Qur'an and experienced directly by every individual. Qutb dwelt on the aesthetic richness and moral depth of the Qur'an and pointed the way to its discovery by the method of *tafsir* (Qur'anic exegesis) which he adopted. This placed his own subjective opinions and impressions at centre stage. His was to be the interpretative consciousness which would lead others to a new understanding of the text through his own subjective judgements. He referred to the works of others, but less to the writings of traditional jurists than to the works of contemporary figures, such as the South Asian writers Abu-l-'Ala Mawdudi and Abu-l-Hasan 'Ali Nadvi, or the Egyptians 'Abbas al-'Aqqad and 'Abd al-Qadir 'Awdah. Qutb judged them to have made the same journey of discovery as he had made.

This journey was intensely ideological. Qutb wanted to derive a programme of action from the Qur'an, not simply moral guidance. At the same time, he believed that this programme would be effective only if Muslims internalised the norms and rulings to be found within its pages. He was seeking, therefore, to clarify the powerful moral obligations of the Qur'an and to convince people that the force expressed in the words of the Qur'an is sufficient to overcome the malign logic of the material world. This would provide mankind with the means of moral self-reinvention, opening up the path for the changes desired by God.[2] Intuition and a direct approach would, he believed, maintain the symbolic and the epistemological purity of this exercise.

Qutb's approach was therefore unashamedly subjectivist, in some respects therefore going against long-established criteria of philosophical validity and the rules of exegetical reasoning. He made a virtue of this, arguing that only such an approach would allow the individual, through direct action and in the company of others, to refound the political and social order by recreating the 'Qur'anic generation'. Qutb was trying to recapture the spirit of the early Muslim community whose members had undergone the dramatic experience of personal conversion, leading to the foundation of an Islamic order in Medina. For him, it was this fierce and transfiguring faith that had given Islamic principles such power under the early Caliphs. For this to happen, direct, unmediated encounter with the Qur'an was not only necessary, it was sufficient. Indeed, it was the very self-sufficiency of this project which Qutb wanted to emphasise in the twentieth century.

Qutb was challenging not simply the apparatus of power, but also the very reasoning on which the justification for most kinds of worldly power rested, defying the dominant forms of common sense. It was a bold endeavour, given

---

[2] See the chapter 'Jil qur'ani farid', in Qutb, *Ma'alim fi al-tariq*, pp. 14–23.

the odds apparently stacked against the project, and his use of the analogy of the first generation of Muslims was therefore both symbolic and instrumental. It was symbolic because it was intended to remind Muslims, through representation of a shared history of Muslim expansion, of the power of faith to transform the world. It was instrumental insofar as Qutb believed that this would be the means whereby Muslims in the contemporary world could be mobilised to take on and overthrow powers that confronted them – states, organisations and ideologies. In doing so, the forces of the *jahiliyah* would be dispersed and Islam would become the foundation of the dominant world order.[3]

As others have pointed out, Qutb had been much influenced by the ideas of the South Asian intellectuals Mawdudi and Nadvi in his thinking about contemporary *jahiliyah*, the indivisible sovereignty of God and the duty of *jihad* to restore the Islamic *shari'ah* to its rightful place in society. He acknowledged this influence and had done much to ensure that a wider Arabic-speaking public was aware of their writings through the journal *Al-Muslimun* in the early 1950s.[4] However, his imprisonment by the government of Nasser in the 1950s sharpened his attitude to the moral deficiencies of existing state power. From his prison cell he witnessed not only the brutal and authoritarian nature of the regime, but also the growing adulation of Nasser by the Egyptian population as he became a towering figure in the Middle East of the time. Yet Nasser claimed to be Muslim, as did the vast majority of those in Egypt and beyond who had elevated him to the status of hero, and he used Islamic symbols and authorities to enhance his authority.

For Qutb, the answer to this paradox was provided by his conclusion that neither the rulers of Egypt, its religious establishment, nor even the majority of its inhabitants could properly be called Muslim. On the contrary, he saw them as dissembling representatives of the very *jahiliyah* which the Islamic message had been intended to confound. Furthermore, this had been made possible not simply by the evil intent of those concerned, and by the structural logic of material power, but also by the insidious way in which the ideas of the *jahiliyah*, their methodologies and their values, had shaped the thoughts even of those who genuinely believed that they were rethinking Islam for the modern world.[5]

---

[3] Qutb, *Fi zilal*, part 3, pp. 70–9; part 4, pp. 19–32; part 5, pp. 148–50 and 195–202.

[4] Isabella Camera d'Afflitto, 'Note sulla rivista Al-Muslimun: analisi di alcuni temi della pubblicistica dei Fratelli Musulmani', *Oriente Moderno* 57 (Jan.–Dec. 1977), pp. 259–67; Y. M. Choueiri, *Islamic Fundamentalism* (London, 1990), p. 95.

[5] Sayyid Qutb, *Jahiliyat al-qarn al-'ishrin* (Cairo, 1980), pp. 54–97, 196–200; Y. Y. Haddad, 'Sayyid Qutb: ideologue of Islamic revival', ch. 4 in J. Esposito (ed.), *Voices of Resurgent Islam* (Oxford, 1983), pp. 85–7.

It became all the more imperative, therefore, that he should alert people to the delusion under which they were suffering. They had assumed that in coming to an understanding of the 'other' and even adapting some of its criteria to a modern Muslim outlook, they were helping to renovate Islam. For Qutb, nothing could be further from the truth. For him, the principles of Islam stood in direct antithesis to the world as it had developed historically, both before and after the capitalist revolution. He returned again and again to this theme, stressing not only the moral superiority of the Islamic message, but also its sharp differentiation from everything that owed its origins either to other faiths or to the presumed autonomy of human reason.[6]

It was in his final book, *Ma'alim fi al-tariq* (Signposts on the Road) (1964) that he expressed these sentiments most forcefully, addressing it to 'the vanguard which is resolute and which must take the road, through the vast extent of *jahiliyah* in this world'.[7] This book seems intended less to explain or persuade than to exhort and to guide those who already shared his own disgust at the ambient society and the condition of the Muslim world. It is a call to like-minded Muslims to engage fearlessly with the powers of the world through the practice of direct action, rather than through reasoned debate. As Qutb states:

setting up the kingdom of God on earth and eliminating the kingdom of man, means taking power from the hands of its human usurpers and restoring it to God alone . . . and [establishing] the supremacy of the *shari'ah* alone and the repeal of all man-made laws . . . This general call to liberate mankind on earth from all power that is not the power of God . . . was not a theoretical, philosophical or passive one . . . it was a dynamic, active, positive call.[8]

The contempt Qutb shows for what he dismisses as 'philosophical reasoning' reinforces his highly subjectivist approach to Qur'anic exegesis and his exhortation to Muslims to apprehend their faith intuitively. It is also consistent with his call for wholesale rejection of the forces of the *jahiliyah*. There is a trace here of the unease felt by Qutb about the seductive power of

---

[6] This forms one of the principal themes of the following works: *Hadha al-din* (Cairo, 1955), *Al-Mustaqbal li-hadha al-din* (Cairo, 1956), *Khasa'is al-tasawwur al-islami wa-muqawwamatuhu* (Cairo, 1960) and *Al-Islam wa-mushkilat al-hadarah* (Cairo, 1960).

[7] Qutb, *Ma'alim*, pp. 12–13. The book is composed of a number of chapters, some of which – such as the one on *jihad* – are extracted from his commentary *Fi zilal al-Qur'an*. Others he wrote explicitly for this work. It was first published in Egypt in 1964, possibly because the censors did not see it as different from the rest of his Qur'anic commentary. However, its potency as a text was recognised a couple of years later by the Egyptian authorities when they used the book as part of the evidence which served to condemn Qutb to death at his trial on charges of treason and subversion. It has since become a powerful influence on new generations of Islamist activists.

[8] Qutb, *Ma'alim*, p. 68.

the world and the danger of succumbing to forms of action based on other than Islamic principles, evident when he states: 'there is an abyss [between the *jahiliyah* and Islam] which is not spanned by a bridge to allow for a meeting half-way between the two, but to allow for the people of the *jahiliyah* to come over to Islam'.[9] Determined to preserve the distinction between two different ways of imagining and thinking about the world, and to stress the autonomy of a self-sufficient Islamic ethic and order, Qutb represents the struggle between Islam and other principles as an existential one, in which there can only be one victor: 'Islam did not come to condone people's desires . . . rather, it has come to eliminate these completely . . . and to found human existence on a particular basis. It came to organise life once and for all. To construct a life which will spring wholly from [Islam] and which will be firmly united with the very core of Islam itself.'[10]

Qutb was aware of the contingency of reason, having criticised Islamic jurists for allowing Greek and other traditions to shape their own understanding of the word of God. He was equally wary about contemporary concerns shaping approaches to the Qur'an, influencing the interpretative outcome before the text could be apprehended on its own terms. This may explain his insistence that the beauty of the Qur'an should be appreciated directly, bringing people into unmediated contact with the word of God.[11] For Qutb the elevation of human reason and human autonomy, although morally desirable, brought with it the danger that man-made rules for establishing mutually understandable communication might prevail, making Muslims vulnerable to the very epistemologies of the *jahiliyah* that he believed it imperative to combat. This was a radical position, containing a tension not easily resolved between an imagined spontaneity theoretically free of preconceptions (the frame of mind urged on those who were to approach the Qur'an 'directly') and the inescapable conditions of structured cognition (the imaginative and intellectual frameworks which must mediate anyone's apprehension of reality, textual or otherwise).

Qutb's attempt to square this circle leads him to place great stress on 'dynamic' *fiqh* and on the privileged understanding of the 'activist'. This can be and has been read as a revolutionary manifesto, encouraging like-minded Muslims to overthrow the systems of power that prevent the establishment of a truly Islamic order. However, Qutb also makes it clear that the precondition for this is the reconstruction of the Muslim self, if all other forms of imagination and reasoning are to be avoided from the outset. As Qutb says:

[9] Qutb, *Ma'alim*, p. 177.
[10] Qutb, *Ma'alim*, pp. 165–6.
[11] Binder, *Islamic Liberalism*, pp. 194–5.

'There is no doubt that we suffer under the social pressures, images, customs and leadership of the *jahiliyah* . . . especially within ourselves. We must not be seduced by this *jahili* society, nor should we give it our loyalty . . . Rather, it is our task first to change ourselves, in order then to change society.'[12] If the main task was to induce Muslims to approach the Qur'an in a direct and unmediated way, enabling them to appreciate its beauty and power, the first target of reconstruction must be the individual imagination.

The focus on the imagination is to protect Muslims against the pernicious, but potentially seductive, arguments of the *jahiliyah* and to ground the Islamic community on solid epistemological foundations. Direct apprehension of the Qur'an was to be the shield behind which a truly Islamic consciousness was to be developed, allowing thereafter a programme of social and political action immune to decay since it would have made no accommodation with the hegemonic power of materialism and secularism, whether working through capitalism or the linked phenomenon of communism. The power of individuals to shape their fate through the force of their beliefs was a powerful symbol of a reinvigorated Islam and held out the promise of a future that did not need to depend either on the material or the imaginative resources of other systems of social organisation and belief. The guarantee was to be the faith of individuals: 'When the number of believers reaches three, then the faith itself says to them: "You are now a society, an independent Islamic society, separated from the *jahili* society" . . . In this way, the Islamic society comes into being.'[13] To his own satisfaction at least, Qutb had thereby escaped from the baneful logic which had dogged the steps of all those – including himself as a social critic of the 1940s and early 1950s – who had 'discovered society' and, in discovering it, had found themselves conforming to the imaginative framework implied by this way of looking at human association.

At more or less the same time, in the different setting of the Pahlavi kingdom of Iran, the writings of Ali Shari'ati show evidence of a similar set of preoccupations, although expressed in a way distinctive to him and influenced by the intellectual and cultural background of Shi'ism and of Iranian intellectual history. Some of his later works, compiled from lectures given not long before he died in the late 1970s, contain a detailed indictment of Marxism, suggesting disillusionment with a creed which had once enthused him. Like the young Sayyid Qutb, Shari'ati had initially been repelled by what he saw as the cruel indifference and distorting greed of capitalism. For him, the power of capital to shape and impoverish human relationships was

[12] Qutb, *Ma'alim*, p. 22.
[13] Qutb, *Ma'alim*, p. 129.

fearsome since it had become hegemonic through the prosperity it had selectively established and through the normative order associated with it.[14]

His was a revolt against the violation of the moral economy perpetrated by capitalism, driven by his anger at the social injustice, greed and dehumanising aspects of the features of capitalism that he singled out for particular condemnation: the institution of private property, the commodification of labour, the alienation of individuals from their spiritual and moral selves, and the consumerism of a morally bankrupt society that only knew how to produce, counting merely the economic cost and not the cost to human sociability and the human spirit. It was scarcely surprising, therefore, that he should have found in some of Marx's writings an echo of his own disgust at the kind of world which capitalist enterprise was bringing into being.[15]

From the outset, Shari'ati had spoken and written in allegorical terms, within an Islamic idiom, using Qur'anic example and episodes from the early history of Islam to make his arguments vivid and comprehensible. His purpose was partly strategic. He was trying to persuade a younger generation, beguiled by European ideologies and values, of the relevance of Islam to contemporary social and political issues.[16] However, it also came from the way in which he saw the world. For Shari'ati, the symbolic was that which represented universal truths and conditions, within the idiom of specific religious and cultural settings. At first sight this might seem like cultural relativism, but in practice it was his acknowledgement that ethics were generally about the same kinds of concerns. Different answers might be returned to ethical questions, depending upon the place and the time, and some might be more confused or internally contradictory than others, but the areas of concern were broadly similar. For Shari'ati, Muslims were uniquely fortunate in that they had the words of God to guide them through the complexities of the world, as long as they read them and interpreted them in an enlightened spirit.[17]

---

[14] Shari'ati had been influenced by the Centre for the Propagation of Islamic Truths and by the 'God-worshipping socialists' in Iran in the late 1940s: Rahnema, *An Islamic Utopian*, pp. 30–4, 50–7.

[15] Shari'ati believed there were several 'Marxes' – and, to the anger of some Iranian Marxists, was most attracted to Marx's critique of capitalism as moral corruption. See Ali Akbar Akbari's attack on Shari'ati's *Islam-shinasi* (Islamology), cited in Rahnema, *Islamic Utopian*, pp. 201–3.

[16] It was also an indictment of those intellectuals who had become so taken with Western intellectual trends that they neglected their own heritage and opened themselves and their societies up to 'westernsickness' (*gharbzadegi*), following Jalal Al-i Ahmad – see Jalal Al-i Ahmad, *Plagued by the West* (Gharbzadegi) tr. P. S. Delmar (New York, 1982); see Shari'ati's lecture on 'Ideology', in Ali Shari'ati, *Man and Islam*, tr. F. Marjani (Houston, TX, 1974), pp. 82–101.

[17] Shari'ati, *Man and Islam*, pp. 16–20.

In this respect, like Sayyid Qutb, Shari'ati found himself between a social relativism which would have to acknowledge the validity of criteria of worth, of social utility and of expediency derived from non-Islamic sources, and an absolute conviction of the unique rectitude of the path laid out by God in the Qur'an for the regulation of human affairs. The reconciliation of these two stances was not always easy, as seen in his praise for Jean-Paul Sartre – the 'enlightened soul' who would liberate the West from its selfish, consumerist culture.[18] From his perspective, the allegorical or symbolic approach helped to bridge this gap, whilst at the same time bringing to bear a distinctively Islamic sensibility – and sometimes a distinctively Shi'i Muslim sensibility – to the problems associated with the global spread of capitalism.

It is in this context that Shari'ati elaborated upon his theme of the struggle between Cain and Abel as an explanatory metaphor that both encapsulated a distinctive form of social conflict and linked it directly to the moral framework set out in the Qur'an.[19] In his view, Cain stands for exploitation, injustice and oppression, whilst Abel represents the exploited, the oppressed and the disinherited. On the basis of this binary opposition running through the moral and material order, he constructed a history of humanity that had strong – and not coincidental – echoes of the opening sentence of the Communist Manifesto: 'The history of all hitherto existing society is the history of class struggles.' Thus, for Shari'ati, ever since the Fall, history has been the story of the struggle between the only two possible forms of human society: that of Cain and that of Abel. In this reading, 'the system of Cain' stands for 'economic monopoly and private ownership . . . slavery, serfdom, feudalism, bourgeoisie, industrial capitalism and imperialism (the culmination of capitalism)'. By contrast, the system of Abel has been represented in history by 'economic socialism (collective ownership), pastoral and hunting modes of production and the industrial mode of production (in the classless post-capitalist society)'.[20]

Applying this binary analysis to the contemporary world, Shari'ati identified what he called 'the pole of Cain' with political, economic and religious manifestations which took the shape of the king, the aristocracy, the bourgeoisie and the reactionary clerics. He saw them as manifestations of the

---

[18] Ali Shari'ati, 'Where Shall We Begin?', lecture, November 1971, in *Daftar-i asar-i Shari'ati* (Tehran, 1981), vol. II, pp. 286–94; *What Is To Be Done?*, ed. Farhang Rajaee (Houston, TX, 1986), pp. 9–10.

[19] Although not mentioned by name in the Qur'an, Cain and Abel (Qabil and Habil in Islamic tradition) are depicted in the story of the two brothers and the murder of one by the other – see Heribert Busse, 'Cain and Abel', in J. D. McAuliffe (ed.), *Encyclopedia of the Qur'an* (Leiden, 2001), vol. I, pp. 270–2.

[20] Ali Shari'ati 'The dialectic of sociology' (translated from *Islam-shinasi*, vol. I, pp. 85–94) in Ali Shari'ati, *On the Sociology of Islam*, (tr. H. Algar) (Berkeley, CA, n.d.), pp. 111–14.

kinds of power and greed indicted in the Qur'an – an indictment which they merited through their domination, exploitation and deception of the people. By contrast, 'the pole of Abel' referred to the people (*al-nas*), dominated and exploited by the ruling classes of kings, owners and clerics. Going further than his clerical critics – and many of his contemporaries – could tolerate, he effectively equated the people with God, calling the subjects of domination 'God-the-people' and asserting that 'In class society God stands in the same rank as *al-nas* . . . Whenever in the Qur'an social matters are mentioned, God and *al-nas* are virtually synonymous. The two words are often interchangeable, and yield the same meaning.'[21] From this he derived the argument that when the Qur'an mentioned the rule of God, it really meant the rule of the people. Equally, when the Qur'an states that property belongs to God, it means that capital belongs to the people as a whole. The 'system of Abel' is therefore a negation of the exclusions and exploitation associated with private property under capitalism. Similarly, it negates the coercive state structure and the ideological apparatus that polices and justifies capitalist systems of exploitation.

In laying out this view of history and of a world in which capitalism was the latest manifestation of a long line of systems which catered to the greed and power of the few at the expense of the many, Shari'ati was approaching the idea of the general will and associating it with the 'discovery' of society. As he put it:

Al-nas does not denote a mere collection of individuals. On the contrary, it has the sense of 'society' as opposed to 'individuals'. The word *al-nas* is a singular noun with the sense of a plural; it is a word without a singular. What word could better convey the concept of 'society', something possessed of an identity totally independent from all its individual members?[22]

The question arose, however, about how 'the people' could and should act in history. Thus a symbolic map of the moral contours of history and human society needed to be supplemented by a sense of social dynamics.

The question was how to ensure that power was exercised to benefit the people as a whole and to establish the foundations of a truly moral order on earth. As others have discovered before and since, Shari'ati was confronted with the fact that the romanticisation of 'the people' in a symbolic universe did not necessarily correspond to the actuality of human beings' diverse and contradictory interests. It is here that Shari'ati turned to the leading role of the intellectuals – or, rather, of the 'enlightened souls', in case the category of 'intellectual' might imply those whom he had indicted for having become too

---

[21] Shari'ati 'The dialectic of sociology', pp. 115–16.
[22] Shari'ati, 'The dialectic of sociology', p. 117.

seduced by secular Western thought. Nor did he want them to be mistaken for the traditional intellectuals, the *'ulama* whom he regarded as too blinded by their own narrow concerns to understand what was happening to society at large. Thus, it was to be the responsibility of the *roshanfikran* (lit. 'enlightened thinkers') to identify social problems, to propose rational solutions to those problems and to enlighten the masses about the nature of those solutions, as well as about their own role in bringing them about. They were to be the catalyst that would mobilise the people. Once this key task of transforming the imaginative and normative environment was achieved, 'society will take it from there', as Shari'ati rather cheerfully stated.[23]

The 'enlightened souls' would give intellectual direction to the people, initiating a revolution in knowledge which will give 'the great God-given gift of self-awareness [*khud-agahi*] to the general public' and which Shari'ati regarded as vital to transform the masses into a creative and dynamic force. Nor did their task end there. They must guide the people on the right path thereafter, ensuring that there was no backsliding or deviation from the values laid down in the path ordained by God. Shari'ati wished to distinguish this kind of knowledge from other forms, suggesting that it was tantamount to man's direct apprehension of the 'divine light and the source of consciousness and of the social conscience'. The enlightened soul would become aware of this through a personal epiphany, avoiding entanglement with conventional forms of knowledge and their associated institutions. He would thereby come to understand the 'inner pains of his society and thus generate self-awareness in people'.[24]

In some contexts, he suggested that such an individual should also rule in order to oversee the project of creating an ideal society, transforming 'institutions, social relations, culture, ethic, outlook, tastes, wants and values of society on the basis of a "revolutionary doctrine" and a "reformist ideology"'.[25] Tyranny would be avoided because, by definition, the 'enlightened soul' could not serve the forces of darkness and would be a perfect human, innately aware of the principles of Islam and the revolutionary Islamic programme. Despite his elevation of *al-nas* (the people) morally, and the role

---

[23] Shari'ati, *What Is To Be Done?*, pp. 16–17; Ervand Abrahamian, 'Ali Shari'ati: ideologue of the Iranian Revolution', ch. 14 in Edmund Burke III and Ira M. Lapidus (eds.), *Islam, Politics and Social Movements* (Berkeley, 1988) pp. 292–3.

[24] Shari'ati, *What Is To Be Done?*, pp. 16–17. Shari'ati had earlier suggested that this process was the discovery of the already given: 'society has been established on the basis of God-given norms and patterns . . . Man has the responsibility of recognising the norms of society and of improving those norms for the advancement of his society.' The norms themselves could not be changed since 'in its Qur'anic usage, norm is unchanging'. Ali Shari'ati, 'Approaches to the understanding of Islam', lecture given at the Husainiya Irshad, October 1968, in Shari'ati, *On the Sociology of Islam*, pp. 51–2.

[25] Cited in Rahnema, *Islamic Utopian*, pp. 236–7.

he assigns them in his account of history, it was clear that Shari'ati had little time for 'the democracy of heads' (by which he meant numbers) and 'the irresponsible and directionless liberalism which is the plaything of social forces'. Instead, he extolled the 'purity of leadership', not necessarily of an individual, but of a 'committed and revolutionary leadership responsible for movement and growth of society on the basis of its world view and ideology, for the realisation of the divine destiny of man'.[26]

It was almost inevitable that Shari'ati should have moved, like Qutb, towards the idea of the upright, enlightened revolutionary vanguard as the catalyst of revolutionary transformation.[27] This parallel becomes even more obvious in the place Shari'ati assigns to *vahdat* (unity) in his scheme, and its radical differentiation from *shirk* (polytheism). As with Qutb, this was the dividing line between justice and injustice, between faith and unbelief, between the permitted and the forbidden – in short, between Islam and the rest of the world. In keeping with his view of the nature and the role of the 'enlightened soul' this crucial frontier was to be manned by the *movahed* – the person who, through their understanding of Islam and direct apprehension of the true nature of society (and thus its ills), would be unaffected by the seductions and intimidation represented, respectively, by capitalism and tyrannical power. As Shari'ati described him, this was to be a hardworking, effective, fearless and selfless person who acknowledged only God's authority.[28] Given his role, it was not surprising that the *movahed*, seen primarily as a preacher, should become a more active ideal: the *mojahed* or the struggler on behalf of Islam. As an activist, he was charged with moving the revolution forward against the forces of tyranny, capitalist exploitation and the official clergy. All of these forces were now identified with *shirk*, the feature that must be uprooted if an ideal Islamic society was to be built.

Faced by the institutional power of polytheism, and aware also of the emerging guerrilla movement in 1970s Iran, some members of which were his students, Shari'ati became more outspoken on the need for violent confrontation between the holders of the 'monotheistic world outlook' (*jahanbani-ye towhidi*) and the champions of *shirk*, the false gods of capitalism and state power. The ideal figure was no longer someone who engaged in debate and sought to persuade others by the power of reason. Instead, the *mojahed* must be armed not only with the Qur'an and sound judgement, but also with weapons. In an apparent reversal of his previous assertion that faith and ideas

---

[26] Ali Shari'ati, 'The ideal society – the umma' (translated from *Islam-shinasi*, vol. I, pp. 97–8) in Shari'ati, *On the Sociology of Islam*, pp. 119–20.

[27] Ali Shari'ati, *Payam-i umid bih roshanfikr-i mas'ul* (Solon, OH, n.d.); Qutb, *Ma'alim*, pp. 54–7.

[28] Ali Shari'ati, *Islam-shinasi* (Mashhad: Chap-i Tus, 1968) pp. 87–97.

alone would be sufficient to transform the world, he now claimed that the ideal society could not be achieved without armed struggle. Dramatically underlining this point to his students, he declared in a speech in April 1972: 'Die! So that others may live.'[29]

Violence and the armed struggle were praised by Shari'ati as much for their symbolic weight as for any immediate political result that might come from armed revolutionary action. He seemed to believe that the spectacle of armed clashes between small dedicated groups of virtuous Muslim guerrillas and the forces of the overweening state would have an effect on public consciousness. It would be a catalyst, awakening the people to the violence and injustice implicit in the state, causing them to look anew at things they had long taken for granted. The outcome of a particular encounter was less important than the longer-term effects of the spectacle. Indeed, Shari'ati was not convinced that armed struggle would achieve the immediate goal of overthrowing the regime or seizing the state. Possibly he was wary of such easy victory. Instead, he made a virtue out of the fact that the rebels would almost certainly be crushed by the forces of the regime, holding up the example of Imam Husain's doomed struggle and death at Kerbala as an inspiration to those contemplating resistance to the Shah's state in Iran. He saw the death of *mojahedin* in the armed struggle as both a wake-up call to the masses and also a way of shaming the state itself. In an argument redolent of the Shi'i tradition, Shari'ati was extolling martyrdom as the means of undermining the edifice of apparently all-powerful *shirk*, since the self-sacrifice of the few would have shown it to be hollow.[30]

His apparent enthusiasm for the steadfast *mojahed* has been seen by some as the characteristic twentieth-century intellectual's romanticisation of revolutionary violence. There may well have been an element of this at work. However, it is also contemporaneous with the distance he was placing between himself and some of his earlier writings on social and economic reform. By the early 1970s he was openly contemptuous of his former idea of seeking to put forward his message on the basis of 'scientific research' and the scientific method. Instead, he invoked the outspoken companion of the Prophet, Abu al-Dharr al-Ghaffari, as someone who did not engage his opponents in

[29] Cited in Rahmena, *Islamic Utopian*, p. 294.
[30] Ali Shari'ati, 'Shahadat' lecture given at the Husainiyah Irshad, Tehran, 9 Muharram 1970, in Mahmud Taleqani, Murtada Mutahhari and Ali Shari'ati, *Jihad and Shahadat*, ed. Mehdi Abedi and Gary Legenhausen (Houston, TX, 1986), pp. 168–74, 178–80, 192–4, 199–214: '*shahadat* [martyrdom] is the only reason for existence, the only sign of being present, the only means of attack and defense and the only manner of resistance so that truth, right and justice can remain alive at a time and under a regime in which uselessness, falsity and oppression rule' (p. 213); Ali Shari'ati (writing as Ihsan Khurasani), *Du shahid* (Tehran, 1977); Rahnema, *Islamic Utopian*, pp. 277–9, 287, 294, 307–9.

reasoned debate when faced with blatant injustice, but took direct action. In the late twentieth century, Shari'ati claimed that he could not apply 'the scientific approach' in the face of 'people's hunger and the pillage of the capitalists'.[31]

By turning his back on the 'scientific method', Shari'ati was following a path which Qutb had trodden before him when he had renounced the utilitarian arguments of his earlier writing in favour of a direct and unmediated approach to the texts, based primarily on faith. In Shari'ati's more obviously 'scientific' work, especially *Islam-shinasi*, he had already expressed his unease at the influence of those Westernised Iranian and Muslim intellectuals who had been so taken by Western thought, its values and its forms of argument, that they had neglected their authentic Islamic heritage. Yet the tenor of that book showed that Shari'ati himself had been equally influenced and had introduced into his reasoning arguments derived from his close knowledge of and sympathy for Western intellectual trends, particularly socialist critiques of capitalism. In these later writings of the 1970s, Shari'ati seems to have seen the road down which this was leading him and – like Qutb – reacted with considerable vehemence.

Shari'ati's mistrust of his own responses to Marxism, and other intellectual trends that he had initially found so appealing, helps to explain the strength of his denunciation of Marxism in these years. These views, in his writings after his release from prison in the mid-1970s, seemed so much at odds with his previous opinions that there has been speculation about a deal to ensure his release with the state authorities given their obsession with the threat of Marxism in Iran at the time. However, his critique of Marxism bears many of the hallmarks of his earlier writings. It shows quite clearly that what he once admired, he still admired, namely 'philosophical Marxism', a humane view of mankind which paid particular attention to the importance of the human spirit. However, he denounced 'sociological Marxism' as materialist and economistic, making it unsuitable as a path to be followed. More than that, it was deeply disappointing and illusory in pretending to present a genuine alternative to capitalism. As he remarked: 'Is not Marxism really just the other side of the coin of Western capitalism?'[32] This was a theme he explored at length.

---

[31] Cited in Rahnema, *Islamic Utopian*, p. 196; on Abu Dharr, see Shari'ati, *Du shahid*, pp. 3–44; Shahrough Akhavi, 'Shari'ati's social thought', in Nikki Keddie (ed.), *Religion and Politics in Iran* (New Haven, 1983), pp. 129–35. But see his contrasting attitudes to the purely intellectual responses to oppression contained in his denunciation of 'Abdallah ibn 'Umar on one hand, and his praise for Imam Ja'far al-Sadiq, Shari'ati 'Shahadat' in *Jihad and Shahadat*, pp. 163–4 and 173–4.

[32] Ali Shari'ati, *Marxism and Other Western Fallacies*, tr. R. Campbell (Berkeley, CA, 1980), p. 43.

In his view, Marxism was a form of bourgeois thought which embodied all the values of the very capitalist society which it claimed to dissect. Both represented an economism which, at its crudest, could be reduced to a mere search for power, understood in material terms. Both, he argued, as their ultimate objectives, wished to create a bourgeois society. In order to underline the fundamental similarities (and to stress the gulf separating them from an Islamic order), Shari'ati claimed that the sole difference 'between the two theses "Capital will be at the disposal of a single class" and "Capital will be at the disposal of the state" is the difference between two systems, not that between two philosophies or two different conceptions of life, humanity, moral values, or the universe'.[33]

Shari'ati agreed with those who claimed that the more Marxism tried to counter capitalism on its own terrain, by asserting its ability to deliver a better material future than any form of capitalism, the more vulnerable it made itself. This would apply both to the possible failure of those places which had consciously adopted a Marxist path to economic development, as well as to the weakness of an argument that had not established new and radically different criteria of value, but had essentially derived them from the same philosophical traditions against which it tried to define itself.[34] Equally important for the position now adopted by Shari'ati was the realisation that the same could also be said of those Muslim intellectuals, including himself, who had tried to set forth a counter-thesis to capitalism which was over-reliant on capitalism's own autocritiques, in the shape of socialism and Marxism. Thus, regardless of the effect of Shari'ati's imprisonment, he was aware that his earlier flirtation with socialism, with its economism, materialism and infatuation with the state as agent of change, was seen as less and less likely to lead to the establishment of a just society, let alone one that would be compatible with Islamic principles.[35]

Equally, by the mid-1970s, Shari'ati saw some of the disadvantages of armed struggle, appealing as it was in a symbolic and even romantic sense. Political violence had real and often terrible consequences. It rarely threw up leaders of the idealised kind he had envisaged, involved as they were in the processes of resistance and secretive armed conspiracy. As in other forms of engagement with the world, his conclusion was that unless the individuals concerned were protected by inner fortitude, they would succumb to the logic

---

[33] Shari'ati, *Marxism*, p. 71.

[34] Shari'ati, *Marxism*, p. 73.

[35] Shari'ati approvingly quoted Proudhon's warning to Marx that socialists were in danger of creating a new cult: 'I am afraid that tomorrow this school of yours will assume the form of a state religion, and that worship of the state will replace worship of God': Ali Shari'ati, 'Mysticism, equality and freedom', in Shari'ati, *Marxism*, pp. 106–8.

of systems of action, as well as of thought, that they could not control and which would lead them further from an understanding of the truth.[36]

Thus, confronted by the power of the world and by the apparent hegemony of its practices and beliefs, Shari'ati returned to direct, self-abnegating immersion in the beauty and truth of the Islamic message. Again echoing Qutb, a strong mystical flavour can be detected in his later writings, since he is advocating direct personal experience of divinity, through a transforming personal experience such as the one he claimed to have undergone himself. This was gnosticism in the service of a social ideal – one which would not be susceptible therefore to corruption by other forms of worldly power, or by the seduction of other value systems. In Shari'ati's view the direct approach to Islam – and indeed to God – was to be the key strategy that would insulate the Muslim from the temptations of the world, whether this was represented by the material promise of capitalism or by Marxism's powerful critique. Only by extensive and deep acquaintance, not simply with the values of Islam but also with the gnostic way of apprehending those values and principles and their truths directly, would Muslims be able to organise an effective defence and thus response to what the world had become.[37]

5.2   The 'guarded sphere': gender and action

Having recourse to the symbolic and the self-referentially Islamic was a way of creating secure boundaries between the world as it was constituted and a world in which distinctively Islamic values would form the parameters of the imagination. Capitalism as a disruptive and transformative process had intruded everywhere and it seemed important to many Muslim intellectuals, therefore, to construct a 'guarded sphere' impervious to the norms of an alienating ideology, encouraging the development of the strong 'Islamic personality'. Nowhere has this been more in evidence than in modern Islamist discourses on gender.

A preoccupation with the comportment of men was intended to define a sanctioned way of being a man, as well as to suggest the means by which a Muslim man could protect himself against an intrusive, sometimes seductive world beyond his control. Forms of dress, of speech, of gesture, as well as ways of acting in a great variety of situations, some intimately private, some open and public, have been prescribed in detail. This is to remind men of their obligations to God, of their identity as Muslims and of the importance of always placing Islam – the service of God – at the forefront of their

[36] Ali Shari'ati, *Khvud'sazi-i inqilabi* (n.p., 1978), pp. 23–55; Rahnema, *Islamic Utopian*, pp. 346–8.
[37] Rahnema, *Islamic Utopian*, pp. 157–60.

thoughts.[38] In this respect, the concern of Muslim writers is by no means unique. Rituals, such as prayer or fasting, have long been associated with all religious practice precisely to remind the believer of his or her connection to the spiritual world, creating a sphere of action and reflection deliberately separated from the mundane.[39]

Some of these writings focus on the comportment of men, but a very substantial proportion concern the behaviour of women. Indeed, this forms a burgeoning field of contemporary Islamist discourse and literature. It is part of the response to the conditions created by the kind of modernity experienced by the Islamic world, in which capitalism and the constructions of gender it encourages loom large. The very ambivalence of industrial capitalism in this regard sharpened the need for a response. Capitalism promised to free women from unpaid servitude within the home, opening up the possibility of a full role as producers and consumers in a market-driven economy which was theoretically gender-blind. Yet, at the same time, it devalued women's traditional skills as producers, replacing a range of domestically produced goods with industrially manufactured output. It also demonstrated that a socially embedded market was by no means gender-blind: women were regarded as a cheaper form of labour and were incorporated as commodities into the thriving global market of the body.[40]

The use of symbolic markers to maintain a separation between the sexes and detailed prescriptions about the proper spheres in which men and women can act autonomously have been integral to many Muslim intellectuals' response to the promise and threat of capitalist modernity. Focusing on those attributes of women which differentiate them from men in society, these writings treat women as the terrain for the symbolic expression of a certain kind of Islamic identity, but also as key players in the defence against the intrusion of other belief systems. Echoing contemporary secular nationalist discourses, there is stress on the functional role of women in maintaining and reproducing a distinctively Islamic society, through the act of giving birth and

---

[38] See, for instance, the impressive range of activities for which there are prescribed forms of action in Ruhallah ibn Mustafa Khomeini, *A Clarification of Questions*, tr. J. Borujerdi (Boulder, CO, 1984). In the case of the Daudi Bohras, for example, orthopraxy and dress codes are a key part of community as well as gender differentiation: see J. Blank, *Mullahs on the Mainframe: Islam and Modernity among the Daudi Bohras* (Chicago, 2001), pp. 186–95.

[39] C. Bell, *Ritual* (Oxford, 1997), pp. 120–8, 191–7; W. E. Paden, *Religious Worlds* (Boston, 1988), pp. 93–120; R. A. Rappaport, *Ritual and Religion in the Making of Humanity* (Cambridge, 1999), pp. 23–57.

[40] S. Lewenhak, *The Revaluation of Women's Work* (London, 1992), pp. 1–19; J. White, 'Women and work in Istanbul', *Middle East Report* 173 (Nov./Dec. 1991), pp. 18–22; B. Fine, *Women's Employment and the Capitalist Family* (London, 1992), pp. 45–86; M. Mies, 'Capitalist development and subsistence production: women in rural India' in M. Mies (ed.), *Women: The Last Colony* (London, 1988), pp. 27–50.

educating children. The security of the domestic environment becomes the guarantee of a truly Islamic society, since it is the site for the production of the strong 'Islamic personality' who does battle with the world in the service of Islamic values. This places a heavy historical and sociological responsibility on women, making their comportment and actions a matter for general concern by the largely male cohort of concerned Muslim intellectuals.[41]

At the same time, women themselves found a voice and engaged in the debate. For some, the symbolism of gender-specific comportment and dress was seen as identity-affirming, both in terms of their gender and their religious faith. It was also seen by some as a practical means of engaging with the world. Equally, the roles prescribed for them were accepted by many as appropriate to Muslim daughters, sisters, wives and mothers, since they too shared the belief in the centrality of the household in the reproduction of an Islamic society – and for the most part appeared to share the view of the division of labour within the household itself.[42] For others, however, confident in their Islamic identity and as critical as their male counterparts of the intrusions of a certain kind of capitalist modernity, much that was being prescribed for them by men was seen as the outcome not of Islamic reflection, but of patriarchal anxiety. Disconcerting as it was for some of the men who had turned women into symbols of a certain kind of Islamic identity, women were now determined to inscribe themselves into the narrative, not as ideally constructed clusters of virtues, but as active interpreters of their own fate.[43]

This perspective was very much in line with Shari'ati's writings. He deplored the restrictive roles assigned to women by conservative clerics, arguing passionately that women should be much more than symbolic and reproductive beings, urging them to challenge the complacency and dominance of men, to educate themselves and to become fully responsible participants in the political and economic life of an Islamic society.[44] By contrast, Qutb, in his later writings, conflated the symbolic with the practical when

---

[41] Cook, *Commanding Right and Forbidding Wrong*, pp. 545–8; for an indictment of male-dominated traditions of writing about women, their sexuality and their role vis-à-vis men in distinctively Islamic discourses historically, see Fatna A. Sabbah, *Woman in the Muslim Unconscious*, tr. Mary Jo Lakeland (New York, 1984), pp. 13–19, 63–118.

[42] Some typical exemplars of this are Fatima Umar Naseef, *Women in Islam: A Discourse of Rights and Obligations*, ed. S. M. Abedin (New Delhi, 1999), pp. 107–16, 185–247; Zainab al-Ghazzali has also argued along these lines, although her autobiography would suggest that this is by no means synonymous with seclusion or inactivity in the public sphere – see *Ayam min Hayati* (Cairo, 1989).

[43] Ziba Mir-Hosseini, *Islam and Gender: The Religious Debate in Contemporary Iran* (London, 1999), pp. 3–18, 86–102; V. Moghadam, 'Islamic feminism and its discontents: toward a resolution of the debate', in T. Saliba, C. Allen and J. A. Howard (eds.), *Gender, Politics and Islam* (Chicago, 2002), pp. 23–7, 35–7.

[44] Ali Shari'ati, *Fatimah Fatimah ast* (Tehran, 1971), pp. 79–93; Ali Shari'ati, *Zan musalman* (Tehran, 1967), pp. 3–40.

he inveighed against women's 'adornment, enticement and enchantment' as symptom and cause of lax morals, family collapse and a marker of the 'backwardness of civilization'. For him, this was the world introduced by industrial capitalism and its voracious drive to open up new markets, identify new sources of labour and transform all relations, even the most intimate, into commodities. It was to guard against its effects that women must return to the home, the site of their prime responsibility, and forgo the better pay, prestige and respect which he admitted that capitalist society accorded to those who took a full part in the production of commodities.[45]

In this he was again echoing Mawdudi's response to the growing engagement of Muslim women in the industrial, urban world of capitalist development. Mawdudi had extolled the virtues of *purdah*, claiming that the physical segregation of men and women in public spaces, and the symbolic differentiation and seclusion of women's bodies through dress and comportment, were the means by which an Islamic ethical order could be restored and defended against capitalism.[46] This was to be a dominant theme in the writings of many who have helped to shape the contemporary Islamist discourse on women – a discourse prompted by the transformations of capitalist development in much of the Islamic world, but which was also sustained by a range of beliefs and traditions that relied more on patriarchal than on strictly textual Islamic authority.[47]

Islamic scholars and commentators retrieved a range of texts to support their positions on such things as the prescribed dress for women, their behaviour in public places, their roles in society and, inevitably, their subordination to the patriarchal hierarchies of family, home and polity. The symbolic order was to be restored through the reinforcement of rules intended to determine the behaviour of women, represented as indicators of the moral health of society more generally. In Iran after 1979, in Saudi Arabia, and in Afghanistan under the Taliban, the legal system enforced conformity with dress codes or with rulings defining the comportment of women in public. These were intended to preserve the distinctiveness of the society in question, but whether as one which was marked by an authentically Islamic ethic, or by a tribal, patriarchal system of values, was open to question.[48]

---

[45] Qutb, *Ma'alim*, pp. 123–6.
[46] Abu al-A'la Mawdudi, *Purdah and the Status of Women in Islam*, tr. Al-Ash'ari (Lahore, 1972), pp. 39–60, 145–71, 175–215; H. L. Bodman, 'Introduction', in H. L. Bodman and N. Tohidi (eds.), *Women in Muslim Societies* (Boulder, CO, 1998), pp. 15–16.
[47] Haideh Moghissi, *Feminism and Islamic Fundamentalism* (London, 1999), pp. 44, 72–3.
[48] Afsaneh Najmabadi, 'Hazards of modernity and morality: women, state and ideology in contemporary Iran', pp. 63–76, and Ayesha Jalal, 'The convenience of subservience: women and the state in Pakistan', pp. 77–114, in Deniz Kandiyoti (ed.), *Women, Islam and the State* (Basingstoke, 1991); J. L. Esposito, 'Women in Islam and Muslim societies', pp. xii–xvii and Laurie Brand, 'Women and the state in Jordan', pp. 104–13, in Y. Y. Haddad and J. L. Esposito

Some Muslim intellectuals treated women on a purely symbolic level, writing about them largely as ciphers: passive participants on whom could be inscribed all the moral preoccupations of their male counterparts. This attitude expressed a recurrent male unease about female sexuality – its disordering and potentially transgressive nature – visible throughout history, in the writings not only of Islamic scholars, but of many other male-dominated traditions. In this case, however, it was reinforced by fears that capitalism, imperialism and the dominant discourses of liberalism had constructed a world which spoke directly to this disruptive side of the female and would develop it to the detriment of social order generally and specifically of Islamic society. In this, it echoed the concern of many Muslim intellectuals about the effects of capitalism in giving unrestrained licence to greed, acquisitiveness and self-interest. Thus the adoption of allegedly 'Islamic' forms of dress and behaviour by women was judged to be symbolically important, in that it represented a cluster of values and the defence of a certain order against forces inimical to Islamic values. At the same time, as the writings of Ayatollah Khomeini demonstrate, by concentrating on the symbolic, the argument was framed in Islamic terms, avoiding the risk of making it vulnerable to the logic of the very systems they were trying to counter.[49]

For other writers, however, it was the functional role of women as believers and as active, engaged human beings which received the most attention. Women were expected to play a full part in a gender-determined division of labour, bringing up and educating children and inculcating Islamic values within the home. The family and the home thus become a bastion against the moral compromises and turpitude of the public arena, given the power of the systems which had come to dominate the polity and the economy. Their role was to safeguard and reproduce Islamic society, just as in positivist sociology the family had been cited as the foundation of social order. It was the responsibility of all Muslims, men and women, to ensure that it functioned as a unit capable of carrying out this task. According to some writers, the family even constituted a strategic point of departure for the recreation of a more general Islamic order – a kind of revolutionary cell which, in concert with others, would organise effective resistance to the structures of political and economic power.[50]

(eds.), *Islam, Gender and Social Change* (New York and Oxford, 1998); Valentine Moghadam, 'Reform, revolution and reaction: the trajectory of the "woman question" in Afghanistan', in Valentine Moghadam, *Gender and National Identity* (London, 1994), pp. 84–109.

[49] Ruhollah ibn Mustafa Khumaini, *Jaigah-i zan dar andishah-i Imam Khumaini* (Tehran, 1999), pp. 55–106, 199, 279; see also the 1980s re-publication in Cairo of Ibn Taimiyah, *Fatawa al-nisa'* (Cairo, 1983).

[50] For some, the actual family, with its different generations and hierarchies, was too complex or irreducible a sociological phenomenon to be cast in this role, so the 'family' needed to be created from scratch to serve these revolutionary purposes – see the example of the Egyptian

Despite the common view that women must raise children and hold to-gether the family, there exists a wide range of opinion about the implications of this for women themselves and their life chances. Some, such as Mawdudi, seemed to suggest that the social institution of *purdah* and rigorous segrega-tion were sufficient to sustain the Muslim family through women's perform-ance of their allotted roles. Others, such as the Egyptians Qasim Amin and Hasan al-Banna in the earlier period, and Zainab al-Ghazzali and the Tunisian Rashid al-Ghannoushi in the latter part of the twentieth century, argued that the key role assigned to women demanded that they have full access to education. Without it, women would not be able to teach their children anything worthwhile, let alone instruct them adequately in the faith.[51] This implied the extension of women's lives beyond the home to public institutions of learning, whether segregated or not. For some, this also implied that women could become full members of the scientific and intellectual commu-nity, capable of independent analysis and original interpretation. For others, this is a disconcerting prospect and they seem to suggest that women's education should be restricted to very specific forms of knowledge.[52]

However, the view that women should take full advantage of the opportun-ities offered by modern education led a number of Muslim intellectuals to endorse the view that women should form a respected part of the labour force in order to safeguard the family and maintain an Islamic society. There was a tendency to restrict women to particular forms of work, such as nursing or teaching, because of the alleged suitability of their natures and physiques, but there was an acknowledgement that women often needed to work outside the home. This need, however, was nearly always phrased in terms which privileged the requirements of the family or of the society as a whole.[53] The

Islamist group, Al-Takfir wa-l-Hijra in Gilles Kepel, *The Prophet and Pharaoh* (London, 1985), pp. 86–91; Abdelwahab Bouhdiba, *Sexuality in Islam*, tr. Alan Sheridan (London, 1998), pp. 231–5.

[51] Mansoor Fahmy, *La condition de la femme dans l'Islam* (Paris, 1990; first published 1913); Qasim Amin, *The Liberation of Women*, tr. S. S. Peterson (Cairo, 2000), pp. 3–34, and *The New Woman* (Cairo, 2000), pp. 179–98; Muhammad 'Abduh, *Al-Islam wa-l-mar' ah fi ra'i al-imam Muhammad 'Abduh*, ed. Muhammad 'Imarah (Cairo, 1975), pp. 55–69; Esposito, 'Women in Islam and Muslim societies', pp. xiv–xv.

[52] Y. Y. Haddad, 'Islam and gender: dilemmas in the changing Arab world', in Haddad and Esposito (eds.) *Islam, Gender and Social Change*, pp. 19–20; Rashid al-Ghannoushi, *Al-Mar'ah baina al-Qur'an wa-waqi' al-muslimin* (London, 2000), pp. 77–88 – although, for some, their view of men's education was not that different: instruction in the truth, established by others.

[53] Y. Y. Haddad, 'Islam and gender: dilemmas in the changing Arab world', pp. 7–9. As Haddad makes clear, citing Muhammad Khamis, even these reasons were not sufficient for some writers; whilst even a writer like Abbassi Madani, who argues for a much more active and engaged role for women in the creation of an Islamic order, tended to fall back on the 'default' position that, all other things being equal, men should have priority over women in access to

idea that women might need to work for reasons of their own individual satisfaction was not mentioned – but became part of the developing women's *ijtihad*.

Once the principle of women's participation in the labour market had been allowed, it opened up possibilities for their participation in public life to a degree which some clearly found disconcerting. There was concern about close physical contact with male colleagues, about women as competitors and even in positions of authority over men. As in other spheres, these fears also reflected unease about the way that arguments from social utility and material advancement shaped the reasoning itself, making acceptable or even commendable that which other interpretations of the Islamic tradition suggested was dubious, if not forbidden.[54]

Qutb's writings demonstrate this shift on the position of women. He had originally taken the view that, although women's primary responsibility was in the home, they needed access to education and to the world of work, recognising the full role they must play in the Islamic movement. However, as his views on the dangerous logic of social utility hardened, so his views on women's roles became more restrictive. He came to deplore the participation of women in the labour force, seeing it as distracting from their prime duties and inviting morally perilous interaction with men in the workplace.[55] In *Fi zilal al-Qur'an*, he suggested that, by going out to work, women were contravening the rules of nature (*fitrah*) and threatening the very foundation of social life. Citing *Surah* 4 (*al-Nisa'*), verse 34 he claimed that the licence now given to women to join the labour force on a par with men went against the divine order itself.[56]

Similar 'arguments from nature' have been used in Europe and the Americas, by both secular and religious authorities, to limit women's roles, particularly insofar as they were likely to impinge on those associated traditionally with men. They share with Qutb and other Muslim intellectuals the idea of an identity between a supposed natural order and an ethical order. The introduction of the topic of women's physiological and even psychological constitution – and the differences from those of men – was intended as a telling proof of the divine order itself. Thus the Qur'an is being read as a text that is in harmony with nature since both are of divine origin. Their congruence is further testimony to divine inspiration. However, it is clear that

---

employment since 'the woman can take care of the home'. Olfa Lamloum, 'Les femmes dans le discours islamiste', *Confluences Méditerranée* 27 (Autumn 1998), pp. 25–32.

[54] Al-Bahi al-Khuli, *Al-Islam wa-l-mar'ah al-mu'asirah* (Kuwait, 1984).

[55] Qutb, *Ma'alim*, p. 123; Sylvia Haim, 'Sayyid Qutb', *Asian and African Studies* 16 (1982), pp. 151–2.

[56] Qutb, *Fi zilal al-Qur'an*, part 5, pp. 9–38.

'nature' in this context is a gendered construction, according with predomin-antly male views of proper social order and the subordinate role of women. Qutb and others are determined to see this in the Qur'an, and so this is the way in which they read it. This is in marked contrast to those women in Iran, Malaysia and Turkey who have taken on the task of *ijtihad* themselves and whose very existence, as well as approach, stands this view of nature on its head.[57]

Nowhere have these debates, on both sides, been better represented than in Iran, both before and after the revolution. Thus, in the 1960s, Ayatollah Yahya Nuri made great play of the biological differences between men and women, in which he included psychological differences, to support his view that in Islamic jurisprudence and society women are inferior to men in terms of rights and status. Using arguments familiar from Europe and elsewhere, he claimed that since women were biologically geared to reproduction and child-rearing, men must have prior claim in the labour market. Furthermore, women's emotional and unstable cast of mind disqualified them from full participation in fields marked out by analytical reasoning and thus assured the primacy of men in the sphere of knowledge and education.[58]

These views were later echoed by Ayatollah Morteza Motahhari. Intri-guingly, his justification for restraints on women's behaviour, as well as for polygamy, is based on man's uncontrollable sexual appetite. In this version of 'nature' it is men who are portrayed as the slave of their passions and women who must therefore use calculating strategies of proper comportment not to arouse them. Yet he also claims that women's powerful emotional natures disqualify them from acting as judges, and thus, by implication, as independ-ent *mujtahids* or as rulers. He leaves open a number of occupations for women, alleged to be more in harmony with their 'nature', such as teaching, nursing, child-minding and medicine, should social and economic conditions demand this. As Motahhari is careful to point out, however, this would only be allowed for the greater good of society, not for the gratification of the woman as an individual.[59]

---

[57] Afsaneh Najmabadi, 'Feminism in an Islamic republic', in Haddad and Esposito, *Islam, Gender and Social Change*, pp. 62–84; Anne Sofie Roald, 'Feminist reinterpretation of Islamic sources: Muslim feminist theology in the light of the Christian tradition of feminist thought', in K. Ask and M. Tjomsland (eds.), *Women and Islamization* (Oxford, 1998), pp. 25–44; Amina Wadud-Muhsin, 'Qur'an and woman', in C. Kurzman (ed) *Liberal Islam: A Sourcebook* (Oxford, 1998), pp. 127–38.

[58] Ayatollah Yahya Nuri, *Hughughe-zan dar islam va jahan* (Tehran: 1964), quoted in F. Hussain and K. Radwan, 'The Islamic revolution and women: quest for the Quranic model', in Freda Hussain (ed.), *Muslim Women* (London, 1984), p. 46.

[59] Murtaza Mutahhari, *The Rights of Women in Islam* (Tehran, 1981), pp. 14–18, 68–71, 113–25, 173–5, 225–34, 340–76. As Hojjatulislam Muhammad Taqi Mesbah points out, if the effect of women joining the labour market is that the family is neglected, then this should be

A similar argument mixing 'nature' with social expediency emerges in the writings of Ayatollah Ruhollah Khomeini. From the 1960s onwards he had been responding to enquiries concerning the status of women, sexuality and sexual behaviour. As he became more of a public figure, he pronounced on the role of women in society generally, and here the criteria of social utility come to the fore. He frequently referred to the biological differences between men and women which provide 'naturalistic' evidence for the inequality of the sexes prescribed in the Qur'an and in other readings from the Islamic tradition. He also insisted on the veiling of women and on their modest dress and behaviour, demonstrating that unease with female sexuality that was so integral a part of the wider discourse amongst both established religious scholars and Muslim intellectuals and social commentators.

However, he also stressed the role which women had to play in reproducing an Islamic society. Women and the family were considered 'pillars of the nation' and 'strong bastions of virtue and chastity', mixing both the symbolic appropriation of women and their prescribed social functions in a striking way. Amongst the most important of these were motherhood and the education of their children – women were the 'instructors of society'. Khomeini vehemently attacked what he regarded as the degradation of women encouraged by the capitalism and consumerism which he blamed the Pahlavi regime for bringing upon Iran. Women were urged to take part in the movement to overthrow the Pahlavis, in order to retrieve their dignity and help to reconstruct the country. These views, and the implications for the role women were expected to play after the revolution, were made plain both in the symbolic act of segregation prescribed by the veiling decree of March 1979, and in the preamble to the 1979 Iranian constitution. This stipulated that 'the family is the fundamental unit of society and the main centre of growth and transcendence for humanity'. Within such a unit, it was necessary to free 'woman from being regarded as a "thing" or as a tool serving consumerism and exploitation', so that she could accept 'a more serious responsibility' by 'regaining her important duty and most respectful role of mother'.[60]

Understandably, many women refused to be regarded as objects, whether by the commodification of consumerist capitalist society or by the Islamic

---

discouraged. He cites family breakdown as one of the hidden ills and consequences of industrial capitalism, since it is capitalist commerce and industry that draw women out of the home and thereby, in his view, encourage a trend that goes against 'nature', with understandably catastrophic results. Muhammad Taqi Mesbah, 'Women or half of the body of society', in *Status of Women in Islam* (Tehran, 1985), pp. 16–27.

[60] Hussain and Radwan, 'The Islamic revolution and women', pp. 48–51; Ruhallah Khomeini, *Islam and Revolution*, tr. H. Algar (Berkeley, 1981), pp. 171–3, 222–3, 263–4; Islamic Republic of Iran, *The Constitution of the Islamic Republic of Iran*, tr. Hosein Elahi Qomshei (Tehran, n.d.), pp. 14–15.

scholars who wished to transform women into symbolic objects. However, in Iran, as elsewhere, they faced a dilemma. They could draw on a rich repertoire of secular critical thought, some but not all specifically feminist, which provided telling critiques of the alienating effects of global capital, and of the gendering of knowledge in societies still in the grip of patriarchal structures and values. For some in the Islamic world, these were powerful and appealing ideas and had been drawn upon to argue for greater empowerment and equal rights for women. The discourses of secular nationalism, ambiguous though they often were on the question of gender, of social reform and of a post-Enlightenment critique of religious knowledge, promised a series of effective rationales for greater participation by women and equality with their male fellow citizens.

The problem arose, however, not simply because practice rarely matched these promises. It was also sharply felt by women who shared the desire to take an active part in determining the futures of their societies, but who felt, with some justification, that the dominant discourses of feminism, liberalism, secular nationalism and socialism marginalised or discounted their identity as Muslims. They were nevertheless aware that much of the traditionalist Islamic discourse did not allow them much space in which to act – and some of the more contemporary Islamic trends seemed to restrict them still further. However, the proliferation of Islamic discourses and the widening repertoire available to those Muslims who were determined to engage with the world, yet retain their Islamic identities, provided opportunities for women to take part in the emerging movements of reinterpretation.

In Egypt, Zainab al-Ghazzali became a prominent advocate not simply of the importance and role of women within the Islamic movement, but also of the importance of the movement itself in the transformation of society. Her organisation of the Muslim Women's Association (founded in 1936) and her writings drew her close to the Muslim Brotherhood, under Hasan al-Banna and his successors. Her position on the role of women followed the line advocated by other Islamic intellectuals, seeing women as responsible primarily for the maintenance of the home and the education of children, whilst recognising that work outside the home was sometimes necessary for the good of the family and of society. In this respect, she seemed to be endorsing the subordinate, if socially vital, role for women in creating bastions of Islamic values that would help to regenerate an Islamic society. As some have remarked, however, this theoretical attitude seemed to be contradicted by the active public role she played, giving it priority for much of the time over the purely private family life which she seemed to hold up as the ideal.[61]

---

[61] See al-Ghazzali, *Ayam min hayati*, pp. 35–8, 143–67; Ruth Roded, *Women in Islam and the Middle East* (London, 1999), p. 258.

Other women have engaged directly with the symbolic, in particular through the conscious adoption of distinctively 'Islamic' dress, of varying kinds. Whilst the veiling and clothing norms might have been devised by men uneasy about women's sexuality, and anxious to segregate women from a world in which their own power was under threat, women have been able to adapt them in practical and symbolic ways more in keeping with their own concerns. By some, therefore, the *hijab* has been extolled as a form of resistance to Western cultural and economic domination – defending against the cultural beliefs that accompany the invasion of 'consumer commodities, the transformation of our countries into markets'.[62] Others have combined this idea of the *hijab* as a bastion against capitalist consumerism with its representation as an instrument which in fact empowers women by allowing them to participate in public spaces and to control their own bodies and guard their privacy.[63]

In Iran, for instance, since the compulsory introduction of the *chador* and various forms of veiling in the aftermath of the revolution, some women have used the dress codes imposed upon them to subvert the male, clerical intent that lay behind it. Elsewhere, 'Islamic' dress has been transformed into high fashion controlled by women themselves, but technically conforming to the modesty enjoined by the clerical rulings. Others have used it to reinforce and extend their presence in the public world, coming out of seclusion to play an increasingly active public role, sanctioned by the very dress code that was intended to segregate them.[64]

Beyond this – and many have recognised the ambivalence of conformity in this regard, however subversive the intent – there has been a more determined effort to go beyond the question of dress, symbolism and identity, and to engage directly with the very sources from which the rulings on comportment, as well as the roles and rights of women, are historically derived. This has involved women increasingly in independent *ijtihad* in many parts of the Islamic world, most notably in Turkey and Iran. Some question the interpretations of the Qur'anic verses which have been used to justify limitations on women's spheres of activity and scrutinise *hadith* traditionally deployed to buttress views which denigrate or devalue female participation in public life. They sharply criticise those Islamic scholars and writers who have fallen back

---

[62] Mona Fayyad Kawtharani in an article in *Al-Safir* (Beirut) 1985, quoted in Nadia Hijab, 'Islam, social change and the reality of Arab women's lives', in Haddad and Esposito, *Islam, Gender and Social Change*, p. 48.

[63] Fadwa El Guindi, *Veil: Modesty, Privacy and Resistance* (Oxford, 1999); Gema Martin, Muñoz, 'Islamistes et pourtant modernes', *Confluences Méditerranée* 27 (Autumn 1998), pp. 33–43.

[64] N. Tohidi, 'The issues at hand', in Bodman and Tohidi, *Women in Muslim Societies*, p. 284; Linda Herrera, 'Downveiling: gender and the contest over culture in Cairo', *Middle East Report* 219 (Summer 2001), pp. 16–19.

upon the 'naturalistic fallacy' of using biological difference to support systems of discrimination against women. However, it is noticeable that a number of secular women writers will also use the Islamic idiom to defend the rights of women. In part this is because of the resonance this has among many of the women whom they are seeking to inform about their rights. In part it is because of the fear that those who are attracted by the authenticity of a distinctively Islamic response will find themselves obliged to accept a peculiarly restrictive and discriminatory interpretation of Islamic order.[65]

Precisely to counter this, and to give voice to an unease felt no less sharply by women about the effects of globalisation and capitalist development on their condition and their identities, an effort has been made to devise an 'Islamic feminism'. This challenges simultaneously both the idea that an Islamic identity is necessarily that interpreted and dictated for women by men, and the ideas of a Western, liberal feminism which would effectively privatise a woman's religious beliefs.[66] Thus, there are journals in Iran which publish women's *ijtihad*, where the Qur'an and the *hadith* are examined in the light of a concern to bring them into line with the Qur'anic injunction that men and women are equal as believers in the sight of God.[67] In Turkey, there are discussion circles led by people like Cihan Aktas, Sibel Eraslan and Gülsen Ataseven who subscribe to many of the moral codes of the Islamist movement, but nevertheless assert their right as women to interpret the sources of their faith, even if their opinions on aspects of women's behaviour diverge from the consensus of male-dominated scholarship.[68] Naturally, the attempt to construct an agenda of women's rights on a par with those demanded by men, yet within a framework based on the Qur'an and *hadith*, has attracted substantial criticism, both from liberal feminists, who regard it as a doomed endeavour, and from conservative clerics and Islamists perturbed by this independence. At the same time it has won support from those who recognise the force of some of the arguments put forward and by those

---

[65] Fatima Mernissi, *The Veil and the Male Elite*, tr. Mary Jo Lakeland (Reading, MA, 1991), pp. 49–81; Moghissi, *Feminism and Islamic Fundamentalism*, pp. 134–40; Asma Barlas, *'Believing Women' in Islam* (Austin, TX, 2002), pp. 1–28; Moghadam, 'Islamic feminism', pp. 15–46. See also Khadijah Sabbar's examination of the meaning of 'hijab' in a similar vein in *Al-Islam wa-l-hijab* (no place, 1994), pp. 85–103.

[66] Moghissi, *Feminism and Islamic Fundamentalism*, pp. 141–2.

[67] See, for instance, the use made of *Al-Qu'ran*, 16 Surah (*al-Nahl*) verses 97–100; but also of Surah 9 (*al-Tawbah*) verses 71–2 and Surah 16 (*al-Nahl*) verse 72.

[68] Nilufer Narli, 'The role of the Islamist women in the political parties', unpublished report submitted to the Istanbul Women Studies Centre and the Friedrich Neumann Foundation, May 1999, available at http://www.geocities.com/evrimkurami/nnarlidin3.html.

who see this as an important way of drawing women into playing a full and vital role in public life and the national economy.[69]

For some of its proponents, in Iran in particular, the writings of Ali Shari'ati are particularly inspiring. His critique of the thought of the religious establishment had linked it and its interpretations to the class conditions and patriarchal structures of their societies. Equally liberating was his assertion that many of the Qur'anic injunctions themselves were contingent upon the conditions of Arabia in the seventh century and should be seen as such, rather than as a set of commands applicable at all times and places.[70] This contributed to the controversy which greeted his interpretations, but it greatly increased the appeal of books such as *Fatima Fatima ast* to a public fearful of the materialism and consumerism accompanying Western capitalist domination, and yet unwilling to accept the strictures of the conservative clerics in an age of increased women's education, social awareness and engagement in the labour force.

The significance of these developments for the symbolic response to capitalism throughout the Islamic world has been the emergence of women as actors in spheres the contours of which are not necessarily dictated by men. 'Women' or rather 'the Islamic woman' was invested with the symbolism of resistance and the function of family-oriented guardian in an Islamic society, generally by men anxious about women's sexuality and the shifting gender roles encouraged by capitalist development. The outcome of these transformations, and also of the responses which became so much a part of the wide-ranging Islamist, re-interpretative discourse, has been that women soon emerged as actors, eager to use their own interpretative skills to understand their obligations as Muslims and determined to take their fate into their own hands as the shapers of their own destinies. Thus, from being a symbolic arena under the control of the Islamic imaginary and its male 'guardians', the question of women and their role has opened up key questions about social roles, equal rights, social utility and the gendering of knowledge.

This is difficult for some of the more tradition-minded to accept, and is still part of an ongoing struggle for the right to autonomous expression both as women and as Muslims. However, it is a characteristic contemporary feature of the responses of Muslims to a world brought into being through capitalist development. It also demonstrates, as did the imaginative constructions of Qutb and Shari'ati, that the symbolic, whilst often projected as creating a guarded sphere, free of the intrusions and the logic of material power, cannot

---

[69] Mervat Hatem, 'Gender and Islamism in the 1990s', *Middle East Report* 222 (Spring 2002), pp. 44–7; Tohidi, 'The issues at hand', pp. 284–7.

[70] Hussain and Radwan, 'The Islamic revolution and women', pp. 61–3; Shari'ati, *Fatimah Fatimah ast* (Tehran, 1971).

in fact be so well insulated, either imaginatively or practically. Unless it remains a wholly idealist exercise with no ambitions to alter behaviour, it must engage in some form with the world in which Muslims exist, even if it is merely to persuade them to see that world differently. Thus, whilst women and their roles in society could be imaginatively constructed, deploying the symbolic repertoire of a particular view of Islamic tradition, a rather different set of priorities took hold of the interpretation once it became part of the way in which women themselves sought to think about their roles as women and as Muslims in the modern world.

5.3   Violence and meaning

Where reasoned engagement with a world formed and dominated by the hegemonic power of a hostile system such as capitalism is felt to be dangerous, the question of response is critical. Symbolic reconstruction of the guarded sphere is one possibility. However, there is the question of how best to defend that sphere and of the strategies to limit the influence and reach of a system that provokes moral indignation and repugnance. In these circumstances, it is not surprising that some have seen violence as a possible resource – an answer to the question of 'What is to be done?' in an idiom appropriate to the context and scale of the problem.[71]

In this respect, Muslim intellectuals and activists have found themselves facing issues – and dilemmas – familiar from other historical encounters between hegemonic power and its challengers. Relative structural weakness, but also the reflection of institutional violence, as well as subordination and moral outrage, have combined to provoke violent reactions in a variety of settings. Capitalism as industrialisation, the enclosure and privatisation of land, as well as the framework of order associated with private property and the operation of the market have been violent in their impact on pre-capitalist societies. They have, in turn, provoked violent protest by those who felt marginalised and impoverished. Furthermore, the implicit violence at the heart of the capitalist enterprise has only been addressed piecemeal over the years, as the disruptive consequences of the ruthless logic of the commodification of labour was felt through insurrection and revolution.

---

[71] In his comprehensive study of the Islamic doctrine regarding the moral duty of 'commanding right and forbidding wrong' (al-amr bi-l-ma'ruf wa-l-nahi 'an al-munkar), Michael Cook outlines the ways in which action appropriate to the 'wrong' has been viewed throughout Islamic history. He describes contemporary interpretations of the duty which have condoned violence against prohibited practices and their practitioners, as well as the nervousness of many about the implications of making such violence a personal duty, rather than that of a specific organisation: Cook, *Commanding Right and Forbidding Wrong*, pp. 523–30, 533–42.

This has made the act of defiance more complex. The targets are no longer so obvious and the use of violence enmeshes people in the logic of the state, whether as a repressive apparatus that helped to shape the responses, or as something to be captured in the hope of making it the instrument of social transformation. Historically, this proved to be illusory. The state, far from providing the means of overturning or challenging a capitalist order, became the principal means of shaping and invigorating capitalist enterprise, facilitating its adjustment through regulation. Where those who had captured the state attempted an alternative course, the record was not a happy one.[72]

For some, therefore, violence aimed at seizing the state and turning it to their own purposes was already a doomed enterprise since the target – capitalism – was so protean and its power so hegemonic. The nature of this power suggested that a purely instrumental response would fail. Instead, the aim would be to break the hold that the insidious common sense associated with capitalism had over the imaginations of those whom it sought to control. Thus, the terrain of combat could no longer be the structures and institutions of the state or industry, but the wider ground of imagination and belief – finally enlightening those whose complicity or acquiescence served the hegemonic project of capital. In these circumstances violence begins to take on a set of meanings in and of itself: it provides a repertoire of symbolic forms and suggests a narrative that resonates with the meaning of the struggle itself – a struggle between good and evil, between spiritual integrity and the formidable bulk of materiality.[73]

In doing so, however, the allegorical aspects can invest acts of violence with a purpose and significance that supersede the particular cultural setting. The targets may have a resonance specific to a particular place, but the annihilating act of violence itself has a ferocious universality. In this respect, the symbolic act can resemble ritual. It provides a moment that fixes values or holds them up according to a scale that escapes the flux of a present shaped by the forces acting upon the world to transform it unceasingly. Against the setting of 'world-devouring' and restless capital accumulation, the certainty and fixity of these values is held to be a shining example of integrity.

---

[72] Most obviously visible during the twentieth century in the communist and socialist alternative inspired by Marx's critique of capitalism. These experiments either decayed or imploded, or made significant compromises with capitalism, not simply as the dominant world economic powers, but also as a way of organising economic life internally, such as in post-Mao China, or in the 'state capitalist' economies of the USSR and the Eastern Bloc.

[73] See particularly Mikhail Bakunin: 'The urge to destroy is also a creative urge' or 'We must first of all purify our atmosphere and transform completely the surroundings in which we live, for they corrupt our instincts and our wills, they constrict our hearts and intelligences. Therefore, the social question appears first of all as the overthrow of society', cited in George Woodcock, *Anarchism* (London, 1971), pp. 139 and 144.

Paradoxically, however, violence and its effects on people's lives generally negate the values being extolled. Yet this is integral to the very theatricality of symbolic violence. It is intended as a performance designed to shock and, through shock, to draw attention to a particular narrative. A version of the world, charged with opposing values, is being presented, and the violence of the presentation is aimed at jolting people out of their everyday understanding of the world, obliging them to confront the issues at stake and to see them in a new light.[74]

Violence, therefore, highlights the role of passion in politics. Through the commitment of those willing to use it and through the effect it has on the victims, it presents itself as both a simplification of the issues at stake, free of ambiguity and ambivalence, and a deliberate rejection of the criteria of rationality by which the discursive logic of hegemonic power eventually enmeshes even those who oppose it.[75] It is not surprising, therefore, that some Muslim intellectuals, concerned about the way their world is changing, vehement about the forces responsible for change, yet fearful of the outcomes of reasoned engagement, should follow the course others had taken before them in different settings and advocate the use of violence in symbolic as much as in instrumental ways.[76]

The instrumental use of violence in this context was particularly fraught with danger. This was not so much the obvious physical danger facing any who challenged the dominant world powers, armed as they are with ferocious means of coercion. Rather, the danger lay in the tendency of instrumentalism to involve the participants in distinctive rules of engagement, obliging pragmatic compromises to ensure success, but thereby compromising in some measure the nature and imagined purity of that success. Mawdudi and others had argued that the ultimate objective of violent struggle by Muslims should be the establishment of a universal Islamic order which would use the spirit of *jihad* and the instrument of revolution to capture power through the existing state system and thereby guarantee the rule of Islam.

Yet the experience of engagement with existing state structures was ambivalent. In some cases, as with the movement Al-Jihad in Egypt in the 1980s, there was little doubt that its followers were determined to use violence against the government, seeing in it the concentration and symbol of all that it abhorred. Yet the understanding of some of its members about the nature of state power and the force needed to undermine it was clearly

---

[74] J. Zulaika and W. A. Douglass, *Terror and Taboo* (London, 1996), pp. 66–7.

[75] Zulaika and Douglass, *Terror and Taboo*, pp. 83–6; C. Besteman (ed.), 'Introduction', in *Violence – A Reader* (New York, 2001), pp. 6–9.

[76] Olivier Roy, *The Failure of Political Islam*, tr. C. Volk (London, 1999), pp. 65–7.

inadequate.[77] However, even where Islamists took control of a government which then projected itself as distinctively Islamic, the results were very mixed, as the experiences of both Iran and Sudan in the last two decades of the twentieth century show.[78] Indeed, the working out of the secular logic of the state, with its latent – sometimes manifest – organisation of violence, caused Mawdudi, for instance, to shy away from intimate involvement in the modern state and to focus instead on the apparently safer, more abstracted goal of transforming nothing less than world order itself through the message of Islam.[79]

There was a further feature which helped to lessen the appeal of instrumentalist violence and heighten that of the symbolic. Historically, violent responses by Muslims acting as Muslims to the advent of industrial capitalism had followed patterns common elsewhere when the dislocating, alienating and emiserating effects of these new procedures and technologies had made themselves felt. The most obvious example is the early nineteenth-century 'Wahhabi' movement in India which used the idiom of Islam to mobilise people to attack the spinning machines and factories threatening the livelihoods of local weavers – a similar reaction, naturally in a different idiom, to the Luddites of the industrial revolution in England.[80] However, this was a localised reaction.

Assaults on state power and its symbols during the twentieth century were also localised, even if they sprang from general concerns recurrent throughout much of the Islamic world which stemmed from the identification of particular governments with the larger phenomenon of the *jahiliyah*, or the *munafiqin* (hypocrites). The hegemonic power of Western capitalism, on the other hand, made it an enemy of a different order entirely. It is ubiquitous and diffuse, possessing no administrative heart, no centre that can be captured and subdued. Furthermore, its power comes as much from its hold on people's imaginations, shaping their wants and values, as through deploying conventional instruments of power. In this respect, as with the state itself, it seems to call forth a reaction that mirrors its own representation of itself.

---

[77] Kepel, *Prophet and Pharaoh*, pp. 191–215; J. J. Jansen, *The Neglected Duty* (New York, 1986), pp. 1–34; interview with Tal'at Fu'ad Qasim by Hisham Mubarak, 'What does the Gama'a Islamiyya want?' in Joel Beinin and Joe Stork (eds.), *Political Islam* (London, 1997), pp. 314–325.

[78] See Mehdi Moslem, *Factional Politics in Post-Khomeini Iran* (Syracuse, NY, 2002), pp. 11–46; Burr and Collins, *Revolutionary Sudan*, pp. 210–30, 253–80.

[79] Abu al-A'la al-Mawdudi in Abu al-A'la al-Mawdudi, Hasan al-Banna and Sayyid Qutb, *Al-Jihad fi sabil Allah* (Beirut, 1969), pp. 5–56 – where he is careful not to use the term '*dawlah*' (state), but rather '*al-nizam al-ijtima'i*' (social order); see also Tripp, 'Secular logic of the state', pp. 51–69.

[80] See chapter 1, footnote 46.

For some, therefore, spectacular violence came to be seen as the most appropriate response. It matched the nature of the enemy; it avoided engagement with capitalism on a terrain already shaped by its own formations; it also appealed to those whose view of the world and its conflicts was largely idealist in nature, privileging the symbolic and the affective as the most effective – and the least contaminated – way of acting. In Egypt in the 1970s, the group led by Shukri Mustafa and labelled by the Egyptian authorities 'Al-Takfir wa-l-Hijrah' (pronouncing unbelief and holy flight) was extraordinarily sensitive to the pitfalls of engagement, not simply with the ambient secular society of Egypt, but also with contemporary Islamic scholarship. Migration to the desert fringes of Egypt and the establishment of pure and uncontaminated Muslim communities was the ideal, but this was accompanied by violence against those who represented the corrupting influences they were hoping to avoid. Violence was thus part of a strategy of symbolic as well as physical dissociation.[81]

Symbolic performances, whatever the idiom, are forms of communication intended to inform and involve. They present a certain narrative, outlining a version of reality, particularly the ethical contours of the world, of which the audience may have been unaware, or which had become obscured by the dominant discourses to which they had been habitually subjected. However, they are also involving, in the sense that the symbolic repertoire is meant to engage the spectators' emotions, evoking responses which make them see the world in a different light, possibly mobilising them as actors themselves. This is the idea of performance as catalyst: a spectacular event that goes beyond mere spectacle to induce people to reinterpret the world, and in doing so to act to change it. The members of the audience thus become participants in a drama that began with an eye-catching, possibly terrifying act.

In the case of political violence used in this symbolic way throughout history, there are generally two intended audiences: those whom the group is seeking to educate and mobilise and those who are responsible for the dominant and reviled order. In this respect, groups that have defined themselves as distinctively Muslim, working to an Islamist agenda, are no different from many of their precursors and contemporaries who have used violence with similar intent in very different cultural and historical settings.[82] The

---

[81] J. J. G. Jansen, *The Dual Nature of Islamic Fundamentalism* (London, 1997), pp. 75–93. Although their violence was generally very purposive and structured, similar sentiments were voiced under the rule of the Taliban in Afghanistan in the late 1990s – see, for instance, the slogan seen on the wall of the Ministry for the Prevention of Vice and the Promotion of Virtue in Kabul 'Throw reason to the dogs. It stinks of corruption', cited in Jason Burke, *Al-Qaeda* (London, 2003), p. 111.

[82] Saad al-Din Ibrahim, 'Egypt's Islamic militants', in Saad al-Din Ibrahim and N. S. Hopkins (eds.), *Arab Society: Social Science Perspectives* (Cairo, 1985).

notion of 'propaganda by deed' so familiar from the anarchists and social revolutionaries of late-nineteenth-century Europe in their fight against the hegemony of the capitalist state, has been taken up as strategy and rationale by some Islamists in the late twentieth century.[83]

For someone like Muhammad al-Farag, the author of *Al-Faridah al-gha-'ibah* (The Neglected Duty – i.e. *jihad*), and ideologue of the organisation Al-Jihad in Egypt, violence was purposive: the 'extermination of infidel leaders' was intended to be the first step on the road to the creation of an Islamic order. However, it was also exemplary and symbolic in the sense that its prime targets were asserted to be 'the idols of this world [which] can only disappear through the power of the sword'. For him, there was little doubt that this task, whilst it was to be accomplished initially by a dedicated vanguard, would not only bring about the downfall of the false beliefs and material seductions that had so mesmerised Muslims, but would also thereby act to alert Muslims to their plight and wake them to a new reality in which the vanguard would act as role model in the transformation of their situation.[84]

This rationale was equally evident in the writings of 'Abdallah 'Azzam, an influential and articulate figure among the Arab Muslims who joined the struggle against the Soviet occupation of Afghanistan. In his book *Al-Difa'a 'an aradi al-muslimin ahamm furud al-a'yan* (Defence of the land of the Muslims is the most important individual duty), he saw violent struggle, and particularly the readiness for martyrdom on the part of the *mujahidin*, as being a way of bringing Muslims to consciousness of their true situation. It was intended to strip away the layers of false consciousness that had blinded them to the reality of the struggle between good and evil, and would restore the lost honour of Muslims, hitherto compromised by the world powers. From his perspective, it was not the scholars who would guide Muslims along the correct path in a confusing and corrupt world. They were themselves too easily corrupted, too susceptible to the seductions of other forms of reasoning and of the material world. Instead, it was 'the people of the battlefront' who can see clearly through the lies and obscurities of the world, because, in the final analysis, 'they are the closest to God'.[85]

---

[83] See the Italian anarchist, Malatesta (1876): '[the Italian Federation of Anarchists] believe that the insurrectionary deed, destined to affirm socialist principles by acts is the most efficacious means of propaganda': Woodcock, *Anarchism*, p. 316; or Gallo's attempt to put this into practice by his attack on the Paris Stock Exchange in 1886 – see James Joll, *The Anarchists* (London, 1969), pp. 124–38.

[84] Muhammad al-Farag, *Al-Faridah al-gha'ibah*, translated in Jansen, *Neglected Duty*, pp. 185–7, 192–207, 225–7.

[85] 'Abdallah 'Azzam, *Al-Difa'a 'an aradi al-muslimin ahamm furud al-a'yan* (San'a', 1990), pp. 82–4, 101–7; a similar message was driven home in another publication by 'Abdallah 'Azzam, *Jihad sha'b muslim* (San'a', 1992), in which he sought to inspire Muslims to *jihad* in the face of all oppression (*zulm*), whatever form it took and wherever it might be found.

Unsurprisingly, given the proximity of 'Azzam to 'Usama bin Ladin and others associated with the network of Al-Qa'idah, similar views about the purpose of violence began to surface here, shaping the targets and the nature of the spectacle. In the aftermath of the 1991 Gulf War, with the continued presence of US forces in the territory of Saudi Arabia, bin Ladin's advocacy of violence had been largely instrumental. The task of the *mujahidin* was a local one which was intended to expel US forces from Saudi Arabia and to institute a truly Islamic order there. Increasingly, however, the violence planned and executed seemed to be geared to more ambitious, symbolic and spectacular ends, as bin Ladin stressed: 'These blessed attacks [referring to the attack on the World Trade Center on 11 September 2001] have great meanings, for they clearly showed that this arrogant and supercilious power, the Hubal of the age, America, is fragile and, thanks to Almighty God, collapsed so quickly despite having great economic power.'[86]

Although greatly overestimating the effect of such attacks upon the substance of American or Western power, he was largely correct about the significance of the spectacle. Part of the intention was to recruit like-minded Muslims to the cause which bin Laden and his associates were defining, by encouraging those Muslims to see the world in the polarised way that was so prevalent in the writings of the people close to Al-Qa'idah. Bin Ladin's and Ayman al-Zawahiri's comments both before and after the events of 11 September indicated that this and similar acts were meant to mobilise a notional global Muslim community, graphically indicating the location of the enemy and the true nature of the struggle, in the hope that this would cause them 'to get up and liberate its land, to fight for the sake of God and to make the Islamic law the highest law and the word of God the highest word of all'. As bin Ladin was to say about the hijackers of 11 September, '[they] said in deeds . . . speeches that overshadowed all other speeches made everywhere in the world'.[87]

Part of the message of 11 September and other acts of violence against symbolic targets identified with the US in particular, but also with Western power more generally, has been to demonstrate the relative weakness of the apparently all-powerful institutions of these countries. Whilst in part the audience for this was the Muslim world in general, partly the intended audience was the Western states and their supportive institutions. Here two particular meanings seemed to be attached to the violence. One was an

---

[86] 'Usama bin Ladin, interview for programme 'First war of the century', *Al-Jazirah* satellite channel, 27 December 2001, tr. FBIS.
[87] Cited by Burke, *Al-Qaeda*, pp. 34–7; Gilles Kepel, *Jihad: The Trail of Political Islam*, tr. Anthony Roberts (London, 2002), pp. 371–6. See also the excerpts purporting to be from bin Ladin's 'will' of 14 December 2001, in *Al-Majallah* 27 October – 2 November 2002.

implicit threat, common to many organisations – Islamic and non-Islamic – seeking to unnerve an apparently stronger opponent, denying it security and possibly obliging it therefore to negotiate an end to the violence. In some cases this was to be amplified not simply by the spectacular size of the explosions caused, but also by the fact that Muslims were willing to die to carry them out. Their disregard for their own safety in the service of a larger cause is the implicit threat to those who might think that the danger could be averted through co-option and appeals to self-interest.[88]

However, there was also a second layer of meaning, possibly more specific to the distinctive discourses of this form of Islamic response. It is connected to the use of martyrdom and violent self-immolation in the struggle against the enemy as a signifier of the enemy's shame and humiliation. Shari'ati voiced a similar sentiment when he extolled the willingness of the *mujahidin* to sacrifice themselves in their doomed encounters with the security services of the Shah's state in Iran in the 1970s.[89] In this context, violence is a vocabulary which stresses the faith of the person happy to die in committing an act of terror and, in doing so, allegedly shames and humiliates those whose power is associated with the target. Such a notion of self-destructive violence adds layers of meaning to the act beyond those of the instrumental calculation of its political effect. It does not, of course, void it of such calculations, since whatever normative values are associated with the act by the perpetrator, it may nevertheless be organised as part of a much larger set of calculations concerning threat, negotiation and resistance, depending upon the context.[90]

The example of the martyr, and the act of violence against an enemy defined as part of an iniquitous worldly order, brings out another meaning often stressed in certain Islamist discourses. This derives from the portrayal of such performances as supreme acts of worship in which the main audience is neither one's own people nor the enemy, but God. In this reading, the targets

---

[88] Interview with 'Usama bin Ladin, May 1998, on programme 'Frontline', Public Broadcasting Service, available at http://www.pbs.org/wgbh/pages/frontline/shows/binladen/who/interview/html; bin Ladin 'First war of the century'. See also interview with Tal'at Fu'ad Qasim by Hisham Mubarak, 'What does the Gama'a Islamiyya want?', in Beinin and Stork, *Political Islam*, pp. 314–25. It can plausibly be argued that it is this sentiment or ambition that lies behind, for instance, Islamic Jihad's use of suicide bombs in Palestine and Israel. John Esposito, *Unholy War* (Oxford, 2002), pp. 95–101.

[89] See footnote 30 above.

[90] The Islamist movements in the Israel–Palestine conflict, or the resistance in Iraq following the US-led invasion in 2003, organised such acts, often explicitly in the name of 'Islam', but also as part of a strategy of resistance in an ongoing political struggle. However, the normative environment and apparent motives of many of the bombers themselves extend beyond immediate calculations and bring in larger, even otherworldly themes and values, helping to rationalise the violence committed against others and the certainty of self-destruction. See Anne Marie Oliver, *The Road to Martyrs' Square: Inside the World of the Suicide Bomber* (Oxford, 2005).

are portrayed as pleasing in the sight of God because they embody the kind of corruption and evil power that all Muslims are urged to combat in their daily lives with all the means at their disposal.[91] Alternatively, the claim is that the targets are associated with such power through complicity or co-option – a form of reasoning used particularly when the victims of violence are by no means the power brokers themselves and are killed or maimed chiefly because they happen to be in the wrong place at the wrong time. It is precisely such an outcome which has turned many away from those who advocate or rationalise these acts of violence, whatever their sympathy for other aspects of the struggle. This was evident, for instance, in Egypt, following the massacre of tourists at Luxor in 1997.[92]

It is also argued by some that the act of self-sacrifice is a form of offering to God, testifying to the strength of a person's faith, determined to serve the cause of God even unto death.[93] Whether cynically exploited or genuinely believed, the view that the measure of a person's commitment to a cause lies in his or her willingness to ignore their own self-interest, to the extent of going against the basic instinct of self-preservation, has long been a staple of political struggles, and has formed the stuff of historical epics since time immemorial. In the Islamic context, it engages more specifically with the idea of *jihad* and with the kinds of meanings attached to the term by those who see it as legitimating, indeed commanding, armed struggle in the name of God and in defence of the faith.

Naturally, the conduct of political violence, as opposed to writing about its general principles and conditions, happens in very specific contexts and with ascertainable outcomes and responses. The symbolic may well play a part in this, but so too does the strategic organisation of material resources, both human and inanimate, to give shape, structure and targets to the use of violence. In many instances, this has led to the trapping of the system of violence itself in the logic of local conditions. Efforts to organise violence successfully involve the organiser in a host of contingent calculations, such as the location and strength of the security forces, the arrangements necessary to procure the weapons or explosives, the financial resources required, as well as the sociology of recruitment. The case of the bombing of the World Trade

---

[91] In this regard, frequently cited verses of the Qur'an are those from Surah 4 (*al-Nisa'*) verses 74–6, beginning 'let those fight in the cause of God who sell the life of this world for the hereafter' – see, for instance, Ayatullah Sayyid Mahmud Taleqani, 'Jihad and Shahadat', in Taleqani et al., *Jihad and Shahadat*, pp. 50–3 or Ayatullah Murtada Mutahhari, 'Shahid', pp. 125–9; Hasan al-Banna, 'Risalat al-Jihad', in Abu al-A'la al-Mawdudi et al., *Al-Jihad fi sabil Allah* (1969), pp. 86–8.

[92] Fawaz Gerges, 'The end of the Islamist insurgency in Egypt? Costs and prospects', *Middle East Journal* 4 (Fall 2000), pp. 592–5.

[93] Qutb, *Ma'alim*, pp. 83–91; Burke, *Al-Qaeda*, pp. 33–4, 69–72.

Center in New York in February 1993 exemplifies this. Here a curious and disparate group of individuals came together to organise an act of violence largely for symbolic reasons, mostly to do with the support of the US government for the state of Israel, under the sanction of the exiled Egyptian cleric Shaikh 'Umar 'Abd al-Rahman, who appeared to license such acts under the rubric of an all-embracing global sanction.[94] What begins as an ambitious symbolic struggle, with large and world-relevant targets and resonance, may become increasingly confined to the particular places where it remains possible to organise and to fight, limiting the potential, as well as the significance, of the *jihad* in question.[95]

Thus capitalism as a catalyst of symbolic violence can become lost from sight in the concerns and preoccupations of particular times and places. However, it remains relevant in important ways. From the testimonies of some of those who have been central to the organisation of symbolic violence, it seems that the impulse to reorient the world in a distinctively Islamic direction stemmed partly from their revulsion at the damage capitalism had done to their own societies – or to what they believed their own societies should be. Thus, Muhammad Atta, the principal organiser and suicidal hijacker in the events of 11 September 2001 had been outraged by government plans in his native Egypt to clear and reconstruct part of the old city of Cairo. For him this was to dismantle a site of historical and distinctively Muslim sociability and to replace it with a substitute, commodified arena for the benefit of tourism. At the same time, he was allegedly angered by the social injustice and glaring inequality which had become a tolerated, even encouraged, feature of Egyptian society under the *infitah* – the economic liberalisation policies pursued since the 1970s by presidents Sadat and Mubarak. Such inequalities had, of course, existed for years, but in the 1990s the forms of capitalism in Egypt – the explicit denial of opportunity to the majority of the population in the name of economic advantage, the consumerism and the cultural changes associated with it – were highly visible and, for some, deeply alienating. It is thus not too much of an exaggeration to suppose that the dark side of capitalism, its exclusions and forms of discrimination, contributed to

---

[94] This has led to numerous theories about the real intentions behind this deliberate act of symbolic terror – see the report of the trial of Ramzi Yousef in 1997, available at http://www.cnn.com/US/9801/08/yousef.update/; see also profiles of those involved at http://www.lib.umich.edu/govdocs/text/socpsy.txt. For Shaikh 'Umar 'Abd al-Rahman's views on the legitimacy of violence see his publication *Kalimah haqq* (Cairo, 1987), pp. 25–80, which contains his testimony at his trial in Egypt for complicity in the assassination of President Sadat in October 1981.

[95] Interview with Tal'at Fu'ad Qasim by Hisham Mubarak, 'What does the Gama'a Islamiyya want?', p. 325, where, having spoken of the importance of the group's activities in the Islamic world, Qasim is obliged to say finally that 'the centre of our activities has always been the *Sa'id* [Upper Egypt]'.

the sentiments that drove Atta towards the transnational networks which became so characteristic of Al-Qa'idah.[96]

The direction of these transnational networks underlines another way in which anti-capitalism may have influenced the nature of symbolic violence. This follows on from the possibility that the effects of capitalist development in specific sites can lead not merely to local protest and opposition, but to more global forms of resistance. Thus, during the 1990s, transnational forms of Islamist protest shadowed the networks of globalisation itself, whether in the movement of individuals, the transfer of funds or the flow of information. A modern irony lies in the fact that the facilities created by capitalist enterprise to help the immense capitalist transformation of lives across the globe also allow the proliferation of transnational organisations hostile to the globalisation of capital. Thus groups and individuals intent on inflicting damage on the symbols and institutions of global capital can communicate through the internet, fostering, through vastly improved and instantaneous communication, a sense of global solidarity amongst Muslims as a transnational community.[97]

In some respects, the internet, as an anonymous channel for conveying powerful messages and arresting images, is ideally suited to the elaboration of alternative and critical views of the status quo, anchored chiefly within the realm of semiotics. The communicative and affective intentions of those who use the medium stand out as one of its chief characteristics and this allows, even encourages, the formation of 'virtual communities' of people bound together through their common adherence to particular world views and to specific configurations of symbolic representation of the world. As any visit to some of the vast number of Islamist internet sites demonstrates, their specific and often individual characters exemplify the fact that their very construction has been based on putting together a vocabulary and grammar of symbolic power from the rich alphabet of Islamic discourse and history. Furthermore, the detachment of the sites and their many scattered members from pre-existing social organisations, institutions or forms of instrumental collective action allows such self-defined 'Islamic communities' to float free

---

[96] Similar sentiments were voiced by people close to bin Ladin when they attacked the US for environmental pollution in pursuit of profit, and specifically for refusing to sign the Kyoto agreement. As Burke points out, the idiom may be distinctively Islamic, but the criticism is similar to that of secular anti-globalisation and anti-capitalist protestors: Burke, *Al-Qaeda*, pp. 24–5, 214–17; Olivier Roy, *Globalised Islam* (London, 2004), pp. 44–50.

[97] Esposito, *Unholy War*, pp. 151–2, 157–8; see, for example, the multiplicity of Islamic websites on the internet, based in various countries, but clearly intended to appeal to an international Muslim audience in terms of the issues they address, the languages used and the engagement with the world which they project: see Lawrence Wright, 'The terror web', *The New Yorker*, 2 August 2004 (posted on the internet 26 July 2004 at http://www.newyorker.com/fact/content/? 040802fa_fact).

from the demanding, confining and transformative logic of a world that remains impervious to their demands.[98]

This very feature, which those geared to more conventional forms of 'concrete' action find deeply exasperating, liberates these emerging virtual communities from the forms of compliance and co-option that have so beset those who have tried to work upon the world of institutional reality. From this perspective, everything can be selectively incorporated into the symbolic realm, made all the more powerful by an absence of contradiction within the guarded sphere of the website. A world view composed of news items, images, *fatwas*, interviews and statements can be put together in a string of mutually reinforcing and reassuring forms which link individuals across the world. Of course, its very virtue as a means of bringing people together may also be its greatest weakness as a basis for the organisation of collective action. Any given site may attract large numbers of like-minded people, but they will be browsing, visiting an array of sites, some with similar messages, others quite differently configured.

In many respects, therefore, the virtual community may be a transitory community: a conglomeration of people gathered around a specific site over a given period of time, but in itself bereft of the possibility of capturing and disciplining its visitors, of giving them coherence as a group geared to social action beyond participation in the virtual community itself. In this sense, the internet shares features with the historical print media. These have been hugely influential, helping to shape imaginative communities, but they re-quired alliance with more engaged forms of social action in order to change behaviour or, specifically, to redress power balances in the world.

At the same time, the global spread of capitalism, and the multifaceted nature of global capitalist enterprise, offers a rich array of symbolic targets and may therefore encourage transnational collective action, however organ-ised, aimed at their destruction. Some of the symbolic targets may be associ-ated with the economic power of particular nation states. Others may simply be made to stand for the practices which capitalism has encouraged and has made an accelerated part of the 'world-devouring' nature of its onward momentum.[99] These could be represented by international financial

[98] D. Lyon, 'Cyberspace sociality: controversies over computer-mediated relationships', in Brian Loader (ed.), *The Governance of Cyberspace* (London, 1997), pp. 23–37; Peter Mandaville, 'Reimagining the ummah? Information technology and the changing boundaries of political Islam', in Ali Mohammadi (ed.), *Islam Encountering Globalization* (London, 2002), pp. 61–90; Jon W. Anderson, 'The internet and Islam's new interpreters', in Dale F. Eickelman and Jon W. Anderson (eds.), *New Media in the Muslim World – The Emerging Public Sphere* (Bloomington, 2003), pp. 45–60; Gary R. Bunt, *Islam in the Digital Age* (London, 2003), pp. 1–36.

[99] 'World-devouring' is a vivid and apt epithet used by the Iranian leadership since the revolution of 1979 to describe great worldly power, most recently used of the US and its allies – see, for

institutions based on an interest-bearing profit motive, or by the many examples of the commodification of culture and of sex that often accompanies global tourism. The bombing of the tourist centre in Bali in 2002 and the bombing of the HSBC building in Istanbul in 2003 carried part of this symbolic freight, as became clear in the post facto rationalisations of those associated with these spectacular acts of violence, even if a series of specific circumstances determined the selection of these targets at the time and in the place that they occurred.[100] The same could be said of the abortive 'Bojinka Plot' aimed at destroying up to twelve airliners in the skies of the Pacific in 1994, or the successful plot which led to the destruction of the twin towers of the World Trade Center in New York in September 2001.

In all of these cases, the acts of violence had real and terrible consequences. However, these seemed to weigh less for the organisers and perpetrators than the resonance of the acts themselves. The demonstration of resolve, even if it meant self-destruction, the selection of targets taken to represent the kind of power and corruption alleged to be threatening Islamic values across the world, and even the enormity of acts of violence that killed so many – these were meant to convey messages to Muslims and non-Muslims alike. It may have been supposed that these messages would work a change upon the world, altering the way that people respond to the forms of power and corruption surrounding them. However, if there was to be a cumulative process of consciousness raising and mobilisation, it was far from systematic. It was almost as if the acts were intended to speak for themselves, to open up the way for the subsequent glosses, rationales and post facto justifications which appeared on websites, in publications and in the rhetoric of a limited number of Islamist preachers. By provoking discussion of these events, there was of course no guarantee that Muslims, or anyone else, would share the same perspectives as the perpetrators; nor was there any means of ensuring that this would be the case. Indeed, the very unsystematic nature of any

---

instance, Ayatollah Khamenei's speech on 26 April 2005, warning of the plots of the 'world-devouring powers' against the Islamic world, IRNA 26 April 2005, available at http://www.irna.ir/en/news/view/menu-236/0504260319142300.htm.

[100] See, for instance, the statements by one of the principal defendants in the Bali bombing trial, Amrozi bin Nuhasyim, who told the court that the attack 'had positive aspects because it encouraged people to re-embrace religion and weakened the corrupting influence of foreign tourists', cited in BBC News Timeline: Bali bomb trials, and BBC News Profile: Amrozi http://news.bbc.co.uk/1/hi/world/asia-pacific/3126241 and 2632043.stm. In the case of the Istanbul bombing of the HSBC building (but also the British Consulate and two synagogues) the linking of these three kinds of target obviously had symbolic resonance for the group that may have carried them out (Islami Buyuk Dogu Akincilar Cephesi – the Great East Islamic Raiders Front (IBDA-C), but may also have been due to the fact that the targets were more accessible than US military bases in Turkey. See http://www.cdi.org/friendlyversion/printversion.cfm?documentID=2535; http://www.fas.org/irp/world/para/ibda-c.htm.

follow-up is testimony to a belief in the power of example, as well as to the weakness of the organisations and groupings concerned.

In some respects, therefore, such actions have much in common with the articulation of primarily symbolic, possibly violent, responses to a world transformed by capitalism and all that it seemed to represent by writers such as Sayyid Qutb and Ali Shari'ati. Their understanding of the power of the word, but also of the image of the act and its capacity to link disparate individuals by connecting them to a common repertoire, shares many of the features of more recent forms of resistance to symbols of capitalist power. However, as their writings and the engagement of large numbers of other Muslim intellectuals demonstrate, violence is obviously not the only language of symbolic riposte to the apparently inexorable advance of capitalist values and practices. The terrain of gender relations and, specifically, the behaviour of women, and the disposition of their bodies and their lives, have also been seen as appropriate sites on which to construct symbolic resistance that would have a powerful social impact. This idealised resistance and thus the role assigned to Muslim women may or may not have been internalised by women themselves, but in some respects its importance lies in the part that has been written for it in the larger repertoire of distinctively Islamic signs.

However, in neither instance can these forms remain entirely within the symbolic realm. Their connection with a material world of social organisation, of human desires and actions and of substantial consequences subjects them to some of the logic of everyday life. Those assigned to take part in these tableaux of symbolic resistance are not ciphers, but need to be persuaded, enthused or even cajoled into playing the roles that will fit them for a task mapped out for them by others. They bring their own interpretative reason to the part, and in doing so they may seek to rewrite the role entirely, to inscribe themselves and what they believe they stand for in a radically different way, escaping therefore from their status as object and becoming the subject of their own story. This has happened in many of the diverse spheres of women's action, where Muslim women have been equally concerned about the effects of capitalism and its associated values on their communities. For some it has meant accepting the symbolic role ascribed to them as inhabitants of the 'guarded sphere', but there are many others, equally committed to the preservation of the values of their faith, who have seen their roles differently, and have therefore negotiated a particular and often contentious path through the symbolic and institutional setting of their world.

Conclusion

In reflecting upon the way in which Muslim intellectuals have responded to the transformative power of capitalism during the past hundred or so years, it becomes clear that many of them were having to think in new categories. The changes they were experiencing demanded not simply a new vocabulary of description and analysis, but new ways of imagining the very world itself. In particular, the social world, in the sense of the variety of human relations, required new ways of thinking about boundaries in space, function and status, with all that this implied for identities and for human potential. In order to achieve this, those involved in the project drew upon a repertoire of seemingly analogous terms of reference from the rich tradition of Islamic jurisprudence and ethics. This constituted the alphabet of appropriation, providing a readily understood and ethically acceptable resource that could be used selectively to meet the challenges of the age. In doing so, it also provided the settings of a moral compass that could guide the believer in ways that appeared consonant with his or her beliefs.

However, as became apparent in the century or so of voiced responses to the phenomenon of capitalist development and the globalisation of capitalist practice and power, this undertaking could neither be as self-sufficient nor as autonomous as some of its originators may have hoped. The terms deployed came with a dual legacy. There was the meaning conferred upon them in the works of jurisprudential scholarship and commentary over some thirteen centuries. But there were also the meanings they took on when applied to forms of behaviour and organisation that had been unimaginable to those whose definition of them had located them within a distinctively Islamic tradition over the centuries. Furthermore, the principles of selection and usage or, to continue the analogy, the rules of grammar under which the new vocabulary was to be constituted, drew a large part of their coherence from the imaginative resources associated with capitalist practice, whether as reinforcement or critique.

The imaginative organisation of these responses within a self-consciously Islamic idiom to a system as ubiquitous and hegemonic as capitalism, provides an example of the way in which the response may be shaped by its object. This study has been intended, therefore, to throw light onto an important aspect of the establishment of a hegemonic discourse, the various strands that go into its constitution and the institutional patterns it generates and which also reinforce its plausibility – the sanctions of discursive practice. It also underlines the tension between the desire to resist encroachment and the limitations on organising sufficient resources for doing so.

In this respect, the negation of that discourse is imaginable, since its terms can be represented almost by definition, and thus a priori, as a cluster of phenomena antithetical to a given moral order, the identification and value of which are taken for granted. In an idealist universe, this is more or less sustainable. Capitalism as process and its associated values and ideologies are represented as the negative imprint of distinctively Islamic values. Thus, the features that distinguish capitalism as a system of organising economic life and of disciplining social relations are portrayed as the opposite of a specifically Islamic order. Logically clear and – to some degree – immune from the epistemological and ethical challenge embodied in capitalist practices and their underlying social ontology, such a response could still be seen by its adherents as authentically Islamic and thus true to the values which inform an Islamic ethical order.

As the examples have shown, as long as this could be maintained as a response imagined mainly in symbolic terms, the self-sustaining and self-affirming values of an idealised Islamic order could be thought of as exclusive and immune to corruption. Of course, the implications for alternative ways of construing a response that is also claimed to be distinctively Islamic can be severe and may lead to contestation. However, the real problem emerged in the attempt to make the leap from the imagined realm of symbolic encounters to actual engagement with the world. The translation of a vocabulary bearing the reassuring markers of a distinct Islamic identity and system of values into a strategy of social mobilisation and effective transformation exposes the self-sustaining ideal to the harsher logic of praxis.

Thus, imaginatively constituting the world in such a way that engagement with it becomes meaningful and effective may well have unforeseen consequences. The direct impact of the dominant institutions that structure social life may have a reciprocal influence. For those Muslim intellectuals determined to craft responses to capitalism, their own ideas and writings have been influenced by three such institutions: 'society' itself, the nation state and the market economy, themselves bounded and distinctive notions inextricably connected with the historical development of capitalism. Each constitutes a repository of power imagined and exercised. In many respects, those who were responding to the capitalist domination of these fields from a distinctively Islamist position were, like their predecessors and contemporaries working in secular idioms, trying to match that power and indeed to harness it for the service of their own ideals.

It is here that the organisation of power shows how susceptible it is to the 'logic' or implicit ontology of the field or framework in which it is imagined and constructed. Discursively, the realms of society, of the state and of the economy have the capacity to order people's lives according to the assumptions of the dominant system of power. That which has been effective in transforming the world becomes influential in shaping the way the world is seen. It conditions the lives led within it, bringing sanctions to bear in its encouragement of conformity. Of course, this is neither a static, once-and-for-all process nor one which goes uncontested, since, as well as reproducing itself, these processes also create grounds for opposition and subversion, even for significant transformation. However, as those with an Islamist alternative in mind were to discover, whilst their activities might contribute towards the reconfiguration of capitalist practice in certain areas, they could do little to shake the underlying assumptions and drives which underpinned capitalist expansion. The imaginative and social power concentrated in the particular conceptions of society, state and economy was so great that it helped shape the Islamist responses themselves, sometimes in ways which were both implicitly and explicitly linked to a global capitalist system and infused with some of the values underpinning it.

The imaginative construction of society began by way of analogy with the faith-based community of the *ummah*. Gradually, however, in the light of both the vocabulary and the metaphors of positivist sociology, as well as of the social transformations experienced by Muslims, it came to represent something different, both more universal in scope and more mechanical in conception. Those who wrote about the effects of industrial capitalism on their own societies were aware of the similarities between these experiences and those of other, non-Muslim peoples, caught up in the great transformations of the nineteenth and twentieth centuries. This was not simply a matter of empirical observation. The very language and analytical tools upon which they drew were implicitly comparative in nature, laying heavy stress on the universality of the underlying functions of any human social organisation. The gaze of Muslim intellectuals was thus to a large degree directed towards the observation of that which the functionalist model assumed must be there. It was scarcely surprising, therefore, that these functions were found, but to ensure that the character of the society remained one which was inalienably Islamic, it was necessary to recast the terms of reference in language redolent of Islam. In some senses, therefore, these intellectuals were re-identifying their societies as Islamic, reconnecting them to an identifiable and identifying tradition.

In doing so, however, they were obliged to reformulate the Islamic identity of that society in its new configuration. The imaginative trajectory from *ummah* to 'Islamic society' to – a reconfigured – *ummah* has implications for the way in which the latter is conceived. In some respects, it is an understandable adaptation, highly influential in shaping the variety of Muslim responses in different settings and variously engaged with the forces of a world that might otherwise have come into being ignorant of the centrality of their faith. From this perspective, the imagination of an Islamic society as an outcome of the transformations brought about by expanding capitalist enterprise has much in common with similar imaginative exercises elsewhere, making Islamic responses recognisably part of a general modern concern about sociability, rationality and ethics in a market society, where all human relations become susceptible to commodification.[1]

Again, as elsewhere, the formal political framework in which this was happening – the legal field of enforced social order represented by the nation state – suggested for some Muslim intellectuals a possible remedy for the social disintegration encouraged by the apparently unrestrained acquisitiveness of an all-devouring capitalism. The state's concentration of centralised power, based upon the assumption of a collective unity of purpose, made it an important bulwark in the imagined response to capitalist encroachment. It is in this context that the re-imagination of the 'Islamic state' begins to take shape, differing in many ways from the historical experiences of the caliphates, emirates, sultanates and kingdoms of Islamic history. Ironically, despite the mistrust of the state and its arbitrary and rapacious nature which had been so evident in much of the juridical literature, these examples provided a reference point for the new construction. Yet it was the model of the modern nation state which proved to be the more decisive. It shaped thinking about what could be expected of a state in the organisation of society and in the maintenance of social security and solidarity. It also brought with it, as was the case with 'society', a way of thinking about the world, about community, welfare, productivity and participation.

The debates which ensued – as in the case of Nasser's Egypt, King Faisal's Saudi Arabia or the Islamic Republic of Iran – followed closely the lines of similar debates in the non-Muslim world between the advocates and opponents of state planning, for instance, or between those who stressed the individual's right to property and those who emphasised its social dimensions. The fact that these debates were being conducted in a distinctively Islamic

---

[1] See the thesis about reciprocity developed by Roxanne Euben, *Enemy in the Mirror: Islamic Fundamentalism and the Limits of Modern Rationalism* (Princeton, 1999).

idiom could not disguise the imaginative and structural reality behind this phenomenon. Essentially, the debate came down to a general, secular question of the most appropriate and effective role for the state in the organisation and regulation of the economy. This ongoing feature of global politics continues to inform power relations within and between states in large part because of the fluid and changing nature of the varieties of capitalism in the sites of its historical origins and in the new territories it has colonised. In this respect, states inhabited by Muslims and those designated specifically as 'Islamic states' have been no exception to the processes, imaginative and political, which capitalism has introduced.

The nature of these debates and, in some cases, concerns about the reach and power of the state, as well as about the power of the market economy, have produced a further imaginative response. The 'Islamic economy' was to play the role which had earlier been played by the 'Islamic state' as the formation which would allow effective engagement with the world by Muslims, whilst still retaining, indeed reproducing, the core values of a distinctively Islamic system. Those who devoted themselves to the theoretical elaboration of an Islamic economy began with an idealised set of principles which would, by definition, safeguard the spiritual and ethical values of the community, protecting its identity as a distinctively Muslim community. It lent to their writings a curiously moralistic air, but also an idealist flavour, since they were more concerned to refer their prescriptions to an established body of Islamic jurisprudence, or even to new interpretations of existing Islamic law, than to the actual workings of the global economy. Underpinning much of this genre of writing was the assumption that an Islamic economy would work better than any other economic system in safeguarding the fundamental values of Islam, whilst also providing a basis for profitable transactions amongst Muslims.

These arguments were internally coherent, since they were based on the a priori assumption that any arrangement which secured the moral economy of an idealised Islamic community must be better in all senses than any alternative, let alone one driven by the acquisitive egotism and commodity-based logic of capitalism. However, this imaginative exercise seemed frustratingly divorced from practice and a distinct shift takes place in the literature, evident in those Muslim intellectuals who challenged capitalism directly, not simply on ethical grounds, but also on those which appealed to 'neutral' criteria of economic efficiency. The claim thus emerged that an Islamic economy would be both morally superior to market capitalism, and more effective at delivering the material benefits of economic development. This had the effect of drawing those seeking to elaborate an Islamic economy into the disciplinary field of economics, which had itself been discursively constructed largely in the context of the emergence of market capitalism. It was not simply the materialist thrust which began to make its mark on these writings, but also the utilitarian calculus, the criteria of efficiency and therefore the measurement of success. Furthermore, underlying much of this was a set of sometimes unexamined assumptions relating to markets, commodities and the human beings whose individual and collective preferences were driving the process forward. Concern about the potential dangers of such an approach led in turn to two distinct forms of response amongst Muslim intellectuals to the capitalist nature of the global economy.

One was the development of specifically Islamic banks. These institutions were intended to embody some of the principles outlined in various prescriptions for an Islamic economy, as well as to safeguard Muslims in their identity and their transactions within the financial sphere. At the same time, however, they were and remain signs of a determination to engage with the dominant capitalist economy in a positive, rather than a confrontational way. The Islamic banking sector has sought and gained recognition as an established part of the global economy, with a specified role to play within financial markets, both international and domestic. Far from representing an alternative to the capitalist economic system, it is a full player within it, offering to its customers a distinctive way of making a profit that may separate it from the conventional banking sector in some respects, but which is clearly in conformity with it in many others. For those who have helped to develop the banks, these are positive features which neither compromise their identities as Muslims nor the values they espouse. On the contrary, whether on jurisprudential grounds, or on grounds related to the welfare of the communities of Muslims associated with particular economies, these institutions are seen as an important way of ensuring that a Muslim can be true to his or her faith, but can also benefit from the advantages of a market economy. Islamic banking may alert people to the ethical implications of their financial transactions, but, despite the hyperbole that attended the inauguration of Islamic banking in the 1970s, this is now seen as a means of engaging successfully with the forces of global capital, rather than the first step on the road to the undermining and overthrow of the capitalist system.

Possible disappointments generated by this and other institutional forms of engagement lie at the root of another kind of contemporaneous response to capitalism. This focuses its attentions on the individual Muslim – the *Homo islamicus* in the writings of those touched by economistic language, or, more simply, the believer. Whatever the designation, the intention has been broadly the same, in the sense that the focus has been on the imaginative creation of an individual who will internalise the very values which the intransigence of the external world may compromise and threaten. As with any such imaginative construction, where the teleology is so much a part of the process, the projected virtuous believer can have a rather 'thin' appearance, in the sense that he or she will reflect the immediate preoccupations and interpretations of the progenitor. However complex these may be, they are unlikely to match the richness, the ambiguity and the complexities of socially grounded individuals.

For some Muslim intellectuals, therefore, the priority is to determine the appropriate space in which conformity can be established, and to decide upon the most effective means of doing so. The intention is to build up the inner resources of the individual Muslim, in the final analysis projected as the main bastion of resistance to a world driven mad by the pursuit of profit, the gratification of material desires and the alienating effect of a market-driven commodification of human qualities. Re-connection with the self, imagined as a repository of identifiably Muslim virtues, and through the self to a specific understanding of God's command, becomes the principal undertaking. Different spaces and different methods have been associated with this drive to reconstitute the Muslim as the prime agent of resistance to the power of the material world embodied in capitalism. For some, the key struggle needs to take place in the individual conscience, the site finally of the human capacity to make moral choices. This is seen as a matter of inner reflection and, although circumstances can be imagined which would be conducive to reflection along lines which would finally be helpful to the project, it is for the individual to decide.

Others have placed a more social construction on this endeavour, seeing the family and gender roles within it as the proper arena for the education of a new generation capable of defending itself against the lures of materialism. Precisely because this may prescribe for both men and women roles which they themselves might question, the project of social reconstruction also becomes one of political power and the persuasive or coercive resources required to determine the outcome. Finally, the issue of political mobilisation and the education, even illumination, of the individual come together in the realm of symbolic politics – the use of spectacle and shock to reconnect the individual with his or her Islamic obligations, opening up the possibility of the overthrow of the deceptive and misguided status quo. In all of these areas, the multiple meanings attached to the term *jihad* have been widely deployed in contemporary Islamist discourses, each usage implying at root the struggle of Muslims to follow the path laid down by God, but their individual and contrasting forms stemming from sharply different ideas about the nature of the obstacles in their way.[2]

In this sense, therefore, Muslims concerned about the power of capitalism to transform their communities have been able to draw upon a distinctively

---

[2] Fawaz Gerges, *The Far Enemy: Why Jihad Went Global* (Cambridge, 2005) pp. 3–15.

Muslim repertoire to make sense of the experience and to organise a response in ways which connect with defining values and symbols of an Islamic inheritance. However, in practice this has yielded a variety of responses, each of which can plausibly claim an Islamic genealogy, yet each of which may differ markedly from the other, both in its evaluation of the nature of the threat and in the consequences for subsequent courses of action. This diversity stems from three major processes that have been at work in the shaping of such responses.

There are the different assessments about the severity of the threat of capitalism, if threat it is judged to be, based in part on judgements about the vulnerabilities of Islamic societies. There is also the variety of factors which have contributed to the selection and deployment of specific examples, models and symbols from the rich, sometimes contradictory array to be found in the narratives of Islamic history and Islamic jurisprudence. These factors may be the product of a history and of a way of looking at the world which owes little or nothing to a distinctively Islamic inheritance, but which nevertheless shapes the evaluation of that world. Finally, and inevitably, there is the range of differing judgements about the most effective ways of engaging with the world in order to protect those interests defined as distinctively Islamic – differences often sharpened by the plurality of views associated with the other two processes.

In the global reach of capitalist expansion which has drawn the whole world into a field of power defined and maintained by systems largely alien to the moral economy of pre-existing forms of sociability, it should come as no surprise that resistance should develop. However, as the unfolding of the varieties of Islamic response to capitalism has demonstrated, that resistance may take a number of forms, some violent, but others not. Equally, and of greater potential significance for the future, resistance to the general principle of capitalist accumulation may not be the chief form of response. On the contrary, Muslims have seized upon the opportunities offered by the restless innovations of capitalist enterprise to assert new ways of being Muslim in the world. This has been combined with articulate, sometimes violent resistance to specific injustices caused by states and enterprises furthering their own self-interested agendas, but this does not imply resistance to capitalism as a system. For Muslims and non-Muslims alike, part of the challenge for the future will be to create the space, imaginative and actual, in which acceptance is not read as subordination and in which active engagement becomes part of a process of self-definition.

Bibliography

WORKS IN ARABIC AND PERSIAN

al-'Abbadi, 'Abd al-Salam Dawud, *Al-Milkiyah fi al-shari'at al-islamiyah*, 3 vols. (Amman: Maktabat al-Aqsa, 1977).

'Abd al-Halim, Mahmud, *Al-Ikhwan al-muslimun – ahdath sana'at al-ta'rikh* (Alexandria: Dar al-Da'wah, 1986), part 3.

'Abd al-Karim, Fathi Ahmad, *Al-Nizam al-iqtisadi fi al-islam* (Cairo: Maktabah Wahbah, 1980).

'Abd al-Rahman, 'Umar, *Kalimah haqq* (Cairo: Dar al-I'tisam, 1987).

'Abduh, 'Isa, *Al-Iqtisad al-islami: madkhal wa-minhaj* (Cairo: Sharikat al-Tiba'at al-Fanniyat al-Muttahidah, 1974).

'Abduh, Muhammad, *Al-Islam wa-l-mar'ah fi ra'i al-Imam Muhammad 'Abduh*, ed. Muhammad 'Imarah (Cairo: al-Qahirah li-l-Thaqafah al-'Arabiyah, 1975).

 Al-A'mal al-kamilah, 3 vols., ed. Muhammad 'Imarah (Beirut: Al-Mu'assasat al-'Arabiyah li-l-Dirasat wa-l-Nashr, 1980).

Abu al-'Ila, Husain 'Abd al-Muhid Hasanain, *Fiqh al-riba* (Cairo: Matba'at al-Amanah, 1989).

Abu 'Ubaid, *Kitab al-amwal* (Cairo: Dar al-Fikr, 1975).

Abu Yahia, Muhammad Hasan, *Iqtisaduna fi daw' al-Qur'an wa-l-sunnah* (Amman: Dar 'Ammar, 1988).

Abu Yusuf, *Kitab al-kharaj* (Cairo: Matba'ah Salafiyah, 1972).

Abu Zahra, Muhammad, *Al-Milkiyah wa-l-nazriyat al-'aqd* (Cairo: no pub., 1939).

 Al-Takaful al-ijtima'i fi al-islam (Cairo: Dar al-Fikr al-'Arabi, 1964).

al-Afghani, Jamal al-Din, *Al-A'mal al-kamilah*, ed. Muhammad 'Imarah (Cairo: Dar al-Kitab al-'Arabi li-l-Tab'ah wa-l-Nashr, 1968).

 Al-Radd 'ala al-dahriyin, ed. Shaikh Muhammad Abu Rayyah (Beirut: Dar al-Zahra', 1981).

Al-Ahram al-Iqtisadi, *Al-Fatawa al-islamiyah fi al-qadayat al-iqtisadiyah*, Kitab Al-Ahram al-Iqtisadi XXVI (Cairo: Mu'assasat al-Ahram, 1990).

'Ali, Majid Ibrahim, *Al-Bank al-islami li-l-tanmiyah* (Cairo: Dar al-Nahdat al-'Arabiyah, 1982).

Amin, Galal, *Mihnat al-iqtisad wa-l-thaqafah fi misr* (Cairo: al-Markaz al-'Arabi li-l-Bahth wa-l-Nashr, 1982).

 Al-Iqtisad wa-l-siyasah wa-l-mujtama' fi 'asr al-infitah (Cairo: Maktabah Madbuli, 1984).

Antun, Farah, *Al-Din wa-l-'ilm wa-l-mal*, ed. Adonis al-'Akrah (Beirut: Dar al-Tali'ah, 1979).

al-'Arabi, Muhammad 'Abdallah, *Al-Dimuqratiyat al-qawmiyat al-'arabiyah baina al-dimuqratiyat al-shuyu'iyah wa-l-dimuqratiyat al-ra'smaliyah* (Cairo: Maktabat al-Nahdat al-Misriyah, 1961).

Al-Milkiyat al-khassah wa-hududuha fi al-islam (Cairo: al-Majlis al-A'li li-l-Shu'un al-Islamiyah, 1964).

Al-Iqtisad al-islami wa-siyasat al-hukm fi al-islam (Cairo: Matba'at al-Sharq al-'Arabi, 1967).

Al-Tanzim al-hadith li-l-dawlat al-islamiyah (Cairo: Ma'had al-Dirasat al-Islamiyah, 1969).

Arslan, Shakib, *Limadha ta'akhkhara al-muslimun wa-limadha taqaddum ghairuhum* (Cairo: Matba'ah 'Isa al-Babi al-Halabi, 1939).

al-'Ashmawi, Muhammad Sa'id, *Al-Islam al-siyasi* (Cairo: Dar Sina, 1987).

Al-Riba wa-l-fa'idah fi al-islam (Cairo: Madbuli al-Saghir, 1996).

al-'Assal, Ahmad and Fathi Ahmad 'Abd al-Karim, *Al-Nizam al-iqtisad fi al-islam* (Cairo: Maktabah Wahbah, 1980).

'Atiyah, Jamal al-Din, *Al-Bunuk al-islamiyah baina al-hurriyah wa-l-tanzim* (Doha: Matab'at al-Duha al-Hadithah, 1886).

al-'Awadi, Rif'at al-Sayyid, *Al-Iqtisad al-islami wa-l-fikr al-mu'asir* (Cairo: Majmu' al-Buhuth al-Islamiyah, 1974).

Fi al-iqtisad al-islami (Cairo: Mu'assasah Akhbar al-Yawm, 1990).

'Awdah, 'Abd al-Qadir, *Al-Islam wa-awda'na al-siyasiyah* (Cairo: no pub., 1967).

Al-Mal wa-l-hukm fi al-islam (Cairo: Matba' al-Mukhtar al-Islami, 1977).

Al-Islam wa-awda'na al-qanuniyah (Beirut: Mu'assasat al-Risalah, 1988).

al-'Awwa, Muhammad Salim, *Fi al-nizam al-siyasi li-l-dawlat al-islamiyah* (Cairo: al-Maktab al-Misri al-Hadith, 1983).

al-'Azm, Rafiq, *Tanbih al-afham ila mutalib al-hayat al-ijtima'iyah wa-l-islam* (Cairo: no pub., 1899)

'Azzam, 'Abdallah, *Al-Difa' 'an aradi al-muslimin ahamm furud al-a'yan* (San'a': Maktabat al-Jil al-Jadid, 1990).

Jihad sha'b muslim (San'a': Maktabat al-Jil al-Jadid, 1992).

al-Bahi, Muhammad, *Al-Islam wa-nuzum al-hukm al-mu'asirah* (Cairo: Maktabah Wahbah, 1965).

Tahafut al-fikr al-maddi al-ta'rikhi baina al-nazr wa-l-tatbiq (Cairo: Maktabah Wahbah, 1975).

Bakr, 'Abd al-Rahman, *'Alaqat al-'amal fi al-islam* (Cairo: al-Hay'at al-'Ammah li-Shu'un Ijtima'iyah al-Matba' al-Amiriyah, 1970).

al-Ba'li, 'Abd al-Hamid Mahmud, *Maqasid al-shari'ah wa-mushkilat al-hajjat fi al-iqtisad* (Cyprus: International Institute for Islamic Banks and Economy, 1987).

al-Banna, Hasan, *Majmu'ah rasa'il al-Imam al-Shahid Hasan al-Banna* (Beirut: Al-Mu'assasat al-Islamiyah li-l-Tab'ah wa-l-Sahafah wa-l-Nashr, 1984).

al-Barrawi, Rashid, *Al-Qur'an wa-l-nuzum al-ijtima'iyat al-mu'asirah* (Cairo: Dar al-Nahdat al-'Arabiyah, 1975).

Al-Qisas al-qur'ani: tafsir ijtima'i (Cairo: Dar al-Nahdah, 1978).

Al-Iqtisad al-islami (Cairo: Dar al-Hurriyah Li-l-Sahafah Wa-l-Tab'ah, 1986).

al-Bishri, Tariq, *Al-Hiwar al-islami al-'ilmani* (Cairo: Dar al-Shuruq, 1996).

al-Dumi, Ahmad 'Abd al-Jawwad, *Al-Minhaj al-ishtiraki 'ala daw' al-islam* (Cairo: Mu'assasat al-Khanji bi-Misr, 1964).

Fahmi, Mahmud, *Madhahib islamiyah: madhhab iqtisadi fi itar min mantaqat al-'asr al-hadith* (Cairo: Matba' al-Shuruq, 1983).

al-Fanjari, Muhammad Shawqi, *Dhatiyat al-siyasiyat al-iqtisadiyat al-islamiyah* (Cairo: Maktabat al-Salam al-'Alamiyah, 1981).

Al-Madhhab al-iqtisadi fi al-islam (Cairo: al-Hai'at al-Misriyat al-'Ammah li-l-Kitab, 1986).

Farraj, Ahmad, Ahmad al-Sharabasi et al. (eds.), *Al-Islam din al-ishtirakiyah* (Cairo: Al-Dar al-Qawmiyah li-l-Taba'ah wa-l-Nashr, 1961).

Ghanim, Husain, *Al-Sil'at al-iqtisadiyah: dirasah islamiyah fi al-nazriyat al-iqtisadiyah* (Cairo: no pub., 1986).

Al-Madkhal li-dirasat al-ta'rikh al-iqtisadi wa-l-hadari: ru'iyah islamiyah (Al-Mansurah: Dar al-Wafa' li-l-Tab'ah wa-l-Nashr wa-l-Tawzi', 1990).

Ghanim, Ibrahim al-Bayumi, *Al-Fikr al-siyasi li-l-Imam Hasan al-Banna* (Al-Mansurah: Mutarih al-Wafa', 1992).

al-Ghannoushi, Rashid, *Al-Mar'ah baina al-qur'an wa-waqi' al-muslimin* (London: Maghreb Center for Researches and Translation, 2000).

al-Ghazzali, 'Abd al-Hamid, *Al-Arbah wa-l-fawa'id al-masrafiyah baina al-tahlil al-iqtisadi wa-l-hukm al-shar'i* (Cairo: Markaz al-Iqtisad al-Islami, 1990).

al-Ghazzali, Abu Hamid, *Al-Mustasfa min 'ilm al-usul*, ed. Muhammad Mustafa Abu al-'Ala (Cairo: Sharikat al-Tiba'at al-Fanniyat al-Muttahidah, 1970).

al-Ghazzali, Muhammad, *Min huna na'lam* (Cairo: Matba'ah Dar al-Kitab al-'Arabi, 1950).

Al-Islam wa-l-awda' al-iqtisadiyah (Cairo: Dar al-Kitab al-'Arabi, 1952).

Al-Islam wa-l-manahij al-ishtirakiyah (Cairo: Dar al-Kitab al-'Arabi, 1954).

Al-Islam al-muftara 'alaihi baina al-shuyu'iyin wa-l-ra'smaliyin (Cairo: Dar al-Kitab al-'Arabi bi-Misr, 1960).

Al-Islam fi wajh al-zahf al-ahmar (Beirut: Manshurat al-Maktabat al-'Asriyah, n.d.).

al-Ghazzali, Zainab, *Ayyam min hayati* (Cairo: Dar al-Shuruq, 1989).

al-Hanafi, 'Abdallah bin 'Abd al-Ghani, *Al-Nur al-badi fi ahkam al-aradi* (ms. in the Dar al-Kutub al-Misriyah – *fiqh hanafi* 563, 1807).

Hanafi, Hasan, *Al-Din wa-l-tanmiyat al-qawmiyah*, vol. IV of *Al-Din wa-l-thawrah fi misr 1952–1981* (Cairo: Maktabah Madbuli, 1989).

Al-Yamin wa-l-yasar fi al-fikr al-dini, vol. VII of *Al-Din wa-l-thawrah fi misr 1952–1981* (Cairo: Maktabah Madbuli, 1989).

Al-Yasar al-islami wa-l-wahdat al-wataniyah, vol. VIII of *Al-Din wa-l-thawrah fi misr 1952–1981* (Cairo: Maktabah Madbuli, 1989).

Harb, Muhammad Tal'at, *Fasl al-Kitab 'an al-hmar'a, wa-l-hijab* (Cairo: no pub., 1901).

'Ilaj Misr al-iqtisadi (Cairo: Matba'ah Dar al-Kutub wa-l-Watha'iq al-Qawmiyah, 2002).

Hasan, Husain Hamid, *Nazriyat al-maslahah fi al-fiqh al-islami* (Cairo: Dar al-Nahdat al-'Arabiyah, 1971).

Hasan, Zaidan Abu al-Makaram, *Al-Iqtisad al-islami* (Cairo: Maktabat al-Khanji, 1977).

Hasanain, 'Abd al-Mun'im, *Al-Insan wa-l-mal fi al-islam* (Al-Mansurah: Dar al-Wafa' li-l-Tab'ah wa-l-Nashr wa-l-Tawzi', 1986).

Hawwa, Sa'id, *Fusul fi al-imrah wa-l-amir* (Beirut: Dar al-'Ammar, 1988).

Jund Allah (Beirut: Dar al-'Ammar, 1988).

Hazmah, Muhammad Ibrahim, *Ishtirakiyat al-islam wa-l-ishtirakiyat al-gharbiyah* (Cairo: al-Majlis al-A'li li-l-Shu'un al-Islamiyah, 1961).

al-Hudaibi, Hasan, *Du'ah la qudah* (Cairo: Dar al-Fikr al-'Arabi, 1977).

al-Husaini, Abu al-Nasr Ahmad, *Al-Milkiyah fi al-islam* (Cairo: Dar al-Kutub al-Hadith, 1952).

al-Husaini, Samir Muhammad al-Sayyid, *Al-Fikr al-iqtisadi al-islami* (Cairo: Matba'ah Hasan, 1985).

Ibn Taimiyah, Taqi al-Din Ahmad, *Al-Siyasat al-shar'iyah* (Cairo: Dar al-Sha'b, 1971).

Al-Hisbah (Cairo and Kuwait: Maktabat Dar al-Arqam, 1983).

Fatawa al-nisa' (Cairo: Maktabat al-'Irfan, 1983).

Ibrahim, Shaikh Ahmad, *Al-Mu'amalat al-shari'at al-maliyah* (Cairo: Matba'at al-Nasr, 1936).

Imam, Muhammad Kamal al-Din, *Usul al-hisbah fi al-islam* (Cairo: Dar al-Hidayah, 1986).

al-Jabarti, 'Abd al-Rahman, *'Aja'ib al-athar fi al-turajim wa-l-akhbar* (Cairo: Matba'at al-'Amarat al-Sharfiyah, 1905).

Jad'an, Fahmi, *Usus al-taqaddum 'ind mufakkiray al-islam fi al-'alam al-'arabi al-hadith* (Beirut: al-Mu'assassat al-'Arabiyah li-l-Dirasat wa-l-Nashr, 1981).

al-Jamal, Muhammad 'Abd al-Mun'im, *Mawsu'at al-iqtisad al-islami wa-dirasat muqarinah* (Cairo: Dar al-Kitab al-Misri, 1987).

Jami'at al-Azhar, *Al-Muhadarat al-'ammah li-l-mawsim al-thaqafi al-awwal* (Cairo: Jami'at al-Azhar, 1959).

Kamal, Yusuf, *Adwa' 'ala al-fikr al-iqtisadi al-islami al-mu'asir* (Cairo: Majallat al-Da'wah, 1980).

al-Kawakibi, 'Abd al-Rahman, *Al-A'mal al-kamilah*, ed. Muhammad Jamal Tahhan (Beirut: Markaz Dirasat al-Wahdat al-'Arabiyah, 1995).

al-Khafif, 'Ali, *Al-Milkiyah fi al-shari'at al-islamiyah*, parts 1 and 2 (Beirut: Ma'had al-Buhuth wa-l-Dirasat al-'Arabiyah, 1969).

Khalid, Khalid Muhammad, *Min huna nabda'* (Cairo: no pub., 1950).

Al-Dawlah fi al-islam (Cairo: Dar Thabit, 1981).

Khallaf, 'Abd al-Wahhab, *Masadir al-tashri' al-islami fi ma la nass fihi* (Cairo: Ma'had al-Jama'at al-'Arabiyah li-l-Dirasat al-'Arabiyah al-'Ulya, 1955).

al-Khatib, 'Abd al-Karim, *Al-Siyasat al-maliyah fi al-islam wa-silatuha bi-l-mu'amalat al-mu'asirah* (Cairo: Dar al-Fikr al-'Arabi, 1976).

Khudairi, Muhsin Ahmad, *Al-Bunuk al-islamiyah* (Cairo: Dar al-Hurriyah, 1990).

al-Khuli, Al-Bahi, *Al-Islam la shuyu'iyah wa-la ra'smaliyah* (Cairo: Matba'ah Dar al-Kitab al-'Arabi, 1951).

Al-Ishtirakiyah fi al-mujtama' al-islami baina al-nazriyah wa-l-tatbiq (Cairo: Maktabah Wahbah, 1963).

Al-Islam wa-l-mar'ah al-mu'asirah (Kuwait: Dar al-Qalam, 1984).

Khumaini, Ruhollah ibn Mustafa, *Jaigah-i zan dar andishah-i Imam Khumaini* (Tehran: Mu'assasah-i Tanzim va-Nashr-i Athar-i Imam Khumaini, 1999).

Madani, Ahmad 'Izzat, *Al-Idarah wa-iqtisadiyat al-'amal: al-minhaj al-islami wa-l-tatbiq* (Cairo: al-Ittihad al-Islami al-Dawli li-l-'Amal, 1986).

Mahmud, 'Abd al-Halim, *Fatawa al-Imam 'Abd al-Halim Mahmud*, 2 vols. (Cairo: Dar al-Ma'arif, 1990).

Makhluf, Hasanain Muhammad, *Al-Mawarith fi al-shari'at al-islamiyah* (Cairo: Dar al-Kitab al-'Arabiyah, 1956).

al-Marsafi, Hasan, *Risalat al-kalim al-thaman*, ed. Ahmad Zakaria al-Shalaq (Cairo: al-Hai'at al-Misriyat al-'Ammah li-l-Kitab, 1984).

al-Masri, 'Abd al-Sami', *Nazarat fi al-iqtisad al-islami* (Cairo: Dar al-Taba'ah wa-l-Nashr al-Islamiyah, 1986).

al-Masri, Rafiq Yusuf, *Usul al-iqtisad al-islami* (Damascus: Dar al-Qalam, 1989).

al-Mawdudi, Abu al-A'la, Hasan al-Banna and Sayyid Qutb, *Al-Jihad fi sabil Allah* (Beirut: Dar Lubnan, 1969).

Mustafa, 'Abd al-'Aziz al-Hajj, *Mustafa al-Siba'i – rajul fikr wa-qa'id da'wah* (Amman: Dar 'Ammar, 1984).

al-Nabhani, Taqi al-Din, *Al-Nizam al-iqtisadi fi al-islam* (Amman: Dar 'Ammar, n.d.).

Na'ini, Muhammad Husain, *Tanbih al-ummah wa-tanzih al-millah* (Najaf: no pub., 1909).

al-Najjar, Ahmad, *Nahwa istratijiyah jadidah li-l-tanmiyat al-iqtisadiyah fi al-duwwal al-namiyah* (Beirut: Dar al-Fikr, 1969).

Harakat al-bunuk al-islamiyah (Cairo: Dar al-Sahwah, 1993).

al-Nasir, Muhammad al-Hajj, *Al-Islam wa-intiza' al-milk li-l-maslahat al-'ammah* (Rabat: Wizarat al-Awqaf wa-l-Shu'un al-Islamiyah, 1991).

Nur, Mahmud Muhammad, *Al-Iqtisad al-islami* (Cairo: Maktabat al-Tijarah wa Ta'awun, 1978).

al-Qardawi, Yusuf, *Al-Islam wa-l-'ilmaniyah* (Cairo: Dar al-Sahwah, 1987).

Fawa'id al-bunuk hiya al-riba al-haram (Cairo: Dar al-Sahwah, 1990).

Fatawa mu'asirah li-l-mar'ah wa-l-usrat al-muslimah (Cairo: Dar al-Isra', 1991).

Dawr al-qiyam wa-l-akhlaq fi al-iqtisad al-islami (Cairo: Maktabah Wahbah, 1995).

al-Qasimi, Muhammad Jamal al-Din, *Dala'il al-tawhid* (Beirut: Dar al-Kitab al-'Ilmiyah, 1984).

Qutb, Muhammad, *Al-Insan baina al-maddiyah wa-l-islam* (Cairo: Dar al-Shuruq, 1980).

Qutb, Sayyid, *Hadha al-din* (Cairo: Dar al-Kitab al-'Arabi, 1955).

Al-Mustaqbal li-hadha al-din (Cairo: Dar al-Kitab al-'Arabi, 1956).

Khasa'is al-tasawwur al-islami wa-muqawwamatuhu (Cairo: 'Isa al-Babi al-Halabi, 1962).

Fi zilal al-Qur'an, 5 vols. (Beirut: Dar Ihya' al-Dirasat al-'Arabi, 1967).

Al-'Adalat al-ijtima'iyah fi al-islam (Cairo: Dar al-Shuruq, 1977).

Al-Salam al-'alami wa-l-islam (Cairo: Dar al-Shuruq, 1979).

Jahiliyat al-qarn al-'ishrin (Cairo: Dar al-Shuruq, 1980).

Al-Islam wa-mushkilat al-hadarah (Cairo: Dar al-Shuruq, 1988).

Ma'alim fi al-tariq (Cairo: Dar al-Shuruq, 1988).

Ma'arakat al-islam wa-l-ra'smaliyah (Cairo: Dar al-Shuruq, 1993).

Nahwa mujtama' islami (Cairo: Dar al-Shuruq, 1993).

Radwan, Ahmad Muhammad, *Ishtirakiyat al-islam* (Cairo: Dar al-Kitab al-'Arabi, 1950).

Rida, Muhammad Rashid, *Muhawarat al-muslih wa-l-muqallid* (Cairo: Matba'ah Majallat al-Manar al-Islamiyah, 1906).

Al-Riba wa-l-mu'amalat fi al-islam, ed. Muhammad Bahjat al-Bitar (Beirut: Dar Ibn Zaidun, 1986).

Al-Khilafah (Cairo: Al-Zahra' li-l-I'lam al-'Arabi, 1988).

Sabbar, Khadijah, *Al-Islam wa-l-hijab* (no place: Ifriqiya al-Sharq, 1994).

al-Sadr, Muhammad Baqir, *Al-Bank al-la-ribawi fi al-islam* (Kuwait: Jami' al-Naqi, 1970).

Iqtisaduna (Beirut: Dar al-Kitab al-Lubnani, 1982).

al-Saif, Tawfiq, *Didda al-istibdad: al-fiqh al-siyasi al-shi'i fi 'asr al-ghaibah* (Beirut: Al-Markaz al-Thaqafi al-'Arabi, 1999).

Sa'id, 'Abd al-Ghani, *Al-Nizam al-iqtisadi al-ijtima'i al-islami wa-inqadh al-iqtisad al-'alami* (Cairo: Maktabat al-Anjlu al-Misriyah, 1985).

Salih, Sa'ad Ibrahim, *Mubadi' al-nizam al-iqtisadi al-islami wa-ba'd tatbiqatuhu* (Cairo: Dar al-Diya', 1986).

Salim, Muhammad Farraj, *Al-Takaful al-ijtima'i* (Cairo: Sharikat al-Tiba'at al-Fanniyah al-Muttahidah, 1965).

al-Salus, 'Ali, *Radd li-kitab mufti misr 'ala mu'amalat al-bunuk wa-shar'aiyatuha al-islamiyah* (Cairo: Dar al-manar al-haditha, 1991).

Saqr, Muhammad Ahmad, *Al-Iqtisad al-islami mufahim wa-murtakazat* (Jiddah: Kulliyat al-Iqtisad wa-l-Idarah Jami'ah, 1396/1976).

Sarhan, 'Abd al-Hamid Ibrahim, *Al-Iqtisad fi al-islam* (Cairo: Al-Hay'at al-Misriyat al-'Ammah li-l-Kitab, 1987).

Shahatah, Shawqi Isma'il, *Al-Bunuk al-islamiyah* (Cairo: al-Qahirah al-Hadithah li-l-Tab'ah, 1977).

Shalabi, Mahmud, *Ishtirakiyah Muhammad* (Cairo: Maktabat al-Qahirah al-Hadithah, 1962).

Ishtirakiyah 'Uthman (Cairo: Maktabat al-Qahirah al-Hadithah, 1968).

Shaltut, Mahmud, *Al-Islam wa-l-takaful al-ijtima'i* (Cairo: Dar al-Qalam, 1960).

Al-Fatawa: dirasah li-mushkilat al-muslim al-mu'asir fi hayatihi al-yawmiyah wa-l-'ammah (Cairo: Dar al-Qalam, 1964).

al-Sharabasi, Ahmad, *Al-Ishtirakiyah wa-l-din* (*Imanuna* no. 2) (Cairo: Idarat al-Shu'un al-'Ammah wa-l-Tawjih al-Ma'nuwa bi-l-Qiyadat al-'Ammah li-l-Quwwat al-Maslahah, 1962).

Al-Islam wa-l-iqtisad (Cairo: al-Dar al-Qawmiyah li-l-Taba'ah wa-l-Nashr, 1965).

Al-Din wa-l-mithaq (Cairo: al-Dar al-Qawmiyah li-l-Taba'ah wa-l-Nashr, 1965).

Baina al-din wa-l-dunya (Cairo: al-Majlis al-A'li li-l-Nashr al-Islami, 1970).

Al-Din wa-l-mujtama' (Cairo: al-Matba'at al-'Arabiyah, 1970).

Shari'ati, Ali, *Zan musalman* (Tehran: no pub. 1967).

Islam-shinasi (Mashhad: Chap-i Tus, 1968).

Fatimah Fatimah ast (Tehran: Husainiyah Irshad, 1971).

Du shahid (Tehran: Nashr-i Hurr, 1977).

Khvud' sazi-i inqilabi (no place: no pub., 1978).

Daftar-i asar-i Shari'ati, vol. II (Tehran: Daftar-i Tadvin-i Tanzim, 1981).

Payam-i umid bih roshanfikr-i mas'ul (Solon, OH: Ittihadiyah-i Anjuman'ha-yi Islami-i Danishjuyan dar Urupa, n.d.).

al-Siba'i, Mustafa, *Al-Mahadarat al-'ammah 1958–9*, no. 7 (Damascus: Matba'ah Jami'ah Dimashq, 1959).

Ishtirakiyat al-islam (Damascus: Mu'assasat al-Matba'at al-'Arabiyah, 1960).

Akhlaquna al-ijtima'iyah (Beirut: Dar al-Irshad, 1972).

Sultan, Gamal, *Ghazw min al-dakhil* (Cairo: Al-Zahra' li-l-I'lam al-'Arabi, 1988).

al-Tabari, Abu Ja'far Muhammad bin Jarir, *Ta'rikh al-Tabari (Ta'rikh al-umum wa-l-muluk)*, vol. IV (Beirut: Dar al-Turath, 1967).

al-Tahtawi, Rifa'ah Rafi', *Al-A'mal al-kamilah*, ed. Muhammad 'Imarah (Beirut: al-Mu'assasat al-'Arabiyah li-l-Dirasat wa-l-Nashr, 1973).

Tantawi, Muhammad Sayyid, *Mu'amalat al-bunuk wa-ahkamuha al-shar'iyah* (Cairo: Dar Nahdah Misr, 1997).

al-Tirmidhi, Abu 'Isa Muhammad bin 'Isa bin Surah, *Al-Jami' al-sahih*, ed. Ibrahim 'Awad (Beirut: Dar Ihya' al-Turath al-'Arabi, 1963).

al-Tunisi, Khair al-Din, *Aqwam al-masalik fi ma'arafah ahwal al-mamalik*, vol. I, ed. Al-Mansuf al-Shannufi (Tunis: al-Majmu' al-Tunisi li-l-'Ulum wa-l-Adab wa-l-Funun, Bait al-Hikmah, 2000).

al-Turabi, Hasan, *Al-Iman wa-atharuhu fi hayat al-insan* (Jiddah: al-Dar al-Sa'udiyah li-l-Nashr wa-l-Tawzi', 1984).

Hiwarat fi al-islam, al-dimuqratiyah, al-dawlah, al-gharb (Beirut: Dar al-Jadid, 1995).

Al-Siyasah wa-l-hukm: al-nuzum al-sultaniyah baina al-usul wa-sunan al-waqi' (Beirut: Dar al-Saqi, 2003).

'Umar, 'Abd al-Halim 'Abd al-Fattah, *Al-Masalih al-mursalah wa-bina' al-ahkam 'alaiha: dirasah usuliyah* (Cairo: Dar al-Tab'at al-Muhammadiyah, 1990).

'Uthman, Muhammad Musa, *Nazriyat al-infitah al-iqtisadi fi al-islam* (Cairo: al-Dar al-Misriyah li-l-Tab'ah wa-l-Nashr, 1990).

Yahia, Muhammad, *Fi al-radd 'ala al-'ilmaniyah* (Cairo: Al-Zahra' li-l-I'lam al-'Arabi, 1985).

Yusri, 'Abd al-Rahman, *Al-Qimah allati ajaraha* (Cairo: Dar al-Shuruq, 1996).

Zaid, Mustafa, *Al-Maslahah fi al-tashri' al-islam wa-Najm al-Din al-Tufi* (Cairo: Dar al-Fikr al-'Arabi, 1954).

WORKS IN EUROPEAN LANGUAGES

Abd-Allah, Umar, *The Islamic Struggle in Syria* (Berkeley: Mizan Press, 1983).

Abdul-Rauf, Muhammad, *A Muslim's Reflections on Democratic Capitalism* (Washington, DC: American Enterprise Institute, 1984).

Abrahamian, Ervand, "'Ali Shari'ati: Ideologue of the Iranian Revolution', ch. 14 in Edmund Burke III and Ira M. Lapidus (eds.), *Islam, Politics and Social Movements* (Berkeley: University of California Press, 1988).

Abu-Lughod, Ibrahim, *The Arab Rediscovery of Europe* (Princeton: Princeton University Press, 1963).

Ahmad, Aziz, *Islamic Modernism in India and Pakistan 1857–1964* (London: Oxford University Press, 1967).

Studies in Islamic Culture in the Indian Environment (Delhi: Oxford University Press, 1999).

Ahmad, Aziz and G. E. von Grunebaum (eds.), *Muslim Self-Statement in India and Pakistan 1857–1968* (Wiesbaden: Otto Harrassowitz, 1970).

Ahmad, Jalal Al-i, *Plagued by the West* (Gharbzadegi), tr. P. S. Delmar, Modern Persian Literature Series IV (New York: Caravan Books, 1982).

Ahmad, Khurshid (ed.), *Studies in Islamic Economics* (Jeddah: King Abd al-Aziz University, 1980).

(ed.), *Islam: Its Meaning and Message* (Leicester: Islamic Foundation, 1988).

Ahmed, Qeyamuddin, *The Wahabi Movement in India* (Calcutta: Mukhopadhyay, 1966).

Ahmed, Ziauddin, *Islam, Poverty and Income Distribution* (Leicester: Islamic Foundation, 1991).

Ahmed, Ziauddin, Munawar Iqbal and M. Fahim Khan (eds.), *Fiscal Policy and Resource Allocation in Islam* (Islamabad: Institute of Policy Studies, 1983).

Akhavi, Shahrough, 'Shari'ati's social thought', in Nikki Keddie (ed.), *Religion and Politics in Iran* (New Haven: Yale University Press, 1983).

Algar, Hamid, *Mirza Malkam Khan* (Berkeley: University of California Press, 1973).

Ali, Abdullah Yusuf (tr.), *The Meaning of the Glorious Qur'an* (London: Nadim and Co., 1983).

Ali, Ameer, *The Spirit of Islam* (London: Christophers, 1922).

Amin, Qasim, *The Liberation of Women*, tr. S. S. Peterson (Cairo: American University of Cairo Press, 2000).

The New Woman (Cairo: American University of Cairo Press, 2000).

Anawati, G. C. and M. Borrmans, *Tendances et courants de l'Islam arabe contemporain*, vol. I: *Egypte et Afrique du Nord* (Munich: Kaiser-Grunewald, 1982).

Anderson, Benedict, *Long-Distance Nationalism: World Capitalism and the Rise of Identity Politics*, Wertheim Lecture, 1992 (Amsterdam: Centre for Asian Studies, Amsterdam, 1992).

Anderson, Jon W. 'The internet and Islam's new interpreters', in Dale F. Eickelman and Jon W. Anderson (eds.), *New Media in the Muslim World – The Emerging Public Sphere* (Bloomington: Indiana University Press, 2003).

Ansari, Ali, *Iran, Islam and Democracy: The Politics of Managing Change* (London: Royal Institute of International Affairs, 2000).

Appadurai, Arjun (ed.), *The Social Life of Things: Commodities in Cultural Perspective* (Cambridge: Cambridge University Press, 1986).

Aquinas, Thomas, *Selected Political Writings*, ed. A. P. d'Entrèves (Oxford: Basil Blackwell, 1965).

Aricanli, T. and M. Thomas, 'Sidestepping capitalism: on the Ottoman road to elsewhere', *Journal of Historical Sociology* 7/1 (March 1994).

Ariff, Mohamed (ed.), *Islamic Banking in Southeast Asia* (Singapore: Institute of Southeast Asian Studies, 1988).

Aristotle, *The Politics*, ed. S. Everson (Cambridge: Cambridge University Press, 1990).

Asad, Muhammad, *The Message of the Qur'an* (Gibraltar: Dar al-Andalus, 1980).

Ayubi, Nazih, *Political Islam* (London: Routledge, 1991).

Aziz, K. K., *Party Politics in Pakistan* (Islamabad: National Commission on Historical and Cultural Research, 1976).

Al-Azmeh, Aziz, *Ibn Khaldun in Modern Scholarship* (London: Third World Centre for Research and Publishing, 1981).
Islams and Modernities (London: Verso, 1993).
Baljon, J. M. S., *The Reforms and Religious Ideas of Sir Sayyid Ahmad Khan* (Lahore: Sh. Muhammad Ashraf, 1970).
Barber, Benjamin, 'All economies are "embedded": the career of a concept, and beyond', *Social Research* 62/2 (Summer 1995).
Jihad vs McWorld (New York: Ballantine Books, 1996).
Barlas, Asma, *'Believing Women' in Islam* (Austin, TX: University of Texas Press, 2002).
Batatu, Hanna, *The Old Social Classes and the Revolutionary Movements of Iraq* (Princeton: Princeton University Press, 1978).
Baudrillard, Jean, *The Mirror of Production*, tr. Mark Poster (St Louis, MO: Telos Press, 1975).
Selected Writings, ed. M. Poster (Stanford: Stanford University Press, 1988).
Beaugé, G. (ed.), *Les capitaux de l'Islam* (Paris: Presses du CNRS, 1990).
Behdad, Sohrab, 'A disputed utopia: Islamic economics in revolutionary Iran', *Comparative Studies in Society and History* 36 (1994).
Beinin, Joel 'Islamic Responses to the Capitalist Penetration of the Middle East', in B. F. Stowasser (ed.), *The Islamic Impulse* (London: Croom Helm in association with CCAS, Georgetown University, Washington, DC, 1987).
Workers and Peasants in the Modern Middle East (Cambridge: Cambridge University Press, 2001).
Beinin, Joel and Zachary Lockman, *Workers on the Nile* (London: I. B. Tauris, 1988).
Beinin, Joel and Joe Stork (eds.), *Political Islam* (London: I. B. Tauris, 1997).
Bell, C., *Ritual* (Oxford: Oxford University Press, 1997).
Benn, S. I. and G. F. Gaus, *Public and Private in Social Life* (London: Croom Helm, 1983).
Berger, Peter, *The Capitalist Revolution* (Aldershot: Wildwood House Ltd., 1987).
Berkes, Niyazi, *The Development of Secularism in Turkey* (New York: Routledge, 1998).
Bernand, M., *L'accord unanime de la communauté comme fondement des statuts légaux de l'Islam* (Paris: J. Vrin, 1970).
Besteman, C. (ed.), *Violence – A Reader* (New York: New York University Press, 2001).
Bin Muhammad, Abdul Aziz, *Zakat and Rural Development in Malaysia* (Kuala Lumpur: Berita Publishing, 1993).
Binder, Leonard, *Islamic Liberalism* (Chicago: Chicago University Press, 1988).
Bior, Isaac Bior Deng, *Some Reflections on Economic Liberalization in the Sudan*, Sudan Economy Research Group, discussion paper 32 (Bremen: University of Bremen, 2000).
Blank, J., *Mullahs on the Mainframe: Islam and Modernity among the Daudi Bohras* (Chicago: University of Chicago Press, 2001).
Bodman, H. L. and N. Tohidi (eds.), *Women in Muslim Societies* (Boulder, CO: Lynne Rienner, 1998).
Bottomore, Tom, *Theories of Modern Capitalism* (London: Allen and Unwin, 1985).

Bouhdiba, Abdelwahab, *Sexuality in Islam*, tr. Alan Sheridan (London: Saqi Books, 1998).

Bourdieu, Pierre, *In Other Words*, tr. M. Adamson (Cambridge: Polity Press, 1990).

The Logic of Practice, tr. R. Nice (Cambridge: Polity Press, 1990).

Language and Symbolic Power, tr. G. Raymond and M. Admanson (Cambridge: Polity Press, 1991).

Practical Reason – On the Theory of Action (Cambridge: Polity Press, 1998).

Bowen, H., 'Ahmad Djewdet Pasha', in *Encyclopedia of Islam* (Leiden: Brill, 1960), vol. I.

Braudel, Fernand, *Civilization and Capitalism 15th–18th century*, vol. II: *The Wheels of Commerce* (London: William Collins Sons and Co., with Book Club Associates, 1983).

Brown, Daniel, *Rethinking Tradition in Modern Islamic Thought* (Cambridge: Cambridge University Press, 1996).

Brown, L., Carl, *The Surest Path*, Harvard Monographs XVI (Cambridge, MA: Harvard University Press, 1967).

de Brunhoff, S., *La monnaie chez Marx* (Paris: Editions sociales, 1967).

Bunt, Gary R., *Islam in the Digital Age* (London: Pluto Press, 2003).

Burgat, François and W. Dowell, *The Islamic Movement in North Africa* (Austin, TX: Center for Middle Eastern Studies, University of Texas at Austin, 1993).

Burke III, Edmund and Ira M. Lapidus (eds.), *Islam, Politics and Social Movements* (Berkeley: University of California Press, 1988).

Burke, Jason, *Al-Qaeda* (London: I. B. Tauris, 2003).

Burr, J. Millard and R. O. Collins, *Revolutionary Sudan: Hasan al-Turabi and the Islamist State 1989–2000* (Leiden: Brill, 2003).

Busse, Heribert, 'Cain and Abel', in J. D. McAuliffe (ed.), *Encyclopedia of the Qur'an* (Leiden: Brill, 2001), vol. I.

Camera d'Afflitto, Isabella, 'Note sulla rivista Al-Muslimun: analisi di alcuni temi della pubblicistica dei Fratelli Musulmani', *Oriente Moderno* 57 (Jan.–Dec. 1977).

Cameron, A. J., *Abu Dharr al-Ghifari – An examination of his Image in the Historiography of Islam* (London: Luzac and Co., 1973).

Carré, Olivier, *Mystique et politique* (Paris: Cerf, 1984).

Carré, Olivier and G. Michaud, *Les Frères Musulmans 1928–1982* (Paris: Editions Gallimard, 1983).

Castoriadis, Cornelius, *Philosophy, Politics, Autonomy*, ed. D. Curtis (New York: Oxford University Press, 1991).

The Imaginary Institution of Society, tr. K. Blamey (Cambridge: Polity Press, 1997).

de Certeau, Michel, *The Practice of Everyday Life*, tr. S. Rendall (Berkeley: University of California Press, 1988).

Chakrabarty, D., *Provincializing Europe* (Princeton: Princeton University Press, 2000).

Chapra, M., Umer, 'Mawlana Mawdudi's contribution to Islamic economics', *The Muslim World* 94/2 (April 2004).

Charlton, W., T. Mallinson and R. Oakeshott, *The Christian Response to Industrial Capitalism* (London: Sheed and Ward, 1986).

Chatterjee, Partha, *Nationalist Thought and the Colonial World – A Derivative Discourse* (London: Zed Books, 1993).

Chehabi, Houshang, *Iranian Politics and Religious Modernism* (London: I. B. Tauris, 1990).

Choueiri, Yousef, *Islamic Fundamentalism* (London: Pinter Publishers, 1990).

Cleveland, William L., *Islam against the West: Shakib Arslan and the Campaign for Islamic Nationalism* (London: Al-Saqi Books, 1985).

Commins, D. D., *'The Salafi Islamic Reform Movement in Damascus 1885–1914: Religious Intellectuals, Politics and Social Change in Late Ottoman Syria'* (Ann Arbor: University of Michigan Ph.D. dissertation, 1985).

Comte, A., *The Crisis of Industrial Civilization*, intro. R. Fletcher (London: Heinemann Educational Books, 1974).

Cook, Michael, *Commanding Right and Forbidding Wrong in Islamic Thought* (Cambridge: Cambridge University Press, 2002).

Cooper, John, Ronald Nettler and Mohamed Mahmoud (eds.), *Islam and Modernity* (London: I. B. Tauris, 1998).

Crecelius, D. N., *The Ulama and the State in Modern Egypt* (Princeton: Princeton University Ph.D., dissertation, 1967).

Crone, Patricia, *Roman, Provincial and Islamic Law* (Cambridge: Cambridge University Press, 1987).

Cuno, Kenneth M., 'The origins of private ownership of land in Egypt: a reappraisal', *International Journal of Middle East Studies* 12 (1980).

   The Pasha's Peasants – Land, Society and Economy in Lower Egypt, 1740–1858 (Cambridge: Cambridge University Press, 1992).

Dabashi, Hamid, *Theology of Discontent* (New York: New York University Press, 1993).

Dalton, G. (ed.), *Primitive, Archaic and Modern Economics – Essays by Karl Polanyi* (Boston, MA: Beacon Press, 1968).

Davis, Eric, *Challenging Colonialism: Bank Misr and Egyptian Industrialisation 1920–1941* (Princeton: Princeton University Press, 1983).

Davis, John, *Exchange* (Buckingham: Open University Press, 1992).

Dean, Kathryn, *Capitalism and Citizenship: The Impossible Partnership* (London: Routledge, 2003).

van Dijk, C. and A. H. de Groot (eds.), *State and Islam* (Leiden: CNWS, 1995).

Dilley, R. (ed.), *Contesting Markets* (Edinburgh: Edinburgh University Press, 1992).

Dobb, Maurice, *Studies in the Development of Capitalism* (London: George Routledge and Sons, 1946).

Dumont, Louis, *From Mandeville to Marx: The Genesis and Triumph of Economic Ideology* (Chicago: University of Chicago Press, 1977).

Duncan, Graeme (ed.), *Democracy and the Capitalist State* (Cambridge: Cambridge University Press, 1989).

Durkheim, Emile, *Professional Ethics and Civic Morals* (London: Routledge, 1957).

   The Rules of Sociological Method, tr. W. D. Halls (London: Macmillan, 1982).

   Durkheim on Politics and the State, ed. A. Giddens (Cambridge: Polity Press, 1986).

Eickelman, Dale F. and Jon W. Anderson (eds.), *New Media in the Muslim World – The Emerging Public Sphere* (Bloomington: Indiana University Press, 2003).

Eickelman, Dale F. and James Piscatori, *Muslim Politics* (Princeton: Princeton University Press, 1996).

El Guindi, Fadwa, *Veil: Modesty, Privacy and Resistance* (Oxford: Berg, 1999).

Emmet, Dorothy, *Function, Purpose and Powers* (London: Macmillan, 1958).

Enayat, Hamid, *Modern Islamic Political Thought* (London: Macmillan, 1982).

Engels, Frederick, *The Origin of the Family, Private Property and the State*, tr. E. Untermann (Honolulu, HI: University Press of the Pacific, 2001).

Engineer, Asghar Ali, *The Islamic State* (New Delhi: Vikas, 1980).

Entelis, John P. (ed.), *Islam, Democracy, and the State in North Africa* (Bloomington: Indiana University Press, 1997).

Esposito, John (ed.), *Voices of Resurgent Islam* (Oxford: Oxford University Press, 1983).

Unholy War (Oxford: Oxford University Press, 2002).

Esposito, John and John Voll, *Islam and Democracy* (New York: Oxford University Press, 1996).

Euben, Roxanne, *Enemy in the Mirror: Islamic Fundamentalism and the Limits of Modern Rationalism* (Princeton: Princeton University Press, 1999).

Fahmy, Mansoor, *La condition de la femme dans l'Islam* (Paris: Editions Allia, 1990; first published 1913).

al-Farag, Muhammad, *Al-Faridah al-gha'ibah* (The Neglected Duty), translated in J. J. Jansen, *The Neglected Duty* (New York: Macmillan, 1986).

Faust, Elke, 'Islam on tour: Die indo-pakistanische Bewegung Tablighi Jama'at', *Orient* 39/2 (June 1998).

Featherstone, Mike, Scott Lash and Roland Robertson (eds.), *Global Modernities* (London: Sage Publications, 1995).

Fine, Ben, *Women's Employment and the Capitalist Family* (London: Routledge, 1992). 'A question of economics: is it colonizing the social sciences?' *Economy and Society* 28/3 (August 1999).

Fine, Ben and Costas Lapavitsas, 'Markets and money in social theory: what role for economics?' *Economy and Society* 29/3 (August 2000).

Fisher, S. N. (ed.), *Social Forces in the Middle East* (Ithaca, NY: Cornell University Press, 1955).

Fletcher, R., *The Making of Sociology*, 2 vols. (London: Michael Joseph, 1971).

Fortna, Benjamin, 'Islamic morality in late Ottoman "secular" schools', *International Journal of Middle East Studies* 32/3 (August 2000).

Imperial Classroom: Islam, the State and Education in the Late Ottoman Empire (Oxford: Oxford University Press, 2002).

Forward, Martin, *The Failure of Islamic Modernism? Syed Ameer Ali's Interpretation of Islam* (Bern: Peter Lang, 1999).

Foucault, Michel, *The Archaeology of Knowledge*, tr. S. Smith (London: Tavistock Publications, 1972).

The Order of Things (London: Tavistock Publications, 1980).

The Foucault Reader, ed. P. Rabinow (London: Penguin Books, 1984).

Frankel Paul, Ellen, F. D. Miller, J. Paul and J. Ahrens (eds.), *Capitalism* (Oxford: Blackwell, 1989).

Friedland, R. and A. F. Robertson (eds.), *Beyond the Marketplace: Rethinking Economy and Society* (New York: Aldine de Gruyter, 1990).

Frisby, David, *Simmel and Since: Essays on Georg Simmel's Social Theory* (London: Routledge, 1992).

Galloux, Michel, *Finance islamique et pouvoir politique* (Paris: PUF, 1997).

Gerges, Fawaz, 'The end of the Islamist insurgency in Egypt? Costs and prospects', *Middle East Journal* 4 (Fall 2000).

The Far Enemy: Why Jihad Went Global (Cambridge: Cambridge University Press, 2005).

Giddens, Antony, *The Consequences of Modernity* (Cambridge: Polity Press, 1991).

Capitalism and Modern Social Theory (Cambridge: Cambridge University Press, 1991).

Glasier, J. B., *William Morris and the Early Days of the Socialist Movement* (Bristol: Thoemmes Press, 1994).

Gobetti, D., *Private and Public: Individuals, Households and Body Politic in Locke and Hutcheson* (London: Routledge, 1992).

Godelier, M., *Rationality and Irrationality in Economics*, tr. B. Pearce (New York: Monthly Review Press, 1972).

Goldberg, Ellis, *Tinker, Tailor and Textile Worker* (Berkeley: University of California Press, 1986).

Gomez, E. T. and K. S. Jomo, *Malaysia's Political Economy* (Cambridge: Cambridge University Press, 1999).

Gran, Peter, *Islamic Roots of Capitalism* (Austin, TX: University of Texas Press, 1979).

Granovetter, Mark and Richard Swedberg (eds.), *The Sociology of Economic Life* (Boulder, CO: Westview Press, 1992).

Grant, Wyn (ed.), *The Political Economy of Corporatism* (Basingstoke: Macmillan, 1985).

Grelle, B. and D. A. Krueger (eds.), *Christianity and Capitalism – Perspectives on Religion, Liberalism and the Economy* (Chicago: Center for the Scientific Study of Religion, 1986).

Grennan, M. R., *William Morris – Medievalist and Revolutionary* (New York: King's Crown Press, 1945).

Haarmann, U., 'Abu Dharr – Muhammad's revolutionary companion', *The Muslim World* 68/4 (October 1978).

Habermas, Jurgen, *Toward a Rational Society*, tr. J. J. Shapiro (Cambridge: Polity Press, 1989).

The Philosophical Discourse of Modernity, tr. F. Lawrence (Cambridge: Polity Press, 1998).

Haddad, Yvonne Yazbeck, *Contemporary Islam and the Challenge of History* (Albany, NY: State University of New York Press, 1982).

'Sayyid Qutb: ideologue of Islamic revival', ch. 4 in J. Esposito (ed.), *Voices of Resurgent Islam* (Oxford: Oxford University Press, 1983).

Haddad, Yvonne Yazbeck and John Esposito (eds.), *Islam, Gender and Social Change* (New York and Oxford: Oxford University Press, 1998).

Haim, Sylvia G. (ed.), *Arab Nationalism – An Anthology* (Berkeley: University of California Press, 1964).

'Sayyid Qutb', *Asian and African Studies* 16 (1982).

Haj, Samira, *The Making of Iraq 1900–1963* (Albany, NY: SUNY Press, 1997).

Hall, John A. and I. C. Jarvie (eds.), *Transition to Modernity* (Cambridge: Cambridge University Press, 1992).

Hanioglu, Sukru, *The Young Turks in Opposition* (New York: Oxford University Press, 1995).

Hanna, Sami, 'Al-Afghani: a pioneer of Islamic socialism', *The Muslim World* 57/1 (January 1967).

'*Al-Takaful al-ijtima'i* and Islamic socialism', *The Muslim World* 59 (1969).

Hanna, Sami and G. H. Gardner (eds.), *Arab Socialism – A Documentary Survey* (Leiden: Brill, 1969).

Haque, Ziaul, *Riba: The Moral Economy of Usury, Interest and Profit* (Selangor: Ikraq, 1995).

Hatem, Mervat, 'Gender and Islamism in the 1990s', *Middle East Report* 222 (Spring 2002).

Hausman, D. M., *The Inexact and Separate Science of Economics* (Cambridge: Cambridge University Press, 1992).

Hegel, G. W. F., *Elements of the Philosophy of Right*, ed. Allen Wood (Cambridge: Cambridge University Press, 1991).

Heilbroner, Robert, *The Nature and Logic of Capitalism* (New York: W. W. Norton and Co., 1985).

Behind the Veil of Economics (New York: W. W. Norton and Co., 1988).

Henry, Clement M. and Robert Springborg, *Globalization and the Politics of Development in the Middle East* (Cambridge: Cambridge University Press, 2001).

Henry, Clement M. and Rodney Wilson (eds.), *The Politics of Islamic Finance* (Edinburgh: Edinburgh University Press, 2004).

Herrera, Linda, 'Downveiling: gender and the contest over culture in Cairo', *Middle East Report* 219 (Summer 2001).

Heydemann, Steven, *Authoritarianism in Syria* (Ithaca, NY: Cornell University Press, 1999).

Hirschman, A. O., *The Passions and the Interests* (Princeton: Princeton University Press, 1977).

Hourani, Albert, *Arabic Thought in the Liberal Age, 1798–1939* (London: Oxford University Press, 1962).

Humphreys, R. S., *Islamic History – A Framework for Inquiry* (London: I. B. Tauris, 1991).

Hunt, E. K., *Property and Prophets – The Evolution of Economic Institutions and Ideologies* (New York: Harper and Row, 1990).

al-Husry, Khaldun, *Origins of Modern Arab Political Thought* (Delmar, NY: Caravan Books, 1980).

Hussain, Freda and K. Radwan, 'The Islamic revolution and women: quest for the Quranic model', in Freda Hussain (ed.), *Muslim Women* (London: Croom Helm, 1984).

Hussein, Ishrat, *Pakistan – The Economy of an Elitist State* (Karachi: Oxford University Press, 1999).

Ibn Taymiyah, *Public Duties in Islam – The Institution of the Hisba*, tr. M. Holland, ed. Khurshid Ahmad (Leicester: Islamic Foundation, 1982).

Ibrahim, Saad al-Din and N. S. Hopkins (eds.), *Arab Society: Social Science Perspectives* (Cairo: American University of Cairo, 1985).

Inalcik, Halil, 'Turkey between Europe and the Middle East', in *From Empire to Republic – Essays on Ottoman and Turkish Social History*, Analecta Isisiana XIX (Istanbul: Isis Press, 1995).

Inalcik, Halil with Donald Quataert (eds.), *An Economic and Social History of the Ottoman Empire*, vol. II: *1600–1914* (Cambridge: Cambridge University Press, 2000).

International Monetary Fund, *Sudan: Recent Economic Developments* (Washington, DC: IMF, 1999).

Iqbal, Muhammad, *The Reconstruction of Religious Thought in Islam* (Lahore: Sh. Muhammad Ashraf, 1968).

Islamic Republic of Iran, *The Constitution of the Islamic Republic of Iran*, tr. Hosein Elahi Qomshei (Tehran: Hamdani Publishers, n.d.).

Issawi, Charles (ed.), *The Economic History of Iran 1800–1914* (Chicago: University of Chicago Press, 1971).

Itoh, Makoto, *The Basic Theory of Capitalism – Forms and Substance of the Capitalist Economy* (Basingstoke: Macmillan, 1988).

al-Jabarti, 'Abd al-Rahman, *Napoleon in Egypt: Al-Jabarti's Chronicle of the French Occupation of Egypt 1798*, translation of the ms. *Ta'rikh muddat al-faransis bi-Misr* ed. and tr. S. Moreh (Princeton and New York: Markus Wiener Publishing, 1993).

Janowitz, Morris, 'Sociological theory and social control', *American Journal of Sociology* 81/1 (July 1975).

Jansen, J. J., *The Neglected Duty* (New York: Macmillan, 1986).

   The Dual Nature of Islamic Fundamentalism (London: Hurst and Co, 1997).

Johansen, Baber, *The Islamic Law on Land Tax and Rent* (London: Croom Helm, 1988).

Joll, James, *The Anarchists* (London: Methuen, 1969).

Kahf, Monzer, *The Islamic Economy* (Plainfield, IN: Muslim Students' Association of the US and Canada, 1978).

Kamenka, Eugene and R. S. Neale (eds.), *Feudalism, Capitalism and Beyond* (London: Edward Arnold, 1975).

Kandiyoti, Deniz (ed.), *Women, Islam and the State* (Basingstoke: Macmillan, 1991).

Karpat, Kemal, *Studies in Ottoman Social and Political History* (Leiden: Brill, 2002).

   (ed.), *Political and Social Thought in the Contemporary Middle East* (New York: Praeger Publishers, 1982).

   The Politicization of Islam (Oxford: Oxford University Press, 2001).

Kazarian, E. G., *Islamic versus Traditional Banking* (Boulder, CO: Westview Press, 1993).

Keddie, Nikki, *An Islamic Response to Imperialism* (Berkeley: University of California Press, 1968).

   Iran: Religion, Politics and Society (London: Frank Cass, 1980).

   (ed.), *Religion and Politics in Iran* (New Haven: Yale University Press, 1983).

Kepel, Gilles, *The Prophet and Pharaoh*, tr. J. Rothschild (London: Saqi Books, 1985).

   Jihad: The Trail of Political Islam, tr. Anthony Roberts (London: I. B. Tauris, 2002).

Kerr, Malcolm, *Islamic Reform: The Political and Legal Theories of Muhammad Abduh and Rashid Rida* (Berkeley: University of California Press, 1966).

Khan, Syed Ahmad, *Writings and Speeches*, ed. Shan Mohammed (Bombay: Nachiketa Publications, 1972).

Khan, W. M., *Towards an Interest-Free Islamic Economic System* (Leicester: Islamic Foundation, 1985).

Khomeini, Ayatollah Ruhollah, *Islamic Government*, tr. Joint Publications Research Service (New York: Manor Books, 1979).

Islam and Revolution, tr. H. Algar (Berkeley: Mizan Press, 1981).

A Clarification of Questions, tr. J. Borujerdi (Boulder, CO: Westview Press, 1984).

Kirchgässner, G., *Homo oeconomicus: das ökonomische Modell individuellen Verhaltens und seine Anwendung in der Witschafts- und Sozialwissenschaften* (Tübingen: J. C. B. Mohr, 2000).

Kolb, David, *The Critique of Pure Modernity* (Chicago: Chicago University Press, 1988).

Kramer, Martin (ed.), *Shi'ism, Resistance, and Revolution* (Boulder, CO: Westview Press, 1987).

Kuran, Timur 'Fundamentalisms and the economy', and 'The economic impact of Islamic fundamentalism', in M. E. Marty and R. S. Appleby (eds.), *Fundamentalisms and the State: Remaking Polities, Economies and Militance* (Chicago: University of Chicago Press, 1993).

Islam and Mammon – The Economic Predicaments of Islamism (Princeton: Princeton University Press, 2004).

Kurzman, C. (ed.), *Liberal Islam: A Sourcebook* (Oxford: Oxford University Press, 1998).

Lambton, A. K. S., *The Persian Land Reform 1962–1966* (Oxford: Clarendon Press, 1969).

Lamloum, Olfa, 'Les femmes dans le discours islamiste', *Confluences Méditerranée* 27 (Autumn 1998).

Laoust, Henri, *Contribution à une étude de la méthodologie canonique de Taki-d-Din Ahmad b. Taimiya* (Cairo: Imprimerie de l'Institut français d'archéologie orientale, 1939).

Essai sur les doctrines sociales et politiques de Taki-d-Din Ahmad b. Taimiya (Cairo: Imprimerie de l'Institut français d'archéologie orientale, 1939).

Laroui, Abdallah, *Islam et modernité* (Paris: Editions de la Découverte, 1987).

Lash, Scott and Jonathan Friedman (eds.), *Modernity and Identity* (Oxford: Blackwell, 1996).

Latham, J. D. 'Musharaka', in *Encyclopedia of Islam* (Leiden: Brill, 1993), vol. VII.

Le Bon, G., *La civilisation des Arabes* (Paris: Firmin-Didot et Cie., 1884).

Psychologie des foules (Paris: Félix Alcan, 1896).

Letwin, W., *The Origins of Scientific Economics* (London: Methuen, 1963).

Lewenhak, S., *The Revaluation of Women's Work* (London: Earthscan, 1992).

Lewis, Mervyn K. and Latifa Algaoud, *Islamic Banking* (Cheltenham: Edward Elgar, 2001).

Lippit, V. D., *Capitalism* (London: Routledge, 2005).

Lyon, D., 'Cyberspace sociality: controversies over computer-mediated relationships', in Brian Loader (ed.), *The Governance of Cyberspace* (London: Routledge, 1997).

McDonough, Sheila, *The Authority of the Past – A Study of Three Muslim Modernists* (Chambersburg, PA: American Academy of Religion, 1970).

Macfarlane, Alan, *The Culture of Capitalism* (Oxford: Blackwell, 1987).

Macpherson, C. B., *Property – Mainstream and Critical Positions* (Oxford: Blackwell, 1978).

Mallat, Chibli, 'Tantawi on banking operations in Egypt' in Muhammad Khalid Masud, Brinkley Messick and David S. Powers (eds.), *Islamic Legal Interpretation: Muftis and their Fatwas* (Cambridge, MA: Harvard University Press, 1996).

Mandaville, Peter, 'Reimagining the Ummah? Information technology and the changing boundaries of political Islam', in Ali Mohammadi (ed.), *Islam Encountering Globalization* (London: RoutledgeCurzon, 2002).

Mandeville, Bernard, *The Fable of the Bees: Or, Private Vices, Publick Benefits* (London: Penguin, 1970).

Mannan, M. A., *Islamic Economics: Theory and Practice* (Delhi: Mohamed Ahmed for Idarah-i Adabiyati-i Delhi, 1980).

Why is Islamic Economics Important? Seven Reasons for Believing (Jeddah: King Abd al-Aziz University, 1982).

The Making of Islamic Economic Society: Islamic Dimensions in Economic Analysis (Cairo: International Association of Islamic Banks, 1984).

Mardin, Serif 'Ideology and religion in the Turkish revolution', *International Journal of Middle East Studies* 2 (1971).

Religion and Social Change in Modern Turkey (Albany, NY: SUNY Press, 1989).

Marshall, Gordon, *In Search of the Spirit of Capitalism* (London: Hutchinson, 1982).

Martin Muñoz, Gema, 'Islamistes et pourtant modernes', *Confluences Méditerranée* 27 (Autumn 1998).

Marx, Karl *Capital: A Critique of Political Economy*, 3 vols., ed. F. Engels tr. S. Moore and E. Aveling (London: Lawrence and Wishart, 1977–9).

Early Writings, tr. R. Livingstone and G. Benton (London: Penguin Books, 1992).

Marx, Karl and Friedrich Engels, *The German Ideology*, ed. C. J. Arthur (London: Lawrence and Wishart, 1999).

Maurer, Bill, 'Engineering an Islamic future', *Anthropology Today* 17/1 (February 2001).

Mutual Life, Limited: Islamic Banking, Alternative Currencies, Lateral Reason (Princeton: Princeton University Press, 2005).

Mauss, Marcel, *The Gift*, tr. W. D. Halls (London: Routledge, 2004).

Mawdudi, Abul A'la *Purdah and the Status of Women in Islam*, tr. Al-Ash'ari (Lahore: Islamic Publications, 1972).

Witnesses unto Mankind, translation of *Shahadat Haqq* (Leicester: Islamic Foundation, 1986).

Let Us Be Muslims, tr. of *Khutubat* (1940), ed. Khurram Murad (Leicester: Islamic Foundation, 1992).

Towards Understanding the Qur'an (Leicester: Islamic Foundation, 1998).

Mayer, A., 'Islamic banking and credit policies in the Sadat era: the social origins of Islamic banking in Egypt', *Arab Law Quarterly* 1/1 (1985).

Meenai, S. A., *The Islamic Development Bank* (London: Kegan Paul International, 1989).

Meijer, Raoul, *The Quest for Modernity: Secular Liberal and Left-Wing Political Thought in Egypt 1945–1958* (Richmond: RoutledgeCurzon, 2002).

Meiksins Wood, Ellen, *The Origins of Capitalism* (New York: Monthly Review Press, 1999).

Mernissi, Fatima, *The Veil and the Male Elite*, tr. Mary Jo Lakeland (Reading, MA: Addison-Wesley, 1991).

Merton, Robert, *On Theoretical Sociology* (New York: Free Press, 1967), vol. II.

Mesbah, Muhammad Taqi, 'Women or half of the body of society', in *Status of Women in Islam* (Tehran: Islamic Propagation Organisation, 1985).

Metcalf, Barbara, *Islamic Revival in British India: Deoband 1860–1900* (Princeton: Princeton University Press, 1982).

Mies, M., 'Capitalist development and subsistence production: women in rural India', in M. Mies (ed.), *Women: The Last Colony* (London: Zed Press, 1988).

Mill, John Stuart, *Principles of Political Economy* (London: Longmans, Green and Co., 1909).

Mir-Hosseini, Ziba, *Islam and Gender: The Religious Debate in Contemporary Iran* (London: I. B. Tauris, 1999).

Mirowski, P., *More Heat than Light: Economics as Social Physics* (Cambridge: Cambridge University Press, 1989).

Mitchell, Richard, *The Society of the Muslim Brothers* (London: Oxford Univessity Press, 1969).

Mitchell, Timothy, *Colonising Egypt* (Cambridge: Cambridge University Press, 1988). *Rule of Experts – Egypt, Techno-Politics and Modernity* (Berkeley: University of California Press, 2002).

Moghadam, Valentine, *Gender and National Identity* (London: Zed Books, 1994). 'Islamic feminism and its discontents: toward a resolution of the debate', in T. Saliba, C. Allen and J. A. Howard (eds.), *Gender, Politics and Islam* (Chicago: University of Chicago Press, 2002).

Moghissi, Haideh, *Feminism and Islamic Fundamentalism* (London: Zed Books, 1999).

Mohammadi, Ali (ed.), *Islam Encountering Globalization* (London: RoutledgeCurzon, 2002).

Mohieldin, Mahmoud, 'On formal and informal Islamic finance in Egypt', unpublished paper presented at MESA meeting in Washington, DC, 6–10 December 1995.

Morris, Brian, *Western Conceptions of the Individual* (Oxford: Berg, 1991).

Moslem, Mehdi, *Factional Politics in Post-Khomeini Iran* (Syracuse, NY: Syracuse University Press, 2002).

Muhammad, S., *Sir Syed Ahmad Khan – A Political Biography* (Meerut: Meenakshi Prakeshan, 1969).

Mulberg, Jon, *Social Limits to Economic Theory* (London: Routledge, 1995).

Mutahhari, Murtaza, *The Rights of Women in Islam* (Tehran: World Organisation for Islamic Services, 1981).

Myers, Milton L., *The Soul of Modern Economic Man* (Chicago: University of Chicago Press, 1983).
Myrdal, Gunar, *Against the Stream: Critical Essays on Economics* (London: Macmillan, 1973).
an-Nabhani, Taqiuddin, *The Islamic State* (London: al-Khilafah, 2001).
The Economic System in Islam (New Delhi: Milli Publications, 2002).
Nader, Albert, *Le système philosophique des Mu'tazila* (Beirut: Institut de lettres orientales à Beyrouth, 1956).
Najmabadi, Afsaneh, 'Feminism in an Islamic republic' in, Haddad and Esposito, *Islam, Gender and Social Change* (1998).
Naqvi, Syed Nawab Haider, *Ethics and Economics* (Leicester: Islamic Foundation, 1981).
Narotzky, S., *New Directions in Economic Anthropology* (London: Pluto Press, 1997).
Naseef, Fatima Umar, *Women in Islam: A Discourse of Rights and Obligations*, ed. S. M. Abedin (New Delhi: Sterling Publishers, 1999).
Nasr, Seyyed Vali Reza 'Towards a philosophy of Islamic economics', *The Muslim World* 77/3–4 (July–October 1987).
'Islamic economics: novel perspectives on change in the Middle East', *Middle East Studies* 25/4 (October 1989).
The Vanguard of the Islamic Revolution: The Jama'at-i Islami of Pakistan (London: I. B. Tauris, 1994).
Islamic Leviathan (Oxford: Oxford University Press, 2001).
van Nieuwenhuijze, C. A. O. (ed.), *Commoners, Climbers and Notables* (Leiden: Brill, 1977).
Nomani, Farhad and Ali Rahnema, *Islamic Economic Systems* (London: Zed Books, 1994).
Norman, E. R., *The Victorian Christian Socialists* (Cambridge: Cambridge University Press, 1987).
Oliver, Anne Marie, *The Road to Martyrs' Square: Inside the World of the Suicide Bomber* (Oxford: Oxford University Press, 2005).
Al-Omar, Fuad and Mohammed Abdel-Haq, *Islamic Banking: Theory, Practice and Challenges* (Karachi: Oxford University Press, 1996).
Ortayli, Ilber, 'Ottoman family law and the state in the nineteenth century', in *Studies on Ottoman Transformation*, Analecta Isisiana X (Istanbul: Isis Press, 1994).
Owen, Roger (ed.), *New Perspectives on Property and Land in the Middle East* (Cambridge, MA: Harvard University Press for the Center for Middle Eastern Studies of Harvard University, 2000).
Owen, Roger and Sevket Pamuk, *Middle East Economies in the Twentieth Century* (London: I. B. Tauris, 1998).
Paden, W. E., *Religious Worlds* (Boston: Beacon Press, 1988).
Pal, Izzud-Din, *Pakistan, Islam and Economics* (Karachi: Oxford University Press, 1999).
Parry, J. and M. Bloch (eds.), *Money and the Morality of Exchange* (Cambridge: Cambridge University Press, 1989)
Pels, Dick, *Property and Power in Social Theory* (New York: Routledge, 1998).
Philipp, Thomas, 'The idea of Islamic economics', *Die Welt des Islams* 30 (1990).

Piscatori, James (ed.), *Islam in the Political Process* (New York: Cambridge University Press, 1983).

Polanyi, Karl, *The Great Transformation* (Boston: Beacon Press, 2001).

Presley, J. and J. Sessions, 'Islamic economics: the emergence of a new paradigm', *Economic Journal* 104/424 (1994).

Rahman, Fazlur, 'Riba and interest', *Islamic Studies* 3/1 (March 1964).

Islam, 2nd edition (Chicago: University of Press, Chicago 1979).

Islam and Modernity (Chicago: University of Chicago Press, 1982).

Rahnema, Ali (ed.), *Pioneers of Islamic Revival* (London: Zed Books, 1994).

An Islamic Utopian – A Political Biography of Ali Shari'ati (London: I. B. Tauris, 1998).

Rahnema, Ali and Farhad Nomani, *The Secular Miracle: Religion, Politics and Economic Policy in Iran* (London: Zed Books, 1990).

Rappaport, R. A., *Ritual and Religion in the Making of Humanity* (Cambridge: Cambridge University Press, 1999).

Rashid, Ahmed, *Taliban: The Story of the Afghan Warlords* (London: Pan, 2001).

Raven, Charles, *Christian Socialism 1848–1854* (London: Macmillan, 1920).

Reeve, Andrew, *Property* (Basingstoke: Macmillan, 1986).

Reid, Donald M., *The Odyssey of Farah Antun* (Minneapolis: Bibliotheca Islamica Inc., 1975).

Richards, Alan and John Waterbury, *A Political Economy of the Middle East: State, Class and Economic Development* (Boulder, CO: Westview Press, 1990).

Roald, Anne Sofie, 'Feminist reinterpretation of Islamic sources: Muslim feminist theology in the light of the Christian tradition of feminist thought', in K. Ask and M. Tjomsland (eds.), *Women and Islamization* (Oxford: Berg, 1998).

Roded, Ruth, *Women in Islam and the Middle East* (London: I. B. Tauris, 1999).

Rodinson, Maxime, *Islam and Capitalism*, tr. B. Pearce (London: Allen Lane, 1974).

Roy, Olivier, *The Failure of Political Islam*, tr. C. Volk (London: I. B. Tauris, 1999).

Globalised Islam (London: Hurst and Co., 2004).

Ruthven, Malise, *A Fury for God: The Islamist Attack on America* (London: Granta, 2002).

Ryan, Alan, *Property and Political Theory* (Oxford: Basil Blackwell, 1984).

Sabbah, Fatna A., *Woman in the Muslim Unconscious*, tr. Mary Jo Lakeland (New York: Pergamon Press, 1984).

Saeed, Abdullah, *Islamic Banking and Interest* (Leiden: Brill, 1996).

Salem, E., 'Arab reformers and the reinterpretation of Islam', *The Muslim World* 55/4 (October 1965).

Saliba, T., C. Allen and J. A. Howard (eds.), *Gender, Politics and Islam* (Chicago: University of Chicago Press, 2002).

Salvatore, Armando, *Islam and the Political Discourse of Modernity* (Reading, MA: Ithaca Press, 1997).

Salvatore, Armando and Dale F., Eickelman (eds.), *Public Islam and the Common Good* (Leiden: Brill, 2004).

Sayer, Derek, *Capitalism and Modernity* (London: Routledge, 1991).

Schacht, Joseph, 'Riba', in *Encyclopedia of Islam* (Leiden: Brill, 1995), vol. VIII.

Schilling, C. and P. A. Mellor, *The Sociological Ambition* (London: Sage, 2001).

Schwartz, Barry, *The Battle for Human Nature* (New York and London: W. W. Norton and Co., 1986).

Scott, James C., *The Moral Economy of the Peasant – Rebellion and Subsistence in South East Asia* (New Haven: Yale University Press, 1976).

Resistance without Protest: Peasant Opposition to the Zakat in Malaysia and to the Tithe in France, 4th James C. Jackson Memorial Lecture, 1986 (Townsville: Asia Studies Association of Australia, 1987).

Searle, P., *The Riddle of Malaysian Capitalism* (Honolulu, HI: University of Hawaii Press, 1999).

Shaaeldin, Elfatih and R. Brown, *Towards an Understanding of Islamic Banking in Sudan*, DSRC Monograph XXI (Khartoum: Khartoum University Press, 1985).

Shari'ati, Ali, *Marxism and Other Western Fallacies*, tr. R. Campbell (Berkeley: Mizan Press, 1980).

Man and Islam, tr. F. Marjani (Houston, TX: Free Islamic Literature–Filinc, 1981).

What Is To Be Done? ed. Farhang Rajaee (Houston, TX: Institute for Research and Islamic Studies, 1986).

On the Sociology of Islam, tr. H. Algar (Berkeley: Mizan Press, n.d.).

Shaw, S. J. and E. K. Shaw, *History of the Ottoman Empire and Modern Turkey* (Cambridge: Cambridge University Press, 1977), vol. II.

Simmel, Georg, *The Sociology of Georg Simmel*, ed. K. H. Wolff (New York: Free Press, 1950).

The Philosophy of Money, ed. David Frisby (London: Routledge, 1990).

Sloane, Patricia, *Islam, Modernity and Entrepreneurship among the Malays* (Basingstoke: Macmillan, 1999).

Smith, Adam, *The Wealth of Nations*, books I–III (London: Penguin Books, 1986).

Smith, W. C., *Modern Islam in India – A Social Analysis* (London: Victor Gollancz, 1946).

Spencer, Herbert, *Structure, Function and Evolution*, ed. S. Andreski (London: Thomas Nelson, 1971).

Staley, C. E., *A History of Economic Thought: From Aristotle to Arrow* (Oxford: Blackwell, 1992).

Starrett, Gregory, *Putting Islam to Work* (Berkeley: University of California Press, 1998).

Stiltner, B., *Religion and the Common Good* (Lanham, MD: Rowman and Littlefield, 1999).

Stowasser, B. F. (ed.), *The Islamic Impulse* (London: Croom Helm in association with Center for Contemporary Arab Studies, Georgetown University, Washington DC, 1987).

Taleqani, Seyyed Mahmood, *Islam and Ownership*, tr. A. Jabbari and F. Rajaee (Lexington, KY: Mazda Publishers, 1983).

Taleqani, Mahmud, Murtada Mutahhari and Ali Shari'ati, *Jihad and Shahadat*, ed. Mehdi Abedi and Gary Legenhausen (Houston, TX: Institute of Research and Islamic Studies 1986).

Tawney, R. H., *Religion and the Rise of Capitalism* (Harmondsworth: Penguin Books, 1938).

Tétreault, M. A. and R. A. Denemark (eds.), *Gods, Guns and Globalization: Religious Radicalism and Political Economy* (Boulder, CO: Lynne Rienner, 2004).

Thompson, H. M. (ed.), *Studies in Egyptian Political Economy*, Cairo Papers in Social Science, 2/3 (Cairo: American University of Cairo Press, 1979).

Thompson, Noel, *The Market and its Critics* (London: Routledge, 1988).

Tignor, Robert, *State, Private Enterprise and Economic Change in Egypt 1918–1952* (Princeton: Princeton University Press, 1984).

Tignor, Robert and Abdel-Khalek Gouda (eds.), *The Political Economy of Income Distribution in Egypt* (New York: Holmes and Meier, 1982).

Tönnies, F., *Community and Association*, tr. C. P. Loomis (London: Routledge and Kegan Paul, 1955).

Toprak, Zafer, 'From liberalism to solidarism: the Ottoman economic mind in the age of the nation state (1820–1920)', in R. Motika, C. Herzog and M. Ursinus (eds.), *Studies in Ottoman Social and Economic Life* (Heidelberg: Heidelberger Orientverlag, 1999).

Tribe, Kenneth, *Land, Labour and Economic Discourse* (London: Routledge and Kegan Paul, 1978).

Tripp, Charles, 'Islam and the secular logic of the state in the Middle East', in Abdel Salam Sidahmed and Anoushiravan Ehteshami (eds.), *Islamic Fundamentalism* (Boulder, CO: Westview Press, 1996).

'An "Islamic economics"? Problems in the imagined reappropriation of economic life', in Kathryn Dean (ed.), *Politics and the Ends of Identity* (Aldershot: Ashgate, 1997).

Troll, C. W., *Sayyid Ahmad Khan – A Reinterpretation of Muslim Theology* (New Delhi: Vikas Publishing House, 1978).

Tröltsch, E., *The Social Teaching of the Christian Churches*, 2 vols., tr. O. Wyon (Louisville, KY: Westminster/John Knox Press, 1992).

al-Turabi, Hasan, 'Principles of Governance, Freedom and Responsibility in Islam', *American Journal of Islamic Social Science* 4/1 (1987).

Turner, Bryan, *Capitalism and Class in the Middle East* (London: Heineman, 1984).
Religion and Social Theory (London: Sage Publications, 1991).
Orientalism, Postmodernism and Globalism (London: Routledge, 1997).
Weber and Islam, Max Weber Classic Monographs VII (London: Routledge, 1998).

Udovitch, A. L., 'Credit as a means of investment in medieval Islamic trade', *Journal of the American Oriental Society* 87 (1967).
Partnership and Profit in Medieval Islam (Princeton: Princeton University Press, 1970).

Vallin, R., 'Muslim socialism in Algeria', in I. William Zartman (ed.), *Man, State, and Society in the Contemporary Maghrib* (New York: Praeger Publishers, 1973).

Vatin, Jean-Claude, 'Popular puritanism versus state reformism: Islam in Algeria', in James Piscatori (ed.), *Islam in the Political Process* (New York: Cambridge University Press, 1983).

Vitalis, Robert, *When Capitalists Collide* (Berkeley: California University Press, 1995).

Wadud-Muhsin, Amina, *Qur'an and Woman* (Kuala Lumpur: Penerbit Fajr Bakti, 1992).

Wagner, P., 'Crises of modernity: political sociology in historical contexts', in Stephen P. Turner (ed.), *Social Theory and Sociology* (Oxford: Blackwell, 1996).

Wahba, Mourad, *The Role of the State in the Egyptian Economy* (Reading, MA: Ithaca Press, 1994).

Wakin, J. A., 'Mudaraba', in *Encyclopedia of Islam* (Leiden: Brill, 1993), vol. VII.

Wallerstein, Immanuel (ed.), *Social Change – The Colonial Situation* (New York: John Wiley, 1966).

Historical Capitalism (London: Verso, 1996).

Warde, Ibrahim, *Islamic Finance in the Global Economy* (Edinburgh: Edinburgh University Press, 2000).

Warriner, Doreen, *Land Reform and Development in the Middle East* (London: Royal Institute of International Affairs, 1957).

Waterbury, John, *The Egypt of Nasser and Sadat* (Princeton: Princeton University Press, 1983).

Weber, Max, *Economy and Society: An Outline of Interpretive Sociology*, 2 vols., trans. E. Fischoff, ed. G. Roth and C. Wittich (Berkeley: University of California Press, 1978).

The Protestant Ethic and the Spirit of Capitalism, tr. Talcott Parsons (London: Unwin Hyman, 1989).

White, Jenny, 'Women and work in Istanbul', *Middle East Report* 173 (Nov./Dec. 1991).

Williams, Raymond, *Keywords* (London: Fontana Press, 1983).

Williamson, Bill, *Education and Social Change in Egypt and Turkey* (Basingstoke: Macmillan, 1987).

Wilson, Rodney (ed.), *Islamic Financial Markets* (London: Routledge, 1990).

Winstanley, George, *The Law of Freedom and Other Writings*, ed. C. Hill (London: Penguin Books, 1973).

Wohlers-Scharf, Traute, *Arab and Islamic Banks* (Paris: OECD, 1983).

Wolfe, W., *From Radicalism to Socialism: Men and Ideas in the Formation of Fabian Socialist Doctrines 1881–1899* (New Haven: Yale University Press, 1975).

Woodcock, George, *Anarchism* (London: Penguin Books, 1971).

Yavuz, Hakan, *Islamic Political Identity in Turkey* (Oxford: Oxford University Press, 2003).

Yousef, Tarik, 'Islamic banking, financial development and growth', *Forum* (Cairo: Newsletter of the Economic Research Forum for the Arab Countries, Iran and Turkey) 3/3 (September 1996).

Zayed, Ahmed, *The Development of Social Science in Egypt*, Cairo Papers in Social Science, vol. XVIII, Monograph 3 (Cairo: American University of Cairo Press, 1996).

Zebiri, Kate, *Mahmud Shaltut and Islamic Modernism* (Oxford: Clarendon Press, 1993).

Ziadeh, Farhat, *Property Law in the Arab World* (London: Graham and Trottman, 1979).

Zubaida, Sami, 'The politics of the Islamic investment companies in Egypt', *BRISMES Bulletin* 17/2 (1990).

Islam, the People and the State: Political Ideas and Movements in the Middle East (London: I. B. Tauris, 1993).

Zulaika, J. and W. A. Douglass, *Terror and Taboo* (London: Routledge, 1996).

Index

'Abd al-Nasir, Gamal (Nasser) 51, 69, 77,
    80, 81, 83, 86, 87, 94, 95, 100, 136,
    155, 197
'Abduh, Muhammad 20, 21, 25, 34, 41, 127,
    128, 133
Abu Hanifah, al-Nu'man ibn Thabit 72
Abu Zahra, Muhammad 89
Adalet ve Kalkinma Partisi (AKP) 9
al-Afghani, Jamal al-Din 19–20, 26, 27,
    33–4, 37, 40, 79, 100
    Refutation of the Materialists 33
    Socialism in Islam 33
Aktas, Cihan 152–3
'Ali, Syed Ameer 40
Aligarh 26
Amin, Qasim 172
Antun, Farah 35
al-'Aqqad, 'Abbas 154
al-'Arabi, Muhammad
    'Abdallah 73, 84
'Arif, 'Abd al-Salam 69
Aristotle 64, 126
Arslan, Shakib 25
Ataseven, Gülsen 178
'Atiyah, Bakri 124
Atta, Muhammad 189–90
al-'Attar, 'Isam 100
al-'Awadi, Rif'at al-Sayyid 111, 112, 116
'Awdah, 'Abd al-Qadir 51, 57, 58–61, 63, 67,
    101, 154
al-'Awwa, Muhammad 82
Al-Azhar 75, 118, 133, 146
al-Azhar, Shaikh 80, 132
al-'Azm, Rafiq 21, 27, 35, 37
'Azzam, 'Abdallah 185

al-Baghawi, al-Husain ibn Mas'ud 66
al-Bahi, Muhammad 92, 95
al-Ba'li, 'Abd al-Hamid Mahmud 110, 121
Bali bombing (2002) 192
Bank Islam Malaysia Berhad 137
Bank Misr (1981) 146

Bank Misr/Misr Group 30–1
Bank of Local Deposits (Mit Ghamr)
    136
al-Banna, Hasan 51, 101,
    172, 176
al-Barrawi, Rashid 112
Bazargan, Mehdi 69
bin Ladin, 'Usama 186
al-Bishri, Tariq 116, 120–1
BNP Parisbas 147
'Bojinka Plot' (1994) 192
Braudel, Fernand 2
Brenner, Robert 3

capitalism
    characteristics of 2–4, 179
    critiques of 7–8, 79, 84, 135–6, 195
    and gender 168
Cevdet, Abdullah 39
chador 177
Chase International Bank 1
Citibank 1, 146
commodification 4–5, 65, 66–7, 84, 95,
    97, 105, 106, 142, 159, 170, 175, 178,
    189, 192, 197, 200
commodities 3–5, 150, 177, 199
communism 46–7, 55, 80, 86, 97–9, 111, 122,
    158, 160
Comte, Auguste 19
Co-operative Bank (UK) 147
Council of Islamic Ideology report
    (1983) 131

Da'bas, al-Hamza 132
Dar al-'Ulum 17
Al-Da'wah (Egypt) 132
derivatives 144
Deutsche Bank 146
Djewdet Pasha, Ahmad 38–9
Dubai Islamic Bank 137–8
al-Dumi, Ahmad 115
Durkheim, Emile 19, 21, 41

225

TOWER HAMLETS COLLEGE
Learning Centre
Arbour Square
LONDON E1 0PT
Tel: 020 7510 7568